THE SECRET

In modern democratic countries, political control is not easily achieved through military power or propaganda. However, by the use of deception and psychological warfare, the public, political elite and local military forces may be deceived into supporting the policies of a major power. Mass media is thus manipulated not by propaganda, but by deception.

Following the stranding of a Soviet Whiskey-class submarine in 1981 on the Swedish archipelago, a series of massive submarine intrusions took place within Swedish waters – later described as the first Soviet military initiative against a west European state since the Berlin crisis. After a dramatic submarine hunt in 1982, a Swedish parliamentary commission stated that six Soviet submarines had 'played their games' in the Stockholm archipelago – one even in Stockholm harbour. The Swedish government protested strongly to the Soviet Union, and relations between the two countries were icy for several years afterwards. Today, however, the evidence for these alleged Soviet intrusions appears to have been manipulated or simply invented. Classified documents and interviews cited in this book point to covert Western rather than Soviet activity. This is backed up by former US Secretary of Defense Caspar Weinberger, who stated, in a Swedish television interview reproduced in this book, that Western 'testing' operations were carried out regularly in Swedish waters, and by former British Navy Minister Sir Keith Speed, who has confirmed the existence of such operations. Royal Navy submarine captains have also admitted to having carried out top-secret operations in the Swedish archipelago.

Ola Tunander's revelations in this book makes it clear that the United States and Britain ran a 'secret war' in Swedish waters to test Sweden's capability and will in the 1980s. Within a couple of years, the number of Swedes perceiving the Soviet Union as a direct threat had increased from 5–10 per cent (in 1980) to 45 per cent (in 1983). In the same period, the number of Swedes viewing the Soviets as unfriendly increased from 30 per cent to more than 80 per cent. This Anglo-American 'secret war' was a deception operation aimed at exerting political influence over Sweden. It was a risky enterprise, but, as the Swedish polls show, perhaps the most successful covert operation of the entire Cold War.

CASS SERIES: NAVAL POLICY AND HISTORY
Series Editor: Geoffrey Till
ISSN 1366–9478

This series consists primarily of original manuscripts by research scholars in the general area of naval policy and history, without national or chronological limitations. It will from time to time also include collections of important articles as well as reprints of classic works.

THE SECRET WAR AGAINST SWEDEN

US and British Submarine Deception in the 1980s

OLA TUNANDER

International Peace Research Institute, Oslo

Foreword by
Brigadier-General Lars Hansson

LONDON AND NEW YORK

First published in 2004 in Great Britain by
Routledge
2 Park Square, Milton Park
Abingdon, Oxon OX14 4RN

Simultaneously published in the US and Canada by
Routledge
711 Third Avenue
New York, NY 10017

Routledge is an imprint of the Taylor & Francis Group

British Library Cataloguing in Publication Data
Tunander, Ola
The secret war against Sweden: US and British submarine deception and political control in the 1980s. – (Cass series. Naval policy and history; 21) 1. Anti-submarine warfare – Sweden – History – 20th century 2. Submarine warfare – United States – History – 20th century 3. Submarine warfare – Great Britain – History – 20th century 4. Cold war – Deception 5. Psychological warfare – Sweden – History – 20th century 6. Sovereignty, Violation of – Sweden – History – 20th century 7. Sweden – History – Carl XVI Gustav, 1973– 8. United States – Military policy 9. Great Britain – Military policy
I. Title
355.9'3'09485'09048

ISBN 0-7146-5322-5 (cloth)
ISBN 0-7146-8275-6 (paper)
ISSN 1366-9478

Library of Congress Cataloging-in-Publication Data
Tunander, Ola 1948–
The secret war against Sweden: US and British submarine deception and political control in the 1980s / Ola Tunader
    p. cm. – (Cass series – naval policy and history, ISSN 1366-9478; 21)
    Includes bibliographical references and index.
    ISBN 0-7146-5322-5 (cloth) – ISBN 0-7146-8275-6 (paper)
    1. Stockholms skègêrd (Sweden) – History, Naval – 20th century. 2. Sweden – Politics and government – 1973– 3. Deception (Military science) – History – 20th century. 4. Submarines (Ships) – United States – History – 20th century. 5. Submarines (Ships) – Great Britain – History – 20th century. 6. Special operations (Military science) – United States – History – 20th century. 7. Special operations (Military science) – Great Britain – History – 20th century.
VA593.T85 2003
359.9'84 – dc21

                                                                                    200305156

Typeset in 11/12pt Classic Garamond by Servis Filmsetting Ltd, Manchester

To Robert Bathurst
In memoriam

Contents

Illustrations

Maps

Map 1 reproduced courtesy of the Norwegian Ministry of Defence. Maps 2–4 reproduced courtesy of the Swedish Maritime Administration. Maps 5–20 are by Ralf Lundberg and Ola Tunander.

Foreword

On 1 October 1982, after four years as chief of division at the Swedish Defence Staff, I entered my new position as Chief of Stockholm Coastal Defence. I took over responsibility for an ongoing wartime forces exercise with 4,000 men in the archipelago, including Special Forces, patrol vessels, mine troops and artillery forces. My first meeting with my new staff was interrupted by a report of a submarine periscope deep inside the archipelago at Muskö naval base. I cancelled the meeting and contacted the regional commander. An intensive anti-submarine operation began, which went on for two weeks. This incident influenced Swedish coastal defence activities for the rest of the 1980s.

We had been anticipating Soviet submarines in connection with an impressive US naval visit to Stockholm in the last days of September 1982. On earlier occasions, Soviet or Warsaw Pact submarines had followed our Western visitors below the surface, also in our territory. We believed the Coastal Defence exercise and our presence in the archipelago would give us an advantage in our battle with intruding submarines.

After a few days of submarine hunting, we were authorized to use our heavy mines against the intruder as long as no civilians were in danger. We detonated mines on 7 and 11 October, in both cases just after clear indications of a passing submarine. The order was not to sink but to stop (or damage) the submarine and force it to the surface. After the 11 October detonation, we received indications of repair works on a damaged submarine. Two days later, we had indications of a submarine once again approaching the mine barrage, but despite full control of the surface, the Commander-in-Chief ordered a ceasefire. Two hours after the submarine had passed the mine barrage we were once again authorized to use force.

As Chief of Stockholm Coastal Defence, I mobilized considerable resources in an attempt to force a submarine to the surface. My task was to rebuff any intruder within my area of responsibility; the nationality of the intruding submarines was not my concern. However, like the Submarine Defence Commission, I was convinced that the submarines originated from the Warsaw Pact. Ola Tunander's research has provided a new basis for settling the question of the intruder's nationality. This is particularly evident for the above incident at the mine barrages in October 1982. Tunander presents a credible account for the course of events: a Western submarine was released during a five-hour ceasefire. Tunander's research, presented in this book, is groundbreaking and should lead to a re-evaluation of the conclusions from earlier analyses.

Brigadier-General Lars Hansson
Former Chief of Stockholm Coastal Defence
June 2003

Series Editor's Preface

Just as the Cold War between the United States and NATO and the Soviet Union and its Warsaw Pact allies was beginning to wind down, a bizarre series of events took place in the Baltic. First, an old Whiskey submarine of the Soviet Union's Baltic fleet, allegedly carrying nuclear-tipped torpedoes, ran aground on some rocks that were well inside Sweden's territorial waters. Shortly afterwards, there occurred a series of strange events in which a number of Swedish citizens, and some military personnel too, began to report seeing signs of mysterious submarines nosing about in Sweden's inland waters. This sparked off a long 'submarine summer' of alarms and concerns.

Around the world, commentators took up their pens to speculate about what it could all mean. First, there was a debate about whether there really were submarines about, or whether it was all the product of fevered imagination and media hype. At some stages, the Swedish submarine issue threatened almost to become another version of Scotland's preoccupation with the Loch Ness monster. Second, there were those who assumed that if there were indeed submarines in Sweden's waters, then they must be Soviet ones. This in turn led to much debate about what the Soviets meant by this. Was it perhaps a coded warning to Sweden not to become too friendly to NATO in the new strategic environment that was rapidly unfolding? Was it free-lance political activity by some of the murkier elements of the Soviet system over whom Mr Gorbachev had less than perfect control? Was it, alternatively, elements in the Baltic fleet who wanted their submariners to get in some realistic practice?

There was even the quite serious suggestion that this was preparation for a *Spetsnaz* campaign to get people ashore to decapitate the Swedish government and air force in the event of an East–West crisis, in which Sweden seemed likely to be moving away from its position of neutrality and getting too friendly with the West. Evidence for this kind of interpretation was, of course, bolstered by the original 'Whiskey-on-the-rocks' affair and by the certain fact that similar events were taking place elsewhere, most obviously of course by the submarines of the North Korean navy.

As this issue dragged on, people on all sides of the argument became frustrated by the absence of proof one way or another and by the miasma of truth and counter-truth that began to envelope the whole issue. Indeed, some even accused the Swedish government and navy of deliberately playing down their anti-submarine measures, partly for the best of humanitarian reasons and partly because they did not want any 'proof', since this could lead to a major crisis and a wholesale re-evaluation of what non-alignment in peace and neutrality in war actually meant in those confusing times. For their part, the Soviet authorities and their Russian successors have steadfastly denied any involvement in the whole affair, except of course for the original incident.

Gradually, the issue died away as the Berlin Wall came down and the Cold War ended, but with this book Ola Tunander with the aid of access to hitherto classified sources and his association with the latest formal and official investigation by Ambassador Ekéus has re-examined the old evidence, looked at the new and come up with an alternative explanation for Sweden's 'submarine summer' which many of his readers will find quite startling. Some will agree with his conclusions, some will not – but all will want to know still more. Either way, with this book the debate upon these strange events will certainly begin a new phase.

Geoffrey Till
Series Editor

Acknowledgements

Like many Swedes, I have been interested in the submarine intrusions into Swedish waters since the early 1980s. In 1987, I wrote a report for the Swedish Defence Research Establishment about US maritime strategy and Scandinavian geopolitics, implying Soviet submarine intrusions into Swedish waters. The report was used as one of two major textbooks for the Swedish Military High School. In 1989, I wrote a larger volume with a similar hypothesis. At that time, I believed that the Soviet Union was responsible for the majority of the incursions, and I accepted the official statements as true. I visited the US Naval War College in Newport and lectured at the Center for Naval Analysis in Washington and at the Naval Postgraduate School in Monterey. However, even in the late 1980s, more and more indications were turning up that pointed to Western activity. Senior US and British officials indicated that they had been involved in operations in Swedish waters. For some reason, US intelligence personnel were interested in my research. My US Navy friends were at first sceptical of my new approach, but they still helped me to find information.

Captain Robert Bathurst, my colleague since the early 1990s, supported me throughout these years. He was Assistant Naval Attaché to Moscow in the mid-1960s, Defense Director for Eastern Europe (Attaché Affairs) in the Pentagon in the late 1960s, Deputy Commander-in-Chief US Naval Forces Europe (CINCUSNAVEUR) for intelligence in the early 1970s, and he held the Admiral Layton Chair of Intelligence at the US Naval War College in the mid-1970s. In 1991, he came to Oslo with his Norwegian wife. I recruited him to the International Peace Research Institute (PRIO), from the Naval Postgraduate School. I worked side by side with him for several years, and he gave me important insights into US Naval Intelligence without revealing classified material. In spring 2000, after former US Secretary of Defense Caspar Weinberger had confirmed US submarine operations in Sweden, Robert went to the USA and checked out with his old colleagues in Naval Intelligence and in the SEAL (US Navy special forces) community what was true about US activities in Swedish waters. After talking to them, he was strongly advised not to ask questions. Two months later, he died, which was a great loss to me and to my friends in every respect. This book is dedicated to Robert for his support and friendship during these years.

I also would like to thank PRIO and its former Director, Dan Smith, for allowing me to write about these issues while I was heading its programme on foreign and security policy, and the Norwegian Research Council for financing the project. I would like to thank PRIO's present Director Stein Tønnesson, the Research Director at the Nobel Institute Olav Njølstad, Research Professor Iver Neumann at the Norwegian Institute of International Affairs and Professor Ole Wæver in Copenhagen for their comments on my manuscript. Many other people have also been very helpful during these years, and in this book I have used hundreds of interviews with Swedish military officers and officials. Many of these officers are mentioned in Appendix I. Some have become friends during the years of interviews.

I have also used a number of interviews with anonymous intelligence officers and naval officers from various NATO countries. In several cases, rank or position has been revealed, at least in general terms. In other cases, I have been more cautious, for example if an officer is still on active duty. To reveal a name or even position might be damaging to him (for the principles used, see Appendix I). Several of these officers have told me about special exercises with US/UK submarines and special forces, though without revealing NATO secrets. I have had long discussions with national and regional commanders-in-chief, chiefs of the navy and chiefs of military intelligence. Some of these officers have reviewed my manuscript for this book. The majority have in general terms confirmed my hypothesis. I am thankful for all these comments.

Interviews have not always been easy. Some officers have been less willing to speak after intervention by the US Embassy. One senior Norwegian diplomat, Einar Ansteensen, told me about a damaged US submarine in Hårsfjärden in 1982. However, I was not able to do the final interviews before he died. Many of the more senior people involved in the incident are now dead. A US Assistant Naval Attaché to Oslo, a former assistant to the US Secretary of the Navy, approached me even before he arrived in Oslo. He was interested in my Italian contacts. The US Embassy was clearly interested in my interviews. In addition, Italian and Swedish military intelligence were interested in my research. I have made a number of interviews with Swedish intelligence officers and naval officers. In this book, most of these officers are referred to by name.

In 1998, the Swedish Minister of Defence, Björn von Sydow, promised me that the Swedish archives on the submarine incidents would be made available for research. In 1999–2000, I received access to formerly classified material – war diaries and intelligence reports – about the Hårsfjärden incident. This material has been very useful. In March 2000, the interview with Caspar Weinberger was broadcast on Swedish TV. It created a lot of fuss. The day after, the Swedish government and the Swedish Commander-in-Chief each launched an investigation, though these had little success. Soon afterwards, the Swedish government appointed Ambassador Rolf Ekéus to carry out a one-man investigation into the political and military aspects of the submarine incidents. The Ekéus Investigation was financed by the Ministry of Defence and the Ministry of Foreign Affairs, but it had its own authority and the right to investigate these ministries as well as the military high command. In winter and spring 2001, Ekéus appointed Ambassador Mathias Mossberg, Director of Foreign Ministry Policy Planning, as his main secretary, and Rear-Admiral Göran Wallén and myself as his experts. This gave Ekéus access to my research, and I got access to some new material. Ambassador Ekéus, Ambassador Mossberg and I made a number of interviews together. However, the interviews referred to in this book were made separately by me with the officers concerned and should not be confused with the interviews made for the Ekéus Investigation. This book represents neither the views of the Ekéus Investigation nor the views of any Swedish ministry.

A Swedish version of this book was published in November 2001, and it should be understood as a draft version of this volume. Rear-Admiral Wallén came up with some critical comments in the journal of the Swedish Royal Naval Society. Most of them proved to be irrelevant, but he also made it possible to weed out a couple of mistakes. I am thankful to Wallén for these comments. I also would like to thank Ambassador Ekéus and Ambassador Mossberg for their support and stimulating discussions, as well as the Swedish publisher Svante Weyler, who supported me during this process.

Abbreviations

ASDS	Advanced SEAL Delivery System
BALTAP	NATO's Command for the Baltic Approaches in Denmark
BÖS	Berga Naval College
CCC	Cellules Communistes Combatantes
CFK	Chief of the Coastal Fleet
CFst	Chief of Staff
CINCUSNAVEUR	Commander-in-Chief US Naval Forces Europe
CM	Chief of the Navy
COMSUBEASTLANT	Commander Submarines Eastern Atlantic
COMSUBIN	Commando Raggruppamento Subacqui ed Incursori
CÖrlBO INT	Chief of Naval Base East, Intelligence Briefings
CÖrlBO	Chief of Naval Base East
CseM	Chief Central Air Section
Csjöop	Chief of Naval Operations, Eastern Military District
CSK	Chief of Stockholm Coastal Defence
DIA	Defense Intelligence Agency
DSRV	Deep Submergence Rescue Vehicle
DSV	Deep Submergence Vehicle
E&E	Evasion and Escape
FMV	Swedish Defence Material
FOA	Defence Research Establishment
FRA	Swedish Signal Intelligence Agency
GRU	Soviet Military Intelligence
IR	infra-red
MAFU	Navy's Experimental Equipment
MBÖ	Commander, Eastern Military District
MSB	Defence Staff

MUSAC	Navy Sound Division
NSCT	Navy Security Coordination Team
NURO	National Underwater Reconnaissance Office
ÖB	Commander-in-Chief
OPG	Defence Staff Operations
ÖrlBO	Naval Base East
OSS	Office of Strategic Services
PRIO	International Peace Research Institute, Oslo
PSYOP	psychological operations
SACEUR	Supreme Allied Commander Europe
SAS	Special Air Service
SBS	Special Boat Squadron/Service
SCÖ	Chief of Staff, Eastern Military District
SCÖrlBO	Chief of Staff, Naval Base East
SCSK	Chief of Staff, Stockholm Coastal Defence
SDVs	SEAL/Swimmer Delivery Vehicles
SEAL	Sea-Air-Land
SEALs	US naval special forces
SISMI	Italian Military Intelligence
SOSUS	sound surveillance systems
SSI	Swedish Military Intelligence

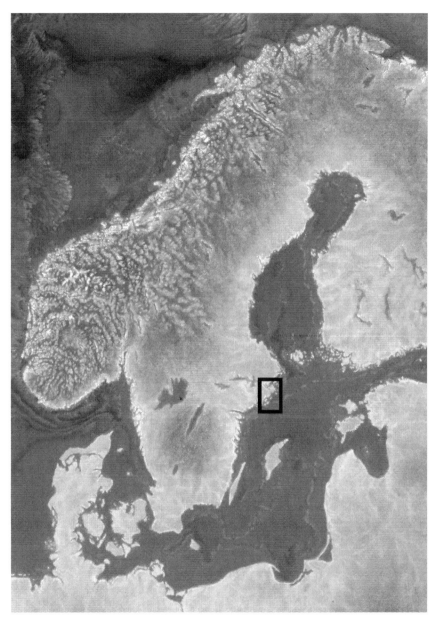

1. Scandinavia, with Sweden, Norway and Denmark, plus Finland and the Baltic coastline of the Soviet Union, Poland, East Germany and West Germany. The marked area around Stockholm shows the area covered by Map 2.

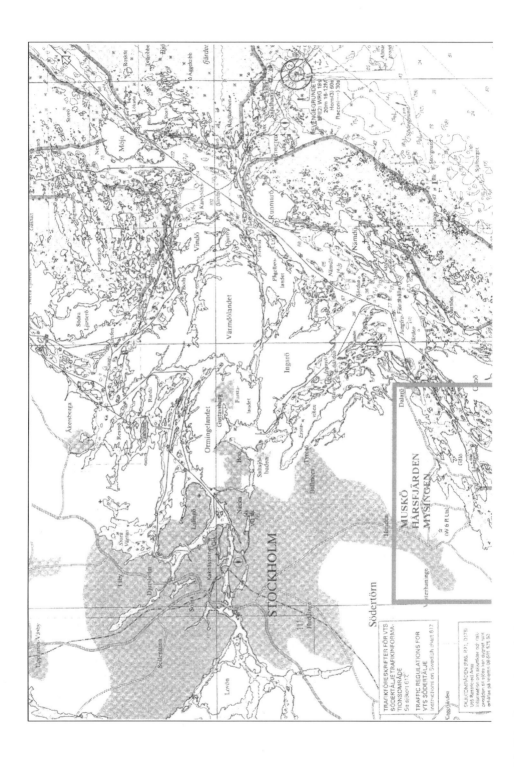

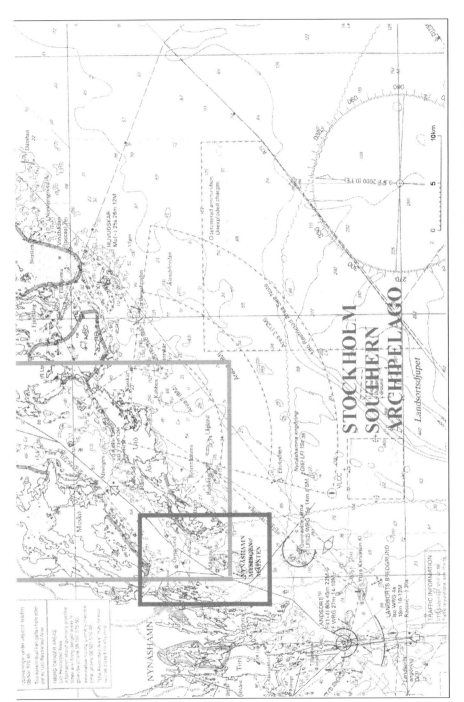

2. Stockholm Southern Archipelago. The map has two marked areas: one covers the area of Map 3 (Muskö, Hårsfjärden, Mysingen) and one the area of Map 4 (Nynäshamn, Mysingen, Mälsten).

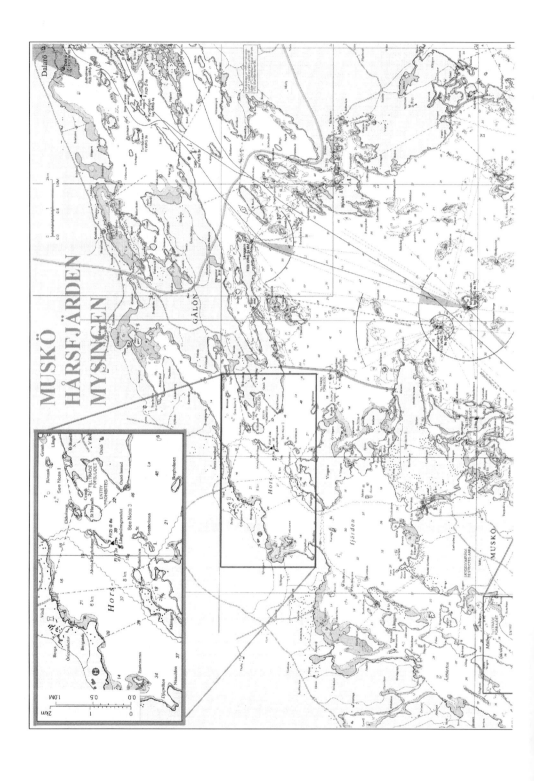

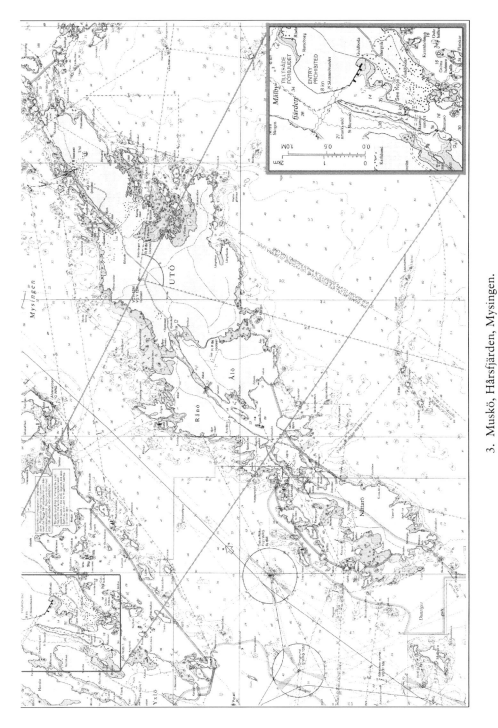

3. Muskö, Hårsfjärden, Mysingen.

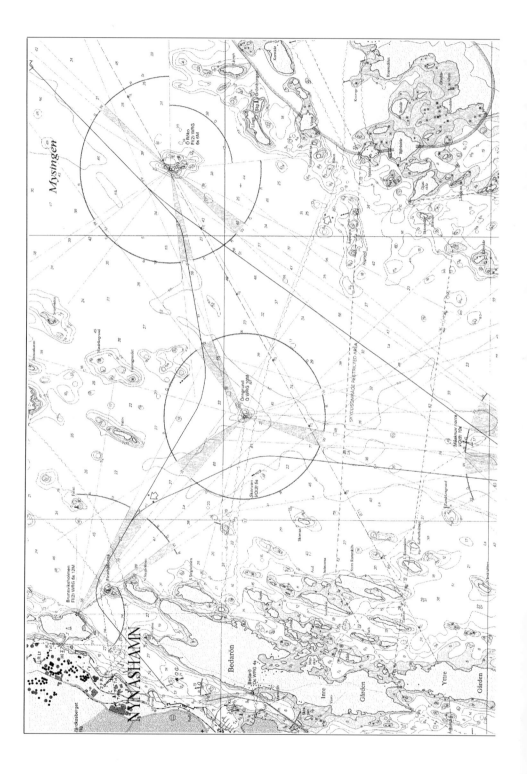

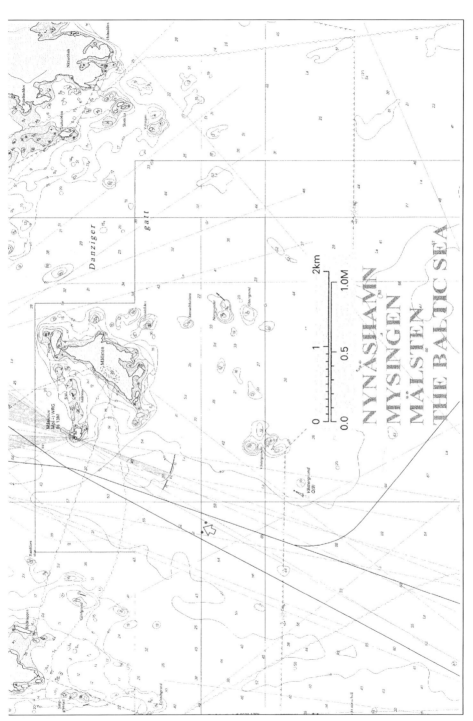

4. Nynäshamn, Mysingen, Mälsten.

1

Introduction

The submarine incidents in Swedish waters during the early 1980s had an enormous impact on the Swedish mentality and perception of threat. After a Soviet Whiskey submarine was stranded in the archipelago close to the Swedish naval base of Karlskrona in October 1981, a number of submarine intrusions took place deep inside the densely populated Swedish archipelagos. The government 'found proof' of large, coordinated submarine operations along the Swedish coasts, and, after one of the most dramatic submarine hunts – in Hårsfjärden in the Stockholm archipelago in 1982 – the government protested strongly against the Soviet intrusions. The Parliamentary Submarine Defence Commission Report stated that six submarines (including three midgets) were believed to have 'played their games' among the islands of the Stockholm archipelago – four of them in the Hårsfjärden area, close to Sweden's Naval Base East at Muskö. In addition, one submersible was observed in the waters of central Stockholm just a few hundred metres from the royal palace, and one midget submarine was able to crawl on the sea floor, as if the Soviets had been coming with 'sub-surface tanks' to attack Sweden from below.[1]

In a report for the US Air Force from 1990, Gordon McCormick writes:

> *Since 1980, Swedish sources indicate that an average rate of between 17 and 36 foreign operations are being conducted per year* . . . For the first time *Soviet intruders began to penetrate into the heart of Sweden's coastal defence zones*, including the harbours and the country's major naval bases. More often than not, *these operations now involved the use of multiple submarines, mini-submarines, and combat swimmers operating in a coordinated manner.*[2] (italics in original)

Within a couple of years, the number of people in Sweden who perceived the Soviet Union as a direct threat increased radically. In the decade up to 1980, between 5 and 10 per cent of the population

1

looked at the Soviet Union as a direct threat, while in 1983, after the official report on the Hårsfjärden hunt had been published, more than 40 per cent perceived the Soviet Union as a direct threat. During the same period, the percentage of people viewing the Soviet Union as hostile increased from around 30 per cent to more than 80 per cent (see below). Sweden changed drastically.

The military leadership reported a large number of submarine observations in the early and mid-1980s: in 1982, there were seven certain, 15 probable and a large number of possible observations; in 1983, there were six certain and 41 probable observations; in 1984, there were 11 certain and 20 probable observations; and, in 1985, there were seven certain and 33 probable observations. They stated, beyond doubt, that tracks had been left on the sea floor by bottom-crawling vessels and that divers had been carrying out sabotage on sub-surface military installations.[3]

The submarine hunts were major media events. During a two-week hunt in Hårsfjärden, 750 journalists from all over the world visited the Navy Press Centre. They filmed helicopters and small Swedish attack crafts carrying out complex operations against the intruder and dropping large numbers of depth charges. The anti-submarine war entered the living room of every Swede, and many people believed that Sweden was already at war with the Soviets. The submarine hunt was front-page news in US and European newspapers, and the Swedish Commander-in-Chief, General Lennart Ljung, talked about using 'war methods in peace time'.[4] Altogether five mines were used and 47 depth charges were dropped during the submarine hunt. This was the first time mines had been used against an enemy since the Second World War. The mine troops and the Air Force were ready to sink the intruding submarines, and Prime Minister Olof Palme said that the state responsible for the intrusions had to consider that Swedish military forces might sink a submarine in Swedish waters.[5]

After one mine explosion, the Swedish Navy Press Officer said: 'We are looking for something we believe is a seriously damaged submarine lying helpless on the sea floor.'[6] Air-defence missiles were moved up to the area. Officers told me that, for the first time, they felt that they had been put into a battle situation. Suddenly, just two days afterwards, the whole submarine hunt was seemingly over: the military press centre was closed down and there were no more official comments, though the government decided to appoint a parliamentary commission to investigate the incident. A month and half later, the newly appointed Minister of Defence, Börje Andersson, left his job and his apartment in Stockholm. He said that he 'felt homesick' and that Stockholm was too large a city for him. No further government statements on the incident were made until half a year later, when the parliamentary commission presented its conclusions about six Soviet submarines that had operated in the Stockholm archipelago.

In a study for the US Office of the Secretary of Defense, Lynn M. Hansen writes that the Hårsfjärden operation – with three midget submarines and three conventional diesel submarines acting as mother-submarines – was a 'Spetsnaz operation' (i.e. a Soviet special forces operation), and he continues:

> [In connection with the presentation of the Submarine Defence Commission Report,] another special Soviet submarine action took place in the territorial waters in the area of Sundsvall, a strategic port and key node in the ground transportation system in the Gulf of Bothnia. On the Norwegian side, the Soviet special operations were taking place at virtually the same time in the Hardanger Fjord . . . [In order to be able to move forward with conventional forces,] the Soviets have been undertaking the special Spetsnaz operations in both Sweden and Norway so that they can move quickly and decisively in achieving naval supremacy in the Baltic Sea by neutralizing Swedish defenses . . . Despite the almost comical nature of Soviet ineptness during the 'Whiskey on the Rocks' incident and the intriguing image of mini-subs crawling along the bottom of the Stockholm Channel within a stone's throw of the royal palace, there was nothing funny about any of these activities.[7]

From early 1984, Swedish Defence Minister Anders Thunborg was given daily briefings about the submarine intrusions as if there were continual reports from the front. Swedish defence authorities seemed to think in terms of a permanent secret war launched against the country. The submarine hunts of the 1980s, particularly the 1982 Hårsfjärden hunt and the subsequent Karlskrona hunt in early 1984, were traumatic events that were formative for Swedish security thinking and for international perceptions about Sweden. Sweden was believed to follow the path of 'flexible neutrality', adapting to the dominant power in the region. Many people saw a parallel between Sweden's 'allowing' submarines in its territorial waters in the 1980s and Sweden's behaviour during the Second World War, when the Swedish government 'allow[ed] the use of Swedish soil for the passage of German troops on their way to Finland'.[8] In 1987, Milton Leitenberg wrote for the Washington-based Center for Strategic and International Studies:

> Between 1980 and 1986 – depending on the accounting criteria used – the Soviet Union carried out some 100 to 200 submarine incursions within Swedish territorial waters. Many of these took place deep in

internal waters, often in the immediate proximity of major Swedish naval bases and within the perimeters of restricted security zones . . . That these incursions have continued over an extended period of time has led to suggestions that their intention may have been either primarily or secondarily to exert political pressure on Sweden. The aim of such pressure would have been to effect changes in Swedish neutrality or foreign policies or to force Sweden to acquiesce to Soviet military movements within its territory both in times of peace and of war . . . The operations are the first Soviet military–political initiatives against a Western European state since the Berlin crisis of 1960–1961.[9]

Still, only on two occasions – after the stranded Whiskey submarine in October 1981 and, in April 1983, after the presentation of the parliamentary report on the Hårsfjärden submarine incident – did the Swedish government point to the Soviet Union and protest against Soviet intrusions. The Hårsfjärden incident was the only submarine hunt during which Swedish authorities allegedly discovered evidence to prove Soviet involvement. In 1985, after four years of continued reported submarine intrusions, Foreign Minister Lennart Bodström told the mass media that only in two cases had it been proven that these sub-surface operations originated from the Soviet Union, and that it was impossible to protest against an intruder that had not been identified. The public, however, was convinced that all of the intrusions originated from the Soviet Union and that the government was adapting to Soviet pressure. According to journalists criticizing Bodström, the Foreign Minister even seemed to express scepticism about the Hårsfjärden incident and the Submarine Defence Commission Report that had already pointed to the Soviets. Bodström's statements were perceived as unacceptable. A few months later, after a harsh political debate, Prime Minister Olof Palme had to sacrifice his Foreign Minister.[10]

The Hårsfjärden hunt started less than two weeks after the Social Democratic Party won a parliamentary election. The controversial Prime Minister Olof Palme had returned to power. In the 1970s, Palme had been an irritant to the USA. Now, in the early 1980s, he had launched a campaign in support of the Sandinistas in Nicaragua and the ANC (African National Congress), the MPLA (Movimento Populas da Libertaçao de Angola) and FRELIMO (Frente de Libertaçao de Moçambique) in southern Africa. This was disturbing to the Reagan regime in the USA, as well as to some industrial and military leaders in Sweden. Palme also supported a campaign for a Nordic Nuclear Weapons-Free Zone and initiated a Western–Soviet dialogue on security and disarmament – the Palme Commission – which was totally unacceptable to the USA and NATO. Since the 1950s, the Swedish Prime Minister had been a guarantee of Sweden's close ties to the USA and of

US access to Swedish territory in wartime.[11] Now, in the 1980s, Prime Minister Palme could seemingly no longer be trusted. For the USA, this led to a dangerous situation. Supported by West German Social Democrats, Olof Palme and the Palme Commission even tried to extend a Nordic Nuclear Weapons-Free Zone to central Europe (see the final report of June 1982),[12] which became a major problem to the US security elite. Secretary of State General Alexander Haig expressed his deep worries. In a book on the future of conflict, the former Director of the CIA and Secretary of Defense James Schlesinger expressed worries about West Europeans turning their backs on the USA.[13] In the same book, William Taylor, Director of Political–Military Studies at the Center for Strategic and International Studies, said that West Germany was moving towards a 'neutral' position, and he warned Europe of possible 'Swedenization'.[14] In the USA, Olof Palme's Sweden became a symbol of a new European 'neutralism' seemingly adapting to Soviet military strength.

However, these Olof Palme initiatives of the early and mid-1980s were largely unsuccessful, particularly his ideas about a reorganized security system for Europe. The submarine incidents made Palme's initiatives look pathetic. His global political initiatives and his European and Nordic disarmament initiatives were no longer credible. While telling others how to solve their security problems, he wasn't able to defend the integrity of his own country. In practical terms, the Swedish example became devaluated. In Sweden, the 'submarine war' was followed by an intense conflict between Social Democratic political leaders on the one hand and some industrial and military leaders on the other. The 'submarine war' totally changed politics in Sweden. It placed the Social Democrats on the defensive and mobilized large parts of the population against the Soviet threat. Conservative Party leader Ulf Adelsohn stated on TV that this was the first time since 1809 that Swedish soldiers had confronted foreign soldiers on Swedish soil.[15] Within a couple of years, the Swedes' reluctance to increase defence spending changed radically: while only 15–20 per cent were in favour of increased military spending in the 1970s, this figure changed to almost 50 per cent after the submarine incidents had started (see below).

After the Hårsfjärden incident, Ulf Adelsohn claimed that the Chief of Staff had ordered the release of a submarine.[16] In 1987, Brigadier-General Lars Hansson, Chief of Stockholm Coastal Defence and the individual responsible for the minefields during the submarine hunt in the Stockholm archipelago, said in an interview that he had been forced by the military leadership to let a submarine escape. He believed there was a Soviet spy in the top leadership.[17] During the submarine hunt, the Italian news agency Ansa said that the Swedes were negotiating in

Geneva with a foreign power responsible for the intrusions, which would explain the release of a submarine. The Social Democratic State Secretary for Foreign Affairs, Pierre Schori, denied any such negotiations, but Ansa claimed to know the positions and the names of the Swedish negotiators.[18] In 1986, Professor John Erickson, a British scholar, Soviet specialist and adviser to the Swedish Submarine Defence Commission, appeared on Swedish TV saying that the Swedes had released a submarine after negotiations with the Soviets.[19]

Within the military forces, naval officers turned against the Prime Minister, and, in the autumn of 1985, a number of naval officers publicly stated that they no longer had trust in him. According to these officers, the Prime Minister no longer took the Soviet threat seriously enough. Former army chief Lieutenant-General Nils Sköld said that this group believed that 'Sweden, in practical terms, was at war with the Soviet Union.'[20] Ever since the Second World War, Sweden had been divided between different elites with different loyalties. Now, this division led to a clash, and not only in the use of words.

In the 1980s, Soviet responsibility for the massive submarine intrusions was evident. The stranded Whiskey submarine in 1981, the Hårsfjärden incident in 1982 and the subsequent parliamentary commission's pointing to the Soviet Union in 1983, and the threatening Soviet rhetoric and military build-up during these years led to worries not only in Sweden. In 1990, Gordon McCormick from the US Rand Corporation wrote: '*The submarine campaign and related Soviet operations ashore can be satisfactorily interpreted only within the context of Soviet military interests and likely wartime goals in Scandinavia and the Baltic area*' (italics in original).[21]

The same year, Jack Anderson and Dale van Atta, writing in the *Washington Post*, argued that Soviet operations in Sweden were an argument for distrusting the intentions of Gorbachev. Referring to CIA sources, they wrote:

> Mikhail Gorbachev is actively courting Western Europe, but the relationship is not all sweetness and glasnost. Soviet mini-submarines and combat frogmen continue to violate the waters of neutral Sweden more than 30 times a year, making US intelligence agencies wonder what Gorbachev is up to . . . In 1982, the Soviet naval Spetsnaz (special forces) conducted operations near Sweden's largest naval base at Muskö. One of the Soviet mini-subs penetrated deep enough into Swedish waters to lay just off Stockholm . . . Another huge operation occurred in 1984, when the Swedes recorded more than 600 detections of foreign intruders in the waters near Karlskrona naval base. There were conventional submarines, small diver vehicles, frogmen and mini-subs. The Swedish army brought out grenades and machine guns to

repel what they suspected were Soviet frogmen . . . US intelligence officials expected that the strange forays would taper off when Gorbachev
came to power in 1985, but they didn't. The incidents have continued
at a rate of 30 or more a year, and they have become even more daring
. . . One has to conclude that Gorbachev is not in control of the strange
forays, or that he sanctions them in the interest of gathering more information. The latter is the more likely.[22]

For the *Washington Post*, or rather its CIA sources, the Soviet operations in Sweden became a proof of Soviet aggressiveness even after the
fall of the Berlin Wall. Today, these large and coordinated submarine
operations along the Swedish coast, deep inside the Swedish archipelagos, with midget submarines and special force divers appearing
among the Swedish summer houses, have become more of a mystery.
Almost nothing has come out of the Russian military system, which has
been leaking information on many other secret operations from the
Cold War. It is now clear that the alleged evidence presented to prove
Soviet involvement in connection with the Hårsfjärden submarine
hunt was invented for political reasons. In this dramatic submarine
hunt, which was presented as the final proof of the Soviets' extremely
provocative nature and demonstrated that all other intrusions most
likely originated from the USSR, the Swedes had nothing on the
Soviets. Rather, the evidence that has since emerged points in another
direction. These high-profile submarine operations appear as a form of
psychological warfare. They may possibly have been what William
Taylor suggested: 'Psychological operations to induce the government
and/or population to resist Soviet intervention or psychological operations to undercut support of an undesirable government.'[23]

This volume presents analysis of the submarine incidents, together
with some hypotheses that are still unconfirmed but which point in the
direction of an ambitious Western deception operation. Appendix I consists of a presentation of the people involved in the submarine hunt, the
documents used in this study and a number of the individuals I have
interviewed. I present a compilation of material from formerly classified
documents (war diaries, private diaries, internal reports, intelligence
briefings, and notes from senior officers and government officials) and
from interviews with officers from Sweden and from various NATO
countries directly involved in these kinds of operations. It seems that the
classified documents totally invalidate the view presented in the official
documents. However, interviews with the people involved make this
picture even more clear, especially since the most sensitive information
was most likely never put down on paper. After some debate in the
Swedish mass media (and particularly after an interview on Swedish TV
with former US Secretary of Defense Caspar Weinberger), the Swedish

government appointed former UN inspector in Iraq and former Swedish Ambassador to Washington, Rolf Ekéus, to investigate the issue. Ekéus invited me as an expert to analyse some of the background for these operations, and thus this volume is written as my own book, but early drafts were also made as an internal report to the Ekéus Investigation.

Chapter 2 deals with the background for the submarine hunt: the so-called Operation NOTVARP (Operation Seine Sweep). Officially, the hunt started after a periscope had been seen in Hårsfjärden on 1 October 1982. This, however, is not true. Secretly, an anti-submarine operation or exercise was planned several months in advance. This Operation NOTVARP was prepared in detail in late September, with US naval ships, including the cruiser USS *Belknap*, acting as a bait to lure Soviet submarines into a trap, but seemingly also with a Western submarine to trigger the hunt. On 26 September, a small submersible was observed in the waters of central Stockholm 'within a stone's throw of the royal palace' and just a few metres from the US naval ships. This, most likely US, submersible was probably the same vessel that, three days later on 29 September, was seen close to the Stockholm harbour a few kilometres further out. Swedish Navy forces were now preparing for an anti-submarine exercise that was due to start early in the morning the following day and were waiting at a narrow passage outside Stockholm. Some hours later a small submarine or submersible turned up in the pre-planned area. Sweden did not have such midget craft at the time, and the Soviets would never have carried out an exercise in collaboration with the Swedes. Thus, it seems more likely that this was a US submersible brought to Stockholm by the US naval ships a couple of days earlier. A Swedish boarding detail of 15 naval special force troops – supposed to take control of the submarine – was fetched by helicopter and brought to the area even before the first confirmed observation of a submarine took place. In the naval base war diary, a submarine was described as 'not Warsaw Pact'. The naval base war diary states: 'not to be reported to the Commander of the Eastern Military District and not to be reported to the Commander-in-Chief'.

Chapter 3 consists of a 'war diary' for the Hårsfjärden anti-submarine warfare operation. The following passage summarizes what can be concluded from an examination of the evidence. On 1 October, two conscripts observed a periscope at close range for more than a minute. The submarine seemingly announced its presence deep inside the restricted area close to the naval base of Muskö as if it wanted to trigger a submarine hunt. Chief of Staff Bror Stefenson ordered the information division to prepare for a press centre with up to 500 journalists. During the following days, a number of observations were made of periscopes, submarine sails and submarines on the

8

surface, almost as if the intruder wanted to play with the Swedes. During the next two weeks, possibly six foreign submarines (including three midgets or small submersibles) seem to have operated in the Stockholm archipelago. Four of these operated deep inside the Swedish waters close to the naval base of Muskö. Two – possibly three – submarines were damaged, one perhaps seriously. All of these submarines appear to have originated from a NATO country. On 5 October, a small submarine (about 40 metres) and a small bottom-crawling submersible may both have been lightly hit by depth charges. On 7 October, a submarine just outside the submarine net may have been hit by six depth charges. It was saved by a ceasefire in the afternoon. On 11 October, a submarine was damaged, perhaps seriously, by a mine explosion further out at Mälsten. During some dramatic hours, it was repaired on the sea floor. Evidence pointed to a Western, possibly US, submarine. The sound signature of the propeller and repair works were tape-recorded. Both tape recordings have since been edited, and other significant information has been blotted out. During this anti-submarine warfare operation, Chief of Staff Vice-Admiral Bror Stefenson gave several orders that in practical terms released two Western submarines. The second submarine was let out at Mälsten during a five-hour ceasefire on the night of 13–14 October. A drop of 16 depth charges was stopped seconds before the launch. This submarine had a damaged propeller, and the sound signature was also tape-recorded on this occasion. However, as early as the morning, it had been decided that this passage had not taken place. At lunch, the Minister of Defence was informed that the mine barrage was indicating wrongly. The Commander-in-Chief was probably never informed about any of the more sensitive details.

In Chapter 4, I present some reflections about the hunt. Most of the organizers of the secret anti-submarine warfare operation probably believed it was a trap for Soviet submarines, and almost everybody involved believed they were hunting Soviet submarines. However, all intelligence briefings of the time speak of low levels of Soviet activity in the Baltic Sea area, and nothing points to any Soviet interest in the damaged submarines in the Stockholm archipelago. In addition, investigation of the sea floor revealed caterpillar tracks from a bottom-crawling vessel believed to originate from an unknown Soviet midget submarine. However, while such submersibles did exist in the West, a Soviet version was not confirmed. The tape-recorded propeller sound was believed to be evidence of a Soviet submarine. However, when these Swedish crown jewels – the recordings – were investigated more closely, they had been polished down to nothing. All important information had been removed from the tapes. Already shortly after the Hårsfjärden incident, Norwegian Military Intelligence, on analysing the tape, found that the submarine recorded was not a Soviet one, conventional or nuclear. Indeed, they believed it was a Western submarine. Later, the Americans confiscated the Norwegian copy of the tape. One hour after the mine explosion, the submarine sent up a yellow/green dye just 150 metres from the place of the explosion, indicating that it was a US submarine or at least under US command. Though kept very secret, the operation seems to have been a Western – US/UK – operation to test Swedish capability and will and to deceive the Swedish government, military officers and public in order to convince them about the reality of the Soviet threat. On the Swedish side, the operation may have been run by the Chief of Staff Vice-Admiral Bror Stefenson, and perhaps by the Chief of the Naval Base Rear-Admiral Christer Kierkegaard, under the supervision of the Chief of the Navy Vice-Admiral Per Rudberg. Afterwards, Western involvement was covered up by Stefenson and by his and Rudberg's private 'chief of intelligence', Commander Emil Svensson, who wrote an extensive secret report prepared for the military leadership, the parliamentary commission and the government. However, almost all sensitive information had been distorted or removed. The Commander-in-Chief and the Commander of the Eastern Military District were probably never informed about the most secret aspects of the operation. The former was believed to have too close ties to the government, and he was not trusted to run the show. Henry Kissinger was impressed by the Swedish government's show of force and its release of a submarine without causing loss of face to the responsible party. However, the Swedish government was seemingly not informed at all. Afterwards, Stefenson became Chief of Staff to King Karl Gustaf and a Swedish 'four-star admiral'; Rudberg was already the secret Swedish top-liaison to NATO and Commander-in-Chief in exile in the event of Sweden being occupied; and Svensson soon was appointed military assistant to Conservative Prime Minister Carl Bildt.

In Chapter 5, I present the Swedish Parliamentary Submarine Defence Commission Report, which concluded that six Soviet submarines had been operating in Swedish waters. This led to a strong Swedish protest against the Soviet Union. However, immediately after the submarine hunt, at a military briefing for Prime Minister Palme, Chief of Staff Vice-Admiral Stefenson explained the submarine activity as 'a testing of Swedish capability and will', in line with US statements about Western submarine activity. Later, the Submarine Defence Commission and its military expert, Vice-Admiral Stefenson, presented a very different explanation: Soviet operative planning for wartime contingencies. Publicly, there was no doubt about the Soviet responsibility. However, nobody in the Swedish government was convinced by the evidence presented by the Swedish Defence Staff. 'But what could we do?' Defence Minister Anders Thunborg said. 'We could not dive ourselves. We had to trust the military officers responsible for this.'[24] In the Swedish government note to the Soviet Union in autumn 1983, Swedish Defence Staff presented a number of 'proofs' of Soviet responsibility, including statements about signal intelligence and tape-recorded propeller sounds. In the early 1990s, Prime Minister Carl Bildt tried to convince Moscow about Soviet responsibility for the intrusions by letting his military adviser Emil Svensson hand over one of the above-mentioned tape recordings, which suggests that he had not been informed about the Norwegian analysis pointing to a Western submarine. Svensson handed over a sequence of submarine sounds, but nobody seemed to know when they had been recorded on the tape. He also gave Moscow a tape recording of a suspected propeller sound from 1992. This latter sound, however, was later believed to originate from a swimming mink, and, when this was revealed, the Social Democratic Minister of Defence at the time, Thage G. Peterson, appointed a new Submarine Commission. This 1995 Submarine Commission found out that all evidence for Soviet intrusions presented by the Defence Staff and the 1983 Commission had been manipulated or just invented. Despite the fact that the Swedish Signal Intelligence had nothing on the Soviets, the Defence Staff (under Vice-Admiral Bror Stefenson) insisted that the contrary was the case.[25] This in turn, according to former Prime Minister Ingvar Carlsson, had been an important argument for the strong Swedish government protest against the Soviet Union in 1983.[26] Thage G. Peterson asked himself why the USA was never interested in Sweden's submarine problem, and he quotes Secretary of Defense William Perry's comment on the submarine intrusions: 'If there is a submarine, it doesn't have to be Russian.'

In Chapter 6, I discuss possible Soviet, West German, British, French, US and even Italian submarine operations in Swedish waters. The Soviets are believed by many to have operated in Swedish coastal waters both for training operations and for preparations for wartime contingencies. But many of the submarine operations in the 1980s were demonstrative. They showed periscopes, sails and surfaced submarines in densely populated areas. This fits neither with training operations nor with war preparations. Soviet lack of interest in the damaged submarines in the Stockholm archipelago also seems to rule out Soviet involvement. When a Soviet Whiskey-class submarine became stranded in southern Sweden in 1981, the Soviet Navy made a powerful demonstration of force. The following year, during the Hårsfjärden incident, there was nothing of that. This led to the hypothesis of possible West German involvement. In the event of war, the West Germans would have difficulty operating their submarines in the Baltic Sea without using Swedish coastal waters. The West Germans, however, were believed to use their numerous port visits to small ports along the Swedish coast primarily to carry out such training for wartime contingencies. Even though I am in no way excluding Soviet or West German intrusions, such activity cannot explain the very high-profile operations in Sweden in the 1980s. Submarines on the surface deep inside the Swedish archipelagos cannot be explained as war preparations, but rather as a kind of psychological warfare and testing of Sweden's defences. Now, several years later, British Royal Navy submarine captains have admitted that they carried out top-secret operations in Swedish waters, that they entered the Baltic Sea submerged through the Danish Straits (which is confirmed by high-ranking Danish officers) with submarines rebuilt for landing of special forces, and that approval was granted at a ministerial level for every single operation. The Prime Minister's Office was briefed regularly about the risks, and the operations along the Swedish coast were perceived as even more secret than operations in Soviet waters. Former British Navy Minister Sir Keith Speed and former Chief of Defence Intelligence Sir John Walker confirmed the existence of these operations. Speed spoke about 'penetration dive exercises' deep within Swedish waters. He was speaking in terms of trying to get in and surface almost in the Stockholm harbour. The point was: 'How far could we get without you being aware of it?'[27] Walker said that they tested Swedish defences and they were allowed 'a certain amount of intrusions within a given period'.[28] In a 15-minute interview, former US Secretary of Defense Caspar Weinberger stated that these operations were carried out 'regularly' in Swedish waters. 'Besides from that one intrusion of the Whiskey-class submarine, there were no violations, no capabilities of the Soviets,' said Weinberger; but Soviet submarines, he continued, 'can get in where they are not wanted, and that is exactly why we made this defensive testing'.[29] According to high-ranking officers, US special forces used Soviet uniforms, Soviet weapons and communication systems, and even a Soviet Whiskey-class submarine to carry out a successful masquerade. In these operations, US Navy SEALs could not be identified as US forces and, on the Swedish side, only a couple of informal contacts loyal to the USA were informed. Einar Ansteensen, the *éminence grise* of the Norwegian Foreign Ministry, told me that a US submarine was damaged in Hårsfjärden. It was a sad story, he said. Senior US officials have confirmed this incident, and a high-ranking CIA officer described it as 'something of an underwater U-2'. The operations seem to have been run by a CIA–DIA liaison office. They were political operations: primarily psychological warfare operations aimed at changing Swedish public opinion.

Chapter 7 discusses the US and British secret war against Sweden in the 1980s. Both the USA and the UK seem to have run secret submarine operations in Swedish waters in order to train their own forces, to train Swedish coastal defences and to test Swedish capability and will to resist a Soviet attack. The Swedish forces became much more alert and much less a 'nine-to-five military defence'. Primarily, however, these US/UK secret operations changed public opinion in Sweden and made Swedish officers and the general public more aware of the Soviet threat. As with the events during the intensified US–Soviet competition of the 1950s, when ghostlike US military aircraft over Sweden created a storm of Swedish reactions against the 'Soviet' intruders, ghostlike US/UK submarines in the 1980s totally manipulated public opinion, and government and military forces in Sweden and made it difficult for the Swedish government to maintain an independent policy. In the first minute of a war, US special forces masquerading as attacking Soviet Spetsnaz forces would make the Swedes turn to the Americans and let US aircraft strike the Central Front and the Soviet heartland from Swedish airbases. This secret US/UK submarine war should primarily be understood as a deception operation to control Sweden politically and to render impotent the anti-US policies of Swedish Prime Minister Olof Palme. Palme's disarmament initiative and his vision about common security and a Nuclear Weapons-Free Zone received little support and proved unrealistic because he was unable to defend himself against 'Soviet aggression'. The Swedish Navy's bombing of 'Soviet' submarines in its internal waters also became the background for the political transformation of Europe in the 1980s. In democratic countries, political control is not easily attained by traditional forms of warfare, not even by the use of traditional propaganda methods. However, through deception and psychological warfare, the public, the political elite and local military forces may be deceived into supporting the politics of a major power. By letting special forces masquerade as 'the other side' while attacking a target force or a target country, one may be able to create 'real experiences' that will influence the emotions, objective reasoning and behaviour of that country. It is possible to manipulate the mass media not by propaganda but by deception, and in the 1980s even the most critical journalists and academic scholars were deceived by the masquerade. By masquerading as the perceived enemy, US special forces have been able to manipulate public opinion in order to change the behaviour of governments. This policy option may be the most important alternative to the use of force in democratic countries. The US Joint Doctrine for Special Operations states that one should create 'indicators', messages tailored to a selective foreign audience 'to influence the emotions, motives, objective reasoning, and ultimately the behaviour of foreign governments'.[30]

In this sense, the operations in Swedish waters, and not least the Hårsfjärden operation, may have been the most successful covert psychological operation of the Cold War. However, the Hårsfjärden operation was also an extremely risky enterprise. If one particular lieutenant-colonel, Sven-Olof Kviman, had had live shells available when a submarine surfaced on 4 October (which he very nearly did have), if the same local commander had chosen to interpret a Commander-in-Chief order about when to give fire with the mines a little bit differently on 11 October (which a less cautious commander might have done) and if the same commander had decided not to follow a ceasefire order on 13 October (which his immediate superior considered) while a submarine passed out over the mines, two (possibly three) US submarines might have been sunk in the Stockholm archipelago within a period of a couple of days, which would have been more than in any other military conflict since the Second World War. We may have to thank Sweden's Chief of Staff, Vice-Admiral Bror Stefenson, for preventing such a catastrophe. It seems that CIA Director William Casey was playing for high stakes.

NOTES

1 SOU (1983); *Rapport*, Swedish TV2 (26 April 1983).
2 McCormick (1990), p. v.
3 SOU (1995).
4 *Svenska Dagbladet* (11 October 1982).
5 KU 1982/83:30, pp. 19–20.
6 *Verdens Gang* (12 October 1982).
7 Hansen (1984), pp. vii–viii, 4.
8 Cohen (1986), p. 12.
9 Leitenberg (1987), pp. 155–7.
10 Lampers (1996); Bodström (2000).
11 Tunander (1999), pp. 169–203.
12 Palme Commission (1982).
13 Schlesinger (1982), pp. 11–18.
14 Taylor (1982b), pp. 411, 415.
15 *Aktuellt*, Swedish TV1 (5 March 1984).
16 ÖB TD (4 January 1983).
17 Kadhammar (1987), p. 106.
18 *Svenska Dagbladet* (11 October 1982).
19 *Aktuellt*, Swedish TV1, 12 January 1986.
20 Sköld (1999), p. 165.
21 McCormick (1990), p. vi.
22 Anderson and van Atta, *Washington Post* (6 May 1990).
23 Taylor and Maaranen (1982), p. 475.
24 Thunborg, in Aland and Zachrisson (1996), pp. 150–1.
25 SOU (1995).
26 Carlsson (1999), p. 115.

27 Speed, on *Striptease*, Swedish TV2 (11 April 2000).
28 Associated Press, 8.38 p.m. (7 March 2000).
29 Weinberger, on *Striptease*, Swedish TV2 (7 March 2000).
30 Joint Pub 3-05 (1998), p. II-8.

2

The Background: Operation NOTVARP

The submarine hunt in Hårsfjärden, close to Muskö Naval Base, started on 1 October 1982. Less than two weeks earlier, on 19 September, the Social Democratic Party had won the parliamentary elections. The new government was due to replace the previous Centre and Liberal Party government on 8 October. Whereas Prime Minister Fälldin's government was on its way out, the new government of Olof Palme had not yet been established. Despite rumours in the mass media about which ministers Olof Palme was going to appoint, the new government did not yet exist.

This change in political leadership was supplemented by a major reshuffling of positions among the military personnel. On 1 October, the Chief of Staff, the Commander of the Eastern Military District and the Chief of Stockholm Coastal Defence were all new appointments. The same was the case with the Chiefs of Operations for the Defence Staff, the Eastern Military District and Naval Base East. Most of Sweden's military chiefs responsible for defence against a foreign coastal operation in eastern Sweden were replaced on that very day. Thus, the operations were initiated on a day when Sweden was most vulnerable to an enemy attack, as if somebody wanted to demonstrate this vulnerability to the Swedes.

Already in spring and summer 1982, a number of submarine incidents had occurred within Swedish waters. There was clear evidence of submarine activities and several indications of midget submarines operating deep inside the Swedish archipelagos, though the intruders had disappeared by the time Swedish naval forces arrived on the scene. There was a feeling within the Swedish Navy that they always arrived too late. Of course, the Navy could not be everywhere. On the other hand, naval commanders wanted to put an end to these activities and looked for alternative strategies. They wanted to show that the Soviet Union could not do as it pleased in Swedish waters. Chief of the Naval Analysis Group Commander Emil Svensson came up with the idea of creating a trap. The only chance of success, he believed, would be if the Swedish Navy was able to concentrate its anti-submarine forces in a certain area, where it was believed the Soviet submarines would turn up and be lured into a trap. According to Christer Larsson's interview with Commander Svensson and Commander Anders Hammar, former Chief of the First Submarine Division, a preliminary plan was made and the go-ahead was given by Chief of Staff Bengt Schuback, Chief of the Coastal Fleet Bror Stefenson, Chief of Stockholm Coastal Defence Brigadier-General Sven-Åke Adler and Chief of First Helicopter Division at Berga Commander Eric Hagström as early as July or August 1982. Nothing was written down on paper, and everything was kept extremely secret.[1] Intensive preparations for this exercise, Operation NOTVARP (Operation Seine Sweep), were made in September. The Chief of the Naval Base, Rear-Admiral Christer Kierkegaard, gave a Naval Staff briefing to about ten commanders involved (including Brigadier-General Adler and his successor, Brigadier-General Lars Hansson) a few days before the operation was to start. Of these central figures, Kierkegaard and Adler are dead, but, according to Hagström, a conversation with Schuback, Stefenson and Adler took place shortly before Operation NOTVARP started. They discussed, among other things, measures against midget submarines and the experience of operations in Swedish waters earlier the same year. Hagström, Adler and primarily Stefenson (as Chief of the Coastal Fleet) assigned forces for the operation. Admiral Schuback said that he did not remember a specific meeting, but the operation 'was run by Chief of the Coastal Fleet [Rear-Admiral Bror Stefenson]', he said. The naval base war diary states that Admiral Stefenson, as the only high-ranking officer, was briefed in the afternoon of 30 September.[2] In 2000, when Commander Lars-Erik Hoff, former Chief of Staff at the naval base, started checking what could be declassified about Operation NOTVARP, he turned to retired Admiral Bror Stefenson, who said that everything was still very secret. Stefenson seems to have been the high-ranking officer 'running the operation'. However, according to Stefenson's testimony for the Ekéus Investigation, he was never informed until afterwards.[3]

Emil Svensson's idea was to profit from the US port visit to Stockholm in late September. The US Navy ships would be used as bait to attract Soviet submarines. Kanholmsfjärden (or rather the sailing routes into Stockholm further north) would be sealed off with submarine nets and mine barrages in an attempt to 'deny the submarines the possibility of escape'. The Coastal Fleet mobilized several vessels with depth charges and passive and active sonar. The First Helicopter Division at Berga was put on alert. Coastal Defence personnel activated the magnetic sensors of the mine barrages. However, personnel were not informed about the background for the operation.[4] From early September, sophisticated listening devices, able to identify submarines, were set up. A boarding detail was mobilized to take care of the submarine. According to Svensson and Hammar, all this was set up as a secret trap for Soviet submarines.[5] This general idea has been confirmed to me by Deputy Chief of Defence Staff Intelligence Commander Björn Eklind and by the local Coastal Defence Commander (Boarding Detail), then Colonel Lars-G. Persson. According to Lars-G. Persson and Commander Bengt Gabrielsson, this was a real anti-submarine warfare operation, but it was also planned as a secret anti-submarine warfare exercise for the Swedish Navy.[6]

In early to mid-September, NATO had carried out a naval exercise, NORTHERN WEDDING, as training in landing operations in Denmark and Norway. On 17 September, this exercise was succeeded by an exercise in the Baltic Sea, BOLD GUARD. On 25 September, when this exercise was finished, some of the US vessels went on a port visit to Stockholm, while others, a cruiser and a frigate, went to Helsinki. The US cruiser USS *Belknap*, the frigate USS *Elmer Montgomery* and the US Navy depot ship USS *Monongahela* stayed in Stockholm from 25 to 27 September. After lunch on 27 September,[7] they left for another naval exercise in the Baltic Sea, US BALTOPS, which ended on 2 October. The political elite was primarily occupied by the change of government. Military matters did not have first priority. To the military elite, however, the US port visit was an important event. It brought a lot of people to the ships. It was the most impressive port visit for years, and, very secretly, the US vessels served as a bait to attract Soviet submarines for Operation NOTVARP. This is at least how it is described by two of the planners of the operation, Commander Svensson and Commander Hammar.[8]

However, Operation NOTVARP did not start until the early hours of 30 September, while already at 14.00 on 28 September the US ships were at a position southeast of Gotland,[9] not far from the Soviet Baltic coast. The idea of using the US ships as a bait does not fit with the actual timetable. The trap was set up several days after the bait had left the area. Furthermore, the early observations do not fit with Soviet submarines. According to a couple travelling on a small ferry boat at 14.00 on 26 September, they saw a small silver-grey periscope in the waters at Kastellholmen in central Stockholm only a few metres from US cruiser *Belknap* and frigate *Elmer Montgomery* and not more than a few hundred metres from the royal palace. They reported that the periscope was 35–40 centimetres high and 10–15 centimetres in diameter. Indeed, several people saw this periscope. It turned around and displayed its aperture, and a detailed drawing of the periscope was made by the couple on the ferry boat.[10] This incident is not mentioned in General Lennart Ljung's diary, and it may not have been reported to him

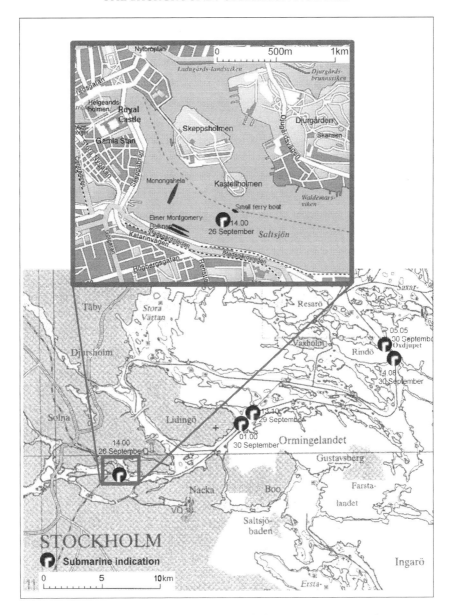

5. Submarine indications in the Stockholm area 26–30 September.
Observations of periscopes and a submarine sail as well as magnetic indications in
mine barrages in the Stockholm area 26–30 September. The periscope seen on
26 September was close to the US ships in the very centre of Stockholm, a few
hundred metres from the Royal Castle.

because the small submarine might have been part of a routine security arrangement for the US ships: there is a long tradition of sabotage in foreign harbours,[11] and US ships would routinely have a sub-surface presence – usually in the form of divers – to protect the ships from sabotage. The periscope seen close to the ships was most likely not that of a Soviet submarine, and, half a year later when the issue was brought up by the Submarine Defence Commission, General Ljung also indicated that there was a link to the US ships (see below).[12] The small submersible might have been released from the US tanker *Monongahela*, which could easily have been adapted for such a purpose.

In the afternoon of the following day, the US ships left Stockholm. On 28 September, they participated in the naval exercise in the Baltic Sea far away from Stockholm. However, at 13.10 on 29 September, a small submarine sail was seen at Lidingö in the Stockholm harbour,[13] a couple of kilometres further out from where the first observation had taken place. The observer saw bubbles, the water was seemingly boiling, and then, for ten seconds, something dark grey, with an antenna – a small submarine sail, 1 metre high and 1.5 metres wide – before it disappeared.[14] Most likely, the 'small submersible patrolling the US ships' had been left on its own in order to exercise its way out from Stockholm in the area already pre-planned for Operation NOTVARP. This occurred on the day before that operation started. Preparations were already more or less finalized. From 09.35 on 28 September, Swedish submarines were not allowed to operate submerged west of a line following the outer archipelago. West of this line, the order was 'one minute between blank ammunition and live ammunition'.[15] From the following day, Swedish forces were deployed along the sailing routes to Stockholm harbour and all the way out to Kanholmsfjärden. The naval base war diary contains the following entry:

18.05 . . . Tomorrow morning, exercise will take place in interesting area . . . Highest alert within the framework of NOTVARP. Concentration of force to the northern area . . . At 20.44, telephone conversation with CSjöop [Commander Bengt Gabrielsson, Chief of Naval Operations, Eastern Military District], who informs about MBÖ's [Commander, Eastern Military District, Lieutenant-General Gunnar Eklund] order to CSK [Brigadier-General Sven-Åke Adler] via CKA1 [Colonel L.-G. Persson] about reconnaissance at Oxdjupet will start 22.00 as well as deployment of a patrol vessel.[16]

At 22.00, forces for the mine barrages were deployed at the narrow channel at Oxdjupet, Vaxholm, outside Stockholm harbour. They were waiting for magnetic indications from a submarine. 'The submarine was expected,' wrote Colonel Lars-G. Persson, Chief of the

Coastal Defence Regiment KA1, in his diary,[17] though this does not mean that he or any of the above-mentioned commanders knew why it was expected.

At 01.00 on 30 September, a radar echo was followed for a 'long time' by a police boat at Lidingö,[18] close to the spot where a small 'submarine tower' had been observed 12 hours earlier. Colonel Persson and others believed that this was a real anti-submarine warfare operation, and Persson was ordered to deploy forces for the mine barrages. A boarding detail – a special force to seize the submarine – was already mobilized and was fetched by helicopter at 01.30. The decision would have been taken just an hour earlier but before the first confirmed observation at 01.00. Patrol boats and additional officers and reserves were also deployed.[19] 'At 01.12, from Night Officer at the Defence Staff: order one helicopter with depth charges start immediately . . . Helicopter II starts in 15 minutes . . . At 02.55, CKA1 [Colonel Persson]: one patrol vessel with depth charges at 15 minutes' readiness.' By early morning on 30 September, all forces involved in Operation NOTVARP had been deployed.[20]

Around 02.00, Chief of Staff Vice-Admiral Bengt Schuback called Commander-in-Chief General Lennart Ljung. There had been two different reports of a small submarine on the surface at Lidingö, close to Stockholm harbour.[21] Admiral Schuback told me that it was a police boat that observed the submarine. There was also a civilian observation and a radar indication registered by the police boat. It is most likely the same submarine that provoked a magnetic indication in Oxdjupet, further out.

At 05.05, telephone call from CSjöop Milo Ö [Commander Gabrielsson]: magnetic indication [in the mine barrages]. We start helicopter. At 05.07, highest alert. [The Naval Analysis Group Report wrote that the object was going out from Stockholm.][22] At 05.40, CÖrlBO [Chief of Naval Base East] order [to fast attack craft *Mysing*]: go immediately to Oxdjupet . . . [One helicopter] in the area for one hour. Conversation between E[mil] Svensson – M[auritz] Carlsson [Chief of Intelligence Naval Base East]: 'a possible submarine in Oxdjupet. Proposal: maximum force now'. At 06.30, Conversation with CKA1 [Colonel Persson] about the situation. At 07.15, the helicopter Y71: no contact . . . At 08.05, conversation with CSjöop [Commander Gabrielsson] about proposal to deploy [more] forces for visual reconnaissance in the archipelago (4–5 places) and for activating the mine barrages. Telephone from H. Neckman [Deputy Chief, First Helicopter Division]: Helicopter 6 is flying in the area from Oxdjupet and further out 09.00–11.00. At 08.25, conversation with Commander [Emil] Svensson about more 'eyes' . . . At 08.40, conversation with crew for [reconnaissance aircraft] GYP: starts 10.30 to cover the [sailing routes] Furusundsleden, Kanholmen, Dalaröleden as well as the entrances to the Stockholm archipelago . . . At 10.08, report from [Chief of Naval Intelligence, Lieutenant-Colonel] R[olf] Malm (police boat): radar echo at Lidingö at 01.00. May fit with later indications . . . At 10.40, called CSjöop [Commander Bengt Gabrielsson] and proposed contact between him and Commander Svensson before the final starting up with pickets. At 11.40, [the helicopters] Y69 and Y71 on 10 min alert. One helicopter 6 starts 13.00 and covers the sailing routes from Oxdjupet and further out up to 15.00 . . . At 12.18, received telegram from the Commander of the Eastern Military District [Lieutenant-General Eklund]: 'Reconnaissance against submarine' . . . At 14.08, the Chief of KA1 [Colonel L.-G. Persson] reports about a new indication. Order to Chief of First Helicopter Division: 'Submarine hunt with sonar in Trälhavet' [outside Oxdjupet]. Start Y71. Y69 on 10 min alert'.[23]

In the evening of 29 September, it was said that an 'exercise' would take place the next morning. At 22.00, personnel were deployed at the mine barrage at Oxdjupet (Vaxholm) to wait for the submarine. Forces were deployed, and others were put on high alert even before the first confirmed observation of a submarine. About 01.00, there were indications further in from Stockholm harbour – probably from the same 'small US submersible' that had been left behind by the US ships. A police boat had followed a radar echo 'for a long time'.[24] At 05.00, a submarine may have passed the mine barrage at Oxdjupet, and the submarine hunt – with helicopters, patrol boats and a fast attack craft – started in the sailing routes out from Oxdjupet. At 14.00, there was supposedly a new indication in the mine barrage at Oxdjupet. A helicopter carried out anti-submarine operations with sonar similar to the operations of nine hours earlier. In the evening, there were indications from Kanholmsfjärden, further out.

It is always very difficult to say anything for sure about all these technical indications and visual sightings, but one or possibly two small US submersibles seem to have exercised an escape operation while Swedish anti-submarine forces exercised a submarine hunt. It is very unlikely that Swedish military authorities would have been willing to use force against a Swedish submarine. Furthermore, from 28 September, Swedish submarines were not allowed to operate submerged in the archipelago. On the other hand, a Warsaw Pact submarine would never have been used in an exercise, and it is unlikely that the presence of such a submarine would have been known in advance. All the preparations on 28–29 September indicate that somebody in the Swedish military leadership knew that one or two foreign submarines were going to exercise their way out from Stockholm. There are several reports of a submarine in Stockholm harbour on its way out. Thus, the submarine(s), or small submersible(s), seem to have been dumped by the US ships in Stockholm harbour and then exercised its/their way out. This hypothesis is supported by the above-mentioned statement of General Ljung, in which he is worried about a link between the submarine and the US naval ships visiting Stockholm.

Alongside the indications from Stockholm harbour and further out, there were further indications of submarine activity from Sandhamn and from the area outside the Stockholm archipelago. On 29 September, the naval base war diary records two possible submarines – one of them close to Korsö (at Sandhamn) in the outer archipelago and one further out (perhaps outside Swedish territorial waters). The Naval Analysis Group Report refers to a visual sighting at 14.10 of waves and a black shadow at Korsö. At 22.25, the fast attack craft *Mode* reported signals[25] possibly indicating a Soviet submarine radar ('Snoop Plate') outside the Swedish archipelago (see below). The naval base war diary states:

[At 14.40 on 29 September, order: two helicopters for submarine hunt east Korsö. The submarine further out] may try to attract attention [from anti-submarine warfare forces, so the first one would be able to act more freely]. Decision: a helicopter for submarine hunt to the Korsö area between 15.00 and 18.00 . . . In the evening: reconnaissance – radar, visual and sonar – in the area. One helicopter on 5 minutes' alert at Berga. Another helicopter on 30 minutes' alert . . .

At 12.35 [on 30 September], *Mode* reports from DQ 4317, bearing 060 degrees: radar indication, 'Snoop Plate' [possibly Warsaw Pact submarine radar] at 12.20. At 13.18 . . . GYP reports oil patch at [the island] Svenska Björn [from the same bearing outside the Stockholm archipelago]. At 12.00 new thin oil. At 13.15, the oil is gone. Conversation with Commander Svensson: 'typically deceptive behaviour. Perhaps active support has been given to the inner submarine [Korsö-Sandhamn] that has difficulties' . . . At 17.00, Rear-Admiral Bror Stefenson is briefed by B. [Lieutenant-Commander Björn] Ljungren. At 17.40, received telegram from the Commander of the Eastern Military District [Lieutenant-General Eklund]: 'Guidelines'. Answer [from Naval Base]: 'We will not change our instructions'. [At 19.35, *Mode* from position DQ 4317 (same position as 12.20) reports West German submarine radar bearing 034 degrees. Visual and radar reconnaissance. No ship. At 20.05, new report from *Mode*: West German submarine radar (from the same position). Visual and radar reconnaissance. No ship.][26] At 20.12, signal reconnaissance contact. Asked for classification. [From *Mode*:] . . . Cannot be classified. Not Warsaw Pact . . . At 21.26, from *Mode*: most likely West German submarine. Has been in contact with SC [SCOrlBO Commander Lars-Erik Hoff, Chief of Staff, Naval Base East]. Should not be reported in the organization 'yet'. Been in contact with Emil [Svensson]: Possible West German submarine at 'Kanan' [Kanholmsfjärden close to Korsö and Sandhamn]. It will not interfere with NOTVARP. Has to be investigated within the framework of VHT [*verksamhet* ('activity'), probably referring to NOTVARP]. Not to be reported to the District Commander [Commander of the Eastern Military District] nor to the Commander-in-Chief. Decision: Y69 will carry out submarine hunt in Kanholmsfjärden with start from south – radio silence. Emil Svensson will participate in a planning meeting at 13.00.[27]

There was one indication of a possible Warsaw Pact submarine radar late at night on 29 September and one at lunchtime on 30 September. An oil patch was observed. No more contacts were made. Both of these radars were later described as possibly being outside Swedish territorial waters, or at least outside the Swedish archipelago. In the evening of 30 September, two 'submarine radar' were identified as belonging to a West German submarine. One is described as possibly being outside Swedish territorial waters.[28] According to the naval base war diary, one submarine radar was identified as being 'not Warsaw Pact': in other words, a Western submarine. According to the 1995 Submarine Commission Report, the observation of possible West German submarine radar may have originated from Swedish territorial waters. However, it may have been confused with the radar of a civilian vessel,[29] even though the fast attack craft *Mode* denies possible confusion with any ship: 'No surface vessel was observed visually or on radar.'[30] Commander Björn Eklind, Deputy Chief of Defence Staff Intelligence, told me that a radar was identified as a West German 'submarine radar', but it may have been confused with a civilian Furuno radar. Naval signal intelligence instruments at the time were not able to make this distinction. Furthermore, it is possible to manipulate a radar so that it will give the characteristics of the other side's equipment. He had once himself modified his radar to show the characteristics of a Warsaw Pact radar while proceeding along the Lithuanian and Latvian coasts (see below). There was no confirmed radar observation of either a NATO or a Warsaw Pact submarine, as indicated by the war diary, he said. Commander Eklind made military briefings on signal intelligence for the Parliamentary Submarine Defence Commission in the winter of 1982–83.

The naval base reaction, however, is interesting: firstly, the alleged non-Warsaw Pact submarine did 'not interfere with' the operation; secondly, the incident was not to be reported to the Commander-in-Chief and the Commander of the Eastern Military District. The

Commander-in-Chief was informed about the reported submarine at Lidingö in the middle of the night, but in the case of the reported Western submarine he was explicitly not to be informed. Chief of Naval Operations at the Eastern Military District, Commander Bengt Gabrielsson, said that he had not heard about it, but added that there was much the naval base never informed them about. Commander Lars-Erik Hoff, Chief of Staff at the naval base, says that there was never a clear indication in Kanholmsfjärden, and that it was simply natural not to report this incident to higher commands.[31] However, there have been hundreds of more or less clear indications of submarine activity and in no other case was it written 'not Warsaw Pact' and 'not to be reported to the Commander-in-Chief'. Furthermore, Hoff could not answer why an alleged Western submarine did 'not interfere' with NOTVARP, because the NOTVARP operation is still considered top secret. He said that NOTVARP referred to the nets north of Kanholmsfjärden and argued that the helicopter started from the south to make the submarine go north into the net.[32]

The Submarine Defence Commission (1983) argued that the Sandhamn-Korsö submarine was most likely the mother-sub that received the small submarine that passed out from Stockholm.[33] This is possible, and there were supposedly indications of a docking operation in Kanholmsfjärden a couple of days later.[34] However, in that case it is not very likely that any of these submarines were from the Soviet Union, which was the conclusion made by the Submarine Defence Commission. The report from the Commission did not discuss Operation NOTVARP, because, according to its secretary Michael Sahlin, they did not want to reveal a concept that the Navy might use on later occasions.[35]

Chief of KA1, Colonel Lars-G. Persson, wrote in his diary: 'The submarine was expected. I was commanding a boarding detail [of naval special forces] – under the Commander-in-Chief and the Chief of Stockholm Coastal Defence – to seize the submarine. This operation is still very secret and I cannot write about it here.'[36] During the night of 29–30 September (at 01.30), more than 35 hours before the first official observation of a submarine in Hårsfjärden and half an hour before the Commander-in-Chief General Lennart Ljung was informed about a submarine at Lidingö, special forces for seizing the submarine had already been deployed and put on high alert. There is no doubt that the organizers of NOTVARP anticipated a submarine, a real submarine. NOTVARP was planned both as an exercise for anti-submarine warfare and as a trap for Soviet submarines. However, if NOTVARP had been primarily a trap for Soviet submarines going for the US Navy bait, the final preparations would have been made at least five days earlier, when the US ships entered the Stockholm archipelago.

The preparations for the hunt and the extreme readiness during these days may have alerted local commanders to real and imagined submarines. But, without a real submarine, the whole NOTVARP operation ran the risk of ending up as a failure, with loss of prestige for the Navy. On the other hand, if the bait or a couple of friendly submarines were used to trigger the hunt, success was guaranteed. In a memorandum signed by the Chief of the Naval Base, Rear-Admiral Christer Kierkegaard, his Chief of Staff, Commander Lars-Erik Hoff, and the Chief of the Operative Section of the Naval Base, Commander Rolf Blomquist, NOTVARP is described as an anti-submarine warfare exercise:

> [NOTVARP was] an 'exercise' carried out in the area north of Jungfrufjärden for special training of forces during the ongoing KFÖ [wartime forces exercise]. They were particularly training in submarine hunting with limited distribution of information to the participants and regional staff personnel. Furthermore, certain principles of leadership – operational and tactical leadership – were exercised. This exercise was carried out until 13.00 on 1 October.[37]

In other words, NOTVARP seems to have been an anti-submarine warfare exercise that the local forces and the regional staff were not informed about. They were obviously to believe that it was a real submarine hunt. Theoretically speaking, a Swedish submarine could have played a foreign submarine during this exercise, but there is nothing about this in the naval base war diary, and, as already mentioned, it is highly improbable that the Swedes would have used forces with live ammunition against their own submarines. However, the submerged passage(s) at Oxdjupet at 05.00 and possibly at 14.00 on 30 September were clearly anticipated. It may very well have been one or possibly two small US submersibles that, for example, the US depot ship *Monongahela* had 'dumped' in Stockholm harbour a couple of days earlier (neither *Belknap* nor *Elmer Montgomery* has space for carrying a midget, though *Monongahela* does). If this is the case, there must have been an agreement between (somebody in) the Swedish Navy and US Naval Command. Operation NOTVARP – understood as a trap for Soviet submarines – was kept extremely secret. Perhaps there was an even more secret aspect to the operation: that it was a secret Western test of Swedish anti-submarine warfare capability.

NOTES

1 Larsson (1987).
2 CÖrlBO WD.

3 SOU (2001), p. 107.
4 Larsson (1987).
5 Ibid.
6 CÖrlBO WD; Kierkegaard, Hoff and Blomquist (1990), p. 8.
7 CÖrlBO WD.
8 Larsson (1987).
9 CÖrlBO WD.
10 MAna Hårsfj, Attach. 2.
11 Compton-Hall (1987), p. 39.
12 ÖB TD (21 April 1983).
13 MAna Hårsfj.
14 *Aftonbladet* (1 October 1982). MAna Hårsfj, Attach. 6.
15 CÖrlBO WD.
16 Ibid.
17 LGP HWD.
18 MAna Hårsfj.
19 LGP HWD.
20 CÖrlBO WD.
21 ÖB TD (30 September 1982).
22 MAna Hårsfj.
23 CÖrlBO WD.
24 MAna Hårsfj, Attach. 9.
25 Ibid.
26 Ibid.
27 CÖrlBO WD.
28 CM/Grandin (1982); SOU (1995), p. 143.
29 SOU (1995), p. 238.
30 MAna Hårsfj.
31 Hoff (2000).
32 Ibid.
33 SOU (1983), p. 34.
34 Larsson (1987).
35 SOU (2001), pp. 110–11.
36 LGP HWD.
37 Kierkegaard, Hoff and Blomquist (1990), p. 8.

3

The Hårsfjärden Hunt: A War Diary

Friday 1 October

The submarine hunt in Kanholmsfjärden continued until 09.00. The naval base war diary states that there were some signs of submarine activity in the morning.[1] At lunchtime, two conscript soldiers in a transport boat made a visual sighting of a submarine periscope. The surface was calm. According to Commander Rolf Blomquist, Chief of Section 1 (Operations) at Naval Base East, these soldiers were travelling in a small boat in northern Hårsfjärden when suddenly they had a clear view of a periscope at a distance of a few metres. The entry for 12.55 in the naval base war diary records the instruction: 'Tpb 457 stay where you are, observe and report.' At 13.05, Tpb 457 was asked to report its position DQ 0904.[2]

The Naval Analysis Group Report states that two observers, L and J, were travelling in a boat from Märsgarn-Furuholmen to Vitså at 12.50 (when they observed a periscope entering Hårsfjärden at the northern entrance at Alvsta Långholmar):

> 200–300 metres from Furuholmen, L and J saw a 0.2–0.3-metre-high wave making a V going towards Berganäs. J saw two dark pipes (0.3 metres high, flat top, 0.1 metres in diameter, and distance from each other about 1–1.5 metres) going towards Berganäs. J observed them for about one minute. After this, the two pipes [periscopes] turned towards Käringholmen [in the south]. Both L and J estimated the speed at 5 knots. W[hiskey], Z[ulu], Q[uebec], R[omeo], and F[oxtrot] all have two periscopes with flat tops. For the W[hiskey], Z[ulu] and Q[uebec] the internal distance is 1–1.5 metres).[3]

This seems like a clear observation of a submarine. However, some of the information is confusing. Why did the submarine show two periscopes close to an observer and for a period of a minute or more? Furthermore, why did it use both periscopes at the same time? There was no reason for this. Also, the attack periscope is often thinner than

6. 1 October.

the main periscope, in order to make the submarine as stealthy as possible during an attack, but this does not fit with the description. Thus, it is possible or rather likely that one of these 'periscopes' was a short-wave antenna or other mast, which makes the estimates made by the

29

Analysis Group irrelevant. It is also clear that the Naval Analysis Group only discussed possible Soviet submarines, and did not consider Western submarines, even though several such submarines would have matched the details gathered in the interviews with the two observers. In the Naval Analysis Group Report and in the internal Navy report on the submarine hunt (the Grandin Report), this sighting is classified as a 'certain submarine'.[4] Officially, this was the first observation of a submarine during the hunt, and this incident supposedly triggered the whole submarine operation. The Parliamentary Submarine Defence Commission stated that the observers had seen 'two periscopes' belonging to a 'conventional submarine'.[5] At 13.00, immediately after this observation of a submarine in Hårsfjärden, Operation NOTVARP came to an end.[6]

This information does not tell us much about the submarine other than that it entered Hårsfjärden through the 200-metre-wide northern entrance. There was a report of a possible periscope at Gålö at 15.00 on 30 September,[7] indicating that this submarine may have waited outside while preparing to enter Hårsfjärden. On 1 October, the Naval Analysis Group Report states that, at about 14.00, an object, a possible periscope, was observed for five minutes going southwards at a speed of 5–7 knots close to Fjäderholmarna in Mysingen not far from the northern exit of Hårsfjärden.[8] This may indicate that this submarine left the area the same way it came in immediately afterwards. According to the Submarine Defence Commission, the 'conventional submarine', which had shown its periscopes, probably had left the area immediately after this observation.[9]

The Submarine Defence Commission also writes that at least one other submarine/submersible had been in Hårsfjärden, when this conventional submarine made its visit. In the morning, there had been indications from one small vessel at Djupviken.[10] At lunch, there was a report of an echo from the same area.[11] In the evening, the Coastal Fleet Staff ship *Visborg* reports about a radar echo with 5–6 knots north-north-west of Enstenarna close to Djupviken/Näsudden.[12] This 'vessel' may have entered Hårsfjärden already two days earlier. The Naval Analysis Group writes that, 'at 04.30 on 29 September, the destroyer *Halland* observed an unknown object at Södra Skramsösund' at the entrance to the narrow southern channel into Hårsfjärden at Muskö Naval Base.[13] The captain of the *Halland*, Commander Hans von Hofsten, said there was a distinct echo and something looking like a rowing-boat turned upside down. This was not a conventional submarine, though it was possibly a small submersible.[14] Half an hour later, the magnetic sensors at Muskö Naval Base registered a passage at Skramsösund.[15]

On 1 October, a third possible submarine may have entered Hårsfjärden. Commander Rolf Blomquist told me that, during the night before, a Swedish naval vessel had seen a submarine sail south of Södra Skramsösund. The crew on the Swedish vessel thought that this was a Swedish submarine and did not take it very seriously. However, they found out soon afterwards that there had been no Swedish submarine in the area. This was also a foreign submarine and clearly a small vessel. At 18.13 on 1 October, there was a 'clear magnetic indication' and a 'diffuse shadow' at the shallow 100-metre-wide Södra Skramsösund,[16] which may indicate that a small submarine entered Hårsfjärden from the south.

On 1 October, according to the diary of General Lennart Ljung, the military leadership's reaction was initially hesitant, but more certain information arrived. The hunt was escalated by the deployment of helicopters and by preparations for sealing off the entire area. One depth charge was dropped. Information regarding the developments was passed on to the Ministry of Defence, and State Secretary for Defence Sven Hirdman briefed Prime Minister Fälldin.[17] Two helicopters were put into operation in the area, and sonar buoys were deployed, one in northern Hårsfjärden (the listening-post at Berga tower) and one in southern Hårsfjärden (the listening-post at the naval base at Muskö). Five motor boats covered the exits and the centre of Hårsfjärden, and the area was sealed off with submarine nets to make passage in and out of Hårsfjärden more difficult.[18] The naval base war diary continues:

> [At 17.00, helicopter] Y64 made sonar contact with possible submarine east Långgarn. . . . At 17.43, Y64 reports: depth charge dropped. [Two depth charges dropped at Brogaholmen south of Långgarn at 17.34 and 17.42][19] . . . At 18.13, clear magnetic indication at Södra Skramsösund. Diffuse shadow. Difficult to see. At 18.16, order: start towards Skramsösund. At 18.18, Skagul leaves ÖHM [the naval base] towards [Södra] Skramsösund. At 18.37, MB 404 replaces MB 410 at Södra Skramsösund. At 18.45, the Commander-in-Chief reports about an analysis group at the disposal of CÖrlBO [the Naval Analysis Group is deployed at Naval Base East to support Rear-Admiral Christer Kierkegaard]. At 19.30, a barrier with weapons plus buoys [and nets] deployed between Alvsta Långholmar and Långholmsgrund [at the northern exit]. Hera is outside the barrier to warn potential traffic. At 20.05, briefing captain of Capella about the barrier at Alvsta Långholmar – Långholmsgrund as well as submarine Sjöhunden [deployed surfaced] west Långholmsgrund . . . At 22.45, from night officer: Visborg reports contact with unknown radar echo north-northwest Enstenarna. Clear echo with 5–6 knots.[20]

Only one Swedish submarine, *Sjöhunden*, was deployed, and *Sjöhästen* was ready to replace it. Lieutenant-Commander Nils Bruzelius, former

Chief of the Submarine Division in Karlskrona, proposed to the staff of Naval Base East that they could use his three, more modern, Näcken-class submarines to cover the exits of Hårsfjärden and Mysingen with their sonars. This would have given the anti-submarine forces more advanced sonars.[21] However, the naval base was not interested in this proposal, Bruzelius said.

On 1 October, there were seemingly indications from perhaps two, possibly three, submarines in Hårsfjärden (one submarine that entered Hårsfjärden at lunchtime and possibly left the area soon afterwards; one small submersible, which may have entered Hårsfjärden two days earlier, left traces at Långgarn and at Näsudden; while a third, small submarine may have entered Hårsfjärden from the south around 18.00). There was possibly still some sub-surface activity in the area of Kanholmsfjärden and Sandhamn. The Naval Analysis Group Report refers to a triangular object seen in Kanholmsfjärden at 18.00.[22] The submarine that entered Hårsfjärden from the north seemingly announced its presence for more than a minute by showing its periscope(s) at close range for the observers. Commander Nils Bruzelius told me that a submarine only has to put up the periscope for a few seconds and not more than centimetres above the surface. Once, on an exercise, he passed through a narrow channel in the archipelago with the whole staff waiting for him at a certain time at a certain place, but nobody saw him. The behaviour of this Hårsfjärden submarine, supposedly showing 'two periscopes' for a minute or more close to the major Swedish naval base of Muskö, indicates that it wanted to demonstrate its presence, he said. To operate like this in an area with only two narrow exits and only one of them more than 15 metres deep (100 metres wide) makes no sense if the intention is not to play with the Swedes and provoke a submarine hunt. It is also interesting to note that, a few hours after this first observation of a submarine in Hårsfjärden, Chief of Staff Bror Stefenson ordered the information division to prepare for a press centre with up to 500 journalists as if he immediately understood that this incident was going to be of international importance.[23] Also at this time, Chief of Naval Base East Rear-Admiral Christer Kierkegaard was given the Chief of the Navy's analysis group – the special intelligence group – as a support in the operation. Geographically, the group, including Commander Emil Svensson, Commander Anders Hammar and Lieutenant-Commander Nils-Ove Jansson, was located with the Intelligence Staff at the naval base and was able to use the base's intelligence officers. A fourth member of the group, Lieutenant-Colonel Rolf Malm, was with the Defence Staff. The group was supported by intelligence personnel at Muskö Naval Base. These were the liaison officer to the Chief of the Navy, Commander Sten Swedlund, as well as Lieutenant-

Commander Ebbe Sylvén and Lieutenant-Commander Maurits Carlsson. The latter was Chief of Intelligence at the naval base.

Saturday 2 October

At 04.50, while still dark, a low submarine sail or rather the top of a sail was observed for 10 minutes at a distance of 100–200 metres in the Oxelesund archipelago some 75 km southwest of Muskö. Lights were turned off when another boat approached it. After some minutes, the submarine left its position and went out towards Hävringe. It was followed by a boat at a speed of 6 knots.[24] The Naval Analysis Group Report states that there had been several indications in that area, and this activity is described as a separate operation.[25] In southern Hårsfjärden, there were several possible submarine contacts. There were low-frequency sounds (a propeller?) and radar echoes in northern Hårsfjärden. Five[26] or eight[27] depth charges were dropped (the latter figure may possibly include the use of blank ammunition). 'At 09.52, GYP reports IR [infra-red] contact east Långgarn. At 11.10, one depth charge dropped towards oil patch and air boil-ups at Jungfruhuvud [south-east Långgarn].'[28] Three depth charges were dropped between 11.08 and 11.12 in the same area.[29] The naval base war diary says:

> At 12.11, Y64: depth charge dropped [at Jungfruhuvud] . . . At 14.30, divers investigated. They report: a rock. At 14.35, the tower at Berga reports: cavitation sounds for 2 minutes registered by the northern buoy. Order: Sjöhunden high alert . . . At 15.10, from Urd: clear sonar contact [at Furuskaten; at 14.19, Urd had sonar contact northeast Furuskaten, east Långgarn[30]] (in bearing 244°), distance 500 metres, possible submarine . . . At 15.30, Y64 drops blank depth charge on Urd's contact, depth 32 metres . . . At 15.58–16.00, Y64 drops [live] depth charges [at Furuskaten] . . . At 17.08, from Väktaren: sonar contact, possible submarine, 0.5M [nautical miles] north-northwest Furuskaten. Helicopter ordered to investigate. At 17.15, GYP has IR contact in the water between Långgarn and Länsman in bearing 150° [north-northwest Furuskaten], ideal IR weather. At 17.20, order to Y71: go towards Furuskaten to investigate Väktaren's and Urd's contacts . . . At 18.40, from Mode: still contact, drops one depth charge . . . At 19.00, order to First Helicopter Division: live depth charge should be dropped without former use of blank ammunition . . . At 19.41, from Mode: checked the place of detonation. Only fish. At 23.05 from Bevb 321: radar echo between Märsgarn and Näsudden. Nothing in the night-vision scope.[31]

A meeting took place between Commander-in-Chief Lennart Ljung, Chief of the Navy Per Rudberg and Chief of Staff Bror Stefenson.[32] At

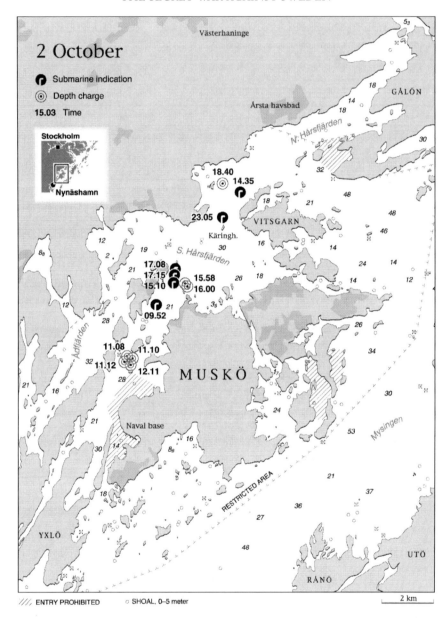

7. 2 October.

19.00, the naval base received the order to use live depth charges without previous warning. The US BALTOPS exercise in the Baltic Sea (which had started on 27 September) came to an end. The first public statement was made at 23.30 on the Saturday night.[33]

Sunday 3 October

There were several indications – radar echoes, sonar contacts and optical observations of waves from possible submarines – in the area around Sandhamn and in Hårsfjärden. Three depth charges were dropped at the southern exit of Hårsfjärden.[34] The naval base war diary contains the following entries:

> At 04.59, from MB 477 . . . echo 400 metres east of Dock One [at Muskö Naval Base]. Disappeared when spotlight was turned towards it . . . At 05.51, from 477: echo between Olångsund and S. Frisholmen. Disappeared, but came back 300 metres from land. At 06.05, from 477: clear echo 100–150 metres north of Långholmen . . . At 13.20, waves and whirlpools at Långholmen–Östra Stendörren at 12.45. Nothing on the surface. At 13.25, from Visborg: intermittent radar echo at the northern tip of Enstenarna . . . [Analysis of oil samples made. Results according to Attachment 20.[35] At 13.45, magnetic indication at Södra Skramsösund [at Muskö Naval Base]. Nothing on the surface. To Snapphanen: go immediately to Skramsösund . . . At 13.55, Y69 on its way. At 14.25, Y69 reports: sonar contact at Gullboda [close to the former position] . . . At 15.05, depth charge dropped, no detonation . . . [At 15.37, another depth charge dropped.[36]] At 15.40, Y69 returns to base. The second bomb detonated . . . At 19.30, from 651: clear radar echo towards Jungfruhuvud, after that waves. Intermittent radar echo for 35–40 seconds . . . At 19.46, clear echo and air boil-ups south of Jungfruhuvud. The echo moved towards the south . . . Helicopter starts . . . At 20.13, 651 reports radar echo towards north entering Olångsund . . . At 21.05, from 651: clear echo west Jungfruholmen . . . At 21.27, patch of mud in the water outside Dock Three.[37]

According to General Ljung, one depth charge was dropped after sonar contact in Hårsfjärden. The Defence Staff discussed the possibility of setting up a press centre.[38] Chief of Staff Vice-Admiral Stefenson went to the naval base 'to deliberate with the naval base chief and the information officer . . . [It was decided to set up] a press centre in the gym hall of Berga naval base.'[39] Two depth charges were dropped.[40]

During the day, there were several indications of submarines in southern Hårsfjärden, as well as a report from northern Hårsfjärden. The magnetic indication at Södra Skramsösund and the following sonar contact at Gullboda (Muskö) indicate that a midget or other small submersible may have entered Hårsfjärden from the south. Depth charges were dropped. The shallow channel, which was less than 100 metres wide, would have made it difficult for a conventional submarine to enter submerged.

The analysis of the oil samples mentioned above is believed to give

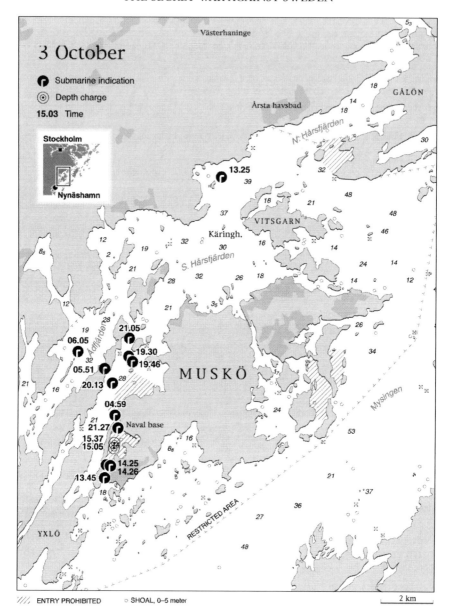

8. 3 October.

clear evidence about the origin of the submarine. In Norway, this
method was used to distinguish between Soviet and Western submarines, because of the different kinds of oil used in the Soviet Union
and many Western countries. However, in the Naval Analysis Group

Report, the attachment about the oil-sample analysis does not state anything about the origin of the oil.[41] Furthermore, in the case of Hårsfjärden, the oil analysis was never used to prove the existence of a Soviet submarine.

Monday 4 October

There were three observations of submarine sails, and several sonar and radar contacts as well as air boil-ups. Twelve depth charges were dropped, and oil (covering 2,500 square metres) appeared on the surface.[42] Chief of the Navy Vice-Admiral Per Rudberg approached Chief of Stockholm Coastal Defence Brigadier-General Lars Hansson and said that they suspected midget submarines.[43] The Norwegian Commander-in-Chief, General Sven Hauge, arrived for an official visit in Sweden. This tied up the Swedish defence leadership for a couple of days.[44] Colonel Persson wrote in his diary:

> Clear [visual] observation of periscope . . . The special force boarding detail and myself are fetched immediately by helicopter. They believe the submarine will soon turn up on the surface . . . [but as] soon as the helicopters start to hover the submarine hides, making the helicopter blind.[45]

The naval base war diary states:

> At 05.13, report from Gullboda: alarm at Skramsösund [magnetic indication], nothing on the surface. A helicopter ordered to go [to Skramsösund] . . . At 05.46, [helicopter] Y69 in Skramsösund . . . [At 09.10, visual observation of submarine sail at Dalarö.[46]] At 09.20 . . . observed with binoculars. It is moving slowly [see below] . . . At 10.45, from Chief of Ekipage [Chief of Muskö Harbour]: oil outside Dock Three. Intensified reconnaissance . . . At 10.57, MBÖ [Commander, Eastern Military District] briefing: first, a naval special force company with 325 men and 40 canoes will most likely be available for CÖrlBO [Chief of Naval Base East, Rear-Admiral Christer Kierkegaard] during the day; second, 40 night-vision scopes are on their way to CÖrlBO . . . [At 12.06, helicopter has sonar contact (high Doppler) at Näsudden.[47]] . . . From 13.20, the helicopter Y71 dropped depth charges after air boil-ups [500 metres from Näsudden, 1,500 metres from Enstenarna (one at 13.20, one at 13.38 and two at 13.46)] . . . [At 14.30, helicopter has sonar contact (high Doppler) at Länsman.[48]] . . . At 15.03, oil patch south of Enstenarna 50×50 metres. At 15.07, from Y71: the oil patch corresponds to where depth charges were dropped . . . At 15.10, fishing with Malin [signal transmitter with a magnet (see below)] . . . At 16.03, Urd reports about a sonar echo 2/10 north of Furuskaten . . . At 16.07, to Y70: go to the contact . . . At 16.11, Y70

is ordered to drop volley of depth charges against visual contact . . . At 16.16, Y70 has dropped two depth charges [500 metres north Furuskaten]. Y70 makes another attack. At 16.18, SC [Chief of Staff, Naval Base East, Commander Lars-Erik Hoff] informs MBÖ [Commander of the Eastern Military District] and ÖB [Commander-in-Chief] . . . At 16.25, Y71 is ordered to drop three depth charges [dropped 16.27 and 16.30] . . . At 17.09, Väktaren has dropped 4 depth charges on Urd's contact [350 metres north-northeast Brudhäll at Furuskaten.[49]] . . . At 18.18, report from Coastal Defence troops at KO [Sandhamn]: suspicious sub-surface object . . . [At 18.15 to 18.20, visual observation of submarine sail at Sandön (Sandhamn).[50]] At 19.00, from Mode: 'certain submarine' at DQ 5218 [close to Sandhamn]. [At 18.45 to 19.00, Mode has sonar contact (high Doppler at Farfars grund, Sandhamn). First blank ammunition and then two depth charges.[51]] At 19.06, to Mode. Order: drop one depth charge. At 19.12, from Mode: one depth charge dropped. At 19.15, from Mode: another depth charge dropped. At 19.17, from Mode: lost contact . . . At 20.45, the hospital ready at Berga [Naval College] . . . At 22.05, report to night officer about clear observation of a surfaced submarine going from Simpviken (Risdal) towards west [in Mälbyfjärden-Hårsfjärden north of the naval base]. At 22.49, from Hebe: clear echo northwest Käringholmen 200–300 metres.[52]

The Naval Analysis Group Report contains the following: 'At 09.10, visual observation of submarine sail at Dalarö ("possible submarine").'[53] In the attachment, it is stated that this was not just a submarine sail but a submarine on the surface seen in a narrow passage between Jutholmen and Aspön, close to Dalarö. It was observed for 15 seconds and was travelling at an estimated speed of 6–8 knots. The depth at this spot is 12 metres, but it had to pass through a 25-metre-wide channel with less than 10 metres depth on each side. The observer had some familiarity with Swedish submarines, and has stated that it was not a Whiskey, of which she had seen pictures. Lieutenant-Commander Nils-Ove Jansson, Chief of Naval Intelligence and a member of the Naval Analysis Group, made a report, suggesting that the observer had confused a surfaced submarine with the top of the sail of a Romeo-class submarine (77 metres, two propellers). This seems far-fetched. The length of the submarine was reported to be two-thirds that of the local Ornö ferry (28 metres and 37 metres), which would make a submarine with a length of 20–25 metres, and most likely 25 metres because the propeller area would not be surfaced. The observer's drawing shows something in the middle of the small sail (perhaps the identification number), a high mast at the very end of the sail or rather just behind the sail, and some specially marked dark

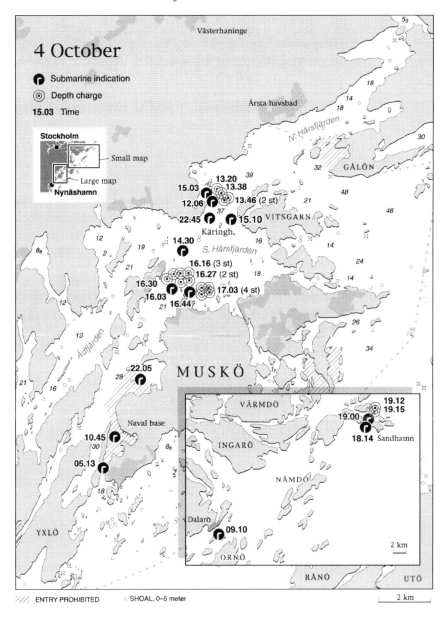

4 October

- Submarine indication
- Depth charge
- **15.03** Time

Stockholm — Small map

Large map — **Nynäshamn**

Västerhaninge

Årsta havsbad

N. Hårsfjärden

GÅLÖN

VITSGARN

Käringh.

S. Hårsfjärden

Ådfjärden

MUSKÖ

VÄRMDÖ

INGARÖ

NÄMDÖ

Naval base

Sandhamn

Dalarö

YXLÖ

ORNÖ

RÅNÖ   UTÖ

13.20
15.03   13.38
12.06   13.46 (2 st)
22.45   15.10
14.30
16.16 (3 st)
16.27 (2 st)
16.30   17.03 (4 st)
16.03   16.44
22.05
19.12
19.15
19.00
18.14
10.45
05.13
09.10

2 km

/// ENTRY PROHIBITED   ○ SHOAL, 0–5 meter   2 km

9. 4 October.

objects – three small squares – on top of the hull.[54] These markings identified by the observer do not belong to any Soviet submarine, but are seen on US and Italian submarines (cf. Strazza Navigation active sonar equipment for narrow waters). The mast just behind the sail is only found on some small Italian submarines, the size of which is consistent with the estimated length of the observed submarine. The small Italian submarines would fit very well in the very narrow and shallow waters at Dalarö. This is not proof of an Italian involvement, but it is interesting that this, the only observation of a surfaced submarine in daylight, does not appear in the Submarine Defence Commission Report or in any other open source.

In the evening, according to this report, there was a clear observation of a submarine at Sandhamn further out. Two depth charges were dropped.[55] The local Coastal Defence commander, Lieutenant-Colonel Sven-Olof Kviman, told me that a large submarine sail – a 'huge wall' – turned up close to the shore only a few metres from his people at Sandhamn. He gave orders to prepare for an artillery attack – to lay a carpet of shells – but the submarine submerged before live shells had been brought up from storage. The attack boat *Mode* was sent out. It made contact with the submarine and dropped depth charges at Farfars Grund. This observation is confirmed by the 1982 internal Navy report made by Rear-Admiral Grandin and by the 1995 Submarine Commission Report. In the internal Navy report, this submarine is described as a 'certain submarine'.[56]

The Naval Analysis Group Report has an attachment covering this incident as it is described by an observer, W. The report states that:

> At 18.15 [dusk], at the western shore of Sandön opposite to Skötkubben, W observes a ship. It is heading straight towards W with its lights on. The distance between the side-lights is about 2 metres and they are 6 metres above the sea. The top-lights are about 1 metre above the side-lights. There is no light in the back. When the ship passes west of Skötkubben, W sees a square [submarine] sail. The height of the sail is about ten metres. The sail is higher than it is wide. The ship is travelling at high speed (about 15 knots). The powerful diesels make a forceful motor sound. W looks for the front and the back of the ship, but there is nothing. W sees waves behind the sail, but nothing in front of it. At 18.20, the sail disappears behind the northern tip of Sandön.[57]

This five-minute observation of a submarine sail is in all documents described as the sighting of a 'certain submarine'. The observer still confirms the 'huge square submarine sail'. The distance between the lights and the height of the sail may be very approximate, but the indication of a conventional submarine with a large and high sail is very clear. However, no Soviet submarine at the time had a sail that would look as though it were higher than it was wide, while several Western submarines had such a design. For example, Soviet Whiskey, Juliet, Foxtrot and Golf submarines all have a rather flat sail, while several British and US submarines have sails that are both large and high. This was never considered by the Naval Analysis Group.

There were a number of visual observations of submarines during this period. In the Hårsfjärden–Sandhamn area, there were four visual observations of a submarine sail or of submarines on the surface (one on 30 September and three on 4 October) and one or two at periscope depth (1 October and 4 October) – all deep inside the Stockholm archipelago. This appears to be a major provocation. Some of these sightings were very clear observations. The periscope on 1 October came so close to the Swedish vessel that observed it that it almost seemed to announce its presence, and it did not dive immediately. In the four cases when the submarine was showing its sail (or even the whole submarine), the provocation is even more obvious.

These submarines seemingly demonstrated their presence, as if they wanted to play with the Swedes, as if they wanted to trigger the submarine hunt to test Sweden's capability and will to defend itself. It is difficult to understand why the Soviets would want to do such a thing. Such an open demonstration would tend to strengthen Swedish resolve. Rather, these observations point to a testing of Swedish will and readiness by Western submarines. Both the Dalarö observation and the Sandhamn observation seemingly point to Western submarines. At the very least, while there is no proof of this, it is indeed the case that the statements made by the Naval Analysis Group about Soviet submarines are unfounded. As with what happened on 1 October, the Naval Analysis Group only discussed possible Soviet submarines and did not consider the possibility of Western submarines. Then, after these incidents, the most publicized submarine hunt in Swedish waters started.

Tuesday 5 October

On Monday night, Swedish Navy and Vice-Admiral Bror Stefenson had given a dinner for foreign guests, including foreign defence attachés, at Berga Castle (at Berga Naval College). About 22.00, Stefenson called the chief of the Navy Information Division, Commander Sven Carlsson, who was in a neighbouring building. Stefenson ordered him to draft a press release about the opening of a press centre in the College's gym hall on 5 October. Commander Carlsson drafted a dramatic statement, but, to his surprise, Vice-Admiral Stefenson rewrote it, making it even more dramatic. It was sent out at midnight at 00.08.[58] The press centre opened two hours after midnight, at 02.00.[59] In the morning, a large number of journalists arrived at Berga and from there they had an excellent view of the submarine hunt. The 'invasion' of foreign correspondents forced Berga Naval College to set

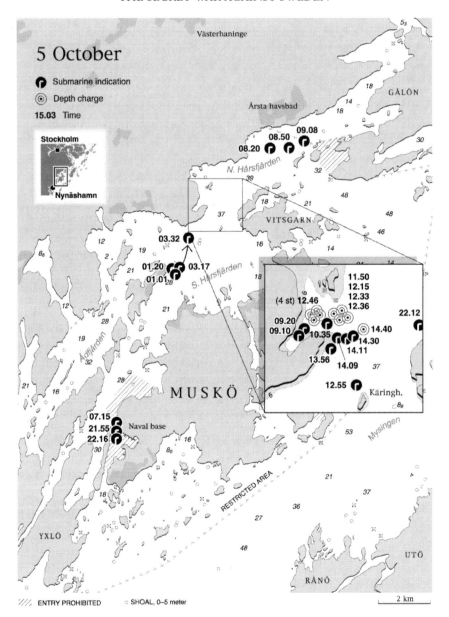

10. 5 October.

up 30 telephone lines and to make the gym hall into temporary lodgings for hundreds of journalists.[60] Commander Hans von Hofsten told the press that the submarine might be a smaller vessel able to crawl on the sea floor.[61] Huddinge hospital had six ambulances on high alert (and the possibility of 20). The hospital was prepared to receive 20 seriously injured and 40 slightly injured submariners.[62] During the day, there were further air boil-ups, oil patches and sonar contacts. Twelve depth charges were dropped.[63] The naval base war diary records the following:

> At 01.01, alarm. Helicopter starts towards [the small island of] Länsman after observation of air boil-ups. Fishing with Malin [a signal transmitter that can be attached to the submarine by a strong magnet. The cord to] Malin was cut loose 0.1M [nautical mile] south of Länsman . . . At 01.20, 321 reports: heavy air boil-ups a couple of hundred metres south of Länsman. Väktaren towards the contact. Helicopter [Y71] in the air in ten minutes . . . At 01.32, Malin attached [to a submarine] (?) . . . At 02.07, [report from] Bevb 321: fishing [with Malin]. 'Boiling water' 2/10 from Långgarn [south of Länsman]. Fishing in the area. The cord to Malin cut off 7–8 metres from the end. [From naval base]: in which direction did the cord go? From Bevb 321: towards position k bearing 330 degrees, towards Länsman . . . at 01.25–01.30 . . . At the contact, the depth of Malin was 4–5 metres above the sea floor . . . At 03.17, Urd report: Malin contact towards Länsman . . . At 03.23, to Urd: Do you maintain the contact? Answer: Yes. [At 03.32, Urd reports: Malin's position more than 1 kilometre north-northeast of Länsman towards Näsudden. Later, at 13.56, mb 464: Malin contact at Näsudden. Y71 investigates. In the evening, at 21.49, a report was given that the cord to Malin was cut off.] It was cut by a sharp object. Not our own propeller. It was most likely cut off by a submarine propeller.[64]

In other words, the Swedish forces went out 'submarine fishing', trying to get a submarine on the hook. In the early hours of 5 October, they succeeded. Malin was attached to a submarine and, according to the war diary, two hours later the Swedish forces received contact with Malin more than a kilometre north of the place where it was dropped and could follow the movements of the submarine for more than 15 minutes.

According to the Naval Analysis Group Report, 'the cord [to Malin] was made of thick nylon. It is impossible that the "fisherman" could have held the rope if it had fastened somewhere. The rope must have been cut off, for example by a propeller.' According to the Naval Analysis Group, this was possibly by *Bevb 321*'s own propeller, but 'it is not possible to rule out that it was cut off by a submarine propeller'.[65] The authors of this document, Commander Emil Svensson and Commander Sten Swedlund, disregarded all the information mentioned above. The naval base war diary continues:

At 07.15 from lookout [at Muskö]: air bubbles and surge waves outside the docks . . . At 08.20, [signal intelligence contact from Visborg (the ship of the Chief of the Coastal Fleet Rear-Admiral Jan Enquist at Vitså close to Berga): 'West German submarine radar'[66]]. At 08.22, report from First Helicopter Div: Leader Boat 95 has reached the position . . . At 08.40, Y70 in the air. At 08.42, all have reached the position . . . At 08.50, from Y70: sonar echo with Doppler close to Visborg 500 metres northwest of Alvsta Långholmar . . . At 08.58, Y70 has lost contact [with the object] . . . At 09.08, Y70: 250–300 metres east Ekholmen. Y70 can direct Snapphanen for the drop . . . At 09.10, Y46 reports: oil bubbles at Djupviken [at Näsudden, north of Länsman]. One Malin dropped. At 09.11, from Y46: new oil patch at the same place . . . At 09.16, Y70 reports: Snapphanen not able to drop depth charge [it was used by FRA as a signal intelligence platform, but this was not known by the officer giving the orders[67]] . . . At 09.20, fresh oil spill, fishing with Malin. At 09.21, . . . 'the oil spill is moving' . . . At 10.08, from MB 95: the echo ranger indicates . . . At 10.35, from MB 95: echo 15 metres above sea floor, length 35–40 metres, height 6 metres . . . At 11.16, Bevb 321 plus boat with divers stays for investigation . . . At 11.40, Y69 keeps contact . . . At 11.47, Y69 directs Väktaren for the dropping of one depth charge m/33 . . . At 11.50, from Väktaren: depth charge dropped . . . At 12.15, from Y69: depth charge dropped [at oil patch at Näsudden.[68] At 12.33–12.36, from Y70: two depth charges dropped at the same place. At 12.46–12.47, from Väktaren: four depth charges dropped (three detonated) 350 metres from Näsudden[69]]. At 12.48, from Y46: the detonation hit in the right area . . . At 12.52, from Y71: after last drop, large suspicious oil patch . . . [At 13.05–13.19, from Y71: light-green patch 100 metres northwest Käringholmen 700 metres from Näsudden. The green patch was first observed at 12.55. It had disappeared some time later when Y71 passed next time.[70]] At 13.30, to Y71: use mechanical sounder 100 northwest Käringholmen . . . At 13.50, to Y70: submarine hunt at Käringholmen. At 13.56, Malin contact at Näsudden . . . At 14.09, 464 has seen a black 'hill' [object] at Näsudden, towards Enstenarna. At 14.11, Y71: 500 m northeast Näsudden. Looks like mud in the water . . . At 14.15, from 464: a 75-cm-long object 20 cm above the surface . . . At 14.30, from Y71: contact. At 14.32, order from Y71 to Väktaren: drop . . . At 14.40, from Väktaren: one depth charge dropped.[71]

This submarine hunt was carried out a few hundred metres from land, while hundreds of journalists followed the events from the new press centre at Berga. TV cameras followed the spectacular 'battle'. This was a TV war – like the Gulf War of 1991, though on a much smaller scale and with an evasive opponent. Deputy Chief of Defence Staff Intelligence Commander Björn Eklind, who was sceptical of the whole operation, told me that the oil spills might have originated from old oil dumps. There is a lot of oil on the sea floor in Hårsfjärden, he said. A detailed investigation of the sea floor, carried out in late October, found a number of oil drums in the area, but also parallel tracks from a bottom-crawling vessel.[72] Thus, we cannot say anything for sure about the oil spills, though fresh thin oil seems difficult to explain as caused by old oil dumps. The first oil patches appeared before depth charges were dropped, and 'moving oil spill' may rather indicate a moving submarine. A Malin signal transmitter moving more than one kilometre definitely indicates a submarine. Sonar echoes, Doppler and forceful air boil-ups also indicate the presence of a submarine. The reading from one echo – indicating an object 35–40 metres in length and 15 metres above the sea floor – together with leaking oil possibly indicates a damaged small submarine. The green patch in the water indicates a signal, a dye sent up from the submarine. A black object on the surface – some 0.75 metres in length, 0.2 metres above the surface and with no sail – indicates a small submersible. Yet nothing of this appears in General Ljung's diary or in the Submarine Defence Commission Report – as if it never was reported outside the Navy.

The figures relating to the echo reading of the other submarine – 6 metres high, 35–40 metres long and 15 metres above the sea floor – are approximate, but the estimates are supposedly more or less correct. These figures have been confirmed by intelligence personnel at the naval base. This may possibly indicate a West German, Danish, Italian or US submarine. The submarine radar indication at 08.20 was interpreted as a West German submarine, though the instruments used by the Swedish Navy for identifying a radar were not very reliable. Furthermore, the hulls of West German submarines were made of a low-magnetic steel alloy, and Malin would not necessarily have been able to attach itself to this. The Italian and US submarines are possible alternatives. At the time, there were, to my knowledge, no Soviet submarines between 20 and 55 metres long. The Soviet Quebec submarine (probably no longer operational in 1982) was 56 metres long. The estimated length of 35–40 metres would therefore seem to rule out a Soviet submarine.

Between 12.15 and 12.47, several depth charges were dropped against this submarine. At 12.46, four heavy depth charges were dropped, and three of these detonated. At 12.48, Y46 reports that the depth charges detonated in the right area. A large oil patch appeared and the submarine may have been lightly damaged. At 12.55, a light-green area appeared on the surface some 700 metres southeast of this spot, close to the island of Käringholmen.[73] It is not very shallow here,

45

and the incident provoked a search for a submarine for more than an hour. It seems to have been a green dye, a chemical substance sent up as a signal from the submarine to communicate its condition and position, a practice employed at the time by both US and British submarines, or possibly by any Western submarine in a US-commanded operation. Soviet submarines did not use this kind of chemical substance: they had other ways of signalling (see below).

Between 14.09 and 14.15, motor boat 464 reported sighting a 75-centimetre-long black object 20 centimetres above the surface, and close to this place an area of mud in the water. The Naval Analysis Group Report mentions an oval object with the same dimensions 400–500 metres northeast of Näsudden. The object is described as looking like a ball partly below the surface, and was observed for five seconds. The observer headed towards the object and reported on it. The Naval Analysis Group reported that the object had been observed earlier.[74] These details do not suggest a submarine sail but rather a small submersible – possibly the one that left 'tank-like tracks' on the sea floor in the same area, and on other occasions stirred up mud in the water. Two weeks later, parallel 'tank-like tracks' were recorded on video, and they were very clear. These tracks must have originated from a small submersible, one much smaller than 35–40 metres. According to an independent study of the sea floor, these tracks in Djupviken close to Näsudden were evidence of a small tracked submersible that operated in the area sometime in the first half of October.[75] (This may also have been the same vessel that was observed by the *Halland* at Södra Skramsösund, possibly entering Hårsfjärden on 29 September.) A few minutes after this vessel had gone down into the water again, at 14.30, *Y71* reported contact, seemingly with the same object, also northeast of Näsudden.[76] At 14.40, the *Väktaren* reports having dropped one depth charge (against the contact). It should be noted that lots of information in the war diary has been 'blacked out'; in addition, more sensitive issues are often not even put down on paper.

The Submarine Defence Commission Report says that the bottom-crawling midget submarine may have been damaged by a depth charge, though without mentioning when this may have happened.[77] However, no other incident in the naval base war diary supports this statement. The captain of the fast attack craft *Väktaren*, Lieutenant-Commander Lars Wedin, says that he knew nothing about what happened afterwards. He just received instructions about the position and dropped the depth charge. However, an intelligence officer at the naval base confirmed to me that the small bottom-crawling submersible may have been damaged at this time. I was interested in this incident because, in 1984–85, I had had a conversation with a diver who had been diving in Hårsfjärden. He said that a Swedish fast attack craft had dropped one depth charge – as happened on the above-mentioned occasion – and by 'mistake' made a perfect hit. When the diver reached the bottom, he found a damaged midget submarine. After this, the diver was put ashore and forced to sign papers that would not allow him to speak to anyone about it. When he did – and I was due to see him the following day – he was removed from his position and from Stockholm within one day. He was thereafter unwilling to speak about the incident.

I have not been able to have the diver's first version confirmed. However, a local officer confirmed the diver's position in Hårsfjärden, and another commander told me that one or two of these divers were borrowed by intelligence personnel to carry out a special mission during the Hårsfjärden hunt. But if it is true that the Swedish Navy had evidence of a damaged submersible in Hårsfjärden, it is difficult to believe that it was a Soviet one. The Navy would have done anything to prove a Soviet presence. According to the naval base war diary, the indications continued during the evening of 5 October:

> At 19.50, from 409 at Dock One: An object close to the destroyer at the western side of Skramsö. A low object, 2 metres long and 10 metres from the ship [possibly canoe from Swedish naval special forces] . . . At 21.55, light below the surface at Dock Three. Increased reconnaissance . . . At 22.12, from Helicopter Division: low-frequency sound from buoy [at Märsgarn and echoes in the Märsgarn area] . . . At 22.16, still light under the water at Dock Three. A boat is going out to investigate . . . At 23.17, all divers have left the sea. At 23.31, from Chief First Helicopter Division [Commander Eric Hagström]: low-frequency sounds, passive sonar buoy at Märsgarn.[78] [From Naval Analysis Group Report: tape recording of low-frequency sound, possibly from propeller with low turns per minute.[79]]

At 22.00, a diver or small submersible with spotlights seems to have investigated the area at Muskö Naval Base. Lights were seen below the surface for up to 20 minutes. Colonel Lars-G. Persson wrote in his diary:

> During the night, 19 canoe patrols and 10 observation posts were deployed all over Hårsfjärden. The waters were covered by 40 night-vision scopes, while all the naval vessels had turned off their engines and listened passively . . . We saw nothing. As a submarine captain, I would probably have been frightened to silence by the silence.[80]

At 21.47, Stockholm Coastal Defence received an order from MBÖ (Commander of the Eastern Military District): 'Deploy immediately forces for mine barrages MS1, MS2 and MS3 [Mälsten 1, 2 and 3] with personnel from Ox [Oxdjupet] and Sa1 and Sa2 [Sandhamn 1 and 2].[81] General Ljung wrote in his diary:

> At 07.30, I called [State Secretary Sven] Hirdman and demanded a meeting with [Defence Minister Torsten] Gustafsson at 09.15 to brief him about the submarine incidents. At 09.15, the meeting started at the Defence Minister's Office with Hirdman, myself, [Chief of Staff] Stefenson and the submarine expert officer [Commander Emil] Svensson from the naval base . . . The minister agreed on the necessity of using force – to force the submarine to the surface.[82]

Later, at 14.40, the Commander-in-Chief and the Chief of Staff gave a briefing to a high-level meeting, including Prime Minister Thorbjörn Fälldin, Minister of Foreign Affairs Ola Ullsten, Minister of Justice Carl-Axel Petri, Minister of Defence Torsten Gustafsson, State Secretary for Defence Sven Hirdman, Acting State Secretary for Foreign Affairs Ulf Dinkelspiel, Conservative Party leader Ulf Adelsohn, Prime Minister-elect Olof Palme and the Social Democrat Ingvar Carlsson. There were no objections to the decision to force the submarine to the surface. The participants expressed unity over detaining the submarine once in Swedish military possession.[83] Sven Hirdman stated just after this incident that they all had a common understanding that the intrusions were unacceptable, that the submarine should be forced to the surface, that this might damage the submarine and risk the lives of the crew and that the submarine should be detained if surfaced.[84] Defence Minister Torsten Gustafsson stated publicly: 'It seems that the only way to force the submarine to the surface is to damage it . . . If foreign powers believe that they can enter Swedish waters safely, they take a great risk.'[85]

On 5 October, there were a number of clear indications of submarines, and even some indications of Western submarines, but none of these indications appeared in the Naval Analysis Group Report. Some of the most important information from the war diary was not included in the Naval Analysis Group Report. The commander of the group, Commander Emil Svensson, appeared together with the Chief of Staff and the Commander-in-Chief at a meeting at the Ministry of Defence to brief the Defence Minister and his state secretary. Commander Emil Svensson was not just any analyst: he had a special role during the NOTVARP operation and, immediately after the Hårsfjärden submarine hunt started, he was in practical terms assigned the role of Vice-Admiral Bror Stefenson's 'chief of intelligence' at the naval base to cover the operation.

Wednesday 6 October

During this day, 300 journalists turned up at the Navy Press Centre at Berga, of which 70 were foreign correspondents (22 from the USA). The next day, there were about 100 foreign correspondents. On one particular day, there were 500 journalists at Berga at the same time, and altogether 750 received accreditation cards from the Swedish military authorities.[86] The *New York Times*, *Washington Post*, *Times* and *Stern* as well as TV channels like ABC, NBC and CBS were all present.[87] The submarine hunt was front-page news. Every day, the *New York Times* and other major newspapers had one or two stories about the Swedish submarine hunt.[88] Commander Sven Carlsson from the Navy Information Division said that his 'private guess' was that the submarine originated from the Soviet Union.[89] Journalists wrote first about one Soviet submarine deep inside the Swedish archipelago, later about two or more.[90] Commander Hans von Hofsten stated that the anti-submarine rockets of the destroyer *Halland* would have been more precise and much more efficient than the depth charges. In spite of this, the *Halland* was retired on the very day that the Hårsfjärden hunt started. Von Hofsten was upset. According to him, the naval base and the military leadership were not willing to use necessary force.[91]

During the morning of the same day, one heavier depth charge was dropped. Later that day a boil-up was observed. Mobile air-defence forces, Swedish special forces and military police were deployed.[92] The naval base war diary reports:

> At 02.40, nets deployed between Rörholmen–Lilla Stenholmen–Stora Stenholmen–Långholmen . . . [At 08.14, sonar echo at Ekeby Näsudden.[93]] At 08.17, from Y70: one depth charge dropped [at Enstenarna] . . . At 08.43, after analysis of sonar contact 150–200 metres from buoy [Märsgarn], bearing 150 degrees: 5- to 10-metre-long echo at a depth of 11 metres, not at 25 metres . . . At 09.21, from Mysing: oil patch in bearing 137 degrees 1,000 metres from [southeast of] Oxnö Udde (DQ 124 035). The patch includes seaweed and air bubbles. From naval base: take oil samples . . . [At 11.50, helicopter sonar 'bottomed' at Frinsholmen 15 metres above the bottom.[94] At 12.40, Swedish submarine rescue vessel] Belos passes Landsort [arrives in the Stockholm archipelago from Karlskrona] . . . At 16.56, from 406: oil outside Dock Three . . . At 19.04, from Mysing: report 18.55 classified as larger vessel . . . At 20.15, from Lieutenant-Commander Heilborn: oil and whirlpools at Dock Two, as well as magnetic indications . . . At 20.16, from Berga Naval College: [radar] echo between Berganäs and Furuholmen. Disappeared suddenly . . . At 20.52 from Mysing: radar echo in bearing 038 degrees. Distance 2,600 metres from Långholmsgrund. At 21.05, the echo is gone . . . At 21.36, from 751 at

49

Frinsholmen between Jungfruhuvud-Märsgarn [should be Långgarn]: large patch of scum. Not from our boat . . . At 21.42, hurry on, very strong air boil-up. [Continued for 5–10 minutes (not methane) in the same area as the sonar had 'bottomed' 15 metres above the sea floor.[95]] Order to Mysing: go immediately to north Jungfruhuvud . . . At 22.37, from Commander S. Hecker [Berga Naval College]: echo at buoy 42 . . . At 23.05, from Berga Naval College: the echo has disappeared and the object that was also seen by binoculars is no longer visible.[96]

This day, 6 October, was not such a dramatic day as some of the others. Only one depth charge was dropped. Some kind of small submersible or midget submarine seems to have operated in the area of Märsgarn-Näsudden, perhaps up to Berganäs. Sub-surface activity seems also to have taken place in the area of Jungfruhuvud and Frinsholmen[97] and possibly at Muskö Naval Base, while one or two indications from another possible submarine were reported from the area outside the northern exit.

Colonel Lars-G. Persson writes in his diary that a group under the command of Lieutenant-Colonel Sven-Olof Kviman was set up at Mälsten to cover the southern exit of Mysingen. The mine barrages were still used for reconnaissance.[98] The Stockholm Coastal Defence Staff Report states:

> [at] 23.39, order from MBÖ: first, CSK deploys forces for MS1, MS2 and MS3 [Mälsten mine barrages 1, 2 and 3], KO1 [Korsö 1] and LB1 and LB2 [Långbälingen 1 and 2]; second, deploy special force and reconnaissance force; third, in cooperation with ÖrlBO [Naval Base East] and CSeM [Chief Central Air Section] prevent [the foreign power] from gaining control of the submarine; fourth, place patrol boats at the disposal of CÖrlBO [Chief of Naval Base East] in agreement with CÖrlBO; fifth, receive platoon 2 × 40 men from KI/FO 44; sixth, receive air-defence forces from Lv3 at BÖS [Berga Naval College]; seventh, after order, from 16.00 tomorrow, deploy mine barrage . . . [northern exit]; eighth, receive reconnaissance force from [the regiments] P10, I1 and Ing1.[99]

General Lennart Ljung writes in his diary that, at 07.55, the West German Defence Attaché, Lieutenant-Colonel Bachelin, handed over a very urgent message from Hamburg. The Commander-in-Chief himself immediately went to the office of the Prime Minister. At 09.00, General Ljung presented the telegram to Prime Minister Fälldin. They both questioned the basis for the information in the telegram, and decided that it should not influence the direction of the ongoing activities. Fälldin, however, told General Ljung to inform the

11. 6 October.

new Prime Minister, Olof Palme. At 09.30, the Commander-in-Chief met Olof Palme in parliament. Both pledged their support. 'We will continue in Hårsfjärden as before.'[100]

I spoke with Thorbjörn Fälldin, who did not want to talk about the telegram because it 'concerned the relationship to a foreign power'. He did not 'remember' anything of its content, he said. Chief of Staff Vice-Admiral Stefenson said that he had 'no recollection of such a telegram, and adds that if it had implications for the hunt he would have known'.[101] I also spoke with Colonel Bachelin, who said that the telegram had been sent from Bonn to the Swedish Defence Staff and that he had been contacted by Vice-Admiral Stefenson. The two of them had also spoken with General Ljung. According to Bachelin, a man in Hamburg – an alleged Soviet civilian captain – had said that the submarines in Swedish waters were armed with nuclear weapons and would detonate their bombs if attacked by the Swedes. Bachelin told me that the captain had earlier come up with false information. 'It was a mistake to send this telegram,' he said. This is one – and perhaps the most likely – interpretation. Another interpretation would be that a Soviet or Western submarine was desperately trying to get out and needed a ceasefire from the Swedish authorities, which the threat of a nuclear detonation might possibly help to establish. For example, the submarine that was under heavy fire on the previous day might have needed a ceasefire in order to escape. In that case, the telegram would have been the result of a (US, British, Italian or West German) deception operation (see below). It might also have been a test to see if Sweden would back out in the event of a nuclear threat. Ljung's and Bachelin's versions do not conflict on any essential points. However, Stefenson's and Bachelin's versions are contradictory.

General Ljung informed Fälldin that he had to go to Kristianstad to accompany the Norwegian Commander-in-Chief, General Sven Hauge, to the command of the Southern Military District, with Vice-Admiral Bengt Schuback as host. General Ljung left Stockholm at 12.45. He kept an aircraft on alert in Kristianstad in case he had to return suddenly. He had a meeting with Hauge until 21.00, when he returned to Stockholm. At 23.00, he briefed Foreign Minister Ullsten.[102] In an interview, Hauge stated that Norway was better equipped to hunt submarines because of its frigates and NATO membership.[103] In Stockholm in the evening, Prime Minister Fälldin, State Secretary Hirdman and Acting State Secretary Dinkelspiel discussed a possible announcement by the government, but, to quote Hirdman, 'we decided at the last minute to wait, because we had no information concerning the nationality of the intruding submarine'.[104] In other words, the government had no clear view on the nationality issue – at least, they were not convinced that it was a Soviet submarine.

Thursday 7 October
Just before midnight, there was a report about an intermittent radar echo west of the northern tip of Skramsö (at Muskö Naval Base)

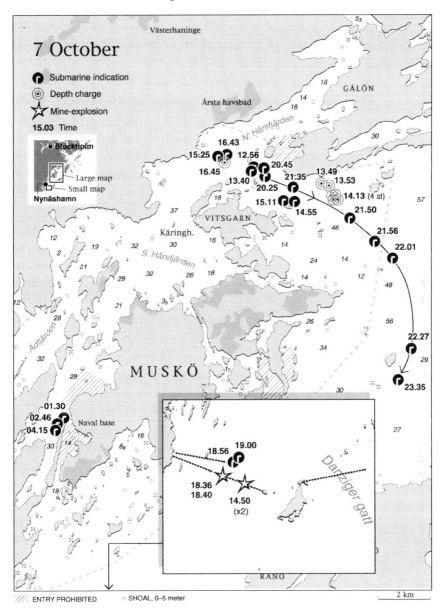

12. 7 October.

close to the retired destroyer *Hälsingland*. There was also some oil on the surface close to the destroyer. At 01.30 there was a report about bubbles in the water north of Skramsö,[105] and the war diary continues:

At 02.46, *751* observes something looking like an antenna [in the water] close to the destroyer. Biscayan is going there . . . At 04.15, from Stenqvist: Biscayan has seen lights on board *Hgd* [the destroyer *Hälsingland*] . . . At 04.20, voices and torches on board *Hgd*. [To] the reconnaissance force: You are not allowed to enter the ship until it is light . . . At 05.58 from Linton: reconnaissance force at *Hgd* has not seen anything. The island will be searched by dogs, when it is light . . . At 08.16, deputy CE [Chief of the Harbour] reports: the dogs have searched northern Skramsö. Nothing to report. There is thin oil outside Dock Three.[106]

In the night, there was some sub-surface activity at Muskö Naval Base at Skramsö close to the retired destroyer *Hälsingland*. There were seemingly even people on board the empty ship. Later, the sea-floor investigation found parallel tracks of a small tracked submersible under the retired destroyer *Småland* at Märsgarn in northern Hårsfjärden. Intelligence personnel believed that this submersible had been hiding under the destroyer to avoid ships (*Mb 95* and others) with echo sounders that covered the area. The empty destroyers might have been used as a base for the submersibles and their crews. The reconnaissance force or the special force for that matter was not allowed to enter the ship until it was light almost two hours after the observation. This 'cautious policy' would indicate a commanding officer who either avoided any risk or actually knew that the destroyers were involved in something that he couldn't touch.

At 10.30, two observers reported the top of a small submarine sail (1.5–2 metres wide and 0.2 metres above the surface) going eastwards at a speed of 10 knots north of Korsö (at Sandhamn). The observers also reported a 0.5- to 1-metre periscope or mast on the sail.[107] The estimated high speed is untypical for such a small vessel. Either the sail is larger or the estimated speed is too high or both. The high periscope or rather mast may indicate a small sail with a fixed mast or a mast erected from a vertical position, which supports the hypothesis of mini-submarine of under 30 metres. This is certainly not the same submarine as the one with a '10-metre-high' sail, which was observed in the Sandhamn area on 4 October.

Concurrently with this incident, the *Belos* investigated the area of the submarine hunt at Näsudden by using the remote-controlled video camera Sjöugglan (Sea Owl). An officer on *Belos* said that Sjöugglan passed over a parallel track on the sea floor, which led to an area of black mud in the water, seemingly stirred up by the above-mentioned bottom-crawling submersible. He also said that, in the sea-floor investigation on 20 October, the tracks of Sjöugglan were found to have crossed the tracks of the bottom-crawling submersible. *Belos*'s investigation, however, was interrupted at lunchtime by dramatic developments at the northern exit of Hårsfjärden. A submarine was believed to be forcing its way through the nets out to Mysingen. Colonel Lars-G. Persson, commander of the special force boarding detail, wrote in his diary that he was on his way to Muskö for a meeting with the staff of the Eastern Military District but had to turn around, because of a (submarine) breakout, or attempted breakout, at the northern exit.[108] The naval base war diary records the following:

At 12.56, from Coastal Defence boat 410: the buoys [linked to the submarine net between] at Långholmsgrund and Alvsta Långholmar are moving. Hercules is ordered to support 410. At 12.59, to Väktaren: go immediately to Alvsta Långholmar–Långholmsgrund. At 13.00, Y70 goes to the area. At 13.01, [order] to Y70: hover east of the buoys. At 13.07, Y68 starts and asks for order. Replace Y70 and receive order from Y70. At 13.09, Y44 in the air. Order: cover the net at Långholmsgrund . . . At 13.40, from 410: the buoys have moved 50 metres towards east, against the wind, and then back and another 50 metres west of their original position . . . At 13.47, to Mysing: attack with depth charge. [At 13.49–13.53 Mysing drops two depth charges at DQ 128 037 northeast Bergholmen. No detonation.] . . . At 14.10, from Mysing: bearing 098 degrees, distance 900 metres, sonar echo, low Doppler, depth 20 metres . . . Order [from naval base]: attack with four depth charges. At 14.12, from Mysing: two depth charges in the water. At 14.13, four depth charges in the water – three detonated. At 14.15, four detonated. Last position: DQ 130 036 [1.5 km northeast of Bergholmen] . . . At 14.55, oil spill to the surface at Bergholmen. At 14.56, 448 drops Malin at Bergholmen [against oil patch] . . . At 15.04, from Y68: Malin is sending where it was dropped . . . At 15.11, [the helicopter] Y64 in the air. Contact with Malin northwest of Bergholmen. Y64 is going there . . . At 15.19, contact with Malin. Belos is ordered to prepare divers for investigating Malin at Bergholmen . . . At 15.25, submarine sail, with something white on the sail, at Berganäs. Alarm: submarine sail at Berganäs. E[mil] Svensson briefed . . . At 15.57, contact with Malin. Y68, Y64 are trying to keep contact with Malin. Order [from naval base]: cease fire. Also to Väktaren. At 15.58, from naval base: units in western Hårsfjärden are given right to fire [because of submarine at Berganäs] . . . At 16.12, from Belos: we have no position for the divers. Order to Väktaren: Give Malin's position to Belos . . . At 16.31, Belos's divers in the water at Bergholmen . . . At 16.43, from Y68: Doppler echo [between Berganäs and Alvsta Långholmar]. At 16.45, from Y68: one depth charge dropped. At 16.48, from Belos: the divers are in the water. Nothing to report. At 16.50, order to Belos: go to position east Långholmsgrund. Prepare for

the deployment of divers . . . At 17.15, order to Belos: anchor east of
the net at Långholmsgrund–Alvsta Långholmar. The divers are to investigate the net. Check if the submarine has tried to force its way through
. . . At 17.46, from Belos: we can start to dive at 18.15 . . . [At 18.31,
to Belos: same order as 17.15] . . . At 18.40, from Belos: 'Shall we
report in plain language?' From naval base: I will come back [to you].
At 18.47, Belos proposes that permission to dive is granted until task is
carried out.[109]

Doppler and sonar echo at a depth of 20 metres indicated the presence of a submarine. The moving submarine nets – first in one direction and immediately afterwards in the other – might also have
indicated submarine activity (the nets were replaced on 8–9 October,
which suggests that they were damaged). Lieutenant-Commander
Hans Kalla, attack diver and later captain of the Belos (1985–87), told
me that there were big holes in the submarine nets, which has been
confirmed by intelligence personnel. After the dropping of six depth
charges targeted on the echo at Bergholmen (or 1.5 km northeast of
Bergholmen and almost 3 km east of the nets), the submarine seemed
to leak oil. Malin was dropped at Bergholmen. General Ljung writes:
one Malin 'was allegedly attached [to the object] and is now sending
signals'.[110] The war diary indicates that Malin was possibly attached
to a submarine. A few minutes later, there was a new contact with
Malin. The position was now reported as northwest of Bergholmen,
and a helicopter proceeded to the location. This helicopter, Y64, made
contact at 15.19. At 15.57, the helicopter was still reporting contact
with Malin, but the helicopters and the small attack craft Väktaren
were ordered to cease fire by the naval base.

Y64 hovered over the 'object' for 40 minutes. Fifteen years ago, I
was told by a conscript from Hårsfjärden that a helicopter had
hovered over a submarine for 40 minutes without receiving any
orders. He believed that the leadership – or perhaps Prime Minister
Thorbjörn Fälldin – had been indecisive and that the helicopter had
to leave because it was short on fuel. The helicopter, however, had to
leave because of a ceasefire. Neither Thorbjörn Fälldin nor General
Ljung seems to have been consulted. Ljung was preoccupied with the
use of mines and about the possible breakout through the nets (see
below). Both he and Fälldin decided to escalate the operation, not to
de-escalate it. It was the naval base – or perhaps the most senior officer
at the base, Vice-Admiral Stefenson – which was first 'indecisive' and
then went for a ceasefire. After this, the Väktaren was ordered to give
Malin's position to the Belos. At that point, this was northwest of
Bergholmen. Half an hour later, the Belos's divers went into the water
where Malin had been located. However, according to the Chief

Diving Officer, Ingemar Lundell, they found no submarine.[111] The *Belos* was soon ordered to check the nets. The captain of the *Belos* asked if he should report in coded or 'plain language'.

Dagens Nyheter reported: 'Divers checked the damaged submarine net. It was found to be cut. A submarine had broken through. A military hospital was made ready to receive people from a damaged submarine.'[112] Lieutenant-Colonel Håkan Söderlindh, Chief of OPG, Chief of Operations Defence Staff (OP2), told me that, according to his information, the most serious incident – directly linked to Hårsfjärden – took place on 7 October after the drop of depth charges at the northern exit.

General Ljung's diary notes that CM (Chief of the Navy Vice-Admiral Rudberg) had been out in Hårsfjärden (either the night before or during the preceding day). The helicopter division reported, according to Rudberg, that the submarine might have been able to escape. There were still high spirits. At 10.00, Ljung had a meeting with Rudberg and Chief of Staff Vice-Admiral Bror Stefenson. They briefed General Ljung about the submarine hunt and discussed possible preparations for a de-escalation of the hunt and new development programmes.[113] At 14.10, Ljung wrote: 'CÖrlBO [Chief of Naval Base East Rear-Admiral Kierkegaard]: submarine breakout at the northern passage. One depth charge dropped. Target lost.'[114] At 14.30, General Ljung decided to use mines against the intruding submarine.

> At 14.30, SCÖ [Chief of Staff of the Eastern Military District, Major-General Gustaf Welin] requested authorization for using mine barrages against submarine. Answer: 'Yes.' At 14.30, I briefed Prime Minister Thorbjörn Fälldin about my decision and he consented ('I understand. Carry on.'). At 14.35, Palme's secretary is given a message for Palme (at press conference). At 14.40, Hirdman is informed about my decision. At 15.00, [Lieutenant-Commander Carl-Johan] Arfvidson [Chief of the Naval Unit at the Defence Staff Operations Division] reported about mine detonated west of Nåttarö [Mälsten]. Oil patch. At 15.10, Chief of Staff [Vice-Admiral Stefenson] from Muskö Naval Base: possibly mistake at Nåttarö. CÖrlBO [Rear-Admiral Kierkegaard]: KA1 [Coastal Defence Regiment] activates mine barrages in the north. At 15.20, order from Commander-in-Chief to Stockholm Coastal Defence and to Naval Base East via [Håkan] Söderlindh [Chief of OPG, Defence Staff Operations]: only use mines when there is no risk to civilian traffic.[115]

Gustafsson and Andersson, the incoming and outgoing ministers of defence, met to discuss the situation. Vice-Admiral Stefenson travelled to Berga and Hårsfjärden by helicopter after lunch when the situation became tense at the northern exit at 13.00. He contacted Ljung from Muskö at 15.10 and stayed at the naval base for six hours[116] – as though he wanted to run the show as a local commander.

Ulf Adelsohn, the leader of the Conservative Party, noted in his diary that General Ljung called him around 15.00: 'The submarine had gone straight through the net.'[117] At 15.30, General Ljung wrote that the breakout would be confirmed within an hour. At 15.50, Ljung briefed Hirdman and Fälldin: breakout still not confirmed. At 16.00, he wrote that it was most likely that there had been a breakout. The *Belos* was going there with divers, which could take some time. At 19.30, there was still no information about the nets.[118] Several times, between 14.10 and 19.30, General Ljung asked if the breakout had been confirmed, but the *Belos* did not start checking the nets until 18.30, perhaps even later. The following day (8 October), General Ljung wrote that it had not been possible to investigate the nets on 7 October because the *Belos* had been investigating Malin, which was attached to another object.[119] Despite his repeated inquiries, the Commander-in-Chief was not informed about the nets in the afternoon, the evening or the night of 7 October. On the following day, he was informed that the nets were going to be checked on that day instead. According to an officer close to General Ljung, Ljung sent his own intelligence people to the naval base because he did not trust the reports he was receiving from there.

A parallel observation of a submarine in the afternoon in northern Hårsfjärden is interesting. This observation is reported in General Ljung's diary, in the naval base war diary and in the Naval Analysis Group Report. Ljung wrote: 'At 16.05, visual sighting: periscope at Berganäs.'[120] According to the naval base war diary, the observation was made at 15.25 (40 minutes before Ljung was informed), but the war diary mentioned a 'submarine sail with something white on the sail at Berganäs'.[121] After this visual observation, a helicopter received a Doppler echo and a depth charge was dropped. This is not just an observation of a periscope. This is, except for the incidents at Lidingö on 29 September and Dalarö on 4 October, the only reports of submarine sails in daylight. A submarine with a damaged periscope may have had to surface its sail in order to prepare for a breakout some hours later (which seems to have taken place at 20.25–20.45), or the submarine may have surfaced because it wanted to help another submarine in trouble, which would fit well with what happened at Bergholmen at more or less the same time. It is, however, very risky to surface in such a way when one is on the wrong side of the narrow passage.

But how could a square submarine sail with some detail become simply a 'periscope' in General Ljung's diary? And why did it disappear from all open sources? This submarine sail appears neither in the Submarine Defence Commission Report (1983) nor in the 1995 Submarine Commission Report. At the naval base, this incident created an alarm: a submarine sail in daylight is remarkable: 'At 15.25, submarine sail with something white on the sail at Berganäs. Alarm. Submarine sail at Berganäs. E. Svensson is briefed.'[122] In other words, this information went directly to the Chief of the Naval Analysis Group, Commander Emil Svensson, which gives an indication of his special role during the hunt. He was immediately informed, and through him most likely Vice-Admiral Stefenson. Stefenson would then have told the Commander-in-Chief, General Ljung, about the 'periscope'. Thus, the information went straight up, but was for some reason modified. There is no indication that this information went through the formal hierarchy, through the Eastern Military District or the Chief of Operations at the Defence Staff. Commander Bengt Gabrielsson, Chief of Naval Operations, Eastern Military District, says that he was informed neither about a periscope nor of a submarine sail on 7 October. He wrote large parts of the material for the Submarine Defence Commission Report, and the war diary for the Eastern Military District was used for writing this report. It is therefore natural that the Submarine Defence Commission Report includes nothing about a submarine sail on 7 October. This information never reached the commission, he said. However, the Submarine Defence Commission also had access to Commander Svensson's classified report from the Naval Analysis Group. This report states: 'At 15.20, an object observed optically west of Alvsta Långholmar (classification: possible submarine – not submarine).'[123] There are no details.

In an attachment to this document, Svensson mentioned a three- to four-metre dark square object. The top of the sail was rugged, possibly because of masts or other instruments. Svensson interpreted the 'white on the sail' as 'white bow-waves', and he concluded: 'such behaviour is unlikely for a submarine in this area'.[124] Despite a detailed report and a Doppler echo he was not willing to give the observation a high priority. True, neither the behaviour of the submarine nor the description of the sail seemed to fit with any Soviet submarine but rather with the 35- to 40-metre submarine reported on 4 October. This is no proof of Western involvement, but it is still remarkable that this information – as with the Lidingö and Dalarö submarines (the only reports of a submarine sail in daylight) – did not appear in any open sources afterwards.

The naval base war diary continues:

> At 20.25 . . . the net between Alvsta Långholmar and Långholmsgrund is moving 100 metres towards east. To fast attack craft: go immediately

. . . At 20.30, to Chief of First Helicopter Division: start one helicopter
. . . At 20.45, from [MB] 457: the buoys [of the net] are moving against
the wind . . . At 21.35, [the helicopter] Y72 reports possible submarine,
low Doppler, speed 8 knots [south Oxnö Udde; classified by the Naval
Analysis Group Report as 'certain submarine'].[125] . . . At 21.38, order to
Väktaren: prepare for drop of four depth charges . . . At 21.44, Väktaren
towards Söderhäll . . . At 21.50, from Y72: contact [object] at high speed
north of Snappudd . . . At 21.56, from Y72: just north of Norrhäll . . .
At 22.01, from Y72: 500 metres northeast Norrhäll . . . At 22.27, from
Väktaren: 0.5M northeast Mysingeholm . . . At 22.41, from Väktaren:
probable submarine. At 22.42, from Y72: certain submarine . . . Order
from naval base: drop four depth charges. From Väktaren: target lost
. . . At 22.52, from Väktaren: sonar contact, no Doppler, possible submarine. At 22.54, from Väktaren: attack. At 22.55, sonar contact lost
. . . At 23.02, order from the naval base: cease fire. At 23.03, from
Väktaren: Does this mean that I should stop and go back? Answer [from
naval base]: Maintain contact. At 23.05, from Väktaren: New contact,
what shall we do? Answer [from naval base]: maintain contact. At 23.06,
contact Mysingeholm in bearing 034 degrees, 1,400 metres. [From
Väktaren: certain submarine – possible submarine] . . . At 23.12, order
from ÖB [Commander-in-Chief] via MBÖ [Commander of the Eastern
Military District]: only one depth charge at the time against confirmed
indication. Ceasefire for the Coastal Defence mine barrages . . . At
23.26, from ÖB: provisional ceasefire for the mine barrages. At 23.28,
Väktaren moves south . . . At 23.35, from Mysing: clear echo in bearing
153 degrees, 200 metres from southern tip of Mysingeholm. At 23.46
from Väktaren: contact at southern tip of Mysingeholm.[126]

According to the Submarine Defence Commission Report, a fast
attack craft had sonar contact with a submarine after the ceasefire had
been declared. The captain was not permitted to drop depth charges
and saw this as a missed opportunity.[127] The ceasefire was ordered by
the Commander-in-Chief on the recommendation of the Chief of
Staff, Vice-Admiral Stefenson (see below). This was the second time
on 7 October that the *Väktaren* received a ceasefire order when it
seemingly was in contact with a submarine. In the 1982 internal Navy
report, the latter submarine is described as a 'certain submarine'.[128] In
both cases, Vice-Admiral Bror Stefenson seems to have taken the
initiative to end the hunting. The captain of the *Väktaren*, Lieutenant-
Commander Lars Wedin, said that, in the first case, the ceasefire was
ordered because of diving in the area. In the second case, it was a
general ceasefire. He added that he had had a clear echo from a submarine in the latter case, but he was denied permission to do anything.
He was never informed about the reason for the ceasefire. 'I dropped

more depth charges then anybody else during the submarine hunt, but I knew nothing about what actually happened', he said. 'I just got the position from the helicopter about where to drop. The journalists knew more than we did. We got our information from the TV.'

Vice-Admiral Stefenson's cautious measures contrast with General Ljung's order to the mine barrages to stop the submarine by force. Up until this point, mines had only been used in wartime. To decide to activate the mine barrages was a clear escalation of the operation. Thus, two seemingly contradictory decisions were taken almost simultaneously, but the decision makers were not the same in each case. General Ljung's decision was taken when Vice-Admiral Stefenson was on his way to Hårsfjärden or had just arrived at Berga. Commander von Hofsten (at Berga) writes that he received a telephone call and the caller asked for Stefenson because mines had been detonated at Mälsten. Stefenson rushed to the telephone. 'The first thing he said: "We had an agreement about not using the mines."'[129] Von Hofsten is dead and he never did reveal who called him. But if von Hofsten's quote about an 'agreement' is correct he is talking about somebody with commanding authority for the mine barrages, who is close enough to Stefenson to call him at von Hofsten's office. This would rather indicate a senior naval officer at the Eastern Military District, because neither Brigadier-General Lars Hansson nor General Ljung himself would have done it. Hansson says that Vice-Admiral Stefenson came up to him on another occasion and asked who had given him the right to use the mines, seeming both upset and critical. Nothing indicates that Stefenson was consulted about this decision.

The sequence of events was as follows: Lieutenant-Colonel Jan Svenhager, Chief of Staff, Stockholm Coastal Defence, and his chief, Lars Hansson, had made a request to General Lehander about getting approval for using the mine barrages. A few minutes after the believed 'breakout' at the net, Major-General Gustaf Welin, Chief of Staff, Eastern Military District, turned to General Ljung and requested the use of mines against the enemy submarine.[130] Major-General Welin says that he and his chief, Lieutenant-General Bengt Lehander, discussed the issue and decided to turn to the Commander-in-Chief to get approval for using the mines. Captain Göran Wallén, the most senior naval officer at the Eastern Military District, was accordingly not consulted. After Lehander's decision, Welin called General Ljung to get approval. The answer was 'yes'.[131] General Ljung then turned to Prime Minister Thorbjörn Fälldin. While Vice-Admiral Stefenson went to the naval base to de-escalate the operation, the chiefs of the Coastal Defence and the Eastern Military District turned to General Ljung to escalate the operation or rather to prepare for an escalation at Mälsten.

The contrast between the two decisions is interesting. In the morning, Vice-Admiral Rudberg and Vice-Admiral Stefenson had already proposed a de-escalation of the hunt, a policy Stefenson seemingly was carrying out in the afternoon and during the following week, while the Coastal Defence and, to some extent, the Eastern Military District went for an escalation. There was a struggle between the two sides about the use of mines, while the use of depth charges, which primarily was under the control of the naval base, was reduced from 45 in the first week to two the following week. Different people influenced General Ljung, which reflects two different 'power networks', which would be more clearly visible in connection with the use of mines at Mälsten in the coming days. After some initial misunderstandings and technical problems, Mälsten soon became the hot spot of the submarine hunt. The Mälsten war diary for 7 October states the following:

At 14.20, from CÖrlBO [Rear-Admiral Christer Kierkegaard]: Alarm, possible breakout [through the nets at Alvsta Långholmar]. At 14.30, from CSK [Chief of Stockholm Coastal Defence, Brigadier-General Lars Hansson]: order to activate the mines. Stop the submarine. All troops are briefed. Order: [The trigger for the mines barrage turned to] automatic against submarine. Conversation with ÖrlBO about getting boats to stop civilian traffic. [At 14.48, repeated order: the system should be switched to automatic.[132]] At 14.50, mine detonation at CM [MS2 at Måsknuv]. Mälsten demanded boats to control the civilian traffic. We got two boats. Stop all civilian traffic. From CÖrlBO: helicopter on its way ... At 16.10, from CSK [Hansson]: do not stop civilian traffic. Stop submarine on its way out, but do not sink it. Graduated use of force [turn off the sensor signals a couple of times before detonating the mine; automatic trigger turned off] . . . At 16.45, after some controversies: civilian traffic to pass through Danziger Gatt. [The civilian traffic was let out through the more shallow eastern passage on the eastern side of Mälsten. The shallower water would make it impossible for a submarine to pass out under a civilian ship. The deeper western side was closed for civilian traffic, because here a submarine might be able to hide under a civilian vessel and thereby escape] . . . At 18.36, detonation of mine RN LI [MS3 at Yttre Gården]. At 18.39, indication MS1. No measures taken. At 18.40, detonation of mine RN LI. At 18.47, radar disturbances Yttre Gården–Mälsten. At 19.05, disturbances ended ... At 21.45, from CSK [Hansson]: Possibly another attempt to break out [through the nets at Alvsta Långholmar]. At 23.20, from MBÖ [Commander of the Eastern Military District, Lieutenant-General Lehander]: cease fire.[133]

Brigadier-General Hansson's version fits rather well with the Mälsten war diary. Hansson went out to Muskö Naval Base in the afternoon. He was informed by Rear-Admiral Christer Kierkegaard, chief of the naval base, that a submarine had just passed out of a narrow channel (a submarine net was damaged) and they had dropped six depth charges in an effort to force the submarine to the surface. Kierkegaard also said that Hansson had received approval from the Defence Staff to use the mines. Hansson immediately called Lieutenant-Colonel Sven-Olof Kviman at Mälsten and gave him an order to use the mines against the approaching submarine. Soon, two mines exploded at Mälsten and later another two mines were detonated.[134]

The commander at Mälsten, Sven-Olof Kviman, says that the first two mines exploded automatically after the triggering mechanism had been turned to 'automatic'. He had, despite warnings, been given the order to switch the triggering mechanism from manual to automatic. Some of the new 'floating mines' were very sensitive and could detonate unintentionally when changed to automatic because a mine might move over iron ore in the earth's crust. This is probably what happened, according to Kviman. Mälsten received the order to switch to automatic at 14.30 and allegedly a repeated order at 14.48.[135] Kviman argued that, soon after having been changed to automatic, at 14.50,[136] two floating mines exploded west of Måsknuv.

The naval base war diary states that 'at 18.36 and 18.40, two mines were detonated . . . At 18.56, transport boat 321 reported strong radar disturbances between Yttre Gården and Måsknuv [Mälsten]. Totally disturbed . . . At 19.05, the disturbances gone.'[137] 'Because of a very careful check of the surface at the mine barrage [it was almost dark] and because of demand to receive the right to use force, a relatively long time passed between indication and detonation . . . Because of the late detonation a possible submarine would not have been damaged' and 'FMV concludes that the indication has been caused by a vessel below the surface'.[138] The disturbances took place just south of 321 in the area of the mine barrage a few hundred metres from the boat. Transport boat 477 reported a very clear radar echo – as large as 321 – visible three times, each time for some 20 seconds, a few hundred metres south of 321 exactly in the area where the disturbances took place. After a few minutes, just after 19.00 when 321 approached the echo at a distance of a couple of hundred metres, the echo disappeared.[139] A clear radar echo (most likely a submarine) appeared just north of the mine barrage, while radar disturbances were directed towards north as if this vessel was blinding the radar of 321 and was transmitting and receiving signals after having survived the passage of the mine barrage 15 minutes earlier. This behaviour is typical for a submarine that needs instructions from a commanding authority. If there was a submarine that had provoked the indication in the mine barrage, it would have survived because the mines were not detonated until about 60 seconds after the 'passage'.[140]

The same incidents are described by General Ljung. At 15.00, Carl-Johan Arfvidson at the Defence Staff Operation Division reported a mine detonated west of Nåttarö (this is not correct;[141] he had been informed by the Chief of Staff at Muskö, Commander Lars-Erik Hoff, who had just called him). At 15.10, Chief of Staff Vice-Admiral Stefenson reported from Muskö that the mine at Nåttarö had possibly detonated by mistake, probably as a result of bad wiring. Rear-Admiral Kierkegaard activated additional mine barrages in the north (Oxnö Udde–Stora Stenholmen).[142] Another set of depth charges and three mines were discharged at Mälsten, outside Hårsfjärden, without results. At 19.30, Vice-Admiral Stefenson was still at the naval base. He reported that there was no information about the submarine nets (even though the *Belos* had reported to the naval base about the nets one hour earlier). At 22.00, he called General Ljung (from Stockholm):[143] three mines had been triggered manually after indications (this was not correct). In his call to Ljung, Stefenson proposed a 'provisional ceasefire' for the mine barrages and for the dropping of volleys of depth charges in order to guarantee security and calm down the operational personnel at the naval base.[144] Ljung writes: 'Order according to Stefenson's proposal.'[145] According to the Mälsten war diary, a ceasefire order for the mine barrages was received at 23.20.[146] The Submarine Defence Commission Report states that the ceasefire was declared at 23.30.[147]

Friday 8 October

The submarine classified as a 'certain submarine' on the previous evening at Mysingeholm may have gone further south in the night, perhaps towards Östra Röko. 'At 02.38–02.58, Mysing and Väktaren have several contacts with an echo 2–3 kilometres north of Östra Röko in southern Mysingen.'[148] The naval base war diary continues:

> At 06.38, from Skarprunmarn: [magnetic] indication in both lines. Something is on its way from Sandhamn to Kanholmsfjärden . . . At 09.28, Belos ready. Has checked the [submarine] nets. Report by telephone. No divers in the water . . . [At 12.50, from Visborg at Vitså: hill in the water towards Årsta Havsbad, 2–3 knots, visible for one minute, 0.4–0.5 metres high and 1 metre in diameter.[149]] At 13.10, from Visborg: strange echo at Vitså . . . To Mode . . . Check radar echo and waves outside Visborg . . . At 13.28, Y72 in the air. Y71 in the air. [A number of oil patches reported during the day] . . . At 16.40, from helicopter division: heard intermittent knocking sounds from the sonar buoy [at the northern exit of Hårsfjärden] . . . At 18.03, Blidö reports about radar echo at low speed in southern Hårsfjärden between

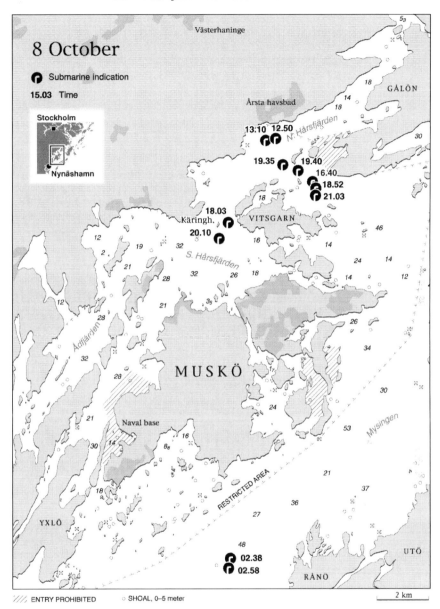

8 October

🏴 Submarine indication

15.03 Time

13. 8 October.

Vitsgarn and Käringholmen . . . At 18.52, helicopter division reports: the knocking sounds are still there. Also heard by Sjöhunden . . . At 21.03, from Väktaren: strange knocking sound in bearing 270 degrees. My position 2/10 north of Bergholmen.[150]

For the evening, the naval base war diary states:

> [At 19.05–19.40, radar echoes and scraping sounds towards the net at Alvsta Långholmar at the northern exit of Hårsfjärden.] At 19.10, from Sjöhunden (west of the choke point]: the scraping sounds are becoming stronger . . . At 19.35, from Sjöhunden: intermittent radar echo in bearing 047°, distance from the net 290 metres. Going towards the net. Scraping sounds . . . At 19.40, helicopter on its way. To Mode and Väktaren [on the eastern side of the net]: high alert, indications [report 21.06: at 19.40, x-band notation, possible submarine, position 0.3M west Oxnö Udde (on the eastern side of the net)]. At 19.47, from Sjöhunden: very strong indication. I want a helicopter . . . 19.58, Y71 in the air . . . At 20.10, from Blidö (passive sonar): sounds like divers breathing, position 0.3M south Käringholmen . . . At 20.47, Y71 returns [no contact].[151]

In the morning, one submarine may have gone towards the southern exit of Mysingen, towards Mälsten. At lunchtime, most likely a small submersible went westwards in northern Hårsfjärden. Later, there was a report from southern Hårsfjärden. From 16.40 until at least 21.00, there were several reports of knocking sounds in the area close to Bergholmen outside the northern exit of Hårsfjärden. In other words, the sounds seemed to originate from the same area that Malin had been located in the day before. The knocking sounds possibly indicated repair work on the submarine damaged the day before. On the other hand, there were still visual observations from inside Hårsfjärden and, later, a number of sonar contacts, radar echoes and then strong indications at the net, and scraping sounds indicating another passage or perhaps a breakout attempt. These indications point to a submersible or midget submarine, not the submarine that went south in the morning and not the one that possibly was damaged the day before. The sea-floor investigation found something believed to be a print from the keel of a midget that had been crawling along the sea floor through the passage between Huvudholmen and Alvsta Långholmar. There were seemingly marks from a keel with propeller marks on either side.[152] However, Cato and Larsson are more sceptical about this observation.[153]

In the morning, the provisional ceasefire from the previous night was terminated. This decision was taken by General Ljung after the morning meeting. Ljung writes:

> At 08.00, briefing: conversation with Chief of the Navy [Rudberg] and Chief of Staff [Stefenson]. At 08.30, [new] order: volleys of depth charges according to the MBÖ rules [end of ceasefire]. Right to use fire

for the mine barrages in daylight under the condition of safety on the surface [this decision did not reach Mälsten until 10.20]. At 08.30, Palme was called and briefed. At 09.00, Adelsohn called. He was briefed. He was irritated and wanted to know [referring to the mine explosions at 18.36 and 18.40 on 7 October] why the mines had been detonated [behind the submarine and] not directly under the submarine.[154] I explained, firstly, that it was not clear if it actually was a submarine that had passed over the mine; secondly, that the policy was still not to sink but to seriously damage the submarine. He seemed to be irritated and asked if I had given such orders. I had not done that. I also told him that, but that I supported the view as to when to give fire.[155]

The Mälsten war diary describes the decision to end the ceasefire:

> At 10.20, order from CSK [Brigadier-General Hansson]: right to use force during daylight in clear visibility. Not against surface targets. Another patrol vessel arrives after lunch. CSK will take over the command from Coastal Defence Staff after lunch. Order from CSK: no graduated use of force [the mine is to be detonated directly under the submarine]. At 10.50, order on fire: prevent submarine from passing.[156]

Dagens Nyheter mentioned a radar contact in Hårsfjärden; the submarine rescue vessel *Belos* was investigating the northern exit; a hospital close to Hårsfjärden was made ready to receive wounded and dead submariners; and a number of ambulances were sent to Berga.[157]

At 12.00, Olof Palme returned to office as Prime Minister after six years in opposition. He introduced his new government, with former trade union leader Lennart Bodström as Foreign Minister and the local Social Democratic leader Börje Andersson as Defence Minister. Both of these appointments came as a surprise, and they indicated that Olof Palme himself wanted to play the dominating role in foreign and security policy.[158] Palme appointed Ingvar Carlsson as Deputy Prime Minister and the former Social Democratic State Secretary for Defence, Ulf Larsson, as his own secretary. Kjell-Olof Feldt became Minister of Finance. In his inaugural speech, Olof Palme said: 'Swedish territory will be defended with all available means.'[159] According to *Aftonbladet*, Palme also said that Sweden 'under certain circumstances might destroy the submarine'.[160] At 16.00, the Commander-in-Chief and the Chief of Staff had a meeting with the new Minister of Defence Börje Andersson and his State Secretary, Per Borg. At 17.00, the Minister, Borg and the Chief of Staff went to Muskö Naval Base.[161]

During the period 6–8 October, Rolf Andersson from FMV (Swedish Defence Material) made the final calibration of the new bottom-fixed sonar system at Mälsten MAFU (Navy's Experimental

Equipment). After several submarine incidents during the summer, Stockholm Coastal Defence had decided to supplement the magnetic systems of the mine barrages with acoustic ones. A system was bought from a Norwegian company, Ocean Research (later bought by Simrad). On 31 August and 1 September, five microphones were deployed along a line south of the mine barrages in Danziger Gatt (southeast of Mälsten from Torskboden and eastwards). Nos 1 and 5 were attached by nylon cords, one to an underwater buoy (2 metres above the bottom) and the other to the sea floor. Nos 2, 3 and 4 were placed on platforms on the sea floor (about 1 metre above the bottom). In September, Andersson visited Mälsten every week in order to calibrate the system. All activities in the waters around Mälsten were followed and tape-recorded from a small house in the southeastern corner of the island of Mälsten. On 6–8 October, Andersson made the final calibrations for this system together with two representatives from Ocean Research. On 9 October, this sonar system set up by FMV and Stockholm Coastal Defence was referred to as 'some FOA tests'.[162] This sonar system was going to play a major role in the following days.

Saturday 9 October

Stockholm Coastal Defence Staff writes:

> At 08.00, order from CSK [Brigadier-General Lars Hansson]: 2.1) Command Persson [Colonel Lars-G. Persson] shall in cooperation with CÖrlBO [Rear-Admiral Christer Kierkegaard] prevent submarine from getting out. In cooperation with CÖrlBO and CSeM prevent foreign power from capturing the submarine. Be prepared to receive air-defence forces from Lv3. Two hours readiness . . . For reconnaissance tasks, take orders from CÖrlBO. 2.2) Command Kviman shall prevent submarine from breaking out. Act as commander for Mälsten and for mine barrages MS1, MS2 and MS3 [Mälsten 1, 2 and 3], LB1 and LB2 [Långbälingen 1 and 2], for the sensor cable station at Stora Stenholmen, for the reconnaissance boats 73 and 77 and for transport boat M . . . 4) The mine barrages have the right to use fire during daylight with clear visibility . . . At 15.15, CSK order: mine troops shall be ready to start to deploy mine barrage at [the northern exit of Hårsfjärden] 06.00 on 10 October.[163]

The naval base war diary states that, during the night, new submarine nets had been deployed at the northern exit of Hårsfjärden:

> At 00.45, nets set out between Rörholmen and Lilla Stenholmen and between Stora Stenholmen and Långholmsgrund on the inner side of and attached to earlier nets. The net between Alvsta Långholmar and

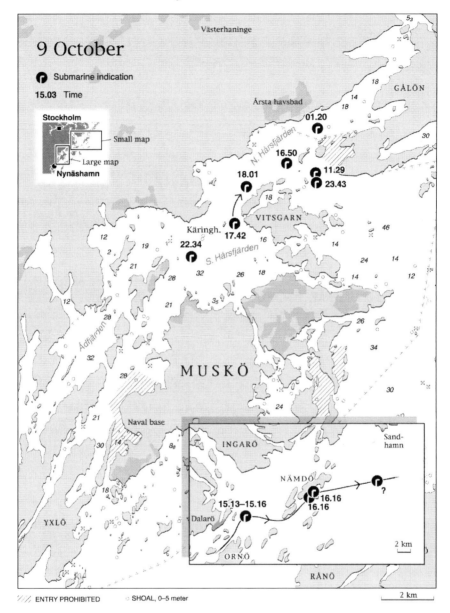

9 October

ⓝ Submarine indication

15.03 Time

Stockholm
— Small map
— Large map
Nynäshamn

Västerhaninge

GÅLÖN

Årsta havsbad

01.20

N. Hårsfjärden

16.50

18.01

11.29
23.43

VITSGARN

Käringh. **17.42**

22.34

S. Hårsfjärden

MUSKÖ

Naval base

INGARÖ

Sand-hamn

NÄMDÖ

15.13–15.16

16.16
16.16

?

Dalarö

2 km

YXLÖ

ORNÖ

RÅNÖ

▨ ENTRY PROHIBITED   ○ SHOAL, 0–5 meter   2 km

14. 9 October.

Stora Huvudholmen is in production and will be put out in the morning of 9 October . . . [In the early morning, there were several echoes and magnetic indications. At 01.20, Mode and ATB2 reported intermittent radar echo 2/10 north of Lilla Huvudholmen] . . . At 06.15, from

69

Mälsten: clear visibility. We activated the mine barrages. At 07.00, from [ammunition transport boat] ATB2 . . . strange indication in the echo ranger. Something passed under the boat . . . At 11.29, from Stenholmen: abnormal magnetic indication.[164]

In the afternoon at 15.15, a periscope was observed in Jungfrufjärden, and, at 16.15, there were two different observations of a periscope east of Nämdö.[165] The Naval Analysis Group Report states: 'At 15.13–15.16, optical observation of "pipe" [periscope] in Jung-frufjärden. At 16.16, two observations of object southeast Västra Kyrkskär (east Nämdö) . . . At 20.15, GYP has IR contact north of Nämdö.'[166] The periscope or mast was described as dark and 1 metre high, and the diameter was compared to the mast of a sailing boat (about 0.2 metres). The observers at southeast Nämdö described a small, dark, narrow submarine sail going out at a relatively high speed. The sail was reported to be extremely narrow (2 metres high and 0.5 metres [sic] wide) but wider at the base.[167] If we accept this observation, we should rather think in terms of a small, narrow submarine seen from behind, but the sail would be 1 metre, not 0.5 metres, wide. The high mast and the narrow sail fit with the report from Dalarö on 4 October.

General Ljung wrote about observations in Jungfrufjärden and at Bullerön east of Nämdö.[168] These observations indicate that the submarine was coming from Jungfrufjärden, or rather from Mysingen and Dalarö, and was entering open sea outside Bullerön. In the 1982 internal Navy report, this submarine was described as a 'certain submarine'.[169] The naval base war diary reported about a periscope at 15.05.[170]

At 15.45, [Coast Guard reconnaissance aircraft] GYP is sent to Jungfrufjärden–Fjäderhällan–Smådalarö. At 15.55, helicopter [Y72] towards Jungfrufjärden. Observation south of Östra Stendörren . . . At 16.17, Y72 reached its position. Cooperation with GYP. [At 17.30, Defence Staff report about suspicious object seen at 16.16 at Ekholmen Nämdö . . . Classification: possible submarine] . . . At 16.50, from Sjöhunden: transmission 4 ping per second 100 kHz for 20–30 seconds . . . At 17.42, Blidö reported: sonar contact [in Hårsfjärden], possible submarine between Käringholmen and Märsgarn. Helicopter on highest alert. At 17.46, from Blidö: position Käringholmen, sonar contact, motor sound. At 17.51, from Sjöhunden: metallic sounds direction Furuholmen [close to Märsgarn] . . . At 18.01, from Blidö: sonar contact close to Flygviken [Märsgarn] . . . At 18.09, from Y71: position Märsgarn . . . At 18.37, new net between Alvsta Långholmar and Långholmsgrund . . . At 18.46, from Blidö: first contact position

DQ 080 025 and last contact DQ 082 035 [Blidö reported that a sub-surface object had moved from one position in the area between Käringholmen and Märsgarn to another position off Märsgarn closer to Furuholmen] . . . At 19.08 . . . from Blidö: after first contact lost, clear propeller sound – with low turns per minute – for 10 seconds . . . At 22.34, from Blidö: echo at the distance of 150 metres . . . At 23.43, from Stenholmen: [magnetic] indication. Nothing on the surface. At 23.45, to Mode and Snapphanen: probable passage at Stenholmen–Oxnö Udde [at the northern exit of Hårsfjärden].[171]

Several clear indications on 9 October point to a submarine passing Jungfrufjärden, Nämdöfjärden and later Bullerön further out. According to Commander Björn Eklind, Deputy Chief of Defence Staff Intelligence, this submarine was believed to have passed out from Mysingen through its northern exit at Dalarö on the night of 8–9 October. It was believed to have followed the western side of Ornö Island (Ornöströmmar) to reach Jungfrufjärden. This channel is narrow and shallow, less than 10 metres deep at its most shallow point. If this submarine was the same as the one attacked outside the nets on 7 October, it would have had to surface when passing Dalarö, as did the submarine on 4 October. After this exit, there are still several indications of a midget in northern Hårsfjärden between Märsgarn and Käringholmen. The submarine nets between Alvsta Långholmar and Långholmsgrund were damaged in the afternoon on 7 October, and new nets were deployed at 18.00 on 9 October. Late in the evening of 9 October, there was a probable passage between Stenholmen and Oxnö Udde (the northern choke point) a few hundred metres east of the nets. This may have been the same small vessel that had tried to pass out the night before. No serious incident seems to have taken place on 9 October.

The Naval Base East intelligence report for 9 October states:

> 1. Briefing 09 12 00. 1.1. *Foreign Naval Vessels:* There are no known foreign naval vessels in the area except for possible submarines. British frigate F72 Ariadne visits Copenhagen 7–12 October. 1.2. *Foreign State Vessels:* The Soviet Prof. Uchov has permission to pass southern Kvarken on 10 October to visit Piteå [some 1,000 kilometres further north]. Return on 14 October. 1.3. *Warsaw Pact Merchant Ships:* At 12.30, Soviet ML Volgobalt 126 [position] at 12.00 CP 5030 destination Gdynia. No other ships in the area. 1.4. *Conclusion:* The naval vessels and signal intelligence ships that were active in the early part of the week participated in the celebration of Constitution Day on 7 October. After this, Warsaw Pact merchant ships appear to have taken over signal intelligence tasks. 1.5. *Foreign Submarine Activity:* Since

27 September, there have been a large number of reports of foreign submarines. Our analysis concludes that, in addition to the object (probable submarine) in Hårsfjärden, there has most likely been one submarine in the Sandhamn area. It is also possible that one submarine has been in Mysingen. We have received indications that one submarine may have passed through the northern barrier [the net at Alvsta Långholmar]. Investigation of the barrier and other indications point to the possibility that one submarine still operates inside the barrier [CÖrlBO INT/CörlBO, from the Chief of the Naval Base, Rear-Admiral Christer Kierkegaard].[172]

This intelligence report is not very alarming. The sharp contrast between this report about low Soviet activity and the dramatic submarine hunt in Hårsfjärden is striking. There is no Soviet mobilization of force. If we believe the Swedish Navy was hunting Soviet submarines, it is difficult to understand why these dramatic incidents were not reflected in Soviet behaviour in the Baltic Sea. However, the events are more easy to understand if we think in terms of Western submarines.

At 12.00, Brigadier-General Hansson, Chief of Stockholm Coastal Defence, was ordered to appear at the office of the Commander-in-Chief, General Lennart Ljung. When he arrived, Vice-Admiral Stefenson and the Commander of the Eastern Military District, Lieutenant-General Bengt Lehander, were also present in the room, but the Chief of the Navy, Vice-Admiral Per Rudberg, was not. There was, according to Hansson, no fighting spirit. The Commander-in-Chief and the Chief of Staff were gloomy. Hansson says that he was ordered not to use the mines unless he had indications from the magnetic sensors of at least three mines. The larger the ship or submarine, the larger the magnetic field, which would cause a greater number of mines to indicate and a larger number of lamps to turn on in the control room, he argued.[173] Many submarines, however, are more or less demagnetized, and they will create only a small magnetic field and provoke indications from perhaps just one or two mines.[174] Hansson believed that this order would have made it possible for a submarine to pass out without the personnel at Mälsten being able to do anything. Hansson was also ordered not to use the mines at night even though their night-vision scopes made it possible to see any surface vessel in darkness. According to Hansson, Chief of Staff Vice-Admiral Stefenson said: 'We don't want to have a massacre of submariners.'[175]

General Ljung's version is a little bit different:

At 12.00, meeting at the Defence Staff building with CFst [Chief of Staff Bror Stefenson], MBÖ [Bengt Leander], CSK [Lars Hansson]. We discussed the question of the use of mines in the submarine hunt. My decision was: Continued prohibition against activating mines in darkness or poor visibility (reason: security on the surface); if a submarine passes the mine barrage, we will allow detonation of a single mine directly under the submarine; additional fixed mines will be deployed at the northern choke point [see above]; start a legal investigation on how information about the fixed mines at Mälsten has leaked out; CFst will find out about some FOA [Defence Research Establishment] tests [with sonar systems mentioned on 8 October].[176]

After having read Ljung's diary, it seems obvious that the experience of 7 October and the talk with Adelsohn the day before might have provoked the meeting. Ljung seems to have changed his views about where the detonation should be, allowing the 'detonation of a single mine directly under the submarine'. The mine should now be detonated without the personnel turning off the signal. This appears as more of a 'hardline policy'. At 13.40, Mälsten actually received such an order. 'Order from CSK [Lars Hansson]: use of force in daylight and clear visibility. No delay [they should no longer turn off the signal]. Fire with one mine.'[177] Ljung does not mention any restrictions other than that of the ceasefire during the night. 'At 18.05, to [the mine barrages at Mälsten] MS1 and MS3: cease fire because of darkness . . . At 18.30 to MS2: cease fire.'[178]

At Mälsten, Lieutenant-Colonel Kviman decided that this order was not technically feasible. To avoid further mistakes – such as what happened when the system was turned to automatic on 7 October – they had to turn off the signal at least once, twice to be on the safe side. Instead of demanding three indicating mines, which was of no relevance, they interpreted the order as meaning that they should turn off the signal twice and then, on the third time, give fire. This procedure might damage the submarine but not necessarily sink it. Kviman said that Hansson and the staff meeting had misunderstood the problem. The sensor signals of one mine had to be turned off to check if there was a constant magnetic field over the mine, not just some problem with the magnetic sensor system. On 7 October, Mälsten had followed an order that led to unnecessary mine explosions, and they had been criticized for what happened afterwards. They were not going to let the same thing happen once more.

Hansson was upset after the meeting at Ljung's office. He did not understand the mood of his superiors. The new night-vision scopes had been proved to be efficient in darkness. The command at Mälsten had tested the control of the surface by towing a small rowing-boat to the other side of the narrow passage. The experiment had been satisfactory. In daylight, one could monitor the narrow passage without binoculars. With the new night-vision scopes, one had full control of the surface even in darkness. A ceasefire in darkness would just make the submarine hunt more difficult. Something seemed to have happened during the last day or two that had changed the mood of the military leadership. Vice-Admiral Stefenson also spoke with Hansson in confidence in a separate room. He said: 'There are rumours about a NATO submarine. We have to stop those [rumours].' Hansson was surprised. Two days earlier, in an interview for *Aftonbladet* on the national origin of the submarine, Hansson had said: 'We can only make guesses ranging anywhere from a Russian submarine left behind after the US naval visit to a NATO submarine that wanted to test us.'[179] However, he had heard nothing about a possible NATO involvement, either before or after Stefenson brought it up.

The above information forces us to look once again at the previously mentioned telegram from the Italian news agency Ansa, which was also on 9 October. This stated that the Swedes were negotiating with a foreign power in Geneva. In the early 1980s, it was 'obvious' that this foreign power was the Soviet Union, and Sweden was believed to have negotiated a release of one or more submarine(s) with them. Still, this information was never taken seriously. If the foreign power was a NATO country, such negotiations would be more easy to explain. At the time, the Italian radio news actually talked of Swedish negotiations with a NATO country.[180] I later spoke to a source of this information. He said that there were two Swedes in Geneva (one industrialist and one military officer, but no one from the Foreign Ministry). The meeting had taken place on 8 October. He claimed that the original source was Italian Military Intelligence (SISMI) and confirmed that the submarine(s) originated from the USA. On the US side, there were two military officers and two civilians at the meeting. There was also an Italian representative present, a lieutenant-colonel from SISMI. This telegram is still not confirmed, but a possible Italian involvement in Hårsfjärden – with, for example, one or two Italian special force submarines operating together with US submarines under US general command – might explain an Italian presence in Geneva. In high-risk operations, the USA may prefer to use forces from other nations, and the Italian naval special forces were indeed qualified for the task.

Another fact that supports this hypothesis is the presence of the large US tanker *Mormacsky* (210 metres). In the afternoon (14.30–16.00) of 9 October, the reconnaissance aircraft *GYP* reported nine civilian ships altogether outside the southern Stockholm archipelago, including a couple of Swedish and Finnish ships, a Danish and a Dutch ship, and the US tanker *Mormacsky*.[181] The latter has been used by the US Navy and the CIA as a support ship for covert operations, and it is most probably able to transport smaller submarines or submersibles in a hidden hangar below the surface similar to what was done during the Second World War (see below on Italian operations). If this ship was supposed to pick up one or two of the smaller submarines, it might have been necessary to have a meeting, for example in Geneva, to facilitate a release of these submarines before the ship was supposed to pass the area.

Sunday 10 October

Between 00.00 and 01.15, the naval base war diary reported on the continued submarine hunt with several indications, including magnetic indications close to the net at Alvsta Långholmar.

> At 01.20, Pingvinen reports: echo between Alvsta Långholmar and Årsta Havsbad. Moving slowly towards [bearing] 040 [degrees (northeast). After this, several further indications]. At 01.58, Pingvinen reports: lost contact . . . At 02.15, IR contact east of Gunnarstenarna in bearing 089 degrees, distance 7,500 metres [southeast of Mälsten].[182] . . . At 05.30, about contact 02.15: may be periscope . . . At 05.48, from Sjöhunden: echo in bearing 346 degrees, distance 840 metres [west Alvsta Långholmar]. At 05.55, from Sjöhunden: increase of low-frequency sounds on my microphone [propeller sounds?] . . . At 13.31, the Commander-in-Chief reports: the Chief of the Navy places the mine diver division [under the command of Kent Pejdell] at the disposal of the Commander of the Eastern Military District . . . At 14.09, [from Sjöhunden]: transmissions at 100 kHz. [At 14.16, Sjöhunden reports about special sonar for sub-surface transmitting.][183] . . . At 15.40, report from a reconnaissance aircraft: a bow of waves moving towards southwest between Sjöhunden and Berganäs [at 14.00].[184] . . . At 16.00, [Chief of the Naval Base] asks for analysis of the photos taken . . . At 18.57, from 514: indication on the radar 100 metres south of Oxnö Udde . . . At 21.45, [magnetic] indication. At 21.47, to Mode and Snapphanen: search at Stora Stenholmen – Oxnö udde [at the northern exit of Hårsfjärden].[185]

The waters between Alvsta Långholmar and Årsta Havsbad are no deeper than 20 metres – in some parts just 10–15 metres deep. New indications in the area appeared in the afternoon. We are thus talking about a submersible or a midget still operating in Hårsfjärden. An IR contact (and a possible periscope sighting) was made southeast of Mälsten at the Swedish territorial border. A submarine seemed to be 'parked' outside the final checkpoint at Mälsten. At the northern exit of Hårsfjärden, there were also registered very high frequency (VHF) signals that may have been used by the submarines for communication with a land-based network.

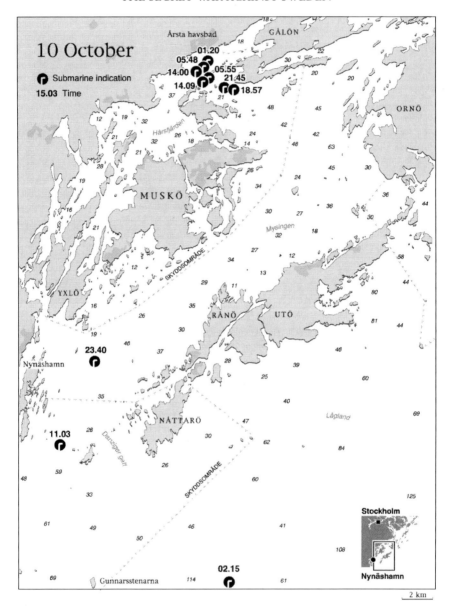

15. 10 October.

At 02.55 Mälsten reported an aircraft without navigation lights over Yttre Gården. Between 01.00 and 03.30, a large civilian ship, *Dalasand/Dalsund,* was anchored in the area of Örngrund-Östra Röko 4 kilometres north of Mälsten. The captain reported that it had anchored to fill its tanks,[186] which is unusual for a commercial ship. Afterwards, we were not able to find the ship in any public register. The Chief of the Information Division, Commander Sven Carlsson, said later that he was informed that a large crane had operated in the area at this time (later, after the hunt, the submarine rescue vessel *Belos* commuted between Måsknuv (see 11 October) and the area of Östra Röko-Örngrund).[187] 'At 23.40, TP79 reports IR contact at Örngrund (in Mysingen [in the same area]).'[188] One submarine was possibly ready to leave Mysingen at Mälsten for the open sea (see 11 October).

At Mälsten, civilian traffic had had to pass on the eastern side of the island – through Danziger Gatt – since 16.45 on 7 October, because on the deeper western side a submarine might hide under a ship when passing out. Before leaving Nynäshamn or before passing the area, pilot authorities gave the captains of the merchant ships strict orders to follow the eastern route. For 10 October, the Mälsten war diary reported that the ceasefire in darkness ended at 05.25 for MS1 and MS2 and at 05.45 for MS3.[189]

> At 10.55, [the West German merchant ship] Borkum Riff was 5 km north of Mälsten ... At 10.59, indications from radar and from lookout that Borkum Riff would not go through Danziger Gatt. Called ÖrlBO [Naval Base East] to make the pilots stop the ship. Tried to contact the pilots via telephone (engaged). Tried to contact the ship via VHF (no answer). Sent out a patrol vessel to stop Borkum Riff. No answer via radio. At 11.03, Borkum Riff passed the mine barrage. Three mines indicated (Måsknuv). Two mines indicated 50 metres behind the ship, but the one in the middle was not turned on. Conclusion: disturbances.[190]

I discussed this with Lieutenant-Colonel Kviman, who said that there may have been disturbances in the magnetic field that explained this incident. On the other hand, the West German captain acted in a strange way. At 11.10, the naval base war diary confirmed this passage and the lack of radio contact.[191] At 21.50, the Mälsten war diary reported a clear indication in the magnetic sensor system. The mine barrage indicated at 21.35. At 22.00, a report was sent to Naval Base East about the possible passage of a submarine.[192]

Lennart Ljung's diary mentions a Polish submarine rescue vessel (or assumed submarine rescue vessel) on route in the Baltic Sea towards the Gulf of Finland. A radio amateur, who recorded the transmission and delivered the tape to the Swedish Signal Intelligence Agency (FRA), intercepted its radio traffic. On the tape could be heard: 'Permission to rise to depth 8 metres?' FRA made an immediate request to the Eastern Military District for night-vision air surveillance. The request was denied, but Vice-Admiral Stefenson overturned this decision. The air surveillance resulted in nothing. FRA analysed the tape: it did 'not concern submarines'.[193]

Monday 11 October
Just after midnight, at 00.12, Naval Base East asked Mälsten to identify an echo at Östra Röko. 'There are two echoes. One at DP 04 55 [at Örngrund, close to Östra Röko, in the area in which an IR contact had been received just before midnight]. Bevb [73]: Nothing on the surface.'[194] This seems to have been a submarine ready to leave Mysingen at Mälsten. At 03.10, the naval base war diary reported a stationary echo at DP 1248 (3.5M south of the island of Grän) southeast of Mälsten (in the area in which an IR contact and a possible periscope sighting had been reported one day earlier (see above)). A patrol boat, *Bevb 77*, was sent to the area and reported that there was nothing on the surface where a constant echo had been showing for three hours.[195] From the night of 10 October, a sub-surface object, most likely a submarine, was 'parked' outside Mälsten in Swedish territorial waters (close to the territorial sea border) at the main exit from the Stockholm southern archipelago. This submarine may have been deployed to support a submarine in the Hårsfjärden/Mysingen area or possibly to receive a midget from this area. The newspaper *Expressen* quoted a high-ranking Swedish officer as saying that a 'NATO submarine' (but not a West German submarine) was 'parked' outside Mälsten at the territorial sea border.[196] A British or US submarine seems to have been deployed outside Mälsten from at least 10 October.

In Hårsfjärden, there were still some indications of sub-surface activity. The Naval Analysis Group Report speaks about 'visual observation of a "pipe" [periscope] in Mälbyfjärden [between Muskö and Herrön] at 06.00–07.00'.[197] The 'dark pipe' was seen for 20–30 seconds before it disappeared. One minute later it appeared 50–100 metres further south.[198] This indication is not found in the naval base war diary, which contains a report of an oil patch and an echo east of Bergholmen from about 05.00.[199] The same war diary states:

> At 06.52, 752 reports: intermittent echo . . . in the oil patch [at the northern exit]. At 07.00, clear magnetic indication at Stenholmen. At 07.42, Väktaren reports: will pass the [sensor] cable [at the northern exit] in one minute . . . At 08.16, Väktaren reports: possible submarine . . . east of Bergholmen. At 08.17, from Väktaren: new position bearing 104 degrees, distance 2,000 metres east of Bergholmen. At 08.20, order to Väktaren: start fishing with Malin . . . At 08.32, from Gullboda: alarm from the sensor cable at Skramsösund [at the southern exit]. At 08.39,

alarm in the other direction . . . At 11.32, Gullboda reports: 'something white' turned up [in the water] outside Risdal [Mälbyfjärden]. Distance 150 metres. [Fast VIP boat] Smuggler goes out to check it . . . At 12.25, visual report from Berga: high narrow object [periscope?] at Länsman. Going towards west. TV 105 investigates . . . At 15.33, from Sjöhunden [at the northern exit of Hårsfjärden]: pulses of several hundred kHz [possibly indicating VHF communication between submarine and other foreign forces (see above) . . . At 18.55, from Mysing: radar echo 0.2M north-northwest of Snappudd [about 2,000 metres east-southeast of Bergholmen] . . . At 19.03, from Mysing: echo is moving in bearing 010 degrees [towards north].[200]

Indications in the sensor cables at the southern entrance to Hårsfjärden, and observation of a periscope and of 'something white' on the surface close to Muskö Naval Base may indicate that a partly white submersible (which would tend to indicate a Western vessel) was still operating in southern Hårsfjärden. There were several indications of a possible submarine at the northern exit going towards Mysingen. None of these observations were reported in the Naval Analysis Group Report.

At Mälsten, the ceasefire during darkness ended at five o'clock (MS1 at 04.45, MS2 at 04.50 and MS3 at 05.00).[201] Just before midnight, an IR contact was received at Örngrund,[202] some 4 kilometres north of Måsknuv/Mälsten. After midnight, an echo indicating a submarine was received from the same area.[203] It seems that a submarine was ready to leave Stockholm archipelago at Mälsten. From 04.56, the Mälsten sonar system operator registered short low-frequency sounds (25–800 Hz) with 30-second intervals. [According to the submarine sound expert at Mälsten, Anders Karlsson, this is typical sound from a submarine propeller working in short intervals to avoid detection.] At 06.35, a report was made to Commander Emil Svensson at Naval Base East. These low-frequency sounds continued irregularly up to lunchtime.[204] At 10.30, the personnel at Mälsten registered a bang.[205] At 10.31, Mälsten reported a loud bang. The naval base war diary states that this originated from the US reconnaissance aircraft SR-71.[206] The Submarine Defence Commission Report says that a bang was heard at 11.00, originating from a US aircraft.[207] At 10.37, the Commander of Naval Base East ordered one helicopter for a submarine hunt at Mälsten.[208] At 11.10, the bottom-fixed sonar system at Mälsten registered a 'ping', an active sonar, either from a helicopter or from a foreign submarine.[209]

At 12.20, the personnel at the mine station at Måsknuv/Mälsten registered a clear indication in the mine barrage west of Mälsten (MS2). The magnetic sensors of a mine some 75–100 metres west of Måsknuv

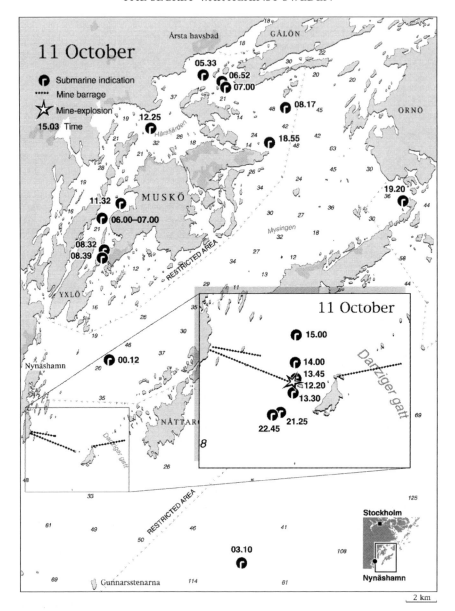

16. 11 October.

indicated a submarine, a magnetic field passing out from Mysingen. There was nothing on the surface. The sensor signals were turned off twice, but the magnetism was still present, indicating a clear magnetic field for ten seconds; this was most likely a conventional submarine, the Commander at Mälsten, Lieutenant-Colonel Sven-Olof Kviman, said. The Mälsten war diary states:

> At 12.20, mine detonated at MS2 [at Måsknuv] after several [magnetic] indications that were not possible to turn off. Depth 37 metres. One indicating mine. At 12.23, report to ÖrlBO [Naval Base East]. At 12.32, report to Stockholm Coastal Defence.[210]

The naval base war diary states: 'At 12.24, from Mälsten: Mine detonated at Måsknuv.'[211] The Stockholm Coastal Defence Staff report contains the following:

> At 12.30, Command Kviman reports: 1–2 mines detonated at MS2. Detonation at 12.25 by MS2 (G1M2) after three indications. The first two indications were turned off. After that, the system was turned to automatic and the main switch was turned to 'on'.[212]

Immediately after this incident, Captain Per Andersson, Deputy Commander at Mälsten, wrote a special report:

> [Telephone conversation 12.17–12.22 between Captain Per Andersson and Captain Johan Eneroth (E), the local commander of the mine troops MS2.] At 12.20, I could hear the alarm from the mine instruments starting to howl. E said immediately: 'Indication in one mine – I am turning it off.' E turned off the indication. The howl from the alarm stopped while the button was pushed in. After that I could once again hear the alarm howling. E said then that he would turn it off once again, and the howling stopped while the button was pushed in. E said then that it was impossible to turn it off. I intended to give fire. I ordered E to detonate the mine. Time from first indication to detonation: about 10 seconds.
>
> The fact that I, as a superior commander, was having a telephone conversation with the chief of the mine barrage when the incident started is irrelevant, because he already had the right to use fire and he would have acted in the same way without my order. When questioning E afterwards, he reported that there had been no disturbances of this mine and that it was not possible to turn the indication off. In order to detonate the mine, he acted in the following way: the system was turned to automatic and the main switch was turned to 'on'. Because the indicating object was within reach of the sensors of the mine, the mine was detonated automatically.
>
> My conclusion: there were no disturbances of the indicating mine. The fact that the indication was still present after having been turned off several times must be understood as meaning that something within

the range of the sensors was affecting them. A mine sensor that is disturbed will usually return to normal after 0.5 seconds. What caused the indication, a submarine, torpedo or other metallic object, is not yet clear.[213]

Most probably, a demagnetized submarine was passing the mine barrage, and the submarine was probably damaged by the mine explosion. This view is supported by the Grandin Report, which states: 'A reasonably demagnetized submarine passing straight over [the mine barrage] at low speed will create 1–2 indications [or indicate in one or two mines].'[214] The explosion of the 600-kilogram mine created a pillar of water some 60 metres above the surface, Lieutenant-Colonel Kviman told me. Not only Mälsten but also the underground naval base at Muskö 15 kilometres north was shaking. According to Commander Rolf Blomquist, Chief of the Operational Section, Naval Base East, you could feel the explosion several tens of kilometres from the place of the incident. At the Seismological Institute in Uppsala, some 100 kilometres further north, the explosion was registered to have taken place at 12.22.10.[215]

Anders Öhman, *Dagens Nyheter* journalist and former civilian captain, was in the town of Nynäshamn. He heard the mine explosion at Mälsten and understood what had happened. The windows in Nynäshamn were vibrating. He immediately got a boat and a photographer, and they went out to Mälsten. One hour after the explosion, they arrived with their boat at the waters between Yttre Gården and Mälsten, southwest of Måsknuv. They went into a bright-yellow patch 20 × 30 metres, a yellow chemical substance that they believed came from the mine explosion. Afterwards, they went home disappointed at not having seen the submarine. In *Dagens Nyheter* this yellow patch and a radio buoy (believed to have been discovered north of Mälsten by the Swedish Coast Guard) were linked to the incident. A former submarine captain was interviewed, and both the yellow patch and the buoy were believed to originate from a damaged submarine. *Dagens Nyheter* had listened to (and even tape-recorded) a military radio conversation about this radio buoy between the naval base and a helicopter ordered to take a photograph of the buoy (see below).[216]

The Mälsten war diary states that:

> Naval Base East was briefed about the mine explosion at 12.23 and Stockholm Coastal Defence at 12.32. At 12.40, transport boat 334 was sent out to search. At 12.55, report from Naval Base East, reconnaissance flight [GYP] has seen thin oil [on the surface]. At 12.57, patrol boat 77 is sent out.[217]

The naval base war diary continues: 'At 12.57, GYP reports: mud from the sea floor and thin oil at Måsknuv, bearing 330 [degrees], distance 6/10. Drifting with the wind.'[218] *GYP* used the metric system at the time, which means that the oil patch was 600 metres north-northwest of Måsknuv, drifting north. At 13.05, *Bevb 77* left Mälsten to take oil samples after the mine explosion.[219] 'At 13.12, report to Mälsten: light helicopter [Y46] will arrive for reconnaissance at 13.30 . . . At 13.46, from Y46: negative report. Returned to base [Berga].'[220] Anders Öhman and his photographer Folke Hellberg would most likely have arrived in the area around 13.20–13.30. Minutes afterwards, Öhman and Hellberg went into a small, bright-yellow patch of 20×30 metres (green at a distance against the blue sea (see below)). They saw the yellow substance at a distance of 1 metre. At 13.45, about 15 minutes later, the helicopter Y46 observed a green-coloured area in the water (according to Y46's drawing about 50×150 metres) at Måsknuv 'about 10 metres from land' – north-northwest of the small island.[221] Some time after 13.25, probably at 14.00, Chief of Måsknuv mine barrage (MS2) Captain Johan Eneroth wrote in his war diary: 'a yellow cloud in the water 200 metres north, extension 300×100 metres. Report to VM [Mälsten].'[222] To the officers at Mälsten, however, it looked more greenish. The Mälsten war diary states:

At 14.09 from MS2 [Måsknuv], green-coloured area in the water north of [Måsknuv. It covers an area of] 300×100 metres. Drifting towards N[orth]. Was small from the beginning; expanded. [After 'expanded', the hand-written version states something unreadable and then] green . . . At 14.35,[223] . . . order: take samples.[224]

I have spoken with the three most relevant commanding officers at Mälsten/Måsknuv, Lieutenant-Colonel Sven-Olof Kviman, Captain Per Andersson and Captain Johan Eneroth, who all confirm a green, yellow-green or yellow-green-grey patch. Andersson said that they went out (in a boat at 14.35) to collect the yellow/green substance by using a couple of clean towels. Ambassador Rolf Ekéus's report notes that no result from this analysis has been found. However, 'it was noted when samples were taken that the layer of the patch was thin, that the patch kept together, was floating as a film on the surface for hours, and that it consisted of a fine substance that did not mix with water'. It was described as 'artificially green'.[225]

At 14.30, *GYP* reported from Mälsten[-Måsknuv]. At 14.35, the Chief of Naval Base East ordered 'a light helicopter [Y46] to take a photo of the green patch on the water at Måsknuv'.[226] Y46 went back to Måsknuv and took 36 pictures of the patch. At 15.00, personnel on Y46 made a drawing of the expansion and movement of the patch.[227]

Y46 states: 'the patch had [now at 15.00] moved further north since we were there last time [13.45]: about 1 kilometre',[228] and, according to the drawing, expanded from 50×150 metres to about 150×450 metres.[229] After the naval base had been informed, its Chief of Staff, Commander Lars-Erik Hoff, called about the green patch to Lieutenant-Commander Carl-Johan Arfvidson at OPG's Naval Unit at the Defence Staff, who reported to his Chief of Staff.

> At 14.47, the sonar system registered low-frequency sounds, 20–100 Hz for 15 seconds [seemingly propeller; one minute and a half before this, a bang]. At 15.30, the green patch still visible. Concentrated. At 16.00, it is still there. At 16.08, from the sonar operator: at 16.05, low-frequency sounds for 25 seconds.[230]

After that, there were no further reports of the yellow/green patch. It was probably more or less dissolved. The artificially yellow/green patch indicates a dye from a submarine giving a signal about its condition and position. The first position of the dye indicates that a probably damaged submarine was hiding maybe 100 metres south-southwest of Måsknuv. The use of a yellow/green dye also indicates that this was a Western submarine, or rather a submarine under US command, which would pick up the signal from a satellite (see below).

At 15.00, the journalists at the Berga Press Centre were asked by Commander Carlsson to elect among themselves a small group to go out with the Navy. (This decision was criticized by a superior command.)[231]

> Anytime now, we can go out to look at the submarine . . . You have to choose a TV team, a radio journalist, a photographer and a newspaper journalist, [Carlsson] said. They have to represent the others. We can only bring a small group with us to look at the possible submarine.[232]

The Mälsten war diary continues:

> At 16.30 [from Naval Base East], Belos will arrive at Mälsten at 19.00. At 17.30, order from the Commander-in-Chief at 16.40: ceasefire for [the mine barrages] MS1, MS2, MS3, LB1, LB2 and Ox [Långbälingen 1, Långbälingen 2 and Oxdjupet] until investigation is made . . . At 18.30, from Chief Stockholm Coastal Defence [Lars Hansson]: end of ceasefire. At 19.20, LB1 reports: explosion is shaking the rocks. At 20.48, from Belos . . . Order to MS2 and MS3 to turn off the electrical system for the mine barrages.[233] At 20.50, Belos arrives at the place of the mine explosion.[234]

The bottom-fixed sonar system registered a lot of sounds during the night, apparently work on a damaged submarine. The Mälsten war diary and the naval base war diary state that, at 21.25, the sonar system station registered 'hammering' sounds or 'metallic hammering', which was 'tape-recorded'. Two patrol vessels went out to the area. At 21.50, they were supported by helicopter Y68.[235] During the night, knocking sounds, metallic sounds and, from 22.45, high-frequency sounds (12.5–20 kHz) could be heard. Some of these sounds continued more or less irregularly for the whole night and the next morning (see below). General Ljung says in his diary: 'Mine detonated at Mälsten – directly under [the indicating object/submarine] – green patch. Ceasefire for the mine barrages until investigation is made.'[236] By saying that the mine was activated 'directly under' the submarine, General Ljung implied that the submarine may have been damaged or even sunk. The next day, he wrote in his diary: 'In the afternoon, no new information on a possibly sunk submarine.'[237]

However, it is important to note that Ljung's comment, 'mine detonated at Mälsten – directly under – green patch', was not written on 11 October. It was clearly inserted afterwards. A detailed study of Ljung's hand-written text indicates that this was inserted in the afternoon of 12 October.[238] Even though Mälsten reported everything to Naval Base East and Stockholm Coastal Defence Staff, and even though they supposedly reported to the Defence Staff, General Ljung made no notes about a 'seriously damaged submarine' until up to 24 hours after the incident took place. In the morning, General Ljung was informed (as usual by Chief of Staff Vice-Admiral Stefenson and Chief of the Navy Vice-Admiral Rudberg) that nothing serious seemed to have happened and that the Chief of the Naval Base, Rear-Admiral Kierkegaard, lacked the optimism of the information division. According to Stefenson and Rudberg, there was no submarine that triggered the mine explosion. This is also the conclusion made by Commander Emil Svensson and the Naval Analysis Group.

While Ljung, since 7 October, had in general been preoccupied with the force of the mine weapon and had demanded to be continuously updated on the current events, he was now, on 11 October, seemingly not informed about the results of the mine explosion – what he himself described as a 'possibly sunk submarine' – until the following day. Perhaps it is not until Chief of Stockholm Coastal Defence Lars Hansson personally briefed the Commander-in-Chief that this information was noted in the diary. The information about the submarine passage, where the fire was given, about the green patch and about 'a possibly sunk submarine' seems to have been blocked by a couple of senior officers, most likely the same officers who had already briefed Ljung on the incident.

Furthermore, the typed version of Ljung's diary for 11–12 October is not the same as the hand-written version. The typed version is 'corrected', extended and given a different meaning.[239] Contrary to what Ljung writes in his hand-written text, the typed version says that there was 'no sign of a damaged submarine', and that the indication from the mine barrage was just 'another indication'. The typed version also has a sentence discussing the problems with the mines: 'The mine explosions are mysterious.' The typed version says that the green patch was checked by the *Belos* the same evening, indicating that it was nothing of interest. Finally, the ceasefire was ordered on recommendation of the Chief of Staff, Vice-Admiral Bror Stefenson. Somebody seems to have influenced Ljung to 'correct' his diary to bring it more in line with the official version. All statements indicating a damaged, or even seriously damaged, submarine – particularly statements pointing to a Western submarine – were changed. The Naval Base East intelligence briefing for 11 October states:

> CÖrlBO [Rear-Admiral Christer Kierkegaard] briefing 11 October 1982. 1. Briefing about the Activity of Foreign Powers. 1.1. *Foreign Naval Vessels:* There are no known foreign naval vessels in the area except for possible submarines. 1.2. *Foreign State Vessels:* Danish fishery research vessel Dana is visiting Västervik until 11 October 1982. 1.3. *Warsaw Pact Merchant Ships:* At 12.30, SU [Soviet] merchant ship in DP3518 K=011, V=9 SU Volgobalt IE6 corr. position DM2740 k IE5. No other ships in the area. 1.4. *Conclusion:* Known indications point to normal activity for the time of the year. 1.5. *Foreign Submarine Activity:* Since 9 October, additional reports of foreign submarines. The analysis concludes that except for the one in the Hårsfjärden area, possible submarine(s) have been found in the Sandhamn area.[240]

This intelligence report is not very alarming. The sharp contrast between this report about low Soviet activity and the dramatic incidents with damaged submarines is striking. There is no Soviet mobilization of force, unlike what happened when a Soviet Whiskey submarine had been stranded outside Karlskrona one year earlier. What happened in Hårsfjärden and at Mälsten was much more dramatic, but the Soviet Navy had normal low activity for the time of the year. If anything, this is an indication that the damaged submarine did not originate from the Soviet Union.

Tuesday 12 October

During the night of 11–12 October, the bottom-fixed sonar system at Mälsten registered metallic sounds, apparently work on or in a damaged submarine, and this continued irregularly for more than 12 hours. Around 21.25 on 11 October, it was possible to hear work with a hammer. Later, there were knocking metallic sounds and high-

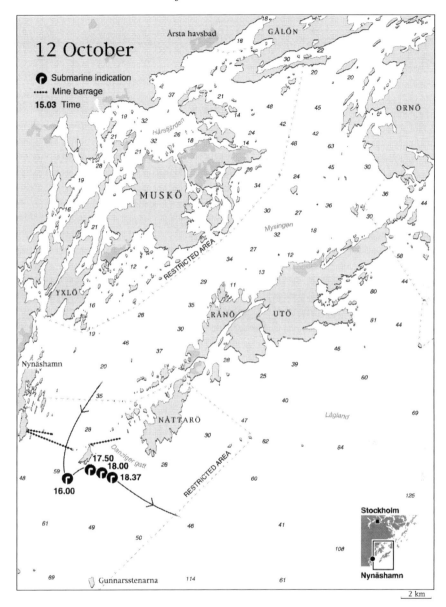

17. 12 October.

frequency sounds. In the morning, there were propeller sounds, and something was shuffling and scraping against the sea floor. The commanding officer at Mälsten, Lieutenant-Colonel Kviman, said in a TV interview: '[after the mine explosion on 11 October] we had

87

tape-recorded sounds that indicated repair works. We heard hammering several times from some kind of activity below the surface.'[241] The Mälsten war diary states:

> At 21.25 [on 11 October], hammering registered by the sonar system. At 21.45, two patrol boats were sent out to the area between MS [Mälsten] and YG [Yttre Gården]. [From 22.45, there were high-frequency sounds (12.5–20 kHz) that continued irregularly for a couple of hours][242] . . . At 01.30, the sonars register sounds similar to a boat with low activity and in a stationary position. At 01.47, the knocking sounds continue. Earlier reported high-frequency sounds (12.5–20 kHz) have now disappeared. The weather is better, which gives better possibility for listening. Low-frequency sounds (propeller?) . . . At 03.10, increase up to 20 kHz from the sonars. At 03.40, alarm from the sonar operators, 20 kHz up to 90 dB . . . At 05.00, Belos is leaving the area. At 06.25, [from the sonar operators: sub-surface] detonation, 90 dB. The lookout on the surface has not heard anything. Nor has the lookout at MS1. NTM [CÖrlBO] informed . . . At 08.21, from the sonars: a motor (weak propeller sounds). At 08.35, the sonar operators report: scraping sounds [against the sea floor], metallic sounds, knocking sounds. At 08.50, the same as 08.35, and going on continuously. At 09.05, [the sonar operators] report: continuous indications from 06.52 to 09.05. After that, silent . . . At 10.07, the ceasefire for [the mine barrages] MS1, MS2 and MS3 is over in daylight and clear visibility [order from the Commander-in-Chief] . . . At 13.38, from the sonar operators: propeller sounds (?) at low activity. Running time about two minutes. After that metallic sounds.[243]

The naval base war diary confirms several of these pieces of information:

> At 21.35, report from Mälsten: at 21.25, metallic hammering registered by the sonar system. Tape-recorded. At 21.45, report to MBÖ [Commander of the Eastern Military District]. Also to ÖB [Commander-in-Chief], CM [Chief of the Navy], CFK [Chief of the Coastal Fleet]. At 21.50, [the helicopter] Y68 sent to Mälsten. Free submarine hunt south-southeast of Mälsten [should be south-southwest of Mälsten (see CMS HWD)]. At 22.17, Y68 arrived. At 22.20, [Y68] returns because of technical problems. New helicopter [Y70] starts at Berga . . . At 01.45, [from Mälsten]: continuous knocking and scraping sounds with variations in amplitude . . . At 03.10, Y70 starts free submarine hunt south of Mälsten . . . At 05.15 Y70 returns to base . . . At 06.16, Belos reports position: northern entrance [Alvsta-Långholmar at the narrow passage Hårsfjärden-Mysingen]. At 06.25, some kind of

sub-surface detonation is registered by the sonar system at Mälsten 90 dB. At 06.40, Belos in Hårsfjärden. Back to the place for earlier activity . . . At 09.35, helicopter is ordered to locate the knocking sounds at Mälsten. At 09.40, the sonar system still registers scraping sounds . . . At 13.45, [Mälsten] reports propeller sounds. At 13.56, helicopter on test flight. Ordered to go to the area of Måsknuv.[244]

All these knockings sounds, scraping sounds, high-frequency sounds and metallic hammering were originally taped and analysed by the sonar operator Rolf Andersson from FMV and by Anders Karlsson from the Swedish submarine *Sjöhästen*. Andersson had set up and calibrated the microphones during September and early October. He visited Mälsten every week (see 8 October). He knew the background sounds and sound environment at Mälsten very well. What he heard in the night of 11–12 October was exceptional. He confirms the above statements in the war diaries. In his report from the same night, it is stated:

> At 21.25, hammering for one minute with 5–6 blows . . . At 22.45, high-frequency sounds 12.5–20 kHz. Two sharp [metallic-sounding] blows. A couple of high-frequency spikes 16–20 kHz. [After this] 12.5–20 kHz [periodically until 01.44]. 23.14, light rain. At 23.53, 12.5 Hz tone from helicopter. [Just around midnight] 12.5–20 kHz. [Just after midnight] Thuds and low-frequency tone. Helicopter at a distance of 3 kilometres. Ferry going out from Nynäshamn. 00.30, Ferry [passing]. 01.04, sharp [metallic] knocking sounds. 01.25, thuds. 01.33, thuds. 01.44, high-frequency 12.5–20 kHz [After 02.00, Andersson was replaced for the night].[245]

The high-frequency sounds for shorter periods in the area between 12.5 and 20 kHz were exceptional. Rolf Andersson had never experienced this, either before or after this incident. A sound expert from Norwegian Military Intelligence said that this frequency (12.5–20 kHz) might indicate work with a high-speed cutting tool, as if the submarine diver had cut loose steel plates (from a damaged outer hull, see below) that disrupted the movement of the submarine. The frequency 12.5–20 kHz might indicate an angle grinder, another specialist told me. Between 21.25 and 01.30, there were a lot of metallic knocking sounds and somebody might have been working with a cutting tool on and off in the waters of Mälsten. Between 03.10 and 03.40, this work continued. According to the Mälsten war diary, the sound was by the end of this period up to 90 dB.[246] There is no natural explanation for these sounds, and they must have originated from a source rather close to the microphones. All of these hammering, metallic and knocking sounds, thuds, high-frequency sounds and sub-surface explosions indicate a seriously damaged submarine repaired during the night after the mine explosion on 11 October.

During the night, Kviman went out to the *Belos*, where he gave a secret briefing for the captain, Lieutenant-Commander Björn Mohlin, about the hammering and other works on a damaged submarine. Chief of the Coastal Defence Regiment KA1, later Lieutenant-General Lars-G. Persson, also confirms these knockings sounds and hammering. This information is confirmed by Chief of Stockholm Coastal Defence, Brigadier-General Lars Hansson, and by his Chief of Staff, Lieutenant-Colonel Jan Svenhager. At 22.05 on 11 October, the Stockholm Coastal Defence Staff Report writes: 'Command Kviman reports about 5–6 hits with a hammer from the sonar system at Mälsten.'[247] The war diaries also speak about continued activity in the morning: metallic and knocking sounds, a propeller sound, a sub-surface explosion, and shuffling and scraping (against the sea floor). Shuffling and scraping, along with knocking sounds, had been registered at Mälsten the whole morning. At 09.35, the naval base sent a helicopter to locate these sounds.[248] However, according to the Mälsten war diary, these sounds had stopped exactly half an hour earlier.

In the Z interview, Lars Hansson said that, after the hit on the submarine, they had heard 'clear metallic knocking sounds as if somebody was repairing something in the water'. But when he told General Ljung and Vice-Admiral Stefenson about this, they were not interested in the information. 'It could be anything,' they said.[249] The local commander Lieutenant-Colonel Kviman, the submarine sound expert Karlsson and the sonar operator Andersson reported to Brigadier-General Hansson and Lieutenant-Colonel Svenhager at the Coastal Defence Staff in Vaxholm, who reported to the Commander of the Eastern Military District, Lieutenant-General Bengt Lehander in Strängnäs, who reported to the Commander-in-Chief General Lennart Ljung (usually via the Chief of Staff Vice-Admiral Bror Stefenson). When Lars Hansson had been to Muskö and Mälsten and briefed by Kviman, he went back to Vaxholm via the Defence Staff in Stockholm and spoke directly with the Chief of Staff and the Commander-in-Chief (without detailed information being given to Lieutenant-General Bengt Lehander at the Eastern Military District). Stefenson, however, was not interested in this information. It was not included in the Submarine Defence Commission Report. What the submarine sound expert had reported – his detailed analysis about work on a damaged submarine during the night and in the morning – was met with Stefenson's: 'It could be anything.'

On 12 October, General Ljung seems to have been informed about the work on a damaged or 'possibly sunk submarine' directly through Hansson, but Stefenson would be the one who kept Ljung continuously informed. Ljung's hand-written diary for 12 October states: 'In the afternoon, no new information on a possibly sunk submarine.'[250] In other words, he was informed that indications existed perhaps even up to lunch, but not in the afternoon. Indirectly, he confirms the information from the sources at Mälsten as well as the fact that he was informed by Hansson at this very time. At 09.00 General Ljung briefed Defence Minister Börje Andersson.[251] Toivo Heinsoo, Andersson's political adviser and close associate, says now that a possibly damaged or sunk submarine was in their focus for a couple of days. The hammering during the night was an important indication. He also remembered the green patch. He said that they considered the situation to be serious and discussed how to act in relation to the foreign power and the media if the damaged submarine were found, but that they never got the indications confirmed. It seems that both the Minister of Defence and the Commander-in-Chief believed in a possibly damaged or even sunk submarine. On the same day, General Ljung made a public statement: 'Anyone who violates Swedish neutrality and Swedish territory is taking a great risk. The only way for us to demonstrate this is to use force. I am sorry.'[252]

I do not know to whom this apology was made. When Prime Minister Olof Palme briefed the Conservative Party leader Ulf Adelsohn a couple of days after this incident, Palme talked about a 'seriously damaged submarine' (in Swedish, 'havererad'; see below).[253] Swedish Navy spokesman Commander Sven Carlsson said: 'The mine that exploded yesterday may have sunk a submarine.'[254] He also said: 'We are looking for something we fear is a seriously damaged submarine lying helpless on the sea floor.'[255] There is no doubt that some people in the military leadership believed in a damaged – or possibly even sunk – submarine and that the green patch was linked to this incident.

The *Belos* had arrived at 20.50 the day before and had been at Mälsten all night. They investigated the mine barrages and the place of the mine detonations. The *Belos* tried to use the remote-controlled video camera Sjöugglan, but was not able to locate the submarine. 'We never found the submarine' and 'we never used the divers', the captain of the *Belos*, Lieutenant-Commander Björn Mohlin, said. It was impossible to anchor because of the risk of mine explosions, and the stream made it difficult to carry out the operation. '*Belos* was given one square at the time, and the submarine could easily have hidden somewhere else', he said. Captain Rodrik Klintebo, Chief of the First Submarine Flotilla, which was responsible for the *Belos*, says that he gave the *Belos* an area to investigate with a radius of 300 metres around the place of the mine explosion. Most of the time was used to check the area around the detonated mines. The *Belos* also checked the mines that had exploded on 7 October in the area close to Yttre

Gården. This was done for a few hours during the night. At 05.00, the *Belos* was removed from Mälsten to search for an unexploded depth charge in Hårsfjärden. At 06.15, the *Belos* informed the naval base that she had arrived at the northern entrance of Hårsfjärden. At 14.45, the naval base war diary states that the *Belos* had been searching for a dud – an unexploded depth charge – since dawn.[256]

Lieutenant-Colonel Kviman told me that the *Belos* reported several steel plates on the sea floor, close to the place of the mine explosion. In his technical report of 12 October, Kviman wrote:

> Belos investigated the area during the night. About 100 metres from the mine barrage (outside [south of]) the place where the mine was detonated, Belos found something that was classified as metal objects about a metre in size ... *Belos's Sea Floor Investigation at Måsknuv*: After detonation of mines at MS2 (Måsknuv) and MS3 (Yttre Gården [on 7 October]), Belos made an [active] sonar investigation according to [enclosed] drawing. Within an area 150 metres south of Måsknuv, Belos found probable metal objects of various sizes (with a diametre of 1–1.5 metres). Belos tried to use Sjöugglan to identify the objects. However, it was not possible to anchor [because of the mine barrage, the stream and bad weather]. Because of this, Belos did not succeed in getting Sjöugglan down to investigate the sea floor. A new investigation with Sjöugglan should be done as soon as possible, when weather conditions have become better or, later, when the incident is over.[257]

This report was received at 16.45 by the naval base[258] and by Stockholm Coastal Defence Staff, who sent it to MBÖ [Commander of the Eastern Military District].[259] The drawing showed these 1- to 1.5-metre metal objects about 100 metres south-southwest of Måsknuv, 150 metres southeast of the place of the mine explosion, which is identical to the place where the yellow/green patch appeared according to our calculations made below.

The captain of the *Belos*, Lieutenant-Commander Mohlin, confirms that they found some kind of steel plates outside Måsknuv, but they were not able to identify what these were. General Lennart Ljung wrote in his hand-written diary: 'Belos in Danziger Gatt [actually on the western side of Mälsten, but the whole area around Mälsten is often called Danziger Gatt]. The divers: possible steel plates on the sea floor. Later found to be oil drums.'[260] Ljung's typed diary states: 'Belos now in Danziger Gatt. Possible steel plates on the sea floor. Later found to be most likely without interest.'[261]

General Ljung seemed first to confirm that steel plates or possible steel plates had been found, but later the same day (12 October) he seemed to have received information suggesting oil drums, or at least something of no interest. This is, however, very different from the report given by the *Belos* and Mälsten. This report states that metal objects of different sizes (a diameter of 1–1.5 metres) were found in an area 100–150 metres south of Måsknuv. However, the bad weather made it difficult to use the remote-controlled video camera Sjöugglan, which made it impossible to investigate what kind of metal objects these were. In other words, General Ljung received a second and totally unfounded report about oil drums that contradicted his first report, but no investigation had been done in the meantime. A senior officer close to Ljung might falsely have informed him that these metal objects were not steel plates but oil drums.

Lieutenant-Commander Hans Kalla, former submarine officer, attack diver and later captain of the *Belos* (1985–87), told me that one of the first things that might happen in the event of a mine explosion is that some steel plates of the submarine would blow off. This even happened to him once during some rough weather conditions. A mine might easily blow parts of the outer hull off, he said. However, without checking out if the possible steel plates belonged to a submarine, the *Belos* was removed from the area. No investigation was carried out until several days later when *Belos* was able to use Sjöugglan to take pictures of such a rectangular plate on the bottom. One officer I spoke with confirms that he had looked at the prints of the pictures taken by Sjöugglan. He did not know what kind of steel plates they were, and it is not clear to me what happened to them afterwards.

The *Belos* was not sent to Mälsten until seven hours after the incident; and even though the *Belos* believed that it had found steel plates at the very same place as the yellow/green patch appeared, possibly indicating a damaged submarine, and even though the sonar system still registered work on the damaged submarine, the *Belos* was, after a few hours' search in darkness, removed from Mälsten for a routine operation to clear up after the submarine hunt in Hårsfjärden, something that could easily have been done the following day. Existing technical evidence should have made it possible to locate the submarine perhaps southwest of Mälsten – actually, in the area where the search for the submarine took place after the hammering late in the evening on 11 October. The *Belos* was not investigating this area.

General Ljung's version is even more confusing: 'At 12.30, *two mines* were detonated in Danziger Gatt after indications.' In the hand-written text, the words 'two mines' were underlined.[262] The same information was given to *Dagens Nyheter* and was printed in the newspaper the following day.[263] It seems that, unlike on the previous day, *two mines* were detonated after submarine indications. In the afternoon, the *Belos* was, according to Ljung, still investigating the sea floor at Mälsten.[264] General Ljung as well as *Dagens Nyheter* seem to have been misinformed, perhaps by a senior officer on the staff, because every local officer knew that no mines had been detonated. Furthermore, Ljung was never told that the *Belos* had already stopped investigating the Mälsten area before dawn and had instead been transferred to Hårsfjärden for a routine task to search for a dud.

Dagens Nyheter reported that they had tape-recorded a radio conversation between the naval base and a helicopter. An emergency buoy had been found north of Mälsten.[265] The *Dagens Nyheter* journalist responsible for this article told me that most of the military communication and orders were given on open frequencies. The *Dagens Nyheter* journalists were sitting in a house close to Hårsfjärden, and they recorded everything of interest, including the communication after lunch between the naval base and a helicopter about a radio buoy found not far from Mälsten in southern Mysingen. The naval base described details of a yellow radio buoy to the helicopter referring to information from the Coast Guard. The helicopter was ordered to take a photo of this buoy. It was believed to have broken loose from the submarine. I have not found any clear confirmation of this incident. However, according to the naval base war diary, *GYP*, the Coast Guard reconnaissance aircraft, had patrolled the Mälsten area before lunch, and at lunch a helicopter was sent for a 'test flight' in the area.[266] Neither Coast Guard nor the Defence Staff was able or willing to deny *Dagens Nyheter*'s story. The Coast Guard denied that they had had a ship in the area, but they had an aircraft and that fits with *Dagens Nyheter*'s story.[267]

The war diaries state that the afternoon was relatively silent, with very few sounds registered by the sonars. At 13.38, the sonar operator reported two minutes of propeller sounds. A helicopter was sent to the area.[268] However, there was seemingly very little activity. For several hours, the Mälsten war diary does not report any sounds from the sonars. At 16.00, there is a report about air boil-ups and oil on the surface at Västergrund, south-southwest of Mälsten.[269] After that, the Mälsten war diary reports:

> At 16.30, twittering (squeaking) sounds with intervals of seconds. The sonar operator on his way. [According to the submarine sound expert, these may have been sounds from a propeller at low speed, working at intervals for short periods of time – as if the submarine was trying to move from its hiding place as silently as possible.] At 17.10, the sound is still there and has become stronger, 2,000–6,000 Hz [still in intervals]. At 17.48, less than 1,000 Hz. At 17.56, BevB 77 is sent out to search [for the submarine]. Naval Base East is briefed. At 18.00, helicopter on its way [from Berga] . . . At 18.30–18.55, helicopter arrives.

Cooperation with HB 7 [T.R. Nilsson, captain of Bevb 77]. According to the tape-recorded sounds, the object is most likely a submarine that has gone out from VM [Mälsten].[270]

The protocol for the speaker channel (of the tape recording) states: 'at 17.50, it is strong . . . [Clear] over the whole register. Conclusion: probable submarine.'[271] The tape recording at about 18.00 was described later, by the Naval Analysis Group Report of late October, the Grandin Report of December, and in the note to Moscow, 10 October 1983, as evidence for a 'certain submarine'.[272] The submarine was seemingly moving towards the microphones and then passed the microphones out from Mälsten. This information in the Mälsten war diary is confirmed by the war diary of Naval Base East:

> At 16.45, Mälsten reports a new sound from the sonars since 16.30: twittering and squeaking, not metallic, sounds with a few seconds' interval . . . At 17.13, Mälsten reports that the twittering sound has continued intermittently for 30 minutes . . . It has become stronger. At 17.45, telegram from CSK [Chief of Stockholm Coastal Defence, Brigadier-General Lars Hansson]: submarine incident. At 17.52, from Mälsten: according to [sonar operator Anders] Karlsson from [submarine] Sjöhästen: possible submarine. One helicopter is sent to the area. Another helicopter is made ready to replace it in one hour . . . At 18.00, from Mälsten: [certain] submarine with a speed of 1–2 knots, closest to microphone no. 5. . . . At 18.20, a patrol vessel at Torskholmen [should be Torskboden southeast of Mälsten, close to microphone no. 1] prepares to drop depth charges [on the submarine] . . . 18.28, the [helicopter] Y69 is in contact with Mälsten. At 18.30, SC [Naval Base Chief of Staff, Commander Lars-Erik Hoff] briefs CÖrlBO [Chief of the Naval Base, Rear-Admiral Christer Kierkegaard]. At 18.37, to Y69, interesting area DP0451 R1 [beyond microphone no. 5]. At 18.45, briefing for the MBÖ [Commander of the Eastern Military District, Lieutenant-General Bengt Lehander] . . . At 19.53, the helicopter Y69 is replaced by Y70. [No more contacts are registered by the war diary.][273]

At 18.00 on 12 October, there was clear evidence of a submarine, and a recording of propeller sounds was made. According to the Mälsten war diary, this submarine sound was followed at least up to 18.30, perhaps up to 18.55, at which point the submarine went out from Mälsten. All this information was immediately reported both to Naval Base East at Muskö, to the Commander of the Eastern Military District and to the Chief of the Stockholm Coastal Defence, who all reported it to the Defence Staff in Stockholm. The Chief of Staff, Vice-Admiral Bror Stefenson, was often informed before the Eastern

Military District. He was most likely informed no later than 19.00 (but probably already around 18.30). At 21.00, Vice-Admiral Stefenson visited General Ljung's home to inform him about the incident.[274] In other words, three hours after clear evidence of a submarine had been registered, and more than two hours after the submarine had disappeared, Stefenson informed Ljung at his home. After that, both of them returned to the Defence Staff. Minutes later, the ceasefire for the mine barrage in Danziger Gatt came to an end. There was no longer a ceasefire in darkness. During the night, two hours after the submarine had left Swedish waters, the ceasefire was ended. According to the Submarine Defence Commission Report, this was because of 'clear indications of a submarine'.[275] It seems that General Ljung had given a green light for the use of mines for something that happened several hours earlier.

In the report from Stockholm Coastal Defence Staff, the following entry is recorded:

> At 20.00, CKA1 [Colonel Lars-G. Persson] reports to MBÖ [Commander, Eastern Military District]: possible submarine is moving close to the mine barrages. The local commander has as good control of the surface during the night as during the day. Proposes right to use fire. At 21.17, from MBÖ: CSK [Chief of Stockholm Coastal Defence] has the right to use fire for MS1 when demanded by Chief of Naval Base.[276]

The report from Colonel Persson was received by the Eastern Military District at least one hour after the incident had taken place, and the decision by the Commander of the Eastern Military District seems to have been slow. In other words, this process seems to have been parallel to Stefenson's briefing of General Ljung. When Ljung and Stefenson arrived at the Defence Staff, they may both just have been informed that the Commander of the Eastern Military District, Lieutenant-General Bengt Lehander, had taken this decision. On the other hand, neither Stefenson nor Ljung found reason to overrule it. The submarine was out and the ceasefire was over. It is interesting, however, that it was the Commander of the Eastern Military District, as on 7 October, who proposed and now decided about the right to use fire for the mine barrages, while it was always Vice-Admiral Stefenson who proposed – or in some cases even decided about – the ceasefires.

According to Lieutenant-Colonel Kviman, no new ceasefire in darkness was declared until the next night. The submarine seemed to have left the area and, soon afterwards, the ceasefire was over, almost as if there had been a causal relationship. The Mälsten war diary states:

At 21.28, end of ceasefire for [the mine barrage] MS1, when demanded by CÖrlBO [Chief of Naval Base East]. At 22.35, report from [Naval Base East], end of ceasefire for NM (MS1). [There is no limitation on this right to use force and no report about a new ceasefire during the night.][277]

The naval base war diary states: 'At 21.35 a telegram from MBÖ [Commander of the Eastern Military District] about end of ceasefire . . . At 22.31, end of ceasefire for MS1 in agreement [with Mälsten].'[278] In other words, there were clear indications of a submarine for 36 hours. There was evidence of (repair) works for several hours, and this was most probably on a damaged submarine. There was even clear evidence of a submarine at the end of this period. Two hours after all this was over, the ceasefire in darkness was terminated. According to the Submarine Defence Commission Report, 'one exception to the rule [about a ceasefire in darkness] was made around 21.00 on 12 October . . . because of clear indications of a submarine'.[279] This is false information.

General Lennart Ljung wrote about Stefenson's visit and the recorded submarine sound at Mälsten:

> At 21.00, CFst [the Chief of Staff, Bror Stefenson] turned up at my home after having visited CM [Chief of the Navy, Vice-Admiral Per Rudberg]. FOA's sonar system at Mälsten has received a positively certain contact with a submarine at a distance of 1,000 metres outside the minefield. We both went to MSB [the Defence Staff].[280]

Per Rudberg confirms that Bror Stefenson visited his place before he went up to General Ljung. Rudberg and Ljung were neighbours at Skeppsholmen in central Stockholm, and Stefenson went to Rudberg to discuss the issue and to 'be given a boost' [in Swedish, 'råg i ryggen'] before visiting General Ljung, Rudberg said. The passage, according to Lennart Ljung, was about 1,000 metres south of the mine barrage, which is a relatively good estimate. This would mean close to, and not more than, 100–200 metres from the microphones. Still, there is something mysterious in Ljung's comment. A large number of radar and sonar contacts were made during the submarine hunt in Hårsfjärden. A sonar contact, or even a recording of the motor sound of a submarine, may not explain why the Chief of Staff, late in the evening and in person, first went to the Chief of the Navy, then to the home of the Commander-in-Chief and, later at night and together with the Commander-in-Chief, to the Defence Staff. This is even more remarkable when we know that the sonar system had registered work on a damaged submarine the whole night before and during the morning of the same day – work that had been going on for more than 24 hours. The sonar contact on 12 October may have included some

very sensitive information that could not be mentioned over the telephone and could not wait until the next day. And why did Stefenson
need 'a boost' before presenting the case to the Commander-in-Chief?
Why was it important to discuss this issue and have a common understanding with Vice-Admiral Rudberg before bringing it up with
General Ljung?

If the submarine was from the West, Stefenson's behaviour is more
easy to explain. A Norwegian senior intelligence officer said to me that
soon after this incident two representatives from FOA came to
Norwegian Military Intelligence underwater division and analysed the
tape: 'It was not a Soviet submarine', he said. 'We believed it was a
Western submarine.' Later, this officer said: 'This was not a known
Soviet submarine. It was neither a conventional nor a nuclear Soviet
submarine. We did not have information on the midgets.' On the other
hand, according to several sources (see below), this was not a midget
submarine. The Norwegians in fact believed that it was a Western submarine. However, nothing of the Norwegian information turned up
in the Submarine Defence Commission Report. The second
Submarine Commission Report of 1995 contains a long discussion
about the incident, but no information regarding a Norwegian analysis. This report only discusses the Swedish Navy analysis and the FOA
analysis (see below).[281] Today, Vice-Admiral Rudberg denies that the
Norwegians analysed the tapes or that the Navy had any contact with
the Norwegians concerning the sonars.

Wednesday and Thursday 13–14 October
At the daily press conference at 18.00 at the Berga Press Centre, the
Commander-in-Chief, General Ljung, and the Chief of the Navy, Vice-
Admiral Rudberg, appeared together with the Navy press spokesman
Sven Carlsson and the Chief of the Naval Analysis Group,
Commander Emil Svensson. Svensson showed a tape with a 'ping'
from an active sonar believed to originate from a submarine. General
Ljung said that 'the likelihood of a submarine's still being in
Hårsfjärden is very small, but they are still searching in the outer archipelago and we will not rule out the possibility that there are several
submarines'.[282] The Chief of the Navy, Per Rudberg, appointed Rear-
Admiral Gunnar Grandin to make an analysis of the submarine
hunt.[283] The Conservative Party leader Ulf Adelsohn called the Chief
of Staff and said: 'Now, we have let the submarine run . . . You have
been too lenient.'[284] According to the naval base war diary, there was
still some sub-surface activity close to Muskö Naval Base. At 21.03 a
reconnaissance boat observed a clear radar echo at the docks and, half
an hour later, there was mud on the water.[285]

At Mälsten, the night became dramatic, but there were also some indications in the early morning and during the day of 13 October. The Mälsten war diary states:

> At 02.40, the sonar system registers propeller sound with high turns per minute . . . At 07.05 Nst [according to hand-written original 'Nssr' (Radar)[286]] reports similar disturbances to earlier [cf. 19.00 on 7 October]. Distance up to 7,000 [1,000] metres . . . [At 11.00, indication in echo ranger west Klövskär in Danziger Gatt, up to 500 metres north of the mine barrage.[287]] At 14.05, the weather is getting worse. Visibility less than half the entrance at CM and RM [MS2 and MS3 between Mälsten and Yttre Gården]. Ceasefire for CM and RM when the weather gets worse. At 15.00, ceasefire limited because of weather conditions. However, all mine barrages have the right to use force for the three groups close to land . . . At 17.40, ceasefire for CM and RM. At 19.00, [better weather, but despite darkness end of ceasefire] right to use force for MS3 [certain mine groups], MS2 [certain groups] and MS1 [certain groups]. At 19.30, HB7 [T.R. Nilsson, *Bevb* 77] left for visual reconnaissance at MS1, MS2 and MS3. [He started with MS1. Conclusion: clear vision.] At 20.05, ceasefire from ÖB [the Commander-in-Chief] in darkness and poor visibility for MS1, MS2 and MS3.[288]

At dusk, the order for Mälsten from the previous night (at 22.35) of using the mines in darkness for MS1 was still in force. From 19.00 there was, according to Mälsten, no ceasefire in darkness. Despite darkness but because of better (but still relatively bad) weather conditions, a partial ceasefire for all mine barrages was introduced at 19.00. Mälsten and Stockholm Coastal Defence had since the previous Saturday requested the right to use force in darkness because the night-vision scopes meant there was no difference between day and night. At 19.30, *Bevb* 77 went out to tow a small rowing-boat to the other side of the narrow passage of Danziger Gatt. The visibility in the area was clear. Mälsten had full control of the surface, and the Commander at Mälsten, Sven-Olof Kviman, intended to give the right to use all the mines of MS1. After that, he was going to check the visibility for MS2 and MS3. However, a new order from ÖB (or rather from the Defence Staff) about a ceasefire was received at 20.05.

At dusk at 17.00 Chief of Stockholm Coastal Defence Lars Hansson requested the right to use force in darkness for MS1 and MS2. The Stockholm Coastal Defence Staff report states:

> At 17.00, CSK [Chief of Stockholm Coastal Defence] requests right to use fire for MS1 and MS2. At 17.49: from MBÖ [Commander of Eastern Military District]: right to use force for MS1 and MS2 according to

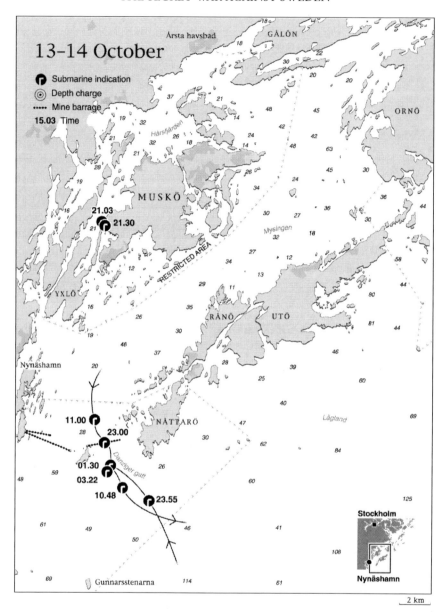

18. 13–14 October.

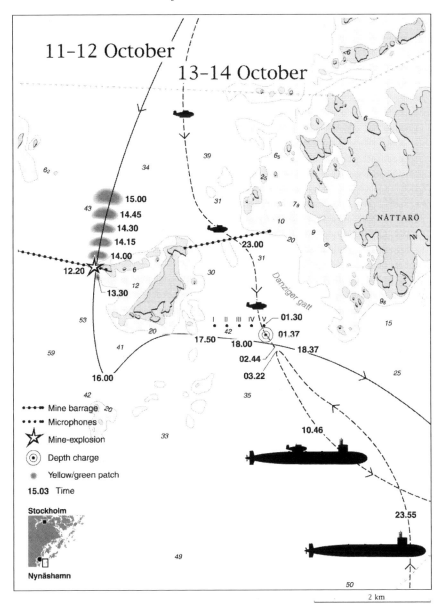

19. 11–14 October.

101

MBÖ order 11.07, 12 October [ceasefire in darkness (this order was never transmitted to Mälsten)]. At 18.22, ÖB [Commander-in-Chief] to [or via] MBÖ . . . right to use fire in daylight and clear visibility for MS1, MS2 and MS3 [ceasefire in darkness]. Otherwise, reconnaissance. Commander Stockholm Coastal Defence asks for clarification. From MBÖ: [order changed to] at clear visibility, right to use fire for MS1, MS2 and MS3 [no ceasefire in darkness]. At 20.15, MBÖ reports new clarification: right to use fire in daylight and clear visibility.[289]

The order from the acting Commander-in-Chief (Vice-Admiral Stefenson) about the right to use force in 'daylight and clear visibility' was, at 18.22, immediately changed by MBÖ to 'clear visibility'. All the mine barrages at Mälsten had the right to use force to stop the submarine even during the night, which was recognized by Mälsten with the order of 19.00. Mälsten received no order about a ceasefire in darkness until 20.05. We may dispute if MBÖ had the right to change the order from the Chief of Staff. MBÖ was the operative command responsible for giving orders about the right to use fire, but this was debated afterwards. At 20.05 (Stockholm Coastal Defence Staff received the order at 20.15), Defence Staff sent the same ceasefire order as at 18.22 directly to Mälsten, and just informed MBÖ and CSK afterwards, probably because of the above-mentioned 'obstructions' from MBÖ and CSK. Despite the fact that the command at Mälsten said that they had full control of the surface even during the night, and despite the fact that Mälsten's control of the surface had been recognized on the previous night and was recognized by MBÖ and CSK, an order for a ceasefire was given.[290]

According to the commander at Mälsten, Sven-Olof Kviman, he received the same ceasefire order from four different points in the chain of command: directly from the Chief of Staff, Vice-Admiral Stefenson, at the Defence Staff in Stockholm; from MBÖ; from Naval Command East at Muskö; and from CSK, Brigadier-General Lars Hansson. Hansson confirms his order and says that he considered refraining from following the order. He believed that Stefenson might be cooperating with the Soviets to release the submarine. According to an interview with Hansson, he told Kviman: 'if you receive indications of a submarine approaching the mine barrage, call me and we will decide what to do'.[291] This lack of trust and MBÖ's change of the Commander-in-Chief order at 18.22 were most likely the reasons for the Chief of Staff's direct orders to the local commander at Mälsten. The same 18.22 order was actually sent directly to Mälsten at 20.05. Lieutenant-Colonel Kviman immediately called Chief of Staff Bror Stefenson. Mälsten had just had a small testing boat in the channel to check visibility. They had total control of the surface. According to

Göran Wallén's quote from Stefenson's diary, Kviman had also said that they had indications in the sonars, and all this influenced Stefenson who decided to terminate the ceasefire later the same night.[292]

The order at 18.22 was given more than one hour (and the order at 20.05 was given almost three hours) after the Commander-in-Chief had left for Berga Press Centre and while he still was at Berga (he travelled back to Stockholm at 22.00).[293] Nothing is mentioned about this order in General Ljung's diary, even though Ljung paid attention to and was involved in all other ceasefires for the mine barrages.[294] This order was not given by General Ljung but by the commander in charge on this evening, Chief of Staff Vice-Admiral Stefenson, and he gave this order seemingly without consulting the Commander-in-Chief himself. Furthermore, it was given without any preparation. According to sources at the Defence Staff, this was the only order during the Hårsfjärden hunt that was given as a command without being prepared at OPG (Defence Staff Operations). Vice-Admiral Stefenson just gave the order as a straight command. Other ceasefires for the mines were ordered by the Commander-in-Chief on the recommendation of the Chief of Staff. In this case, the Chief of Staff gave the order himself.

Minutes after eight o'clock, the local commander Sven-Olof Kviman called Vice-Admiral Stefenson, who used a 25-minute telephone conversation to convince Mälsten that a new ceasefire had to be accepted. After that, Stefenson's subordinate and Kviman's friend from Coastal Defence, Lieutenant-Colonel Håkan Söderlindh, called Kviman to convince him to follow orders. According to other officers at the Defence Staff, Stefenson had said that Kviman might blow up a fishing boat. Stefenson had given the impression that Kviman did not have full control of the surface. This was not the view of MBÖ and CSK. By giving orders, by personally trying to convince Kviman and by using his friends, Stefenson tried to secure a guarantee that the mines would not be used. The ceasefire was not terminated until five hours later. It seems as if Vice-Admiral Stefenson wanted to be directly in charge of what happened at Mälsten during these hours.

During the evening, Lieutenant-Colonel Kviman called Naval Base East at Muskö several times to get approval for using the mines, but it was not possible to have the ceasefire lifted. Instead, Kviman ordered two patrol boats and one transport boat with 16 depth charges to take position south of Mälsten and south of Danziger Gatt to wait for the approaching submarine. He also prepared for a helicopter to lead the attack. If Mälsten was not allowed to use mines, they still had the right to use depth charges. Without reporting to higher commands, Kviman intended to lay a 'carpet' of depth charges over the submarine. Nothing of this was put down in the Mälsten war diary, and Naval Base East was never directly informed.[295]

However, the log-book and the war diary for *Bevb* 77 states: 'At 22.55, has reached position 1 nautical mile south of Mälsten to be prepared to drop depth charges on order from helicopter.'[296] Five minutes later, the submarine passed the mine barrage. The Mälsten war diary states: 'At 23.00, from NH [Lieutenant Bengt Olsson]: the mine barrage [MS1 Danziger Gatt (east of Mälsten)] indicates. Report to NTM [CÖrlBO]. The sonar system indicates. Helicopter arrives.'[297] The naval base war diary has the following: 'At 23.00, VM [Lieutenant-Colonel Kviman] reports: indications in the mine barrage. Nothing on the surface. Increasing noise in the sonars. At 23.02, Y69 ordered to go to the contact.'[298] On the speaker channel on the tape, Anders Karlsson states:

> at 23.02, starting recording because of indication in the mine barrage north of the sonar system. Increased noise (10 dB) for two minutes, particularly for lower frequencies. Not possible to classify. [A minute and a half later:] rather strong dB increase on 16 Hz [low-frequency, possibly propeller].[299]

Lieutenant-Colonel Kviman's technical report from the following day states: 'It was the sixth mine group that indicated. The submarine passed just east of the main sailing route [and just east of the shallow area in the middle of Danziger Gatt; see figure].'[300] Kviman himself told me:

> At 23.00, the mine barrages indicated a submarine. The magnetic field was constant over the mines. It turned on five mine lamps in the control room. The sensor signals were turned off twice. There was no reason to turn them off more than that. Despite the fact that it was obvious that a submarine had passed over the mine barrages, they were denied the use of the mines.[301]

The Grandin Report states that, on 20 October, a test was made with a Swedish submarine passing at an angle of 45 degrees over the same mine barrage. The results were exactly the same as those during the passage at 23.00 on 13 October. The Grandin Report concludes: 'This indication [on 13 October] must accordingly be understood as a very likely passage of a sub-surface vessel over or in the immediate vicinity of the mine barrage.'[302]

When Deputy Chief of MS1, Lieutenant Bengt Olsson, called Lieutenant-Colonel Kviman to report the passage, he heard submarine sound expert Anders Karlsson report about the propeller sound: '120 turns per minute'. Karlsson described to me how the submarine was moving forward in intervals of 10–15 seconds and then stopping in order to avoid detection. The whole sequence was tape-recorded. A propeller blade or propeller axis was damaged, and this was clearly registered on the tape.

Immediately after the submarine had passed the mine barrage, the naval base ordered a helicopter to go to the contact. Lieutenant-Colonel Kviman ordered the helicopter to lead the three small patrol boats to carry out a massive drop of depth charges. Once again, Kviman asked for the right to use fire for the mine barrages. At 00.10, Stockholm Coastal Defence requested the right to use fire for the mines.[303] On the speaker channel of the tape, Anders Karlsson stated:

> I continue the tape-recording. Y69 is in contact with a submarine . . . We had a couple of cavitation sounds. Conclusion: submarine increasing speed. [Half a minute later:] cavitation sounds. [Two minutes later, about 00.15] Helicopter prepares for a drop. [Four minutes later:] Submarine, increasing amplitude. [Four minutes later:] I cannot hear the submarine. [Six minutes later:] the submarine has started again. It is moving forward slowly. [Six minutes later:] It seems that the submarine is going with five-six-seven-eight turns with the propeller and then stops. He is possibly going very close to the sea floor.[304]

The helicopter made contact with the submarine, and the patrol boats prepared the drop. However, the helicopter pilot pushed the wrong button (for the lift and not for fire), and no depth charges were dropped. After that, the helicopter lost contact. The Mälsten war diary states that this incident took place at 00.15 and goes on to say:

> At 00.30, the sonar operator reports: still contact . . . At 00.35, from the sonar operator: contact . . . the sonar operator concludes that the propeller axis of the object is damaged. At 01.06, the helicopter receives contact south Mälsten, and [Mälsten] receives the right to use fire for the mines. NM [MS1] is informed.[305]

In other words, despite darkness, five hours after the ceasefire was declared and two hours after the submarine had passed the mine barrages, the ceasefire was over. The Stockholm Coastal Defence Staff report states:

> At 01.00, MBÖ [Commander of the Eastern Military District] announces: right to use fire for MS1 after consultations with CÖrlBO [Chief of Naval Base East]. At the same time, Command Persson [see 10 October] is calling about another order, now from the Defence Staff, about right to use fire for the mines.[306]

105

The naval base war diary confirms this submarine passage at 23.00, the immediate action, the following submarine hunt and the end of the ceasefire at 01.00, and states:

> At 23.00 indications in the mine barrage. Nothing on the surface. Increasing noise in the sonars ['At 12.33 (on 14 October), Mälsten confirms five indicating mines. The signal appeared again after having been turned off'.[307]] At 23.02, [the helicopter] Y69 ordered to go to the contact. 23.10, Y69 is in Danziger Gatt . . . At 23.55, [the helicopter] Y70 on its way to Mälsten. From Y69: a very clear echo. From MS [Mälsten]: helicopter reports submarine in bearing 180 degrees, distance 1.2M from Nåttaröhals [2.5 kilometres south of Nåttarö] . . . At 00.01, Y69 and Y70 receive the right to use depth charges . . . At 00.19, Y69 receives the order: drop depth charge. At 00.21, Y69 leaves the area . . . At 00.25, MS [Mälsten] to Y70: the submarine is moving forward by intervals towards the deepest area. At 00.31, MS [Mälsten] still has contact [with the submarine] . . . At 00.34, from MS [Mälsten]: the submarine has increased speed . . . At 00.53, Mälsten has lost contact. At 00.55, Y70 has 15 minutes left in the area. At 01.00, CSK [Chief of Stockholm Coastal Defence] has received the right to use the mines [the ceasefire is over].[308]

According to the Mälsten war diary and the naval base war diary, this submarine hunt continued up until lunchtime on 14 October. On the speaker channel on Tape 4, Anders Karlsson stated:

> At 01.19.00, continued tape recording of submarine. It is now 01.19. The amplitude of the submarine has first decreased and then increased to the present relatively high level. At 01.22.55, the helicopter is now preparing for an attack. At 01.25.30, the boats are coming here for the drop. Before this, I am going to turn off the whole system . . . The helicopter had contact [with the submarine] at microphone no. 5, which died. It is very likely that the submarine passed close to the microphone – so close that the fuse melted. After the detonation, the system was turned on. The noise level is back to normal. The low-frequency sounds are back to normal. They decreased to about 30 dB.[309]

The Mälsten war diary states:

> At 01.09, report from the sonar operator: the object is moving forward slowly. Helicopter Y69 informed. At 01.13, the sonar operator: the contact is stronger. At 01.14, Y70 returns. The speed of the object increases. Report to helicopter. At 01.16, from the sonar operator: the contact is stronger . . . At 01.18, the object is quiet . . . At 01.19, the

object is moving forward by intervals. Y69 is informed. Check with NH [MS1]. Mine barrages [MS1 Bengt Olsson, MS2 Johan Eneroth], the sonar operator [Anders Karlsson] and the lookout follow on radio. At 01.21, the patrol vessels are led by Y69 + [transport boat] TpbS. The distance between the patrol vessels discussed. HB7 [T.R. Nilsson on *Bevb* 77] takes the lead. At 01.24, Y70 gives the frequency.[310]

According to Sven-Olof Kviman and T.R. Nilsson, the vessels prepared for a massive drop of 16 depth charges (two patrol vessels with six bombs of 105 kilos and the smaller transport boat with four bombs of 55 kilos). The helicopter had contact with the submarine and was going to give the order to the three vessels. At 01.30, the submarine hit or passed in the immediate vicinity of microphone no. 5 (belonging to the sonar system at Mälsten). The Mälsten war diary states:

At 01.30, one of the microphones (no. 5) out of order. At 01.32 . . . According to Y69, contact close to A = the microphone [no. 5]. Contact close. From the sonar operator: in spite of this, no contact [in the microphone]. Y69 reports: the microphone is eliminated. The sonar operator receives order to close down the system. No. 5 may have been hit [the microphone was fixed by a strong elastic nylon cord between the sea floor and a buoy less than two metres above the sea floor, Rolf Andersson said]. Reported to Y69. From patrol vessel: three depth charges ready. From Y69: increase the speed. [Anders Karlsson tells how he could hear on the radio how the helicopter reported: '150 metres left, 100 metres left, 50 metres left.' Just at this very moment, the helicopter received an order from the naval base to use only two depth charges.] From NTM [the naval base]: you are allowed to use two [depth charges]. At 01.37, Drop! HB5 [George Gustafsson at *Bevb* 73] is disturbed [by the naval base] so the order 'Drop' is not received. He hears 'Don't drop' and drops them later . . . At 01.40, only HB5 dropped two.[311]

This incident is confirmed by the naval base war diary: 'At next contact, drop two depth charges', and, at '01.40, two depth charges detonated'. At 02.02, the Commander of the Eastern Military District was informed about the dropping of depth charges.[312] The massive drop of 16 depth charges was interrupted by an order from the naval base to drop just two. The order was given when there were fewer than 100 metres left, T.R. Nilsson said. According to one participant, a voice suddenly appeared on the frequency, and the helicopter and the patrol vessels did not know who gave the order. They were disturbed and asked the voice to leave the frequency.

When describing this case, the Grandin Report discusses a drop against a 'certain submarine' at 01.38 (helicopter contact). The report states:

> Because of interruption from the naval base, the drop was delayed and limited to just two depth charges in relation to the planned drop of six [actually 16] . . . The dropping of depth charges has to be done massively to have a reasonable chance of success.[313]

After Vice-Admiral Stefenson and Vice-Admiral Rudberg had gone for a de-escalation on 7 October, no drop of depth charges was ordered by the naval base (see above). When the Command at Mälsten ordered a massive drop, the naval base limited the operation so that there was no 'reasonable chance of success', to use the words of the Grandin Report. The Mälsten war diary continues:

> At 01.40, from HB5: both of them exploded. At 01.43, nothing from the microphones. Only our own vessels . . . No low-frequency sounds [no propeller]. The vessel may have been damaged, or keeps totally silent, or the microphones are damaged for lower frequencies . . . At 02.35, [the fast attack craft] Kaparen has arrived to ordered position. The role of the ceasefire and the end of the ceasefire are discussed with CKA 1 [Chief of the Coastal Defence, Vaxholm, Colonel Persson] and with night officer ÖrlBO [Naval Base East]. At 02.39, the helicopter Y68 arrives in the area. At 02.44, from the sonar system: two knocking sounds. At 03.00, CSK [Chief of Stockholm Coastal Defence, Brigadier-General Hansson] is contacted about the ceasefire. He is briefed about the incident . . . At 03.08, consultations with ÖrlBO about landing helicopter Y68 at Mälsten (Y70 out of order) . . . At 03.20, poor visibility because of rain. At 03.22, the sonar operator reports: several knocking sounds close to [microphone] no. 4. Sonar personnel should brief Y68 when landing . . . At 03.50, ÖrlBO asks for position to let Belos start search for the object. The weather is getting worse . . . At 05.30, Belos searches for the object, while the helicopter hovers and tries to receive contact in case something tries to move for protection because of the noise of Belos. If contact is received the helicopter will direct the attack craft [Kaparen] for a drop . . . At 07.12, from Mälsten (direct contact with Belos): go to DP 047 504 and search in an area with a radius of 0.5M . . . At 10.31, from the sonar operator: possible submarine, echo, 2 pings . . . At 10.46, the object is moving. Y71 is informed. At 10.48, from sonar operator: possible submarine . . . At 10.55, from the sonars: silent again. Y71 is informed. At 10.56, Y71 asks for last position of the object. Answer: 1,000 metres southwest Vitingen.[314]

There were no more sounds from the submarine and no more contacts. It may at this point have been on its way out to open sea, out of reach of the microphones. The naval base war diary has a similar presentation of the incidents:

> At 03.30, from the sonars at Mälsten: rattling sounds . . . sounds similar to the closing of a scuttle or a door [submarine hatch (Anders Karlsson)] . . . At 03.41, Y69 in the air. At 03.45 . . . Belos ordered to go to Mälsten [from Hårsfjärden] . . . At 07.45, Belos arrives. At 09.00, Belos continues searching southwest of Vitingen . . . At 11.00, from Mälsten: microphone contact for the previous half-hour (since 10.35). The submarine has been moving since 10.46 (cavitation sounds). Conversation with the captain of Belos [Björn Mohlin]. Search in an area 1 × 1M with the centre being the location of the microphones . . . The submarine will have to be 500–1,000 metres from the microphone for the sound to be registered. Order to put continuous helicopter pressure on the area. [No more contact mentioned.][315]

The submarine most likely left the area around 10.45, and at 11.00 it was out of reach of the microphones. The Stockholm Coastal Defence Staff report states:

> At 04.15, from ÖrlBO [the naval base]: submarine is confirmed. Helicopter has classified object in Danziger Gatt as 'submarine'. At 01.35, two depth charges dropped. At 03.45, sound classified as coming from submarine. At 08.50, SCSK [Chief of Staff, Stockholm Coastal Defence, Lieutenant-Colonel Jan Svenhager] makes a report to MBÖ about muddle-headedness in orders about the use of force [for the mine barrages]. At 17.20, ÖB order to MBÖ about the right to use force for the mine barrages. At 18.30, MBÖ order about right to use force for MS1, MS2 and MS3 under the condition of clear visibility and no risk to civilian traffic.[316]

At 17.20 on 14 October, the ceasefire in darkness was terminated. A new order about ceasefire in darkness was not given until 17.00 on 21 October.[317] After the submarines had passed out, there was a permanent right to use force at night for a week. On 13 October, both war diaries state that there were clear indications of a submarine and that the submarine passed the mine barrage at 23.00 without personnel being allowed to do anything. The five-hour ceasefire for the mines as well as the order about only dropping two depth charges most likely saved the submarine. The internal Swedish Navy investigation by Rear-Admiral Gunnar Grandin *et al.* stated:

> The amount of force used was limited by the number of depth charges local commanders were allowed to drop in every single case . . . The

number of depth charges allowed [in the single drops] shows that super-ior command totally lacked necessary technical competence for such a detailed planning of the operations . . . Ceasefires for [the mines at Mälsten] were also given by higher commands without competence and knowledge . . . On a couple of occasions the order about ceasefires – for depth charges as well as for mine barrages – may have positively contributed to letting the submarine(s) escape.[318]

There is no doubt about a submarine passage, for several reasons. Firstly, the magnetic sensors of the mine barrages indicated a sub-surface object – most likely a submarine – that passed the mines. This was a clear indication – 'a very likely passage', to quote the Grandin Report. Secondly, the microphones at Mälsten indicated a 'certain sub-marine' moving forward by intervals. The speed and the turns per minute were registered. The vessel had a damaged propeller blade or propeller axis (or the blade was scraping a damaged propeller shroud). There were clear cavitation sounds. Thirdly, the helicopter sonars indi-cated a submarine and had contact with the submarine several times. The helicopter classified the vessel as a 'certain submarine'. Fourthly, the sound of the closing submarine hatch at 03.30 could not be con-fused with other sounds, which make it possible to classify the object as a 'certain submarine'. Fifthly, one microphone (no. 5) was hit by the submarine or passed by the submarine at a distance of a metre or less, an event confirmed by the sonar operators involved, as well as by Brigadier-General Hansson. When the submarine's position was given as 'close to the microphone', the sonar system received its maximum signal, the fuse for no. 5 blew and the microphone died. There is no object that could have provoked such an event other than a submarine or submersible operating very close to the bottom. According to general rules, this submarine should be classified as a 'certain subma-rine'. Later, Lieutenant-General Persson characterized this submarine as a 'certain submarine'.[319] The Grandin Report also described it as a 'certain submarine'.[320] Between 02.45 and 03.30, there were reports of several knocking sounds and the closing of a submarine hatch. The sonar operator Anders Karsson interprets this as a docking operation. After that, the submarine kept quiet for several hours. Around 10.45, it was moving (cavitation sounds). It most likely left the area and went out of reach of the microphones, out to open sea.

Commander-in-Chief General Lennart Ljung wrote in his diary on 14 October:

01.00, CFst [Chief of Staff Vice-Admiral Stefenson] called. Contact with bottom-fixed sonars in Danziger Gatt [Mälsten]. Also sonar contact from helicopter. The mine barrages indicated submarine. Two depth charges dropped. The results are not yet clear. At the time, there was a ceasefire for the mine barrages ('daylight and clear visibility'). CFst went to MSB [the Defence Staff]. I stayed at home[321] [to be contacted by telephone].[322]

Ljung confirms the version of the two war diaries – that all systems indicated a submarine – and, immediately after Ljung had been informed about this, the ceasefire was terminated at Mälsten. According to the personnel at Mälsten, they once again received the right to use the mines at 01.06, two hours after the submarine had passed the mine barrages. A five-hour ceasefire at the time of the most clear passage of a submarine and after that a denial of a massive drop of depth charges against the same submarine appeared absurd to the personnel. As already indicated in the war diaries, the Commander at Mälsten, Lieutenant-Colonel Kviman, was upset. The naval base and Stockholm Coastal Defence were contacted. Two days later, Vice-Admiral Stefenson went to Mälsten by helicopter to talk with the personnel, according to Kviman (Stefenson arrived at 13.50).[323] It seems to have been important to Vice-Admiral Stefenson to calm down the personnel, and particularly Kviman. Stefenson sent Kviman's wife hundreds of red roses and a letter of thanks saying that her husband was still needed.

The Submarine Defence Commission Report gives a very different version. The ceasefire for the mines in darkness was declared at 23.30 on 7 October.

> After that, the order was to use fire only in daytime. This ceasefire was in effect until 14 October (at 01.00), when conditions for the right to use fire safely in the night had been achieved, because of better control of the surface in darkness. Before this, one exception to the rule was made around 21.00 on 12 October, when there were clear indications of a submarine similar to what happened on 14 October.[324]

This statement is misleading in every respect. Mälsten had received its night-vision scopes on 8 October.[325] Nothing had changed Mälsten's capability to control the surface after that. From 9 October, Chief of Stockholm Coastal Defence Lars Hansson requested the right to use force even in darkness. The confirmed indications from 12 October were around 18.00 (actually 16.30–18.30, possibly 18.55) and not at 21.00. The ceasefire for MS1 ended at 21.30 (or, formally speaking, at 22.35) on 12 October, just after Vice-Admiral Stefenson had visited General Ljung and informed him about clear indications of a submarine – more than two hours after the submarine had left the area. For the night of 12–13 October, there was no ceasefire during darkness. A partial ceasefire was declared for a couple of hours (17.10–20.05) on

13 October, because of bad weather and poor visibility. At 18.22, the Eastern Military District stated clearly that there was no ceasefire in darkness for MS1, MS2 and MS3.[326] A new ceasefire, however, was declared at 20.05. This ceasefire ended at 01.00 or, at Mälsten, at 01.06, just after Stefenson had called General Ljung and informed him about clear indications of a submarine and two hours after the submarine had passed the mine barrages. As on 12 October, the indications on 13–14 October took place two hours earlier. *In other words, these two ceasefires were both terminated more than two hours after clear indications of submarines had terminated. Somebody has presented consistently false information to the Submarine Defence Commission.* The Commission Report states that 'there was no indication of a submarine' on 13 October,[327] and 'the commission has found no evidence that a submarine would have passed out over the mine barrages in connection with a ceasefire'.[328] This false information was also reported by the Naval Analysis Group under Commander Emil Svensson, and it was most likely given to the commission by its military expert, the officer who gave these orders, Vice-Admiral Bror Stefenson.

Vice-Admiral Stefenson did not call General Ljung until two hours after the submarine had passed the mine barrages. He told Ljung about clear indications of a submarine. After this, at 01.00, the ceasefire was ended and Stefenson went to the Defence Staff. The Ekéus Investigation stated:

> After his conversation with the commander at Mälsten [Lieutenant-Colonel Kviman], the Chief of Staff checked with the relevant commanders and, at about 01.00 in the night, he decided to accept the request for the right to use fire [in darkness]. He briefed the Commander-in-Chief about his decision.[329]

This is Admiral Stefenson's own version. Chief of Stockholm Coastal Defence Lars Hansson was never contacted, and all the others are dead. The only individual the commission spoke to was Bror Stefenson. The conversation between Kviman and Stefenson took place immediately after the order was given at 20.05. Stefenson could easily have contacted the relevant commanders and ended the ceasefire before 21.00. Instead, he waited for another four hours.

Stefenson's activity during this night contrasts with his late order to end the ceasefire and late call to General Ljung, as though Stefenson wanted to keep Ljung uninformed until the submarine was out. Nothing indicates that Ljung had been informed about the ceasefire. The Grandin Report states that the orders about ceasefires did not follow the usual routines.[330] The whole incident was obviously important enough to force the Chief of Staff back to his office just after midnight. There is no doubt that he, at the time, believed these indications. As early as the following morning, however, Vice-Admiral Stefenson denied any passage at Mälsten. He did not inform the Submarine Defence Commission about the passage and has denied the existence of the passage in interviews afterwards (see below).[331] Neither did he mention the counter-order that prevented the massive dropping of depth charges that supposedly saved the submarine.

At 08.00, General Lennart Ljung had a meeting at the Defence Staff. He wrote in his diary: 'Discussion [with Chief of Staff, possibly also Chief of the Navy Vice-Admiral Rudberg]: are the mines manipulated because the mine barrages indicate a submarine (but possibly no submarine)? Electronic disturbances?'[332] After interviews with Vice-Admiral Stefenson, Fredrik Bynander wrote about this meeting: 'An upset discussion took place.'[333] In other words, General Ljung was then given information, most likely by Stefenson (and possibly Vice-Admiral Rudberg), that in all respects contradicted the information he had been given seven hours earlier (at 01.00). Stefenson woke him up in the night to tell him about a serious situation and a 'certain submarine', and then – a few hours later – it was just 'electronic disturbances' even although all the information from the local commanders still supported the fact that it was a 'certain submarine'. There was also the technical evidence of the tape-recorded propeller sound. Either Stefenson totally manipulated the information to the Commander-in-Chief or they together reached a manipulated conclusion. However, the second alternative is not very likely, because why would General Ljung in that case have entered the information about Stefenson's telephone call in his diary in the first place? It seems that Stefenson, and possibly Rudberg, had decided that this passage did not take place. The ceasefire would be too difficult to explain.

After two interviews with Vice-Admiral Stefenson (but none with General Ljung), Fredrik Bynander states:

> Personnel on the site had been confused over what directives were in effect when a strong indication was received and consequently did not fire. Ljung and Stefenson were certain that no ceasefire rule was in effect at the time of the alleged escape.[334]

Stefenson ordered the ceasefire having consulted with – or, more likely, without having consulted with – General Ljung, but Ljung was clearly informed at 01.00. To argue that there was no ceasefire from 20.05 to 01.06 is absurd. It is in every respect contradicted by the Mälsten war diary, the naval base war diary, the Stockholm Coastal Defence Staff report and by interviews with regional and local personnel involved.

Deputy Chief of Defence Staff Intelligence Commander Björn Eklind has told me that Vice-Admiral Stefenson asked him about the technical possibilities for manipulating the mines and whether there were indications of Soviet use of these techniques. After an hour or two Eklind came back to Stefenson and presented some limited evidence for Soviet experiments and the technical possibilities for this. At 13.45, General Ljung briefed Defence Minister Börje Andersson and told him that it was suspected that 'the mines may be indicating erroneously'.[335] Börje Andersson was informed that there was no clear indication of a submarine. The 'certain submarine' about which General Ljung was briefed 12 hours earlier no longer existed. It seems as though Vice-Admiral Stefenson or Vice-Admiral Rudberg had decided that the passage did not take place. Toivo Heinsoo, Börje Andersson's close associate and political adviser at the Ministry of Defence, told me that they several times received reports about strong indications, but afterwards there was no confirmation. Lieutenant-Colonel Håkan Söderlindh, Chief of OPG at the Defence Staff, has said that the criticism of the ceasefire on 13–14 October (and of Stefenson) did not take into account the security–political consequences of the sinking of a submarine. The leaders with the final responsibility had to consider this problem. After allegations that this submarine might have been a Western submarine, Lieutenant-Colonel Kviman said that this would explain Vice-Admiral Stefenson's behaviour.[336] Brigadier-General Lars Hansson said to me in 2002 that he now had more respect for Vice-Admiral Stefenson's orders after having understood that it was a Western submarine. However, he felt that he should have been informed about it beforehand.

The passage at 23.00 (not at 23.01 or 23.02) indicates that the submarine had orders to pass out at a certain hour within a given (five-hour) time window. According to an experienced admiral I have consulted, a five-hour time window is appropriate for such an operation. And if you receive an order to pass at a certain hour, you will do that, he said. You wait until the right minute before you pass the mine barrage. The passage at exactly 23.00 is a clear sign of a pre-planned operation, this admiral said. This view has been supported by other senior submarine officers. This, however, presupposes that a ceasefire had been established giving enough time for the passage. This might explain why the Chief of Staff started to operate as a local commander and why a lot of strange decisions were taken at the Defence Staff, which even made Brigadier-General Hansson believe that Vice-Admiral Stefenson was cooperating with the Soviets. Ambassador Rolf Ekéus found that the pages covering this incident in the Defence Staff (OPG) war diary (from the afternoon of 13 October to after one o'clock in the morning of 14 October) had disappeared in both the hand-written and the typed versions.[337] The tape recording had also disappeared. The 20-minute recording had either been demagnetized or just cut out, said Arne Åsklint, who investigated this issue for the Ekéus Commission (see below).

Three months later, General Ljung wrote in his diary that Henry Kissinger had said: 'it was smartly done by the Swedish government to release the submarine the way they did'.[338] Of course, by first damaging the submarine and then covertly releasing it, Sweden would have been able to demonstrate its resolve to defend its territory without causing a foreign power to lose face. But this does not make sense if the foreign power was the Soviet Union. It seems as though Kissinger was speaking about a Western, or rather US, submarine that Sweden had released after having first damaged it. Kissinger's knowledge about the case may indicate that the submarine originated from the USA. However, the officers who tried to damage the submarine were hardly the same as those who tried to release it. And the government, as well as the Commander-in-Chief, were probably not informed at all.

In the evening of the same day, the press centre at Berga was closed down and General Ljung reported that the submarine had most likely been able to escape. The Naval Base East intelligence briefing for 15 October states:

> 1. Briefing about the Activity of Foreign Powers. 1.1. *Foreign Naval Vessels:* Warsaw Pact naval vessels, among others three frigates of Riga class are having an exercise Ösel–Tallin 1982-10-14–11-14. Possible submarines may be in the vicinity. 1.2. *Foreign State Vessels:* Soviet rescue vessel Loksa FM 4930 151100 [at 11.00, 15 October] . . . 1.3. *Warsaw Pact Merchant Ships:* At 17.11, Soviet merchant ship Volgobalt at EP 4324 . . . 1.4. *Conclusion:* No activity can be linked to the submarine incident. There may be increased interest among even non-engaged nations. 1.5. *Foreign Submarine Activity:* No definite indications during the day.[339]

The sharp contrast between this report about low Soviet activity and the dramatic incidents involving damaged and released submarines is striking.

NOTES

1 CÖrlBO WD.
2 Ibid.

3 MAna Hårsfj, Attach. 15.
4 MAna Hårsfj; CM/Grandin (1982).
5 SOU (1983), p. 34.
6 Kierkegaard, Hoff and Blomquist (1990), p. 8.
7 CM/Grandin (1982), Attach. 2; MAna Hårsfj.
8 MAna Hårsfj, Attach. 16.
9 SOU (1983), p. 35.
10 Ibid, p. 35.
11 CM/Grandin (1982), p. 78.
12 CÖrlBO WD; MAna Hårsfj.
13 MAna Hårsfj.
14 Von Hofsten (1993), pp. 78–9.
15 MAna Hårsfj.
16 CÖrlBO WD.
17 ÖB HWD; KU (1982/83:39), Attach. 7, p. 164.
18 CÖrlBO WD.
19 CM/Grandin (1982), Attach. 2.
20 CÖrlBO WD.
21 CM/Grandin (1982), p. 101.
22 MAna Hårsfj.
23 SOU (2001), pp. 316–17.
24 MAna Hårsfj, Attach. 18.
25 MAna Hårsfj, pp. 1–2.
26 SOU (1983), p. 83.
27 CM/Grandin (1982), Attach. 2.
28 MAna Hårsfj.
29 CM/Grandin (1982), Attach. 2.
30 MAna Hårsfj.
31 CÖrlBO WD.
32 ÖB TD.
33 SOU (2001), p. 317.
34 CM/Grandin (1982), Attach. 2.
35 MAna Hårsfj.
36 Ibid.
37 CÖrlBO WD.
38 ÖB TD.
39 Bynander (1998b), p. 370.
40 SOU (1983), p. 83.
41 MAna Hårsfj, Attach. 20.
42 CÖrlBO WD; SOU (1983); CM/Grandin (1982).
43 Kadhammar (1987), p. 102.
44 ÖB TD.
45 LGP HWD.
46 MAna Hårsfj.
47 Ibid.
48 Ibid.
49 CM/Grandin (1982), Attach. 2.
50 MAna Hårsfj.
51 Ibid.
52 CÖrlBO WD.
53 MAna Hårsfj.
54 MAna Hårsfj, Attach. 21.

55 SOU (1983), p. 83.
56 CM/Grandin (1982), Attach. 2; SOU (1995), p. 140.
57 MAna Hårsfj, Attach. 25.
58 SOU (2001), p. 317.
59 SOU (1983), p. 84.
60 Von Hofsten (1993), pp. 81–2.
61 *Aftonbladet* (5 October 1982).
62 *Expressen* (5 October 1982).
63 SOU (1983), p. 84.
64 CÖrlBO WD.
65 MAna Hårsfj, Attach. 27.
66 MAna Hårsfj.
67 Rylander (draft 2002).
68 MAna Hårsfj.
69 CM/Grandin (1982), Attach. 2.
70 MAna Hårsfj, Attach. 29.
71 CÖrlBO WD.
72 SOU (1995), pp. 243–9; Cato and Larsson (1995).
73 MAna Hårsfj, Attach. 29.
74 MAna Hårsfj, Attach. 30.
75 Cato and Larsson (1995).
76 MAna Hårsfj.
77 SOU (1983), p. 35.
78 CÖrlBO WD.
79 MAna Hårsfj.
80 LGP HWD.
81 SCSK Report.
82 ÖB TD.
83 ÖB HWD; ÖB TD.
84 KU (1982/83:30), Attach. 7, p. 166.
85 *Dagens Nyheter* (6 October 1982).
86 *Dagens Nyheter*; *Svenska Dagbladet*.
87 *Expressen* (7 October 1982).
88 *New York Times* (5–11 October 1982).
89 *Expressen* (7 October 1982), p. 7.
90 *Expressen* (8 October 1982).
91 *Aftonbladet* (6 October 1982); see also von Hofsten (1993), pp. 85–7.
92 SOU (1983), p. 84; *Dagens Nyheter* (7 October 1982).
93 MAna Hårsfj.
94 MAna Hårsfj, Attach. 33.
95 MAna Hårsfj, Attach. 34.
96 CÖrlBO WD.
97 MAna Hårsfj, Attach. 33, 34.
98 LGP HWD; CMS WD.
99 SCSK Report.
100 ÖB HWD; ÖB TD.
101 Bynander (1998a), p. 33; (1998b), p. 405.
102 ÖB HWD.
103 *Dagens Nyheter* (7 October 1982).
104 KU (1982/83:30), Attach. 7, p. 166.
105 CÖrlBO WD.
106 Ibid.

107 MAna Hårsfj, Attach. 35.
108 LGP HWD.
109 CÖrlBO WD.
110 ÖB TD.
111 In the late 1970s and early 1980s, the *Belos* had an experienced US Navy diver as US Navy Exchange Officer. Lieutenant Ingemar Lundell, the *Belos*'s Chief Diving Officer, has described how, from the late 1970s, three or four US divers (among them John Cole, Douglas Brown and Philip Butera) replaced each other on the *Belos*. Master Chief Petty Officer John Cole was on the *Belos* in the period 1977–79 (interview with Cole, *Reportrarna*, Swedish TV2, 9 September 1998). According to the captain of the *Belos*, Lieutenant-Commander Björn Mohlin, the US Navy diver Douglas Brown (replacing Cole) left probably sometime in 1981 and was never replaced. Lieutenant Lundell said that Brown was on the *Belos* during the Hårsfjärden incident. And in 1985–86, when a high-ranking officer visited the *Belos*, there was still a senior US Navy diver there. This was also the case in the early 1990s, he said. However, I spoke with Lieutenant-Commander Hans Kalla, who replaced Mohlin and was captain of the *Belos* from September 1985 to sometime in 1987. He said that he had never had a US diver on the *Belos*. Of course, if a US submarine was involved in these incidents, the nationality of the divers at the time is of some interest.
112 *Dagens Nyheter* (October 1982).
113 ÖB HWD; ÖB TD.
114 ÖB HWD.
115 Ibid.
116 ÖB HWD; ÖB TD.
117 Adelsohn (1987), p. 93.
118 ÖB HWD.
119 ÖB TD.
120 ÖB HWD.
121 CÖrlBO WD.
122 Ibid.
123 MAna Hårsfj.
124 MAna Hårsfj, Attach. 37.
125 MAna Hårsfj.
126 CÖrlBO WD.
127 SOU (1983), p. 51.
128 CM/Grandin (1982).
129 Von Hofsten (1993), p. 83.
130 ÖB TD.
131 ÖB HWD.
132 MAna Hårsfj, Attach. 38.
133 CMS WD.
134 Kadhammar (1987), pp. 102–3.
135 MAna Hårsfj, Attach. 38.
136 CMS WD.
137 CÖrlBO WD; MAna Hårsfj, Attach. 39.
138 CMS Report (12 October 1982).
139 MAna Hårsfj, Attach. 40.
140 CM/Grandin (1982).
141 The Submarine Defence Commission (SOU 1983:13) says one mine exploded in the afternoon (16.00) and two in the evening (20.00). Lennart Ljung (1978–86) says that one mine exploded at 15.00 at Nåttarö and three in the

evening. The correct version is two mines at 14.50 and two at 18.40.

142 ÖB HWD; ÖB TD.

143 ÖB TD.

144 In the typed version of Ljung's diary, it is stated that a ceasefire was declared for the 'duration of the night'. The reason for this was the security of civilian traffic (ÖB TD). The hand-written version talks about a 'provisional ceasefire' without a clear ending to guarantee security for civilian traffic and to calm down the situation on-site (ÖB HWD). The naval base war diary as well as the Staff Report from Stockholm Coastal Defence also talk about a 'provisional ceasefire' (CÖrlBO WD; SCSK Report). The ceasefire did not end at dawn next day, but about five hours later, at 10.20 (the decision was taken at 08.30, but it did not reach the local commander until 10.20 (see below)). The hand-written version of Ljung's diary seems to be more reliable. According to the naval base war diary, the ceasefire for the mine barrages and depth charge volleys was ordered by MBÖ at 23.12 (ten minutes after the naval base had ordered a ceasefire for the *Väktaren* during its attack on a submarine). The telegram about the order from the Commander-in-Chief for a provisional ceasefire for all mine barrages was received by the naval base at 23.26 (CÖrlBO WD).

145 ÖB HWD.

146 CMS WD.

147 SOU (1983), p. 51.

148 CÖrlBO WD.

149 MAna Hårsfj, Attach. 41.

150 CÖrlBO WD.

151 Ibid.

152 MAna Hårsfj RABu.

153 Cato and Larsson (1995); SOU (1995).

154 ÖB HWD.

155 ÖB TD.

156 CMS WD.

157 *Dagens Nyheter* (9 October 1982).

158 ÖB TD.

159 *Aftonbladet* (8 October 1982).

160 *Aftonbladet* (10 October 1982).

161 ÖB HWD; ÖB TD.

162 Ibid.

163 SCSK Report.

164 CÖrlBO WD.

165 SOU (1995), p. 140.

166 MAna Hårsfj.

167 MAna Hårsfj, Attach. 43, 44.

168 ÖB HWD.

169 CM/Grandin (1982), Attach. 2.

170 CÖrlBO WD.

171 Ibid.

172 CÖrlBO INT (9 October 1982).

173 Kadhammar (1987), p. 105.

174 CM/Grandin (1982), p. 130.

175 Kadhammar (1987), p. 105.

176 ÖB HWD.

177 CMS WD.

178 Ibid.

179 *Aftonbladet* (7 October 1982).
180 *Aftonbladet* (11 October 1982).
181 CÖrlBO WD.
182 MAna Hårsfj.
183 MAna Hårsfj, Attach. 47, 48.
184 See also MAna Hårsfj, Attach. 46.
185 CÖrlBO WD.
186 CMS WD.
187 Ibid.
188 MAna Hårsfj.
189 CMS HWD.
190 Ibid.
191 CÖrlBO WD.
192 CMS WD.
193 ÖB TD.
194 CMS HWD.
195 CÖrlBO WD; see also CMS HWD.
196 Brännström and Persson (1983).
197 MAna Hårsfj.
198 MAna Hårsfj, Attach. 50.
199 CÖrlBO WD.
200 Ibid.
201 CMS WD.
202 MAna Hårsfj.
203 CÖrlBO WD; CMS HWD.
204 CMS WD.
205 Ibid.
206 CÖrlBO WD.
207 SOU (1985), p. 85.
208 CÖrlBO WD.
209 MAFU Report (1982).
210 CMS WD.
211 CÖrlBO WD.
212 SCSK Report.
213 CMS Report (11 October 1982).
214 CM/Grandin (1982), p. 130.
215 *Dagens Nyheter* (12 October 1982).
216 *Dagens Nyheter* (12–14 October 1982).
217 CMS WD.
218 CÖrlBO WD
219 Bevb 77 LB; Bevb 77 WD.
220 CÖrlBO WD.
221 Y46 Report.
222 CMS2 WD.
223 'At 14.35, Bevb 77: probably mud from the sea floor' (CMS HWD). This statement certainly refers to the oil/mud patch investigated by *Bevb* 77 after 13.05 (see text). The commander of *Bevb* 77, T.R. Nilsson, told me that, after this check, he was sent south to Järflottalandet to look for oil patches from a possible submarine. He was not in the area of Måsknuv when the yellow/green patch appeared. His log-book states that he returned to Mälsten at 14.30 and did not leave Mälsten again until 16.05. According to his log-book and his war diary, he did not go out at 14.35 or minutes after that. According to Kviman, it was *Tpb*

120

334 that took these samples on the green patch.

224 CMS HWD.
225 SOU (2001), p. 124.
226 CÖrlBO WD.
227 Y46 Report; SOU (2001), p. 124; Wallén (2002), p. 40.
228 Y46 Report; see also Wallén (2002), p. 40.
229 Y46 Report.
230 CMS WD.
231 *Aftonbladet* (12 October 1982); ÖB TD.
232 Eriksson (1982).
233 CMS WD.
234 CMS2 WD.
235 CMS WD; CÖrlBO WD; MAFU Report; SCSK Report.
236 ÖB HWD.
237 Ibid.
238 The comment, 'mine detonated at Mälsten – directly under – green patch' was clearly inserted later, in between the last paragraph for 11 October and the already written first lines for 12 October. In the hand-written original, one can see that Ljung used a different pen and that he has drawn a line separating the inserted sentence from the first line of 12 October. This sentence would otherwise have been 'intruding' into the text of the following day. The colour of the pen is the same as the one used for the 12 October entry, 'In the afternoon, no new information on a possibly sunk submarine' (ÖB HWD), indicating that General Ljung most likely wrote these sentences on the same occasion. He seems to have received information about a damaged or 'possibly sunk submarine' sometime during 12 October.
239 'Possibly sunk submarine' (ÖB HWD) is changed to 'possible damaged submarine' (ÖB TD). Two entries in the hand-written version – 'Mine detonated at Mälsten – directly under – green patch' and 'Ceasefire for the mine barrages until investigation is made' (ÖB HWD) – are made into a whole new paragraph with a different meaning (the new typed text is in italics): '*During the day* a mine was detonated *in the area west of* Mälsten. *This time there was another indication from the mine barrage, and a mine was activated* directly under *the indicating object. There was* a green patch *on the surface. It was investigated during the evening by divers and Belos. There was at that time no sign of a damaged submarine. The mine explosions are mysterious, and I am afraid that this will have long-term consequences for our peacetime-deployed mines, their function and security. On recommendation of the Chief of Staff,* I will not allow any activation of mines until the circumstances surrounding the latest mine explosion have been investigated' (ÖB TD).
240 CÖrlBO INT (11 October 1982).
241 *Aktuellt*, Swedish TV1 (7 March 2000).
242 MAFU Report (11–12 October 1982).
243 CMS HWD; CMS WD.
244 CÖrlBO WD.
245 MAFU Report (11–12 October 1982).
246 CMS WD.
247 SCSK Report.
248 CÖrlBO WD.
249 Kadhammar (1987), p. 105.
250 ÖB HWD.
251 Ibid.

252 *Aftonbladet* (13 October 1982).
253 Adelsohn (1987), p. 97.
254 *Aftonbladet* (12 October 1982).
255 *Verdens Gang* (12 October 1982).
256 CÖrlBO WD; CMS HWD.
257 CMS Report (12 October 1982).
258 CÖrlBO WD.
259 SCSK Report.
260 ÖB HWD.
261 ÖB TD.
262 ÖB HWD; ÖB TD.
263 *Dagens Nyheter* (13 October 1982).
264 ÖB HWD; ÖB TD.
265 *Dagens Nyheter* (13 October 1982).
266 CÖrlBO WD.
267 *Aftonbladet* (13 October 1982).
268 CMS HWD; CÖrlBO WD.
269 MAna Hårsfj.
270 CMS WD.
271 FOA Tape, Band 1.
272 SOU (1995), pp. 140, 145.
273 CÖrlBO WD.
274 ÖB HWD; ÖB TD.
275 SOU (1983), p. 51.
276 SCSK Report.
277 CMS HWD.
278 CÖrlBO WD.
279 SOU (1983), p. 51.
280 ÖB TD.
281 SOU (1995), pp. 201–210.
282 *Dagens Nyheter* (14 October 1982).
283 CM/Grandin (1982); Carlsson (1999), p. 67.
284 ÖB HWD.
285 CÖrlBO WD.
286 CMS HWD.
287 MAna Hårsfj.
288 CMS WD.
289 SCSK Report.
290 The Ekéus Report states that the order about right to use force in darkness from 22.35 the night before was automatically changed at dawn, at 06.00, to the old order: 'daylight and clear visibility'. A new ceasefire would have started at dusk, at 17.15, on 13 October. At 20.05 'the Chief of Staff repeated the order from the Commander-in-Chief' (SOU 2001, p. 117). This is the view presented by Vice-Admiral Bror Stefenson. It has been supported by his associate, Ambassador Ekéus's military expert, Rear-Admiral Göran Wallén (2002, p. 37). However, there is no support for this view in the naval base war diary, the Mälsten war diary or the Stockholm Coastal Defence Staff Report. Mälsten and Stockholm Coastal Defence both had a very different understanding of what happened during these hours.
291 Kadhammar (1987), p. 105.
292 Wallén (2002), p. 38.
293 ÖB HWD.

294 Ibid.; ÖB TD.
295 CMS WD; CÖrlBO WD.
296 Bevb 77 LB; Bevb 77 WD.
297 CMS WD.
298 CÖrlBO WD.
299 FOA Tape 3.
300 CMS Report (14 October 1982).
301 See also *Aktuellt*, Swedish TV1 (7 March 2000).
302 CM/Grandin (1982), p. 131.
303 SCSK Report.
304 FOA Tape 3.
305 CMS WD.
306 SCSK Report.
307 CÖrlBO WD.
308 Ibid.
309 FOA Tape 4.
310 CMS WD.
311 Ibid.
312 CÖrlBO WD.
313 CM/Grandin (1982), p. 139.
314 CMS WD.
315 CÖrlBO WD.
316 SCSK Report.
317 SOU (2001), p. 119.
318 CM/Grandin (1982), pp. 24–5.
319 LGP HWD.
320 CM/Grandin (1982), p. 139.
321 ÖB HWD.
322 ÖB TD.
323 CMS WD.
324 SOU (1983), p. 51.
325 CMS WD.
326 SCSK Report.
327 SOU (1983), p. 85.
328 Ibid., p. 51. The Submarine Defence Commission Report states: 'The commission has found no evidence that a submarine would have passed out over the mine barrages in connection with a ceasefire. In particular, the night of 13–14 October has been discussed. Whether the indications received on this occasion (which led to the end of the ceasefire in darkness after some delay in the decision-making process) should be interpreted as the passage of a submarine is under debate among naval experts. It is, however, very doubtful that a foreign submarine would pass the mine barrages knowing that mine explosions had taken place' (SOU 1983, p. 51). In other words, because mine explosions had taken place, no indications of a submarine should be taken seriously. This is obviously different from the views of General Ljung (as presented in his diary) and the local commanders.
329 SOU (2001), p. 117.
330 CM/Grandin (1982), pp. 24–5.
331 *Dagens Nyheter* (1 February 1994).
332 ÖB HWD.
333 Bynander (1998b), p. 401.
334 Ibid., pp. 379–80.

335 ÖB HWD; ÖB TD.
336 *Aktuellt*, Swedish TV1 (7 March 2000).
337 SOU (2001), p. 118.
338 ÖB TD.
339 CÖrlBO INT (15 October 1982).

4

Reflections after the Submarine Hunt

The official report of the Parliamentary Submarine Defence Commission states with regard to the mine explosion on 11 October: 'the yellow powder was probably green mud from the sea floor'.[1] In other words, there was nothing of interest. According to the Submarine Defence Commission Report, there was no clear indication of a damaged submarine or of a yellow or green patch linked to a submarine. This is all misleading.

The mine detonated at 12.20 was located at some 37 metres in depth on a sea floor of rocks and hard clay up to 100 metres from the small island of Måsknuv. Still, some mud and thin oil were brought up by the explosion, which, according to Lieutenant-Colonel Kviman, created a large patch of maybe 100 metres in diameter. The reconnaissance aircraft *SE-GYP* reported that this patch drifted northwards. Oil samples were taken at 13.05. This patch had nothing to do with the small 'bright-yellow' or green patch that appeared more than an hour after this incident around 13.30.[2] At 14.35, Mälsten went out and collected the yellow/green substance in clean towels, and the Chief of Naval Base East sent a helicopter to take photos of the green patch.[3] The Chief of Staff at the naval base informed the Defence Staff Operation Division, who immediately informed the Chief of Staff. Captain Per Andersson, from his observation at 16.00, reported 'mud from the sea floor or a less concentrated green dye',[4] but by this time the patch was more or less dissolved. Earlier observations mention a 'bright-yellow' or 'concentrated green patch'. The yellow/green patch was clearly something exceptional, and, in the diaries of General Ljung and Lieutenant-General Lars-G. Persson, it was the only thing worth mentioning.[5] When Chief of Naval Staff Major-General Bo Varenius retired in 1983, he received a bottle of water from Lieutenant-Colonel Rolf Malm and the Naval Analysis Group. He was jokingly told that this was the sample from the yellow/green patch on

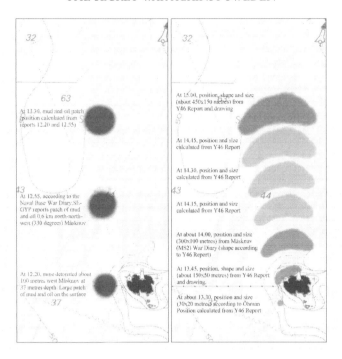

20. At 12.20 on 11 October, a mine was detonated 100 metres west of the island of Måsknuv after clear indication of a passing 'subsurface object'. On the surface, a large patch of mud and oil appeared. It drifted northwards at a speed of 750–800 metres per hour. At 12.55, Swedish aircraft SE-GYP reported the position of the patch about 600 metres north-northwest of Måsknuv. At 13.30, a small yellow patch, most likely dye from a damaged US submarine, appeared just southwest of Måsknuv. This patch also drifted northwards at a speed of 750–800 metres per hour. It followed the currents northeast along the northern shore of the island. After that, it followed the main current northwards. Positions, size and shape of this yellow/green patch are given in the report of helicopter Y46. This report is supplemented by the position and size noted in the Måsknuv War Diary, and by the information from the Mälsten War Diary that follows the expanding patch drifting northwards for two hours.

the water at Måsknuv in October 1982. The yellow/green dye was not a mass-media phenomenon as indicated by the Submarine Defence Commission.

First, the yellow/green patch did not appear immediately after the explosion at 12.20, but more than one hour later (around 13.30). In other words, the patch did not originate from the explosion. The boats ordered out 20 minutes (*334*) and 37 minutes (*Bevb 77*) after the explosion to patrol the area did not report a green or yellow patch, nor did the reconnaissance aircraft *SE-GYP*, which was patrolling the area 35 minutes afterwards, nor did the arriving helicopter, which passed over Måsknuv 65–70 minutes after the explosion.[6] At 13.05, T.R.

Nilsson on *Bevb 77* left Mälsten and went out to take samples from the patch of thin oil and mud reported by *GYP*. He took oil samples, which is confirmed by his log-book.[7] After that he was sent to look for oil patches south of Mälsten. He has said that he never saw the yellow/green patch. At 13.25 Chief of MS2 (Måsknuv), Captain Johan Eneroth reported to Mälsten but not about a yellow/green patch, which he did about half an hour later.[8] Up to over an hour after the explosion, there was no report of a yellow/green patch. The existence of this patch was reported later, at about 13.30 (1 hour 10 minutes after the explosion). The photographer Folke Hellberg and the journalist Anders Öhman went out from Nynäshamn in a small boat and arrived in the area about an hour after the explosion. Shortly afterwards, around 13.30, they went straight into a small 'bright-yellow patch' close to Måsknuv. The two men stayed in the area for only a few minutes. At 13.45, the helicopter *Y46* observed the patch close to Måsknuv.[9] After that, there were several reports about the yellow/green patch. In the afternoon (according to Mälsten about 14.00), MS2's [Måsknuv's] war diary states: 'a yellow cloud in the water about 200 metres to the north, size 300×100 metres. Report to VM [Mälsten]', which was written in the Mälsten war diary at 14.09.[10]

Second, after 13.30, the yellow/green patch expanded rapidly. It was not a biological phenomenon, and it was not mud from the bottom. The Mälsten war diary states at 14.09 that the patch expanded. It started as a smaller patch and became larger and larger.[11] When Öhman saw it about 13.30, it was concentrated and 20×30 metres in size. The estimate made by personnel on *Y46*, at 13.45, was, according to the drawing (and compared with the island of Måsknuv), a size of 50×150 metres.[12] Around 14.00, Måsknuv reported a size of 100×300 metres, which was registered by Mälsten at 14.09.[13] Personnel on *Y46* made a drawing of the patch's further expansion and movement northwards.[14] At 15.00, the size was, according to the drawing, around 150×450 metres.[15] The fact that the patch, in half an hour, expanded about 40–50 times its original size, and in an hour and a half more than 100 times its original size suggests that it was not a biological phenomenon. The size of the patch at the first observation (20×30 metres) implies that it had nothing to do with mud on the sea floor. The Ekéus Report also excludes mud from the sea floor: 'it was noted when samples were taken of the patch that the layer of dye was thin, that the patch kept together, was floating as a film on the surface for hours, and that it consisted of a fine substance that did not mix with water'. It was described as 'artificially green'.[16] Öhman describes it as a 'chemical substance'. 'It was bright yellow,' he said. Taken together, this all suggests that it was a dye, a marking chemical from a submarine, sent up more than an hour after the incident took place.

Third, the speed of the surface water makes any confusion with the patch that appeared with the mine explosion impossible. A large patch of mud appeared on the surface immediately after the mine explosion, and thin oil was also reported, which may have originated from the damaged submarine. This mud and thin oil were drifting northwards. At 12.55 to 12.57 (35 minutes after the mine was detonated), the reconnaissance aircraft *SE-GYP* reported to the naval base that this mud/oil patch had been drifting northwards some 450 metres from the place of the explosion to a position some 600 metres north-north-west of Måsknuv (0.6 km, bearing 330 degrees).[17] The surface water would accordingly have moved northwards at a speed of approximately 770 metres an hour. At 13.45, the helicopter *Y46* observed a green patch about 10 metres from Måsknuv (north-northwest of the island). Around 14.00, it was reported to be 200 metres north of Måsknuv. At 15.00, this patch had moved to a position 1 kilometre further north compared to the position at 13.45.[18] This means that the surface water, in the second case, moved northwards at a speed of about 750–800 metres an hour. Both patches moved northwards at approximately the same speed, perhaps 750–800 metres per hour. By just looking at the speed of the surface water, we can exclude the possibility that the yellow/green patch appeared at the place of the mine explosion at the time of the explosion. When the yellow/green patch was at the place of the mine explosion (at Måsknuv), the patch of oil and mud that appeared at the explosion would have been up to 1 kilometre further north. The yellow/green patch had nothing to do with what appeared immediately after the explosion.

Fourth, the patch did not originate at the place of the explosion, some 75–100 metres west of Måsknuv, but most likely at 13.30 some 100 metres south-southwest of Måsknuv. Öhman saw it just southwest of Måsknuv about 13.30. At 13.45, it was, according to the report and drawing made by Y46, already north or northwest of Måsknuv, but just 10 metres from the small island. The position of the by-then long oval patch indicates that it followed the currents northwards and, for a moment (for natural reasons), eastwards on the northern side of the island. This created its strange form, the long, oval, bow-like patch, which then moved northwards with the currents. It can only have appeared just south or south-southwest of Måsknuv. With an estimated speed of 750–800 metres an hour, it might have appeared around 13.30 about 100 metres south-southwest of the small island (100–150 metres southeast of the place of the mine explosion) roughly at the place where Öhman saw it, and, according to the Mälsten report of 12 October, exactly at the place where *Belos* had found 1 × 1.5 metre possible 'steel plates', which were belived to have originated from the damaged submarine. Öhman and Hellberg probably saw the patch before Måsknuv-Mälsten, because the staff of Måsknuv and Mälsten were located inside the rocks. Only the conscript lookouts, one on each island, followed what happened outside, and they may not have been alert all the time. In other words, the patch did not originate from the place of the explosion. There is no explanation for this patch other than that it was a dye from a submarine sent up to the surface more than one hour after the explosion at the place where the submarine would most likely have bottomed, 100 metres south of the mine barrage.

Fifth, the colour of the patch was most likely dependent on how concentrated it was and from where it was seen. This particular Monday was a calm and beautiful October day with clear visibility. At a distance, from the island of Mälsten, the rather large patch looked green against the blue sea. According to the Mälsten war diary, the patch was first 'concentrated green'.[19] The first report from Måsknuv states: 'a yellow cloud on the water'.[20] In the Mälsten war diary this report from Måsknuv, the 'yellow cloud', was changed to 'green-coloured area' probably because it looked green from Mälsten. The reports following speak about a green patch. The *Dagens Nyheter* journalist and former civilian captain Anders Öhman and the photographer Folke Hellberg went straight into a 20×30 metre yellow patch. They saw the substance at a distance of 1 metre. It was clearly yellow. 'It was nothing biological and definitely not mud from the sea floor. It was a chemical substance. It was bright yellow,' Öhman said. This means that the yellow dye (at a distance) would have looked green against the sea. Johan Eneroth at Måsknuv speaks now about it as 'yellow-green-grey'. The Submarine Defence Commission checked neither with Öhman nor with the personnel at Mälsten/Måsknuv. The commission simply stated that 'the yellow powder was probably green mud from the sea floor'.[21] It was still visible – 'concentrated green' – at 15.30, and even at 16.00, though by then less concentrated. After 16.00, there were no reports of the patch. If it had been a dye, a marking chemical, from a submarine, it would have dissolved within three hours or less, depending on the weather, a high-ranking officer told me. In other words, it would have disappeared sometime around 16.30, by which time the patch actually had dissolved.

Sixth, almost all evidence about the yellow/green patch has disappeared. After 14.35 samples of the yellow/green patch were taken in clean towels. The Defence Staff Security Division believed that the samples were sent to SKL (the State Laboratory for Crime) in Linköping. The Ekéus Report states that, in the Military Intelligence archives, it had 'not been possible to find any results from the analysis of the samples. A helicopter [Y46] was ordered to take photos, but these photos are no longer there.'[22] Y46 actually took 36 colour photos from various altitudes,[23] but it has not been possible to locate any of them in the Military Intelligence archive. However, the drawing made by personnel from Y46 exists as well as the report from the personnel who took the samples, which states that 'it was floating as a film on the surface for hours, and that it consisted of a fine substance that did not mix with water'.[24] During Anders Öhman's and Folke Hellberg's trip to Måsknuv, Hellberg took several photos. He believed he even took photos of the yellow patch, but all his negatives were in Pressens Bild's archive (the newspaper pictures archive), he said. His personal archive is organized chronologically. The negatives were there, regardless of the quality of the pictures. However, in the file for his 11 October trip to Mälsten the whole film with 36 pictures is gone. And from his trip the following day, several negatives are seemingly missing. Almost all physical evidence has for some reason disappeared, and the drawing made by Y46 was never used. It gave the rough expansion and speed northwards of the patch, and it would have made it possible to estimate the position where the dye appeared, but for some reason this information was never used.

Seventh, Mälsten immediately reported the green patch to the naval base, which reported to the Defence Staff and its Chief of Staff, but the latter seemingly did not report it to the Commander-in-Chief. Chief of Staff at the Naval Base East, Commander Lars-Erik Hoff, called Lieutenant-Commander Carl-Johan Arfvidson at OPG about the mine explosion at 12.20. Relatively soon after that, he called about the green patch, Arfvidson said. Arfvidson reported immediately (within 30 seconds) to his superior. Chief of Staff Vice-Admiral Bror Stefenson would have been informed about the incident minutes after Måsknuv/Mälsten had reported it. However, he did not seem to have reported the incident – or at least its significance – to the Commander-in-Chief. General Ljung did not write about the mine explosion, the green patch and the 'possibly sunk submarine' until after lunch the following day. In the early morning of 12 October, he accused the Navy Information Division of allowing its optimism to create unnecessary expectations on the part of journalists, since the Information Division was preparing to take journalists out to a discovered (damaged) submarine. Chief of Naval Base East, Rear-Admiral Christer Kierkegaard, did not show the same optimism, Ljung writes. At 09.00, General Ljung briefed Minister of Defence Börje Andersson.[25] It is not clear whether Ljung told the minister that something had happened or whether he wanted to counter speculations in the media. However, no briefing was given on 11 October. Most likely, General Ljung was not informed about a green dye and a damaged submarine on 11 October, perhaps not until the afternoon of 12 October. After that, he made a public statement about the necessity for Sweden to use force. He ended with the words 'We are sorry.'

There is no other explanation for this yellow/green patch than a yellow/green dye from a submarine. Its appearance as a small, concentrated yellow patch – exactly where a damaged submarine would most likely have bottomed, perhaps 100 metres from the place of the explosion – about an hour or more after the explosion, its expansion to 40–50 times its original size within half an hour, and finally its dissolving after less than three hours all indicate a dye or marking chemical from a damaged submarine. The events are similar to what happened on 5 October, when a green patch appeared on the surface after an attack on a submarine. However, on 11 October there is enough evidence to prove that this patch originated from the submarine. Afterwards, we have to ask why both the typed version of Ljung's diary and the Submarine Defence Commission used false information, and why the Naval Analysis Group or the Grandin investigation never discussed the issue.

Commander Anders Hammar, a member of the two latter groups, who also briefed the Commission, says today that he never had access to my material. However, he says that this material leaves no doubt. He is now supporting my analysis. Commander Bengt Gabrielsson, Chief of Naval Operations, Eastern Military District, says that he wrote drafts for the Commission, but he was never informed about the yellow/green patch; nor did he receive any report about a damaged submarine, though there were many things that he was not informed about. The naval base often reported directly to the Defence Staff, he said. Actually, the naval base reported directly to Carl-Johan Arfvidson at OPG, who reported to the Chief of Staff. But why did the latter not report the yellow/green patch to the Commission? Vice-Admiral Bror Stefenson was the Commission's military expert, a former submarine captain, who would have known the significance of this observation. He would also have known that an analysis was made that excluded mud from the bottom, but despite this he and the Commission talk about 'green mud'. When retired Commander-in-Chief General Bengt Gustafsson mentioned the information about the green patch to Admiral Stefenson in 2000, Stefenson still argued that it was green mud from the sea floor, Gustafsson told me. Ambassador Ekéus's report is at least more humorous: 'The investigation has asked specialists from FMV who could not find any other explanation to the patch than an old container of paint that was lying on the bottom and was destroyed by the mine explosion.'[26] This can hardly explain why this yellow/green substance reached the surface one hour after the explosion. Ekéus also knew about the significance of such a yellow/green patch, but he decided not to bring it up in the report, because there was no 'hard evidence', no photographs and no results from the analysis of samples.

The answer to all the questions raised by the above events may be found further west. When I spoke with Captain Robert Bathurst, a former deputy CINCUSNAVEUR for intelligence, I asked him what instruments the US Navy uses to identify the position of a sunk or damaged submarine. He told me that they use a buoy that sends signals and a 'golden-yellow powder' that creates a patch on the surface so that the location can be identified from the air. 'Soviet submarines do not use this kind of marking that reveals the place of the incident,' he said. Later, after having been presented with the background for my question, he added: 'There is no proof. The Soviets probably had this marking chemical but they had uncertain supply and may not have had it on board. Also, they do nearly anything not to reveal their positions.'

A Norwegian admiral and former Chief of the Navy, said that the dye may look yellow or green depending on where it is seen from. Not only the USA but also Britain uses this kind of buoy, with a green or possibly orange dye or marking chemical in cases of emergency. Furthermore, the chemical is available on the commercial market. The Norwegians have used this kind of dye in anti-submarine warfare training operations, but never as an emergency dye, he said. A Danish admiral and former Chief of the Navy said that both the Danish and the West German navies have used a green dye in anti-submarine warfare training operations, though not as emergency dye. A submarine may send up a dye when a frigate tries to hit the submarine with a rocket. Afterwards, it can be found out if the rocket hit the water in the dye. A Norwegian submarine captain told me that the USA started to use emergency dyes with different colours in the 1970s. The British did not use these dyes until later, or at least not before 1978. They were experimenting with dyes in the early 1980s. Most NATO countries had never used them. The Norwegians used a radio buoy and an orange lifeboat, he said. He had never seen the Russians use a dye. Commander Björn Eklind, former deputy chief of the Swedish Defence Staff Intelligence, told me that the Swedes have used a green dye in connection with anti-submarine warfare training. They dropped a green dye from a helicopter or they shot a small rocket with green marking chemical to check if they were able to hit the submarine. Despite having followed Soviet naval activities in detail from the late 1970s to the mid-1980s, he had never seen the Soviets use this kind of marking powder, he said. They use a chemical that creates smoke on the surface, but not a dye of yellow or green powder. The same view is presented by Captain Bo Rask, Chief of First Submarine Flotilla, in a letter for the Ekéus Investigation. He states that the Swedes have experience of the Soviets sending up a chemical creating red smoke on the surface. The Poles and probably the Soviets also used smoke shells. We have no information of any other methods used, he said.[27] This was not made very clear by the Ekéus Report.[28] The personnel at Mälsten told me that nobody – neither the Swedish helicopters nor any other Swede – used a yellow/green dye or marking chemical during the submarine hunt at Mälsten. The naval base sent up a helicopter to take a photo of the green patch. It was believed to be directly linked to a submarine damaged by a mine explosion.[29]

The Swedes did not use a yellow or green dye at Mälsten, nor did the Soviets. All intelligence personnel I have spoken with have said that it is impossible that the Soviets would have used a bright-yellow or concentrated green dye in a secret operation. They would avoid being revealed at any price. A former colleague of Captain Bathurst, a US specialist on submarine activities and professor at the Naval War College, said that US submarines would automatically release a buoy and a dye if a submarine should sink to a certain level. However, the Russians did not use this technique. In 1989, when the Soviet *Komsomolets/Mike* submarine sank near the Norwegian coast, no dye was released, a Norwegian general told me. A Norwegian senior intelligence officer responsible for following underwater activities within the Soviet Navy for some 20 years said that the Soviets used various kinds of markings (also 'light rockets'), but never a dye, not even in their own home waters. Furthermore, Vice-Admiral Stefenson and the Swedish Defence Staff went to a lot of effort to prove that the submarines in Hårsfjärden originated from the Soviet Union (see below). If the yellow/green powder could possibly have come from a Soviet submarine, it would not have been necessary to manipulate the Submarine Defence Commission Report in order to deny the existence of such a dye.

Two senior Royal Navy officers and former submarine captains told me that their submarines used to have a green dye. It's 'bright light-green', they said. One of them added that they might also have used a purple dye. This fits very well with the Mälsten war diary, the naval base war diary, the Y46 Report and with the Commander-in-Chief's diary, but not with the Måsknuv war diary speaking about a 'yellow cloud' or with Öhman's information saying that the marking chemical was 'bright yellow'. Of course, I don't know if these British officers have only seen their dyes at later stages. Accordingly, the dye at Mälsten could very well have originated from a British submarine. However, it is not very likely that the British (or any other European navy) would expose themselves and reveal their positions with a dye. It is actually much more easy to imagine the more technocratic USA carrying out such an operation. The above-mentioned Norwegian admiral told me that the USA is likely to use a dye in a secret operation in order to get real-time information. It would direct a satellite to focus on the area of operation, and a dye on the surface would immediately tell Washington about the exact position of a damaged submarine. In other words, Washington would be able to act and communicate with and give orders to the submarine before the target country knew about the incident.

This may explain the US use of a dye even in a secret operation, he said. The dye is sent up through a pipe in the submarine, but this has to be done deliberately. The dye is not released by mistake; it is sent up to identify the position of the submarine, he added. In cases where it is not possible to cover the area with one's own aircraft, a dye is sent up to the surface to be picked up by a satellite. This indicates a US operation. A radio buoy would have made it possible for the Americans to have real-time communication with the submarine via satellite. They may have used *SR-71* for communication and reconnaissance before the passage. They may also have sent instructions from the embassy or via a mobile radio. The Norwegian admiral said to the Ekéus Investigation that, if he had received information about a yellow/green dye appearing on the surface after a mine explosion, this information would have been presented to the government the moment he received it. This did not happen in the Swedish case.

Also, the above-mentioned senior intelligence officer said that the Americans might use a dye, because they would have a satellite focused on the area of operation. No one except for the USA would use satellites to carry out a covert operation. Another intelligence officer with experience of CIA operations explained that the CIA used to use a dye in covert special force operations. The meaning of a particular colour of dye would be decided from case to case, he said. This may explain the use of a yellow/green dye at Näsudden-Käringholmen on 5 October and at Måsknuv-Mälsten on 11 October. The patrol of *SR-71* before the submarine passage at Måsknuv and the possible British/US submarine following the activities from a position outside Mälsten also fit into this picture. It would possibly also explain why the photos of the yellow/green patch have disappeared. The concentrated yellow/green patch on the surface one hour after the mine explosion clearly indicates one thing: a US special force operation. Either the captain of the submarine sent up the dye to be picked up by satellite so his headquarters could give him orders before the Swedes knew about it, or he just did not understand how sensitive the operation was and, because of a serious incident, he was willing to reveal his position, or, possibly, he knew about its sensitivity but wanted to show the local collaborators in Sweden where not to look for the submarine.

THE SOUNDS

In autumn 1999, I contacted sonar expert Rolf Andersson of FMV. We made an appointment close to the FMV buildings in Stockholm, and I travelled from Oslo to see him. When he arrived, he told me that his superior, Stefenson's 'right hand', Captain Emil Svensson, had denied him permission to speak to me. He just wanted to tell me that. He was under no circumstances allowed to speak about the Hårsfjärden incident. In 2000, Svensson retired, and I could speak to Andersson. He told me that – more than 15 years after the Hårsfjärden incident – he had received the tape with the alleged repair works from the night of 11–12 October in a package by secret mail. There was nothing that indicated who had sent it to him. In the MAFU protocol, this tape was called 'Tape 2'. In the later FOA protocol, this tape was called 'Tape 0'. In connection with Ambassador Rolf Ekéus's investigation of the submarine incidents, we listened to the tape together with Andersson. Most of the sounds, along with Andersson's commentary on the speaker channel, could be heard clearly, but the more interesting sounds – the hammering, the metallic sounds, the knocking sounds and some of the high-frequency sounds – were gone. The tape was not damaged, but most of the essential sounds registered by the MAFU protocol, the Mälsten war diary and the naval base war diary had been erased. Somebody had seemingly cleaned the tape of more sensitive information. The most significant and dominating sound was now something that sounded like 'a diver breathing and scratching the microphone'. Andersson had never heard this sound before, and it is not found in any protocol or war diary. It seems to have been recorded later, on top of the original recording. Only the detailed protocol and the war diaries help us to see that the tape had been edited. If the 'repair works' had been of no interest, it is difficult to understand why someone had taken the time to edit the original tape.

Commander Emil Svensson's Naval Analysis Group Report says: 'Indication in sea-floor mine at Måsknuv. Mine was detonated. Conclusion: if a submarine had created the indication, it would most likely have been damaged seriously. The following investigation found no traces [of that]. No submarine.'[30] According to Svensson, there were no signs of a damaged submarine and, accordingly, 'no submarine'. Despite the existence of the yellow/green dye and tape-recorded repair works pointing to a damaged submarine, and despite the fact that Svensson would have been one of the first to be informed about all these activities, he and the Naval Analysis Group deny the presence of a submarine. The 1983 Submarine Defence Commission and the 1995 Submarine Commission, which both used the Naval Analysis Group Report, were misinformed.

During the night of 11–12 October and the following day, the damaged submarine was most likely hiding southwest or south-south-west of Mälsten. The position of the submarine would have been possible to locate, because sounds from repair works were registered during the night up until nine o'clock in the morning. However, by the time the naval base had sent a helicopter to locate the sound, it was too late. During the day, the submarine was mostly silent. There is a short sequence of propeller sounds at 13.38 and after that a couple of transients, but nothing else. From about 16.30 in the afternoon, new squeaking and twittering sounds appeared 'with intervals of seconds. The sonar operator is on his way.' This may be sounds from a propeller at low speed, working at intervals for short periods of time as if the submarine was trying to move from its hiding place southwest of Mälsten as silently as possible. At 17.10, the Mälsten war diary states: 'the sound is still there and has become stronger', indicating that the submarine was moving towards the microphones. 'At 17.48, less than 1,000 Hz.'[31] Two minutes later, Anders Karlsson's commentary on the speaker channel states: 'At 17.50, it is strong – over the whole register. Conclusion: probable submarine.'[32] The naval base war diary states:

At 17.52, from Mälsten: according to [sonar operator Anders] Karlsson from [submarine] Sjöhästen: possible submarine. One helicopter is sent to the area [at the time, the Naval Analysis Group and the naval base did not use the term 'probable submarine'] . . . At 18.00, from Mälsten: submarine ['certain submarine'] with a speed of 1–2 knots, closest to microphone no. 5 [the position close to no. 5 might have been an illusion because it turned out to amplify the sound more than the other microphones] . . . At 18.20, patrol vessel prepares to drop depth charges at [Torskboden close to microphone no. 1. Also about 18.20, Karlsson states on the speaker channel: 'continued recording of submarine'] . . . At 18.37, [to the helicopter:] interesting area at DP0451, beyond microphone no. 5.[33]

The Mälsten war diary states at 18.30–18.55: 'according to the tape-recorded sounds, the object is most likely a submarine that has gone out from VM [Mälsten]'.[34] 'Out' [in Swedish, 'utåt'] can, in this case, only mean out towards the sea or the open sea, which means it had to pass the microphones, because of the shallow area south of Mälsten. In other words, Karlsson was reporting to staff at Mälsten that he had tape-recorded a submarine passing the five microphones. According to a former director of the sound institute at FOA, the submarine had been 'limping out' after some kind of damage.

Soon after this incident, the tape was transported to Berga by helicopter and then to the Defence Staff. In a report for the Naval Analysis Group (about 12 October), Commander Erland Sönnerstedt, Chief of Defence Staff Security Division, speaks about an analysis or preliminary analysis made on the same night. In this report, the frequency, speed and turns per minute are identified, supposedly from the incident at 18.00. The sound is classified as 'submarine', in other words 'certain submarine'.[35] At lunchtime the following day, Tapes 1 and 2 were handed over to Bengt Granath at the Passive Sonar Division at FOA. Granath and FOA made a preliminary analysis, which was delivered to Emil Svensson and the Naval Analysis Group on 20 October.[36] However, according to Granath, there was nothing on tape – only noise from the sea – during this sequence. Also these tape recordings seem to have been edited.

The five microphones had been put in a line on the sea floor in Danziger Gatt between Mälsten and Nåttarö (between Torskboden and Vitingen; see map 19, page 101). Microphone no. 1 was close to Torskboden, and no. 5 was closer to Vitingen, with about 100 metres between each microphone. In the early 1990s, FOA analysed a 3.47-minute sequence of propeller sound.[37] On this sequence the sound was registered in microphone no. 1 260 milliseconds before it was picked up by microphone no. 4 (no. 5 was excluded because it amplified the sound too much), and the sound became stronger, which was interpreted as clear evidence for the object being west of the microphones, at a distance of a few hundred metres and moving towards the microphones. The estimate made by FOA in 1993 was that the submarine, travelling at a speed of 2 knots, would have been 550 metres from the western microphone (no. 1) at the beginning of the sequence and 350 metres from the same microphone at the end. At a speed of 5 knots, it would have been 1,120 metres from the same microphone at the beginning of the sequence and 590 metres at the end.[38] After this, the tape recorder was supposedly turned off. The FOA analysts said that, following this route, the submarine would have had to pass the microphones at a distance of no more than a couple of hundred metres (probably less than 100 metres because of the rather narrow channel south of Mälsten), which probably would have made it possible to identify the vessel.

This is of importance, because the 3.47-minute sequence has been presented by the Swedish authorities as the most important proof of Soviet intrusions into Swedish waters. This is the tape recording referred to in the Defence Staff notes of 18 April 1983, in the Submarine Defence Commission Report of 26 April 1983, and in the note to Moscow in autumn 1983. In the early 1990s during the Swedish–Russian dialogue, Captain Emil Svensson presented this recording in Moscow as the major evidence of Soviet intrusions. The Russians accepted that it was a submarine 'as long as there was nothing on the surface', but they denied that it could have been a Soviet submarine.[39] The critical 1995 Submarine Commission accepted only about ten observations in Swedish waters as 'certain submarine'; one of them was this tape recording (see below). All commissions, the MAna Report and the Grandin Report describe the sequence as taking place at 18.00,[40] which was when Anders Karlsson reported a 'certain submarine' close to the microphones. If Karlsson did turn off the tape recorder, he did so while doing the most important recording of his career – while the submarine was approaching the microphones at a distance of a few hundred metres. FOA was told by Emil Svensson that Karlsson had turned off the tape recorder 'because of lack of tape'. This explanation was later supported by Rear-Admiral Göran Wallén.[41]

Anders Karlsson, the sound expert from the submarine *Sjöhästen*, says that he tape-recorded the whole sequence with propeller sounds for about half an hour or maybe more, until the submarine disappeared. In any case it would have been absurd if he had turned off the tape recorder at this moment; it is clearly wrong to say he did. FOA never said that the 3.47-minute recording took place at 18.00. According to the FOA report, this sequence preceded Karlsson's first statement about 'probable submarine' ('at 17.50, it is strong – over the whole register. Conclusion: probable submarine') by at least 10 minutes. From the speaker-channel protocol it is not clear if this sequence actually took place several hours earlier, because the tape recorder has been stopped several times and, unlike on other recordings made by Rolf Andersson and Anders Karlsson, on this tape the time is not announced before the entries. The only statement of time before 17.50 is 09.45, and the only propeller sound that is reported before the squeaking and twittering sound of 16.30 is a sequence of 'about 2 minutes' at 13.38 reported in the Mälsten war diary.[42] This does not mean that the 3.47-minute sequence took place at 13.38, but the sequence had certainly nothing to do with what Anders Karlsson reported at 17.50 and 18.00. At this time, there was, according to FOA, nothing on the tape. There was nothing of interest after 17.50. The submarine sounds on the tape do not correspond to what Karlsson states on the speaker channel or reports in the war diaries.

After 17.50, there is a period of 26 minutes of 'empty tape' (FOA Tape 1) – nothing on the speaker channel and only waves and sea sounds on the other channels – at exactly the period when the submarine is believed to have passed the microphones. The speaker channel of the following tape (FOA Tape 2) from about 18.20 starts with Karlsson's commentary: 'Continued recording of submarine. About four minutes to change of tape.'[43] This commentary only makes sense if Karlsson had recorded the submarine on Tape 1 until the tape was finished. He now speaks about 'submarine' as he did in the war diary at 18.00, not about 'possible' or 'probable submarine', as he did from 17.50 to 17.52. So let us assume that the last 26 minutes of Tape 1 was used to record the submarine passing the microphones. The recording on Tape 2 would then have started at 18.20 (at 17.50 + 26 + 4 minutes). After 17 minutes and 45 seconds of this tape recording or, in other words, minutes before 18.40, the speaker channel on Tape 2 states: 'Helicopter has been in the area for about five minutes.' Just after 18.40, the speaker channel states: 'Very weak sounds from submarine. Possibly lying still.' Six minutes later, it states 'It has started again', but the sonar operator is soon disturbed by a heavy helicopter. At about 19.00, the speaker channel says: 'I cannot hear submarine any longer. Possibly single cavitation sounds.'[44]

If we assume that Karlsson was recording the submarine on the last 26 minutes of Tape 1, the helicopter would have been registered by the sonars at 18.35 or minutes before that. The naval base war diary states: 'at 18.28, [the arriving helicopter] Y69 and Mälsten have made contact with each other'. At 18.37, Y69 was given the position to go to [beyond microphone no. 5].[45] Mälsten war diary states at 18.30 or a few minutes later: 'the helicopter is arriving'.[46] In other words, at 18.35 (or a couple of minutes before that) the helicopter arrived at Mälsten, which means that Karlsson started Tape 2 at about 18.20, and finished the recording of submarine sounds on Tape 1 about 18.16. Karlsson must, accordingly, have been recording the submarine between 17.50 and 18.16 on Tape 1, and during this period he was able to identify the submarine as a 'certain submarine', which is also reported in the war diary at 18.00. The part of the tape recording covering the submarine passing the microphones has been erased and replaced with a recording of waves and sea sounds, or, alternatively, waves and other sounds from the sea have been kept on the tape, while all submarine sounds on these 26 minutes have been filtered away. And this cannot have been done by mistake at Mälsten, I was told by Rolf Andersson who set up the system, because unlike most tape recorders, the one that was used at Mälsten did not have a mechanism for erasing from the tape.

On Tape 2, the speaker channel states that the increased amplitude for the submarine sound was in the area of 80 Hz.[47] It was possible to follow the different amplitudes in real time at Mälsten. Karlsson describes the submarine sound maximum as being around 80 Hz. In the first report classifying this sound as 'submarine' (from the night of 12 October), Erland Sönnerstedt at the Defence Staff Security Division speaks about a submarine frequency, or increased amplitude, at 80–120 Hz (which also includes Tape 1). However, according to the FOA report of 20 October 1982 to the Naval Analysis Group, 'the announced increase of 80 Hz cannot be found on the tape'.[48] If this is true, someone must have edited both Tape 1 and Tape 2 either before they reached FOA or, perhaps, at FOA before Bengt Granath made his detailed protocol.

On 15 October 1982, two of the most senior Swedish submarine sound experts, Arne Åsklint of the Submarine Division, FMV, and Bertil Johnsson of the Anti-Submarine Warfare School were invited as experts to FOA to listen to the tape (according to Åsklint's notes). Åsklint said that the sound was to some extent similar to the Swedish submarine type Hajen (69 metres; two propellers). You could easily hear the hissing hydraulic sounds from the rudder movements, which are typical of a submarine. You could also hear the cavitation sounds and how the submarine stopped and started again, exactly as Karlsson had described it. The following day, Saturday 16 October, Commander Emil Svensson called Åsklint and asked for his conclusion. Åsklint said that it was clearly sounds from a submarine and one that was to some extent similar to a Swedish Hajen. Svensson was, according to Åsklint, very happy to hear his conclusion. On 30 January 1995, Åsklint and Rolf Andersson were at FOA to listen to what was alleged to be the same tape, the 3.47-minute sequence analysed by FOA in 1993–94. He was surprised. It was clearly not the same tape. None of the sounds Åsklint remembered from 1982 were found on the 1995 tape, he said. There were no rudder or hydraulic sounds on this tape. The cavitation sound on the 1995 tape was not that clear, and he could not tell what it was. The turns per minute were high. Only a scientific study at FOA could prove that it was a submarine. Åsklint had not listened to this tape in 1982. In addition, the new tape included a second propeller sound from a motorboat, which was not on the tape he had listened to in 1982. This was not the same tape, or at least not the same part of the tape that he had listened to before.

In 2001, Åsklint and Rolf Andersson listened to the so-called 'original tape'. There were no rudder or hydraulic sounds on that tape. Two representatives of FOA have confirmed Åsklint's reaction when he listened to the tape in 1995. One of them also confirmed that there were no rudder or hydraulic sounds either on the copy of the 3.47-minute tape FOA analysed in early 1990s, or on the so-called 'original tape' that includes the 3.47 minutes. Bengt Granath's report about the tape of 12 October (draft report written on 20 October 1982 for the Naval Analysis Group) speaks about 'propeller and hydraulic [rudder] sounds'.[49] The report is supposed to conclude the analysis made on 14–15 October by the submarine sound specialists Anders Karlsson, Arne Åsklint and Bertil Johnsson, and by the people from FOA, Bengt Granath and Per Schultz. The investigation of the tapes from Mälsten made in 2001 by Arne Åsklint and Chief of MUSAC,

Peter Gnipping, states: 'The rudder and hydraulic sounds reported by A. Åsklint have not been found on any tape.'[50] Today, although many sounds are still clear, the most important sounds registered by the report are no longer to be found on the so-called 'original tape'. All important information has been erased. There is no doubt that the tape has been edited.

When Chief of the Navy Vice-Admiral Dick Börjesson asked Svensson in the early 1990s if it was appropriate to send the tape of 12 October – the 3.47-minute sequence – to the Russians, Svensson reassured him that it was no problem. FOA was asked to analyse the tape, and they were supposed to provide the scientific support in the talks with the Russians. Svensson, at the time military adviser to Prime Minister Carl Bildt, wanted to convince the Russians that it was a Soviet submarine (see below), but the Russians were only willing to accept that it was a submarine if it could be proved that there had been no surface vessel in the area. And the statement that this had not been the case at 17.50 or 18.00 is no longer relevant, because the tape recording did not take place at this time. The 3.47-minute sequence might possibly have been recorded at 13.38, but this recording was, according to the war diary, weak and about two minutes long, which does not fit with the 3.47 minutes. Some transients were reported immediately after the propeller sound at 13.38 indicating that the tape recorder was not turned off during the recording. The only reported propeller sound with high turns per minute was recorded at 02.40 the following night.[51] The more or less constant cavitation and high turns per minute on the 3.47-minute sequence do not fit the description of the sound of the '18.00 submarine', but perhaps with the '02.40 submarine'. However, the only thing we know now is that the origin of this recording is not clear, and that it has nothing to do with the tape recording made by Anders Karlsson at about 18.00, which for some reason has disappeared.

Bengt Granath's report of 20 October 1982 states that the 12 October submarine (the 3.47-minute sequence) had high turns per minute: '190 rpm, probably smaller propeller'.[52] Later, Swedish MUSAC estimated the turns per minute at 192 rpm. A document from the Swedish–Russian talks states: 'about 200 rpm'.[53] The Russian hydro-acoustic centre argued that the turns per minute were 201 rpm and the submarine was believed to have one propeller with three blades.[54] These figures are very different from the estimates made by Karlsson at 18.00. He speaks in an attachment to the MAna Report from 14 October of '1–2 knots. Low turns per minute', which would mean less than 60 rpm.[55] After having listened to the tape on 15 October, Åsklint compared it to a Swedish Hajen that has 25–50 rpm at 1–2 knots, and he said that the 3.47-minute sequence (with 190–200 rpm) was not the same tape as he had listened to on

15 October 1982. In the report of 12 October, in the night shortly after the incident had taken place, Commander Erland Sönnerstedt, Chief of Defence Staff Security Division, speaks about low speed and low turns per minute: '30–40 rpm, large propeller and about 2 knots'.[56] All early reports speak about turns per minute that are lower than 60 rpm (perhaps lower than 40 rpm). The timetable in the Mälsten war diary clearly indicates a low speed – something that, from a tactical point of view, would have been necessary for a submarine in these waters. Anders Karlsson estimated the speed at 1–2 knots.[57] Sönnerstedt says in the report that the turns per minute exclude a Soviet submarine: 'To me, this indicates a submarine from the West.'[58]

A senior Norwegian intelligence officer has told me that the tape-recorded sound signature was analysed in Norway. Two Swedes from FOA appeared in Oslo with the tape immediately after the incident. The quality of the tape was not as high as it might have been, but the Norwegians found out that 'it was not a Soviet submarine' – or, more precisely, 'it was neither a conventional nor a nuclear Soviet submarine'. Another Norwegian intelligence officer involved in this analysis has stated that it was not a Soviet submarine, and he said that it was a Western submarine on the recording. He also indicated that it was a US submarine and that it had been damaged by a mine on 11 October. The Norwegian Underwater Division had a sound signature archive of all conventional and nuclear Soviet submarines. A senior member of the Norwegian Underwater Division research section told me that they were also able to identify some West German, French and British submarines, but did not have an 'organized archive' for these. The former senior intelligence officer told me that, despite having 'fingerprints', the sound signatures of the above submarines, the Norwegian experts were not able to identify the Mälsten submarine. They came to the conclusion that it might have been a Western submarine, but not one of the usual suspects. The Chief of the Underwater Division forwarded this analysis to the Norwegian Chief of Intelligence Rear-Admiral Jan Ingebrigtsen, who has confirmed in public that he helped the Swedes with the analysis of the tape. A fourth Norwegian intelligence source told that Norwegian Military Intelligence had copied the Swedish tape in 1982. However, some time later the Americans confiscated it. According to an agreement signed in the 1960s on information from the SOSUS systems between the USA, the United Kingdom and Norway, Norway should not have access to information on US and British submarines except when risk of collision might occur.[59] In other words, this agreement may be interpreted as if the Americans had the right to confiscate information on US submarines. The fact that the Americans did confiscate the Norwegian copy of the Mälsten tape indicates that this was a US submarine or at least a submarine participating in a US-commanded operation.[60]

One representative from FOA confirms that he was in Oslo with the tape and that the Norwegians were not able to identify the submarine, and that it was 'limping out'. The Norwegians also reported that they had had talks with Commander Emil Svensson. Despite the Norwegian experience of analysing submarine sound signatures, the Swedish naval leadership ignored the Norwegian information. A Swedish source has said to Anders Hasselbohm that the Norwegian personnel analysed the sound of the submarine and stated that the submarine originated from the West.[61] In spring 2000, Sweden declassified large parts of Captain Emil Svensson's report from the Swedish–Russian dialogue of 1992–94.[62] This report includes diagrams and an analysis of the tape of the above-mentioned submarine (Mälsten, 12 October 1982). Svensson argues that the submarine had two propellers and, because of this, was most likely a Soviet Whiskey-class submarine. The Russian side was not willing to accept these statements.[63] The Swedish material did not, according to the Norwegians, indicate a Whiskey-class submarine, a Norwegian senior intelligence officer told me. The Swedish Navy at the time had no ability to distinguish between individual submarine sounds. The Swedes had very little experience, and that is why they turned to the Norwegians in the first place, he said. In 2001, the Ekéus Investigation turned to the Norwegian government asking for a briefing from its now retired intelligence officers about what they had told the Swedes in 1982. However, according to the letter received by the investigation, the responsible (Defence Ministry) official vetoed this. The letter states 'Despite several attempts by the [Norwegian] Foreign Ministry to convince the officials responsible for Norwegian intelligence these officials have considered themselves unable to comply with our wishes, because of the sensitivity of this issue in relation to the USA.'

In a Naval Analysis Group attachment about this tape recording, the 12 October submarine is compared to the 14 October submarine. The report is written by Lieutenant-Commander Ebbe Sylvén, after he had interviewed Anders Karlsson at 23.30 on 14 October.[64] Karlsson had just been at FOA in Stockholm, where he had demonstrated the 14 October-tape to two representatives from FOA, Bengt Granath and Per Schultz and to Commander Anders Hammar from the Naval Analysis Group. In the afternoon, Karlsson went by helicopter to Stockholm. At 16.15, he arrived at FOA,[65] where he analysed the propeller sound, pointed out rudder movements and the cavitation sounds on the tape. The representatives from FOA had, at the time, no experience of submarine sounds. Karlsson demonstrated the damaged propeller shaft or blade, and how the submarine was moving by intervals to avoid being detected. He stayed with Granath and Schultz and discussed details with them for about three hours.[66] However, the report states that a subsequent analysis had also been made of the tape of 12 October, and that this analysis confirmed the classification already made at 18.00 on 12 October, which indicates that Karlsson or somebody else had listened to and analysed the tape already before this report was written. This statement is supported by a report for the Naval Analysis Group of the night of 12–13 October. In this report Commander Erland Sönnerstedt, Chief of Defence Staff Security Division, presents detailed information (including increased amplitude at 80–120 Hz and 30–40 turns per minute) from an analysis of the tape. This senior naval officer says the sound was classified as 'submarine'.[67] This seems to indicate that the tape was analysed at Mälsten, Berga or somewhere else already during the night. Now, 20 years afterwards, Sönnerstedt does not remember where he was on this occasion. In the first interviews I had with Anders Karlsson, he said that he had analysed the tapes and that two senior naval officers had participated. They made no comment during the presentation, Karlsson said. Commander Hammar confirms that he was present during the analysis of the tapes. In 2002, Rear-Admiral Göran Wallén stated that no officer participated in the sessions when the tapes were analysed, and the first analysis of the tapes were made later at FOA.[68] However, in the first report about the two tape recordings, made by Lieutenant-Commander Ebbe Sylvén for the Naval Analysis Group on 14 October, Karlsson states:

> The subsequent analysis made of the tapes recorded on 12–14 October shows that the classification 'submarine' ['certain submarine'] that was done on 12 and 13[–14] October is confirmed. C [Karlsson] says that propeller sounds, turns per minute and cavitation sounds are clearly heard on the tapes. The frequency is about 80 Hz. C [Karlsson] states that the tape-recorded sounds originate from two different submarines. The 12 October [Sylvén writes by mistake 13] submarine is very different from the one tape-recorded on 14 October. The sound of the former is richer, stronger and more distinct than the latter. Also, on 13[–14] October, it is possible to hear how the submarine starts up and moves and, when the helicopter arrives in the area, stops and hides on the sea floor. Then you can hear bumping and scraping sounds. It is also possible to hear sounds similar to the ones when you close a submarine hatch in a Swedish submarine [this is clearly about 14 October]. The submarine on 13[–14] October indicated/was heard [by the sonars] shortly after the mine barrage MS1 had reported the indication. This means, according to C [Karlsson], that the submarine was on its way out. When the sound came closer to the microphones, its effect was amplified, particularly in microphone no. 5. When the submarine was close to it, the effect was so strong in the microphone that C [Karlsson] got the impression that this microphone had been hit by the submarine.

The fuse for this microphone melted. It has not been possible to use the microphone since then. C [Karlsson] estimates that this submarine went towards the southeast. The tape also reveals a 'strange' sound. The conclusion made by C [Karlsson] is that this submarine has a damaged propeller shaft, or one of the blades is broken. Cavitation sounds are also heard. According to C [Karlsson], this indicates changes in the depth. C [Karlsson] concludes that the sounds are different from each other, and that there are two different submarines. He also concludes that the difference in force and 'heaviness' shows that the 12 October [Sylvén writes by mistake 13] submarine is larger than the 14 October submarine. The speed of both submarines is estimated at 1–2 knots. Low turns per minute.[69]

According to Karlsson's commentary on the speaker channel for the 13–14 October submarine, 'the submarine is going with five-six-seven-eight turns with the propeller and then it stops. He is possibly going very close to the sea floor.'[70] The submarine must have gone close to the sea floor, because it hit the microphone a metre above the sea floor or passed it at a distance of less than a metre. This may explain why even a small submarine may have created a very clear magnetic field. Karlsson says that the sound of this submarine indicated that it was a small vessel. Furthermore, a conventional submarine would most likely avoid going along the sea floor, while a small submersible has propeller shrouds to protect the propellers, which makes it able to creep along a rocky bottom. There are strong reasons to believe that this was a small submersible passing out. The sound of the so-called docking operation at 03.30 (and the closing of a submarine hatch) would, according to Anders Karlsson, indicate that this smaller 13–14 October submarine was received (close to microphone no. 4) by another larger submarine, most likely the one that earlier had been located in the area south of Grän, some kilometres southeast of Mälsten (see Chapter 3, 10–11 October). At midnight, during the night of 13–14 October, a helicopter had made contact with a submarine 2 kilometres south of Nåttarö, still southeast of Mälsten but now much closer and close to the position where the sea-floor investigation believed a docking operation may have taken place 100 metres south of microphones no. 4 and no. 5 (see below).

Karlsson argued in the report for the Naval Analysis Group that either a propeller blade or a propeller shaft was damaged on the small submersible. The Mälsten war diary and the Sylvén report also speak about a damaged propeller shaft. On 15 October, Arne Åsklint, the submarine sound expert at FMV, listened to this tape recording (as well as the 12 October tape) at FOA. He confirmed that this was a submarine, but he believed that the circular metal protection of the propeller

(propeller shroud) had possibly been hit and that a propeller blade was scraping this damaged cover. This conclusion was first drawn by submarine sound expert Bertil Johnsson of the Anti-Submarine Warfare School, said Åsklint. They both analysed this tape and made printouts on paper. Karlsson found this explanation reasonable; and it also supports Karlsson's hypothesis that the sounds were made by a small submersible because most of these smaller vessels have such a propeller shroud, while larger submarines usually do not. All these submarine sound experts have agreed with this explanation. In the first report about this tape (by Ebbe Sylvén for the Naval Analysis Group), Karlsson also states that the analysis made at FOA shows that the classification 'submarine' ['certain submarine'] that was done on 13–14 October is confirmed.

Bengt Granath's draft report of 20 October (for the Naval Analysis Group) states something different. It states that the analysis was made by the group of experts Anders Karlsson, Arne Åsklint and Bertil Johnsson. (Per Schultz and Bengt Granath describe themselves as newcomers when it comes to submarine sound analysis.) The report says that the tape has a rhythmic sound that can be heard for 23 minutes with a frequency of 177 rpm. However, 'the group of experts argues that these sounds have too fast an attack to originate from a propeller . . . The group does not rule out the possibility that the sounds are a symptom of an initial electronic dysfunction [in microphone no. 5].'[71] Karlsson and Åsklint have never seen this report and never agreed to it. They clearly have a different view, and both argue that it was a submarine, or rather a small submersible. The third expert, Bertil Johnsson, previously held the same view, but now denies having listened to the tape, and said he has listened to so many tapes that he does not remember. Commander Anders Hammar from the Naval Analysis Group was present during one session. He confirms Åsklint's and Karlsson's version. 'They clearly referred to a submarine with a damaged propeller. The report may state something different, but I did not write it', Hammar said. According to FOA, the argument about an electronic dysfunction was made by Rolf Andersson at FMV. Andersson, however, says that this is a total misunderstanding. Both Karlsson and Andersson say that the electronic problem in microphone no. 5 had nothing to do with the rhythmic scraping sound. FOA has seemingly misunderstood its experts. Granath says that they were in a hurry to make the report. He gave only a hand-written draft to the Naval Analysis Group. The report is dated 20 October, but it includes some observations from 25 and 28 October. It seems that it was Commander Emil Svensson who printed it out and added things he found of interest. Svensson's main report for the Naval Analysis Group concludes that there was no submarine: 'At 23.00, from

Mälsten: indication in the mine barrage and sound from the sonars. Conclusion: Tape is sent for analysis. Preliminary report: [cavi]tation sound not confirmed. Rhythmic thumping from unknown source. Conclusion: no submarine.'[72] For 14 October, the only reported indications that are included in the Naval Analysis Group's main report are: 'At 01.11, helicopter suspects sonar contact south of Mälsten. At 01.35, drop of depth charges.'

Despite a great amount of information from several sources pointing to a 'certain submarine', and despite the evidence mentioned above, Svensson denies any submarine passage, which is in line with the statements by Vice-Admiral Stefenson and Vice-Admiral Rudberg, who from eight o'clock on 14 October were already arguing that there was no submarine. At 13.45, the Defence Minister was informed that the sounds were electronic disturbances: the incident never took place.[74] In other words, this was stated before FOA received the tape for analysis, and, although the three submarine sound experts confirmed that the sound originated from a submarine, the FOA report on this issue concluded that it was 'electronic disturbances' similar to what had been reported to the Defence Minister already on 14 October. The same view has also been presented by Rear-Admiral Göran Wallén, who was the military expert for the Ekéus Investigation and a close associate of Bror Stefenson. Wallén states that there was no submarine passing out either east or west of Mälsten.[75] When Åsklint recently listened to the 'original tape' for the Ekéus Investigation, all the sounds of which he himself had made printouts were gone. Either these sounds had been removed from the tape or this part of the tape had been cut out. On one occasion, there is, according to Åsklint, a voice recorded on top of the original commentary (by Anders Karlsson), and when Karlsson says that the submarine is increasing speed, there is nothing on the tape. There is no correspondence between the sounds on the tape on the one hand and what is stated by Karlsson and by the war diaries on the other. Also this tape seems to have been edited. Sweden's crown jewels had been polished down to nothing.

Rolf Ekéus's report does not mention any of these irregularities despite the fact that he used Arne Åsklint as expert in the analyses of the tapes. The Ekéus Investigation also interviewed Anders Karlsson and Rolf Andersson. As an expert to the Ekéus Investigation, I introduced the three of them to Ambassador Ekéus, and we decided to use Åsklint and Andersson (Karlsson was not in Sweden at the time) to analyse the tapes, because of the discrepancy between the sounds registered by the early FOA report and the present 'original'. In October 1982, Bengt Granath had made a detailed 27-page protocol, and we wanted to compare this protocol with the present 'original'. Both

Andersson and Åsklint were perceived as trustworthy, and they had experience of these tapes from before. In May 2001, the new military expert of the Ekéus Investigation, Rear-Admiral Göran Wallén, took over the responsibility for carrying out this task. When I brought it up with him, he said it was not 'a high-priority issue'. However, he soon understood that Ekéus wanted to investigate this, and he took over the task. According to Åsklint, however, they never used Bengt Granath's 27-page protocol but a later protocol of three to four pages made by Bertil Johnsson. Although Granath had handed in his original detailed protocol to the investigation, Åsklint never saw it and never used it, he told me. Åsklint brought up the same points to Wallén as he had mentioned to me, but Wallén does not seem to have brought this information up to the investigation. And although Åsklint was supposed to be invited to further sessions to analyse the tapes in the autumn, he never heard anything more from Wallén. In the Ekéus Report it is stated that the 'Investigation has not found that the tapes have been manipulated'.[76]

THE PRINTS

Commander (later Vice-Admiral) Dick Börjesson was chief of the Navy's mobile mine-clearing division. He commanded a number of small boats with sonars and mine divers. In the first half of September 1982, this mobile force was deployed on the west coast of Sweden. Börjesson was ordered by Chief of the Navy Vice-Admiral Per Rudberg to go to Hårsfjärden. He arrived on 30 September, the day before the submarine hunt started. From 30 September, all of the mine divers of the Swedish fleet were concentrated in Hårsfjärden. On 10 October, while the submarine hunt was still going on, Vice-Admiral Rudberg put the mine divers at the disposal of Naval Base East.[77] Commander Börjesson was ordered to carry out an investigation of the sea floor. Börjesson had a team of divers placed at his disposal, headed by Chief of the First Diver Division Lieutenant Kent Pejdell. On 20 October, they found a number of parallel tracks while investigating the sea floor at Djupviken/Näsudden, close to where the submarine hunt had taken place on 5 October and where the *Belos* had seen parallel tracks and something on the bottom stirring up mud in the water on 7 October. These prints were believed to be no more than two to three weeks old. They were created in the first or possibly the second week of October exactly at the time of the submarine hunt in the area. In early November, these parallel tracks were already less clear. In early December, they were no longer visible. The caterpillar tracks with a mechanical ribbed pattern were recorded by a video camera. There were clear indications of a bottom-crawling submersible.[78]

In the report made by the sea-floor investigation for the Naval Analysis Group, it is stated that each track was 0.6 metres wide and that there was a distance of 0.5 metres between them, making a total width of less than 2 metres. The prints were clear, sometimes 0.4 metres in depth, with sharp vertical sides and an angle of 90 degrees between the sides and the bottom of the prints.[79] There is no doubt that these prints were created by a bottom-crawling vessel. According to Cato and Larsson's analysis, this submersible was able to avoid various obstacles like oil drums.[80] Lieutenant Pejdell said that it had turned right to avoid a large stone, then turned left again and finally continued along the original track. The submersible seems to have been able to look forward and to navigate on the sea floor. The Soviets are believed to have a couple of bottom-crawling submersibles leaving caterpillar tracks on the sea floor. However, the dimensions of these are supposedly different, and they may rather originate from a vessel belonging to the Italian naval special forces COMSUBIN (see below), which are working closely together with the US Navy SEALs. According to the sea-floor investigation, there were similar tracks at Märsgarn, not far from Näsudden, and prints from the keel of another midget submarine at Huvudholmen-Alvsta Långholmar at the northern exit of Hårsfjärden.[81] After having looked at the video films, Cato and Larsson found these latter tracks less clear and would not rule out the possibility that a buoy-stone had been dragged along the sea floor.[82]

The sea-floor investigation for the Naval Analysis Group is also very detailed when describing the second print. The approximately 0.5-metre-wide keel was composed of two runners creating a characteristic profile of the letter 'u' turned upside down. On each side of the 'keel', the submarine left a pattern from propellers indicating two propellers with an estimated diameter of 0.5 metres with an estimated distance of 2.5 metres.[83] Of course, the estimates may be approximate, but the details of the 'keel profile' indicate that Cato and Larsson were not given access to this information, or to any photo or video film confirming this information. Several Western submersibles have this kind of 'keel' with propellers on each side. The *Deep Quest* (12 metres; two propellers), formally owned by Lockheed but, in the 1980s, used by the US Navy and the CIA in connection with special force operations, has two propellers and runners but the distance between them is too large.[84] A smaller relative to the *Deep Quest* is the *Beaver* (8 metres; two plus one propellers) from 1968 (retired in 1985).[85] Both the keel and the distance between the lower propellers are a bit too large to fit the measurements made at Huvudholmen.[86] Other US submersibles and the Italian midget 3GST9 (10 metres; two propellers) also have a keel and double propellers similar to the Huvudholmen prints. The *Taurus* (10 metres; two propellers) used by the Royal Navy for rescue operations and for setting out divers has the same distance between the propellers and has runners that can be modified to fit the keel profile of the Huvudholmen submersible. Corresponding Soviet/Russian submersibles like the *Sever 2* and others, or special force vessels like the Triton, have neither two propellers nor an external keel or runners.[87] All wet SDVs – Soviet, US, British, Italian, French – have one propeller (except for the US MK IX with two propellers).[88] US submersibles like the *Sea Cliff* and the *Turtle* have a large central propeller plus two smaller propellers (with a distance of about 2.5 metres). It is unlikely that these submersibles would operate without using the central propeller. Also, the distance between the runners is too large and they are too small to penetrate deep into the bottom and to create a pattern of a 'keel'. Their prints would not fit with the prints at Huvudholmen. Still, one of the above-mentioned submersibles may have been involved in the Hårsfjärden operation. This submersible entered Hårsfjärden through the very shallow passage between Alvsta-Långholmar and Huvudholmen and later left the same way perhaps on 8–9 October, when there were a lot of scraping sounds registered by the Swedish submarine *Sjöhunden*.[89] There was no net covering this passage, because it was believed to be too shallow for a submarine.

After having observed a periscope and something stirring up mud in the water on the surface on 6 November, the divers found parallel tracks in Varnäsfjärden in northern Mysingen similar to the ones found at Näsudden some weeks earlier, and, after that, similar tracks were found in Danziger Gatt, close to Mälsten. These prints were less clear than the ones found at Näsudden, because the sea floor is very muddy and soft in Varnäsfjärden and, in Danziger Gatt, the prints were found much later and were already pretty old. The general pattern, however, was the same. In Danziger Gatt, in the middle of these parallel tracks, there seemed to be a print from the 'keel' of a possible conventional submarine, as well as prints similar to the ones found at Huvudholmen-Alvsta Långholmar.[90] In the sea-floor investigation for the Naval Analysis Group, it is stated that the large print from a 'keel' is 60 metres long,[91] indicating that this may have been a conventional submarine less than 100 metres in length and possibly considerably so, because it may have moved along the sea floor. It was believed to have been a docking operation with a small submersible and a mother-sub. Both the prints from a possible keel and the narrow parallel prints from a bottom-crawling submersible were found 100–200 metres south of microphones no. 4 and no. 5, northeast of Norrgrund exactly in the area where the sonar operator Anders

Karlsson had heard sounds from a closing hatch on 14 October and believed that a docking operation had taken place. There were also parallel tracks with a length of more than 100 metres along the microphone line, between these two microphones.[92]

When I interviewed Vice-Admiral Börjesson during 2000, he said that they had not found anything on the western side of Mälsten. They had only investigated the sea floor on the eastern side. When I told him about the reported steel plates southwest of Måsknuv (west of Mälsten), he was surprised and said that that nobody had told him anything about that either before or after their investigation. He thought it was remarkable that, as head of the sea-floor investigation, he wasn't informed about this beforehand. What happened with these reported steel plates is still unclear. There is, however, no doubt that a small tracked submersible operated at Näsudden, and most likely at Varnäsfjärden and at Mälsten.[93]

From the first and second Submarine Commission Reports, one gets the impression that the sea-floor investigation had covered large areas, and that these parallel tracks revealing a bottom-crawling submersible had been found at three or four locations. One gets the impression that Hårsfjärden as a whole must have been covered, along with almost all or at least large parts of the Mysingen-Mälsten area. This is not the case. Except for Hårsfjärden and the Näsudden case, Börjesson and Pejdell were told where to look. They only investigated a couple of small spots outside Hårsfjärden (Varnäsfjärden, the Älvsnabben area and in Danziger Gatt, including Norrgrund, Klövskär and Nåttarö canal). Varnäsfjärden, Klövskär and Nåttarö canal were investigated because of new submarine indications: on 26 October, six indicating mines plus propeller sound in Danziger Gatt; on 29 October, propeller sound and a moving buoy in Nåttarö canal; and on 6 November, periscope and mud in the water in Varnäsfjärden in northern Mysingen.[94] In two of these areas (Varnäsfjärden and Danziger Gatt/Norrgrund), they found parallel tracks from a bottom-crawling submersible.

The place that was investigated southeast of Mälsten, northeast of Norrgrund, was marked with a buoy, Pejdell said. According to the Naval Analysis Group Report, there had been an acoustic indication in late November in the bottom-fixed sonars at Mälsten from what was believed to be a transponder that had transmitted short bursts of high-frequency signals. This had provoked the investigation just south of the microphones.[95] A believed sub-surface transponder, a navigation aid for submarines, had been sending from a certain position 100 metres south of microphone nos 4 and 5, and that position had been located by FMV through mathematical analysis. A submersible docking on another submarine would have needed a transponder to find the exact position, and this place coincided with where the different submarine prints had been found and where the sound from a docking operation on 14 October had been registered.

On 5 December, Dick Börjesson, as commanding officer, Kent Pejdell with a couple of divers, and Rolf Andersson from FMV went out in a small boat to the position given by FMV. An unknown buoy was marking this very position. The whole operation was very secret, even for the people involved. When the divers went down with a Geiger counter, Börjesson wanted to know what was going on. Pejdell then told him that they were looking for a transponder that might have a nuclear source. General Ljung writes that Chief of the Navy Vice-Admiral Rudberg had informed him the following day that they had found what they believed was a transponder. 'This instrument was going to be brought up today or tomorrow,' he adds. Ljung writes that it might be possible to identify the national origin of the object. 'This issue might be very sensitive politically,' he says and continues: 'Together with the Chief of the Navy, I will request a meeting with the Prime Minister to brief him about the issue.'[96] A week later, on 14 December, Prime Minister Palme was informed by General Ljung that they had found parallel tracks on the sea floor and some kind of 'metal object [not yet brought up from the bottom] that might give further information. However, there is still no information about the nationality.'[97]

The alleged transponder, a 30- (or 40-) centimetre-long cylindrical object attached to a square plate was videotaped and a drawing was made.[98] On the drawing, it is stated '40 cm', which seems to refer to the length of the object but it may refer to the width of the plate. The cylindrical object looks to some extent like a thermos, but 5–10 centimetres at each end of the cylindrical object has a smaller diameter. The square plate was supposedly heavy, and the diver was not able to lift it from the bottom. The divers were then ordered not to do anything, because it was believed that it might have contained explosives that would detonate if the object were moved. Commander Börjesson, the head of the sea-floor investigation, says that he was never informed about the significance of the object: 'It was never brought up, at least not by us.' Andersson knew even less. He says that he and his superior, Director Sten Wibeus, went to brief Vice-Admiral Rudberg. They reported that they had found nothing – no sub-surface transponder – at the given position. However, Rudberg told them that they did not have to feel sorry about that, because at this very place – 100–200 metres south of microphone nos 4 and 5, far out at sea, more than a kilometre southeast of Mälsten – the divers had found two-month-old prints from a tracked submersible, something the divers had not told Andersson while the operation was being carried out. Börjesson says that he was responsible for not telling Andersson about the prints, but he was never informed that the divers had found an object that could possibly indicate nationality. The Ekéus Report states that the cylindrical object was brought up and turned out to be an artillery shell, while the signals supposedly originated from an electrical power cable at Mälsten, something that has been underlined by Ekéus's military expert Rear-Admiral Göran Wallén. The latter states that after an electrical transformer had been installed the signals disappeared.[99] However, the drawing made certainly did not indicate an artillery shell, and, if it were, why would it be attached to a square plate? And electrical power cables cannot transmit such high-frequency signals, Andersson told me. And if there was no transponder sending the high-frequency signals, how was it possible to locate a position – more than 1 kilometre out at sea – where the divers were able to find prints from three different submarines. Ambassador Ekéus was not correctly informed.

The three men in the boat knew nothing about one another's activity. The sea-floor investigation raises more questions than it answers. The prints were found where the investigators were told to look. And neither Börjesson nor Pejdell had ever heard any report of possible steel plates or a damaged submarine at Måsknuv. The position of these metal objects was, according to the Mälsten report and drawing, about 100 metres south-southwest of Måsknuv. This position is identical to the position where the yellow/green dye appeared more than one hour after the mine explosion on 11 October. It was from this area that the submarine was 'limping out', according to the analysis of the 12 October tape recording. The position of the docking operation on 14 October, as presented by the sonar operator, is also identical to the position given by the analysis of the transponder signals. At this position the sea-floor investigation found prints on the bottom indicating submarines as well as a docking operation. Physical evidence including drawings of the yellow/green patch, the tape-recorded sounds and the prints on the sea floor all coincide and point to several submarines or submersibles.

THE SUBS

The more one studies the submarine hunt of October 1982, the more question marks one finds. But at the same time, there are also question marks that can be erased. There is a large amount of evidence and indications that point to submarine activities in the Stockholm archipelago. In every submarine hunt you will have a number of false indications, but in this case there is no doubt. There were several visual sightings made by civilians and military officers of submarine sails and periscopes just a few metres away from them; sonar echoes indicating distance from the sea floor as well as length (5–10 metres and 35–40 metres) of submarines; a number of Doppler indications of a moving sub-surface object; registered speeds of submarines (1–2 knots, 5–6 knots, 8 knots, 10 knots and 15 knots); submarines with attached Malin signal transmitters moving more than 1 kilometre (something a Malin could not do by itself); several IR contacts; forceful air boil-ups and continuously moving oil spills; parallel caterpillar tracks on the sea floor from a bottom-crawling submersible; damaged submarine nets that had to be replaced after personnel had clear submarine indications close to the nets; tape-recorded sounds of submarine propellers (including one submarine with a damaged propeller); a maximum signal in a bottom-fixed sonar that made the fuse melt and microphone die when the position of a submarine was 'close to the microphone'; magnetic indications in the mine barrages simultaneous with sonar echoes and tape-recorded propeller sounds; a yellow/green dye released from a damaged submarine; tape-recorded repair works on the same submarine; and reported visual sightings of damaged submarines – all this points to several certain submarines operating in the Stockholm archipelago in October 1982.

However, while this dramatic submarine hunt was going on, all intelligence briefings (on 9, 11, 15 and 22 October) speak of low activity within the Soviet Baltic Fleet – that is, no particular state of readiness. Ships would participate in the celebration of the Soviet Constitution Day, but nothing can be linked to the activities in the Swedish archipelago. Even though two, perhaps three, submarines may have been damaged, the Soviets did not seem to care. And why should officers with very close ties to the Royal Navy and the US Navy release Soviet submarines? All these incidents are much easier to explain if we think in terms of Western, perhaps even US, submarines. Ulf Adelsohn, Chairman of the Conservative Party, writes that he and Carl Bildt were briefed by Prime Minister Olof Palme just after these incidents in October 1982:

> [Palme said that the Navy had had contact with a] 'certain submarine'. It was possibly here to assist another submarine that had been seriously damaged [in Swedish, 'havererad']. When I asked him if they had orders to sink [to kill], he said that 'there are no restrictions'.[100]

This was the information the Prime Minister gave to the opposition leader immediately after the incident had taken place. Palme allegedly stated that two submarines (including one damaged submarine) probably had operated together.

If we look at each serious submarine observation presented in Chapter 3, we get a general hypothesis about which observations refer to one and the same submarine. This gives us a possible scenario with, for example, six submarines, including three small submersibles.

The *first* submarine was observed on 26 September a few metres from the US cruiser *Belknap* and frigate *Elmer Montgomery* between Stadsgården and Kastellholmen, in the very centre of Stockholm. Witnesses had seen a small, silver-coloured periscope, which most likely belonged to a US submersible patrolling the US ships. Commander-in-Chief General Ljung spoke about a link between this submarine and the US ships. The small submersible had probably been dumped in Stockholm harbour by the US depot ship *Monongahela* at Skeppsholmen 200–300 metres from the other ships. At lunchtime on 29 September, two days after the US ships had left Stockholm for an exercise southeast of Gotland, the 'top' of a 1.5-metre-wide submarine sail was seen further out in Stockholm harbour, probably belonging to the same 'US submersible'. On the evening of 29 September, it was stated that an exercise was scheduled for the coming morning. During the following night, Operation NOTVARP started. At 22.00, forces were deployed at Oxdjupet, seemingly waiting for an approaching submarine. Special forces were brought in by helicopter to seize a submarine. About 01.00 on 30 September, the periscope of a small submarine was followed on radar by a police boat for 'a long time' in Stockholm harbour, close to the earlier observation. This was reported by the Chief of Staff to the Commander-in-Chief at 02.00. There were several indications of a small submersible or midget submarine on its way out from Stockholm and heading for the open sea. At five o'clock in the morning, there was a clear magnetic indication at the choke point at Oxdjupet, which actually started the real hunt. Later, there were indications from Kanholmsfjärden further out. There were supposedly indications of a docking operation in this area. The 1983 Submarine Defence Commission believed that this midget then entered its mother-sub in the Kanholmsfjärden-Sandhamn area. There were no indications of a submarine on its way into Stockholm. The final preparations for the hunt (or what the naval base war diary calls an 'exercise') were made hours before the first confirmed observation of a submarine, as though an escape operation with a midget was part of the exercise. Let us assume that this midget was the *Turtle*, the only small US submersible that received an award for bravery in espionage in 1982, or more exactly for an operation from 30 August to 5 November 1982. This period fits exactly with the operation in the Stockholm archipelago. According to one Navy Intelligence source, this operation took place in Scandinavian waters. The small, dark, 1.5-metre-wide submarine sail seen at Lidingö on 29 September fits well with the US *Turtle* or *Sea Cliff*. Furthermore, the *Turtle* has spotlights, which fits with the observation of light under the water

155

close to Muskö Naval Base on 5 October. This would imply that the larger mother-sub would have carried the *Turtle* from the Kanholmsfjärden-Sandhamn area and delivered it to the area of Hårsfjärden-Mysingen before the Mälsten mine barrages were activated on 6 October – most likely on 3 October, when a small submersible seems to have entered Hårsfjärden, or rather Mälbyfjärden, at Södra Skramsösund. This small submersible would then have participated in the operations in the southern area around Muskö Naval Base with several indications from 3 to 7 October with observations of whirlpools, oil patches, magnetic indications, light under the water and an antenna seen close to the retired and empty destroyer *Hälsingland*. Other indications from the destroyer indicate that it may have been used as a 'base', and that this small submersible may have been hiding under the destroyer. After that, it may have left for Mysingen. If this submersible was received by its mother-sub in Mysingen or outside Mälsten is not clear. On 7 October, there is a report from Sandhamn-Korsö about a top of a 1.5- to 2-metre sail indicating that the Sandhamn submersible may have been different from the Muskö submersible. However, the estimated 'high' speed of the former may rather point to another submarine. This small US submersible may have been transported from Swedish waters either by a larger submarine or by a modified civilian tanker (see below).

The *second* submarine was indicated on 29 September at Sandhamn-Korsö and on the following day in Kanholmsfjärden in the same area. This submarine was first believed to have been a West German submarine because of a radar indication. There were also some indications from Kanholmsfjärden on 1 October. The 1983 Submarine Defence Commission believed that this submarine was the mother-sub to the small submersible described above. Of course, there is no evidence for this, but this submersible must have been brought away from the area by some kind of larger vessel, and there is no indication of any other candidate. Furthermore, there was a possible docking operation, with the midget being attached to the mother-sub in Kanholmsfjärden at this very time. This would indicate that the larger 'Sandhamn submarine' was also American, for example USS *Seawolf*, which has operated as mother-sub for the *Turtle*. On the evening of 4 October, there were several observations of and indications from a submarine at Sandhamn, which was possibly the same submarine as the former one (which might have returned having first delivered the small submersible to the Hårsfjärden area). Various reports described this submarine as a 'certain submarine'. A 'large wall', a very high submarine sail, was seen passing at a high speed (15 knots) with 'diesel engines' for five minutes, for a while at close range. The sail was estimated to be up to 10 metres high and 'higher than it was wide'. This may be an exaggeration, but under no circumstances does it fit with any Soviet submarine, which all would have a relatively flat sail. We should rather look at the British Oberon class or various US diesel submarines. However, if we put emphasis on the high sail, we have to look at nuclear submarines like the British *Dreadnought* or perhaps the relatively noisy USS *Seawolf*. The 'Sandhamn submarine' does not easily fit with the submarine in Hårsfjärden on 1 October, nor with the observation of a conventional submarine at the northern passage out from Hårsfjärden on 7–8 October. After 1 October and most likely on 3 October, the 'Sandhamn submarine' may have delivered its small submersible into the Mysingen/Hårsfjärden area and then, after a short return trip to Sandhamn, gone down to the southern exit of Mysingen, to the area south of the island of Grän, a few kilometres southeast of Mälsten, where there were several submarine indications on 10–11 October before the exit of the other submarines. This first Mälsten submarine was seemingly 'parked' at the exit of Mysingen – possibly to help another submarine in trouble or more likely to receive a small submersible or midget, which passed out on 13–14 October. The report of a submarine south of Nåttarö around midnight on 13–14 October indicates that this submarine waited for its midget in the area where a docking operation was later supposed to have taken place. The alleged print of a keel on the sea floor at Mälsten may indicate that this submarine was a British Oberon-class submarine, or possibly a US or Italian Tang-class submarine or the US *Seawolf*. The print of a 'keel' of a small submersible (see the sixth submarine) in the same area may also indicate a docking operation. The submarine southeast of Mälsten has been described by a senior Swedish officer as a 'NATO submarine', though not a West German one and accordingly most probably a US or British submarine. If this submarine was the mother-sub of the above-mentioned small submersible, it was also most likely a US or possibly a British submarine.

The *third* submarine entered Hårsfjärden at noon on 1 October. The periscope and mast were seen heading west for a minute and then turning southwards. This submarine first announced its presence and then left Hårsfjärden, probably in the same way and on the same day as it entered. It is in all reports described as a 'certain submarine'. Let us assume that this submarine later made an excursion up to Dalarö, where a submarine surfaced in the morning of 4 October, perhaps to test the northern exit of Mysingen. It then went back to Mysingen, where it 'parked' outside the approaches to Hårsfjärden. This would have been the same submarine that seems to have appeared in this area on 6 October. After the submarine nets had moved more than 100 metres at lunchtime on 7 October, a contact was made with this submarine outside the nets (in Mysingen), and soon afterwards it was possibly lightly damaged by the drop of six heavy depth charges northeast of Bergholmen. An oil patch appeared. A Malin was dropped and later located northwest of Bergholmen. According to the naval base war diary, a helicopter was hovering over it for 40 minutes before a ceasefire was ordered. On 8 October, there were a lot of knocking sounds that might have originated from repair works from the same area. This submarine may later have passed through the narrow waters at Dalarö or along Ornö Strömmar in the night of 8–9 October, which would indicate a small vessel. On the following day, this submarine would have continued northwards, giving rise to periscope/mast indications in Jungfrufjärden, and a submarine sail at Nämdö going towards Bullerön further out. The ceasefire and the behaviour of the submarine (announcing its presence on 1, 4 and 9 October) seem to indicate a Western submarine. The 'Dalarö submarine' supposedly had 'square objects' (perhaps Strazza Navigation active sonars for narrow waters) on top of its hull, which might indicate a small Italian submarine. According to the drawing made by the observer this submarine had a high mast at the very end of the sail or rather behind the sail, which only fits with the Italian Cosmos, most likely Cosmos SX 756-W. The estimated length, about 25 metres, and the distance between the mast and the periscope (1–1.5 metres) also fits with this submarine. The high mast and the small narrow sail seen from behind on 9 October may also indicate a Cosmos SX 756-W. The size of Cosmos also fits these narrow and shallow waters (10–12 metres at Dalarö and less than 10 metres at Ornö Strömmar). According to *Jane's Fighting Ships*, no Soviet submarine at the time had such a mast and these kinds of 'objects' on top of its hull. Soviet submarines are also rather large for these narrow waters.

The *fourth* submarine was a small conventional-size submarine or mini-submarine, which points to an Italian, US or possibly West German submarine. The fact that the signal transmitter Malin attached to the submarine may exclude a West German submarine, even though its radar was first believed to have been West German. It may have been this small submarine that allegedly was seen surfaced late at night on 30 September south of Södra Skramsösund and then entered at the narrow southern passage to Muskö and Hårsfjärden at dusk on 1 October. Let us assume that this was the same submarine that was hunted on 4 October, observed late at night on 4 October and, possibly after having been lightly damaged on 5 October, sent up a green dye to the surface at Käringholmen, a few hundred metres from the place of the submarine hunt. It seems to have operated primarily in southern Hårsfjärden up to Näsudden (north of the area of operation for the *Turtle*). The green dye indicates that this was a Western submarine under US command. On 5

October, the length of the submarine was measured with an echo ranger. The estimated length of 35–40 metres was close to the length of the US mini-submarine *NR-1*. This may have been the same submarine that, on the afternoon of 7 October, showed its 3- to 4-metre dark square sail with small objects on top – according to the naval base war diary with 'something white on the sail' – at the exit of Hårsfjärden. All this information fits well with the *NR-1*. This submarine may then have left Hårsfjärden at 20.30 the same evening. One hour later, the helicopter *Y72* reported Doppler and an estimated speed of 8 knots. However, the time and positions given by the war diary indicate a speed of 6 knots. But, according to a former *NR-1* officer, even 6 knots is high or too high for this vessel. On the night of 7–8 October, this submarine was followed by Swedish anti-submarine forces from the exit of Hårsfjärden. It passed Norrhäll and Mysingsholm towards Östra Röko in southern Mysingen. The Swedish fast attack craft *Väktaren* had a clear contact at 23.00, but at this very moment the submarine was saved by a ceasefire. It may have been this or possibly another submarine (seen close to the mine barrages on 7 October) that was 'parked' at Östra Röko-Örngrund on the night of 10–11 October, seemingly preparing to pass out from Mysingen at Mälsten. It may also have been this submarine that, at lunchtime on 11 October, was damaged by a mine, perhaps seriously, while trying to pass out at Mälsten. The magnetic indication was constant for 10 seconds despite being turned off twice, which suggests a relatively demagnetized submarine. One hour after this incident, the submarine sent up a yellow/green dye 100–150 metres from the place of the explosion, which also indicates a submarine under US command. Reported steel plates were found at the same position as the yellow/green dye appeared. This submarine was most likely repaired on the sea floor somewhere southwest of Mälsten during the following night. It left Mälsten, and possibly also Swedish waters, on the evening of 12 October. Both the repair work and the propeller sound were tape-recorded. The first two reports spoke about low turns per minute (below 60 rpm; one report states 30–40 rpm). The later FOA analysis (190–200 rpm) refers to a sequence not known by the operator. According to Norwegian Military Intelligence, the propeller sound indicated a Western, possibly a US, submarine. The fact that both tapes have since been edited and significant sequences removed indicates a Western submarine. The fact that the Americans confiscated the Norwegian copy of the tape indicates a US submarine or at least a US operation. The yellow/green dye indicates a Western, probably a US, submarine. The narrow estimated length of the submarine and the sail indicates the US *NR-1*. Afterwards, there were several statements from senior officials about a damaged US submarine and also about *NR-1* participating in this operation (see below). However, these statements may refer to two different submarines.

The *fifth* submarine is the small submersible that left tracked marks on the sea floor. On the morning of 29 September, the destroyer *Halland* saw a small, round object in the water at the southern entrance of Hårsfjärden. Soon afterwards, something seems to have passed the magnetic sensor cable at Södra Skramsösund. The Submarine Defence Commission speaks about an observation on 1 October at Näsudden. On 5 October, *464* reported an area of mud in the water as well as a small round object, a 'black hill', the top of a ball visible above the surface northeast of Näsudden, close to where the submarine hunt had taken place. This was not a submarine sail, but rather the top of a small submersible. It was soon afterwards attacked with a depth charge, and it may have been damaged. On 7 October, the *Belos*'s remote-controlled video camera saw parallel tracks that led to something that was stirring up mud from the sea floor. When the divers checked the area on 20 October, they found parallel caterpillar tracks on the sea floor from a small, bottom-crawling submersible. The total width of the tracks was less than 2 metres, and the width of each of the two tracks was 0.6 metres. Both Submarine Commissions and the Defence Staff describe this as a 'certain submarine'. The prints were clear and fresh, and they most likely originated from the first week of October, from the time of the submarine hunt in the area. This vessel seems to have operated in northern Hårsfjärden, between Näsudden and Märsgarn and further north. On 6 October, the naval base war diary records a 5- to 10-metre-long echo at Märsgarn at a depth of 11 metres. In the following days, there were a number of observations of a small submersible in this area. Similar parallel tracks at Märsgarn under the retired and empty destroyer *Småland* made intelligence personnel at the naval base believe that it had been hiding under the destroyer to avoid the echo sounders of boats covering the area. Similar to the submersible that was operating close to the naval base, which may have used the retired destroyer *Hälsingland* as a 'base', this submersible may have used *Småland*. Tracked marks on the sea floor were later also found in Varnäsfjärden (after indications on 6 November), and after that at Mälsten. This indicates that this submersible stayed in the area for a longer period of time or was transported back to the area. The prints at Mälsten may indicate that this submersible also passed out through the southern exit of Mysingen. This submersible was supposedly operating together with other submarines, which indicates a Western submarine. The analysis made by Swedish Defence Staff described it as a 'certain submarine' and pointed to the Soviet Union, because it was unlikely that such a submersible would have been possible to keep secret in the West.[101] However, the Italian naval special forces COMSUBIN has had such a 'toad', a small bottom-crawling submersible that leaves tracked prints similar to the ones found in Hårsfjärden. This submersible is carried by a civilian vessel. It may have been this submersible that operated in the Stockholm archipelago. The Italians may have sold one or more of these craft to another Western navy. There are reports stating that the Soviets had similar vessels, but I have not had this confirmed. Prints found in northern Norway from what was believed to be a Soviet bottom-crawling submersible had very different dimensions (see below).

The *sixth* submarine is a small submersible that left 'keel' prints or prints from parallel runners on the sea floor between Alvsta Långholmar and Huvudholmen at a depth of less than 10 metres. This might indicate a small US submersible. The width of the 'keel' and the estimated diameter of the propellers (0.5 metres) as well as the distance between the two propellers (2.5 metres) fit with certain US submersibles. However, there are also a couple of other Western submersibles with a similar 'keel' and double propellers (see below).[102] No Soviet submersible has, to my knowledge, such characteristics. This small submersible may have operated in northern Hårsfjärden, north of the area of the former vessel. Some of the small privately owned US submersibles were used by the CIA in connection with special forces operations. One or two of them may have been brought to Swedish waters and to central Stockholm by the *Monongahela*, and then exercised an escape operation out from Stockholm, which would explain the indication at Oxdjupet at both 05.00 and 14.00 on 30 September. After that they would have been transported to the Hårsfjärden area by most likely a larger submarine. The 'keel' prints between Alvsta Långholmar and Huvudholmen might have been created at the passage on the evening of 8 October, when the Swedish submarine *Sjöhunden* reported a lot of scraping sounds at Alvsta Långholmar, or at 23.45 on 9 October, when there was another indication of a passage out to Mysingen. This small submersible would then have left Mysingen at Mälsten, for example on 13–14 October. If we believe the sea-floor investigation, similar prints of a 'keel' south of the microphones may indicate that this submersible was docking to a larger submarine in this area on 14 October. This would mean that this submersible was the same as the one that left Mysingen at Danziger Gatt and passed the mine barrage at Mälsten at 23.00 on 13 October during a five-hour ceasefire. Submarine sound expert Anders Karlsson at Mälsten describes this submarine as a small vessel, a midget. The propeller, or rather the propeller shroud, something that most small submersibles have, was believed to be damaged. This submersible hit microphone no. 5 or passed it at a range of 1 metre, which indicates that it went very close to the bottom, which would presuppose that it was a small submersible having a propeller shroud like most US submersibles have. A couple of hours later, there were indications that this submersible was once again received by its mother-sub, the larger submarine, which had been 'parked' a few kilometres southeast of Mälsten since 10 October and now approached Mälsten. Both the propeller sound and sounds from a possible docking operation were tape-recorded. Divers found indications of a possible docking operation south of microphone nos 4 and 5, more than 1 kilometre southeast of Mälsten. The passage exactly at 23.00 indicates that the small submersible was ordered to pass at a certain hour within a given time window. This clearly points to a Western submarine. If it was a US submersible, the ceasefire is easy to explain.

Almost all indications – and even all available evidence – point to Western submarines. One or two of these submarines may possibly have been Soviet submarines, but indications pointing in this direction are weak. Several submarines seem to have demonstrated their presence by showing periscopes or submarine sails to the public at close range in a relatively densely populated area, and more important within the area of the naval base, as though they wanted to be seen. To operate on the surface in this way was not necessary at all. It is difficult to believe that these were Soviet submarines. Some sources have pointed to Soviet arrogance, but this does not fit with other information. It rather seems to have been a US or US/UK operation in cooperation with Italian naval special forces to give the Swedes some 'subs to play with', to trigger the anti-submarine warfare operation to test 'Swedish capability and will' – words actually used by Vice-Admiral Bror Stefenson in his first briefing to the Prime Minister after the submarine hunt.[103]

From conversations with submarine captains, it appears that there is no operational rationale for going into such narrow waters with several submarines. Usually, one may travel with two submarines operating in tandem, so that one can attract the attention of foreign anti-submarine warfare forces if the other gets into trouble. In these cases, however, one would have one submarine 'park' outside narrow waters, exactly as was done with the submarine 'parked' outside the exit of Hårsfjärden (see 1–7 October) or at Mälsten outside the exit of Mysingen (see 10–11 October). Several naval officers have told me that it is not possible that, for example, a British, Italian or German submarine could operate without US knowledge. It is always necessary to coordinate with the US Navy wherever one is going. This operation with several submarines would have been coordinated at Northwood, outside London, by the British COMSUBEASTLANT (Commander Submarines Eastern Atlantic) and his US deputy. Under no circumstances would this have been a conventional espionage operation – neither a Soviet nor a US/UK one – because one would never enter such narrow waters with several submarines. It may have been an exercise to train coordination in narrow, shallow waters, to train E&E (Evasion and Escape) networks or to 'test Swedish capability and will', but primarily it must have been a political operation to let the Swedes have some 'subs to play with'.

THE ACTORS

The submarine damaged by a mine at Mälsten on 11 October sent up a yellow/green dye about an hour after the explosion. Although the analysis of the yellow/green dye excluded mud from the sea floor, this was mentioned neither in Emil Svensson's Naval Analysis Group Report nor in the Submarine Defence Commission Report with Bror Stefenson as its military expert. The yellow/green dye was described as mud from the sea floor. In official material as well as in secret summaries the existence of both a dye and a damaged submarine has been filtered away. All sonar information on a damaged submarine at Mälsten on 11–12 October (including evidence of metallic hammering, knocking sounds and high-frequency sounds seemingly originating from a cutting tool) has been filtered away from the tape recording and from the report of the Submarine Defence Commission. When Stefenson was presented with Brigadier-General Hansson's report from the submarine sound expert, Stefenson said that 'it could be anything'. When the submarine sound signature was recorded by the Navy, Stefenson went to Vice-Admiral Rudberg to be given 'a boost' before informing General Ljung about it. Rudberg and Stefenson apparently ignored the Norwegian analysis of the sound signature, which pointed to a Western submarine, and Stefenson would have been the one who ensured that this information did not turn up in the Submarine Defence Commission Report. Stefenson and Rudberg have stated afterwards that there was no submarine passage over the mine barrages at Mälsten. Accordingly, there was no damaged submarine. Even though Commander Emil Svensson and the Naval Analysis Group had full access to the war diaries from the naval base at Muskö and from the Coastal Defence base at Mälsten, he states that no submarine passed the mine barrages at Mälsten (on 11 October) since there was no indication of a damaged submarine after the explosion. According to the Naval Analysis Group Report – used as raw information by the 1983 Submarine Defence Commission and by the 1995 Submarine Commission – this incident never took place.

The passage of a submarine on 13–14 October has seemingly also been filtered away by the same individuals. In this case too, the tape and the report of the tape recording have been manipulated. Before this tape was 'edited', it was possible to hear the damaged propeller, its turns per minute, how the submarine went forward by intervals to avoid detection and, later, the shutting of a submarine hatch. Even though the evidence for this submarine is undeniable, and even though Vice-Admiral Stefenson has confirmed that all systems pointed to a submarine, he decided a few hours later to deny the existence of this submarine. The incident never happened. At 08.00 on 14 October, the Commander-in-Chief was informed that there were 'electronic disturbances', and, at 13.45, the Minister of Defence was informed that the mines had most likely indicated in error. Commander Emil Svensson and his Naval Analysis Group Report state that there was probably no submarine passage, and Svensson selects a couple of vague pieces of information from the naval base war diary, while taking out tens of others that clearly state that a submarine is passing. On several occasions, General Ljung received more or less correct information. On a number of occasions, however, this information was immediately afterwards retracted, probably by a senior officer reporting directly to him. According to one source, Ljung even sent his own intelligence people to the naval base to find out what was going on, as though he did not trust the naval base reports or his own Chief of Staff.

Coastal Defence officers have told me that they believed that Coastal Fleet officers ordered the ceasefires and the release of the submarines because they wanted to get the submarines themselves and not to let Coastal Defence get them. Or, as one Coastal Defence officer said, Coastal Fleet helicopters were unable to do anything against the more sophisticated submarines. Senior and relatively senior Coastal Fleet officers, on the other hand, have told me that Coastal Defence's mine barrages were unreliable and that indications from Coastal Defence were not trustworthy. Generalizing from a mistake on 7 October, they argued that Coastal Defence wanted to save its own face, and they doubted that any submarine actually had passed out at Mälsten. Bror Stefenson stated in 1994 that 'there was no [submarine] passage over any mine barrage', referring to the incidents at Mälsten in October 1982.[104] Per Rudberg said to me that he doubted that any submarine had passed the choke point at Mälsten in October 1982. In a criticism of my work, Rear-Admiral Göran Wallén, the military expert to the Ekéus Investigation, stated: 'there is no record of a submarine or submersible passing out either on the eastern or the western side of Mälsten'.[105] The same conclusion is made in the Naval Analysis Group Report under Commander Emil Svensson.[106] This view was also presented to many officers within the Navy.

This 'Coastal Fleet view', however, is confirmed neither by relevant war diaries nor by General Ljung's diary. The documented evidence is pretty clear that one submarine passed out on 11–12 October and another on 13–14 October. It seems that not only the public but also most fleet officers have been kept from vital information regarding those days. Coastal Fleet rumours of what happened must have been formed by somebody at the very top – seemingly Stefenson and Rudberg. On the other hand, Coastal Fleet officers were split between officers believing this version and other high-ranking officers with access to secret information about Defence Staff activities during the submarine hunt. The latter did not believe the above-mentioned 'Coastal Fleet view'. However, the 'Coastal Defence view' is not very credible either. It may have appeared as the most likely explanation to some officers at Mälsten, and even higher up, but the view that high-ranking Coastal Fleet officers would have forced Coastal Defence to release two submarines because they themselves were unable to get them is difficult to take seriously. This story is much easier to explain if we think in terms of two Western submarines that were secretly released by somebody at the very top (for example by Vice-Admiral Stefenson and Vice-Admiral Rudberg), which later led to misunderstandings and increased distrust between the Coastal Fleet and Coastal Defence.

On all of these occasions, Commander-in-Chief General Ljung received information through his Chief of Staff and his Chief of the Navy. Information was passed from the naval base to the Defence Staff, but not always through the Commander of the Eastern Military District, Lieutenant-General Bengt Lehander, who formally speaking should have been the commander in the area reporting to the Commander-in-Chief. The Commander of the Military District, in this case the Eastern Military District, was, according to Swedish regulations, 'the officer in charge of ordering an engagement with effective fire'.[107] In the Hårsfjärden case, this did not happen. General Lehander is no longer alive, but I spoke with his Chief of Staff, Major-General (now Lieutenant-General) Gustaf Welin, who told me that they were often not informed. The information went directly from the naval base to the Defence Staff. Chief of Naval Operations, Eastern Military District, Commander Bengt Gabrielsson said the same. His superior, Captain Göran Wallén, Chief of Operations at the Eastern Military District, has a different view, and he denies that any information presented above has any relevance.[108] But both Welin and Gabrielsson said that the Eastern Military District – the command that formally speaking was responsible for giving orders about fire and ceasefire – was 'shunted aside'. They were kept in the dark. Despite that, Stefenson let them write drafts for the Submarine Defence

Commission Report. Stefenson operated informally. Several times, he went out in a helicopter and acted as a 'local commander', short-cutting the chain of information. After these incidents, he did not report to his subordinates, who were kept uninformed about operations. Several officers describe him as an informal and 'spontaneous personality'. This 'spontaneity', however, may have been instrumental in his carrying out some delicate operations while keeping the formal hierarchy uninformed. His professionalism as a high-ranking naval officer and former submarine officer also gave him an obvious authority. The Commander-in-Chief explicitly mentions that the ceasefires on 7, 11 and 12 October were declared after recommendations from the Chief of Staff, Vice-Admiral Bror Stefenson.[109] The ceasefire on 13 October was most likely decided by Stefenson himself, without consultation with Ljung. The ceasefire order from 17.49 on 13 October was signed by Captain Göran Wallén.[110]

After the believed breakout through the nets at lunchtime on 7 October, Vice-Admiral Stefenson went to Hårsfjärden. At the same time, Major-General Gustaf Welin from the Eastern Military District requested the use of mines against the approaching submarine, something General Ljung supported. Ljung turned to Prime Minister Thorbjörn Fälldin, who also responded positively. The use of these 'wartime weapons' was understood as an escalation of the operation. Stefenson was not consulted on the issue, most likely because he was in a helicopter on his way to Berga and Hårsfjärden. Requests to the Commander of the Eastern Military District were first made by Stockholm Coastal Defence. After the believed breakout on 7 October, the most senior officers at the Eastern Military District, Lieutenant-General Bengt Lehander and Major-General Gustaf Welin, discussed the issue and turned to the Commander-in-Chief. This escalation stands in contrast to the almost simultaneous de-escalation at the naval base. A ceasefire for depth charges was decided by the naval base – or perhaps through influence of the most high-ranking officer at the base, Vice-Admiral Stefenson. Stefenson was allegedly upset about the decision to use the mines, and immediately after the first mine explosion he had argued that there was an understanding not to use the mines. In a telephone conversation with an anonymous officer, Stefenson had, according to von Hofsten, 'exclaimed that we had an agreement about not using the mines'.[111] Logically speaking, a tacit agreement could only have been with somebody at the Eastern Military District, and the only candidate for that would be von Hofsten's trusted former chief, Captain (now Rear-Admiral) Göran Wallén, who was close to Stefenson and also favoured Stefenson's view afterwards.[112] It seems that the escalation of the operation was possible only because Lieutenant-General Lehander and Major-General Welin listened to the Chief of Stockholm Coastal Defence rather than to their own most senior naval officer and because Stefenson, at the time of General Ljung's decision, was absent from the Defence Staff.

On the morning of the same day, Per Rudberg and Bror Stefenson had proposed a de-escalation of the submarine hunt. In the evening, the decision to use mines against submarines was revoked on the recommendation of Vice-Admiral Stefenson, but it was once again accepted the following morning, though with certain reservations, as though a compromise had been reached. At a Naval Staff meeting, Vice-Admiral Rudberg argued against the use of mines. Rudberg said that it was necessary to 'take it cool' (in Swedish, 'ta det lilla lugna'). He argued that the indications in the mines were not trustworthy. Stefenson used the same words and said: 'we had to take it cool for a while'.[113] After 7 October, the naval base did not order any drops of depth charges, despite several indications in Hårsfjärden, at the northern exit, in Jungfrufjärden and at Mälsten. At this point, according to the naval base, the use of depth charges was limited to action against a submarine classified as a 'certain submarine'.[114] Between 1 and 7 October, 45 depth charges (or possibly 48[115]) were dropped, while only two depth charges were dropped between 8 and 14 October, and these two charges were ordered not by the naval base but by the Coastal Defence base at Mälsten. Or, more correctly, Mälsten ordered the drop of 16 depth charges, but the naval base entered the frequency and overruled Mälsten's decision seconds before the drop. After 7 October and Stefenson's and Rudberg's decision to de-escalate the hunt, the use of force was in practical terms over. Only the Coastal Defence base at Mälsten, not fully under the control of Stefenson and the naval base (but partly supported by the Commander of the Eastern Military District), carried out its own war. The crucial question, however, is why did Stefenson and Rudberg try to de-escalate the operation from 7 October. Had something happened, or was something going to happen? There are at least four arguments that might have motivated this decision. First, the incident on 5 October might have been more serious than described above, which might have forced the state responsible for the operations to back out. Second, this state might have desperately needed a de-escalation to save its submarines, which would have difficulty surviving in the Swedish archipelago for a longer time. Third, if one or more submarines/ submersibles were going to be brought away from the area by a civilian merchant ship passing by (see 9 October), an immediate release of these vessels was necessary. Fourth, on the following day, the new Palme government was due to take office. An end to the right to use force from 8 October, in practical terms, would make the Palme government look weak and compliant to the Soviets, which would discredit the government from its first day in office. All these arguments may have supported each other.

At the meeting on 9 October, Ljung seems to have tried to find a compromise between Vice-Admiral Stefenson on the one hand and Brigadier-General Hansson (and perhaps Lieutenant-General Lehander) on the other. On 12, 13 and 14 October, the decisions to accept the use of mines in darkness was taken by the Eastern Military District or by General Ljung on Lieutenant-General Lehander's recommendation, while all decisions about a ceasefire were taken by Vice-Admiral Stefenson or by General Ljung on the recommendations of Vice-Admiral Stefenson. General Ljung seems to have changed his view depending on who influenced him. However, on most occasions, briefings were given by Vice-Admiral Stefenson or by Stefenson together with Vice-Admiral Rudberg. A Swedish intelligence officer told me that it was Stefenson, not Ljung, who was running the Hårsfjärden operation. He said that, within the fleet, Ljung was called 'Grodan Boll' ('Froggie Ball'), a Swedish comical figure who makes comments and supports others.

It was primarily Vice-Admiral Stefenson who ran the Hårsfjärden submarine hunt, and, according to Vice-Admiral Bengt Schuback, Chief of Staff (from 1 October Commander of the Southern Military District, and later Chief of the Navy), it was the Chief of the Coastal Fleet (Rear-Admiral Stefenson) who ran the NOTVARP operation that preceded the hunt in Hårsfjärden. On the other hand, when Stefenson needed advice from a senior officer, he turned to Vice-Admiral Per Rudberg (see 12 October). Almost every morning, Vice-Admiral Rudberg and Vice-Admiral Stefenson briefed General Ljung about the submarine hunt. They almost totally controlled the information to the Commander-in-Chief. But it seems to have been Stefenson who was running the show, assisted by his 'chief of intelligence', Commander Emil Svensson, and perhaps together with the Chief of the Naval Base, Rear-Admiral Christer Kierkegaard (the first Swedish officer at the US Naval War College and Stefenson's predecessor as Chief of the Coastal Fleet), and with Captain Göran Wallén at the Eastern Military District. The whole operation, however, seems to have been under Vice-Admiral Rudberg's supervision. Of course, you may argue that Stefenson and Wallén were under the influence of Rudberg and perhaps of Svensson or the other way around. Still, I have difficulty in believing that they were totally incompetent. On 5 October at the briefing of the Minister of Defence, Stefenson brought Emil Svensson as his anti-submarine expert. When an alleged 'NATO submarine' appeared at Kanholmsfjärden on 30 September, Kierkegaard (or his assistant) wrote that, according to Emil Svensson's advice, the Commander-in-Chief and the Commander of the Eastern Military District should not be informed. Kierkegaard and Stefenson, both former chiefs of the Coastal Fleet, together with Emil Svensson, seem to have filtered away information about possible Western involvement, similar to how Wallén filtered away this information in the Ekéus Investigation. This seems to have been the general approach. In a dispute with a senior officer in the Ministry of Defence, Emil Svensson made a similar statement: 'your minister will get to know what he needs to know'.

The most senior naval officer at Defence Staff Intelligence, its Deputy Chief, Commander Björn Eklind, had been sceptical about the large number of reported submarines in the early 1980s, partly because there was no corresponding activity on the Soviet side and partly because he believed that, in a paranoid climate, people would see things that did not exist. To Rudberg and Stefenson, Eklind was a problem, and they needed their own 'naval intelligence organization', which had been created after the Whiskey submarine had grounded at Karlskrona in 1981. Hours after a submarine had appeared in Hårsfjärden, this Naval Analysis Group was deployed at Muskö 'at the disposal of the Chief of the Naval Base', Rear-Admiral Kierkegaard.[116] When something important took place, the war diaries state: 'contact Emil Svensson'. Commander Svensson played a central role in the submarine hunt. He presented a compilation of all observations or submarine indications in the Naval Analysis Group Report. However, almost all sensitive information and information pointing to Western submarines was excluded. Svensson played as important a role after the submarine hunt as Vice-Admiral Stefenson did during the hunt and for the Submarine Defence Commission. Svensson, however, may not have been fully informed about the role of the Western submarines.

The Naval Analysis Group Report for the Hårsfjärden submarine hunt, became – together with the Grandin Report (see below) – the most authoritative secret document about the hunt. It classified all essential observations from the war diaries as 'certain submarine', 'possible submarine' or 'not submarine'. Or, rather, this is what most inside observers believed to have been the case. The Naval Analysis Group Report was believed to have been a compilation of raw information. However, almost all of the war diaries' most delicate statements were left out of the Naval Analysis Group Report. Commander Emil Svensson was responsible for all these decisions. I will present some examples. The 5 October information about an echo of 35–40 metres, 15 metres above the sea floor (confirmed by intelligence personnel at the naval base), is not reported by Svensson. The 5 October information about the signal transmitter Malin attaching to a submarine (also confirmed by several senior officers) is explicitly denied by the report. The 7 October information about a 'submarine sail with something white on the sail at Berganäs' is changed to just an 'object at Berganäs' and is classified as a 'possible submarine'; it disappears among hundreds of less relevant pieces of information. The 7 October information about damaged nets, about a breakout and about a possibly damaged submarine are all denied by Svensson. The 11 October information about a mine explosion after indications from a submarine passing the mine barrage, the report about a yellow/green patch on the surface an hour after the incident, the repair works the following night, and the reported 'steel plates' on the sea floor are all denied in Svensson's report, which states: 'if a submarine had provoked the indication [in the mine barrage], it would most likely have been damaged seriously. The following investigation found no traces [of that]. Conclusion: no submarine.'[117] Unlike the Mälsten report of 11 October and the Grandin Report,[118] the Naval Analysis Group Report concludes: no submarine. Also, the passage over the mine barrage on 13–14 October is classified as 'no submarine'. The Naval Analysis Group Report states:

> [On 13 October] at 23.00, from Mälsten: indication in the mine barrage and sound from the sonars. Conclusion: the tape is sent for analysis. Preliminary report: [cavi]tation sound not confirmed. Rhythmic thumbing from unknown source. Conclusion: no submarine. [On 14 October] at 01.11, helicopter suspected sonar contact south of Mälsten. At 01.35, attack with depth charges.[119]

In all these cases, information from the war diaries pointing to submarines – and, in several cases, Western submarines – is taken out of the report. During the night and early morning of 14 October, the war diaries speak about a submarine moving and hiding from the Swedish anti-submarine forces. This information is, in Svensson's report, reduced to two sentences of no significance (see my italics below), which lead Svensson to conclude that there was no submarine. The speaker channel on the tape as well as the war diaries state the following: '[Just after midnight], Y69 is in contact with a submarine . . . We have a couple of cavitation sounds. Conclusion: submarine increasing speed. [A minute later: more] cavitation sounds. [Two minutes later:] Helicopter prepares for a drop. [Four minutes later:] Submarine, increasing amplitude. [Four minutes later:] I cannot hear the submarine. [Six minutes later:] the submarine has started again. It is moving forward slowly. [Six minutes later:] It seems that the submarine is going with five-six-seven-eight turns with the propeller and then stops. He is possibly going very close to the sea floor' (Speaker channel, Tape 4). 'At 00.25, Mälsten to Y70: the submarine is moving forward by intervals towards the deepest area' (CÖrlBO WD). 'At 00.30, the sonar operator reports: still contact' (CMS WD). 'At 00.31,

Mälsten has still contact [with the submarine] . . . At 00.34, from Mälsten: the submarine has increased speed' (CÖrlBO WD). 'At 00.35, the sonar operator: still contact . . . the sonar operator concludes that the propeller shaft of the object is damaged' (CMS WD). 'At 00.53, Mälsten has lost contact' (CÖrlBO WD). 'At 01.06, helicopter contact south of Mälsten. At 01.09, report from the sonars: the object is moving forward slowly. Helicopter Y69 informed' (CMS WD). *At 01.11, Y70 has suspected sonar contact* (CÖrlBO WD). 'At 01.13, from the sonar operator: the contact is stronger. At 01.14, Y70 returns. The speed of the object increases. Report to helicopter. At 01.16, from the sonar operator: the contact is stronger . . . At 01.18, the object is quiet. At 01.19, the object is moving forward by intervals. Y69 is informed' (CMS WD). 'It is now 01.19. The amplitude of the submarine has first decreased and then increased to the present relatively high level. At 01.23, the helicopter is now preparing for an attack. At 01.26, the boats are coming here for the drop. Before this, I am going to turn off the whole system' (Speaker channel, Tape 4). 'At 01.30, one of the microphones (no. 5) out of order. No contact. At 01.32, transport boat S reports: distance [from the object] 180 metres. According to Y69, contact close to A = the microphone [no. 5]. Contact close. From the sonar operator: despite that no contact in the microphone . . . The microphone may have been hit [see above]' (CMS WD). *At 01.35, attack with depth charges* (CÖrlBO WD). 'At 01.37, the tape recording stopped because the patrol vessel dropped two depth charges. They were directed by the helicopter. The helicopter had contact [with the submarine] at microphone no. 5, which died. It is very likely that the submarine passed close to the microphone – so close that the fuse melted. After the detonation, the system was turned on. The noise level is back to normal. The low-frequency sounds are back to normal. They decreased to about 30 dB' (Speaker channel, Tape 4). 'At 01.40, HB5 reports: both of them exploded. At 01.43, from the sonar operator . . . No low-frequency sounds [no propeller]. The vessel may have been damaged, or is keeping totally silent, or the sonar system is damaged for lower frequencies . . . At 02.44, from the sonars: two "knocking" sounds . . . At 03.22, the sonar operator reports: knocking sounds close to [microphone] no. 4' (CMS WD). 'At 03.30, from Mälsten: rattling sounds and sounds similar to the closing of a valve or [submarine hatch]' (CÖrlBO WD). 'At 10.31, from the sonar operator: possible submarine, echo, 2 pings . . . At 10.46, the object is moving. At 10.48, from the sonar operator: possible submarine . . . At 10.55, from the sonar operator: silent again. Y71 is informed. At 10.56, Y71 asks for last position of the object. Answer: 1,000 metres southwest Vitingen' (CMS WD). 'At 11.00, from Mälsten: microphone contact for half an hour (10.35). The submarine has been moving since 10.46 (cavitation sounds)' (CÖrlBO WD). It seems that Commander Emil Svensson deliberately excluded everything that clearly indicated a submarine at Mälsten on 14 October. This most clear submarine passage recorded by three different systems (with a contact with the submarine for a couple of hours) is by Svensson reduced to one suspected sonar contact south of Mälsten at 01.11 and a drop of two depth charges.

When the Naval Analysis Group Report considers periscopes and submarine sails it only discusses alternative Soviet submarines. The description of a submarine sail close to Sandhamn on 4 October points instead to a British or US, and definitely a Western, submarine.[120] The observers' description of the sail does not indicate a Soviet submarine. The Analysis Group, however, concludes that it might have been a large diesel submarine, and the Soviet Union was the only Baltic Sea country with such submarines. Prints on the sea floor from two propellers and of a 'keel' and double runners give a clear indication of the dimensions of the small vessel, which points to a couple of possible US submersibles, but Svensson and Stefenson believe that the prints must originate from an unknown Soviet submersible.

A Norwegian admiral asked me if an analysis of the oil was carried out. In Norway, oil from a submarine is always analysed, because the Soviet Union and many Western countries use different kinds of oil. It is possible to identify which refinery the oil originates from, and there is no problem in identifying the national origin. However, in the Hårsfjärden case, although a large number of oil samples were taken, the results from the analysis of these samples were never used as evidence to prove Soviet submarines. I was told that there was a lot of oil on the bottom that might have turned up on the surface after the drop of depth charges, but on several occasions the oil patch appeared far from where the depth charge had been dropped. A first analysis of three samples is reported by the Naval Analysis Group on 3 October in Attachment 20.[121] In this case, it seems as if the chemical composition of the oil did not indicate a Soviet submarine. No other analysis is reported, despite the number of samples taken. Commander Svensson has seemingly filtered the raw information given to both Submarine Commissions. A Norwegian officer had a conversation with Svensson about demonstrating the tape recording (from 12 October) for the Parliamentary Submarine Defence Commission. According to the Norwegian officer, Svensson said: 'I never played the real tape. I played one of the signatures we had in the archive.'

While Commander Emil Svensson always appeared as a naval activist, Vice-Admiral Bror Stefenson acted publicly as a cautious and responsible leader. However, during these incidents, Vice-Admiral Stefenson seems to have been showing two faces: on the one hand, he was the cautious and perhaps overly restrained military leader who under no circumstances wanted to upset the delicate balance and low tension in northern Europe; on the other hand, he seems to have played a political game that might have increased European military tension and guaranteed US support in order to achieve certain political goals. This Janus-type masquerade was repeated three years later in connection with the forced resignation of Commander Björn Eklind. Eklind was Deputy Chief of Defence Staff Intelligence during the hunt in Hårsfjärden; in the winter of 1982–83, he gave several briefings for the Parliamentary Submarine Defence Commission; and in 1985, he became captain of the new Swedish intelligence ship, *Orion*, which was to listen to all Soviet military activities in the Baltic republics. Eklind seemed to be an ideal officer for this task, and he had even participated in Swedish–US talks in order to ensure that Sweden received as capable a ship as possible.

In early 1986, Eklind had to resign as captain of the *Orion*. In his diary, General Ljung writes that Eklind had been an excellent captain, but he had problems in cooperating with the [Signal Intelligence] personnel on the ship.[122] To be more specific, he actually refused to accept US intelligence personnel on board, and he refused to allow Swedish Signal Intelligence officers to prioritize reconnaissance against SA-10s (Soviet low-level air-defence missiles designed for use against US air-launched cruise missiles and low-flying B-1 bombers). The US missiles were programmed to follow paths through the Baltic republics – the Soviet 'soft underbelly' – to Leningrad and Moscow. Eklind did not accept that the *Orion* should become a platform for preparing US strategic nuclear strikes against the Soviet Union. He believed that Swedish support for US strategic attacks against the Soviets would increase tension in northern Europe and would be completely contradictory to Swedish policy.[123]

This view was unacceptable to the Chief of Staff, Bror Stefenson. Eklind had to go, and Stefenson had to get support from the government for removing Eklind. Stefenson, however, could not say that Eklind had to leave, because Eklind was in line with Swedish government policy. The argument for removing him was a very different one. A few months earlier, Eklind had been involved in an incident with a Soviet mine-sweeper, while the Soviets were carrying out the first exercise with a Kilo-class submarine in the Baltic Sea. General Ljung wrote in his diary on 21 February that Eklind had 'done an excellent job during this incident', and this was not a reason for Eklind to step down.[124] Eklind presented a lot of information new to the Commander-in-Chief, which made General Ljung ask Pär Kettis, Director of FRA (the Signal Intelligence Agency), for an explanation, and Ljung wrote in his diary that he had had to brief the Minister of

Defence.[125] However, when Stefenson presented the case to the government, he said that Eklind's behaviour during the incident had been provocative and unacceptable, implying damage to the low tension in northern Europe. In this masquerade, Stefenson put himself on the other side to Eklind. Stefenson presented himself as an advocate of low tension, and the government supported his demand for the removal of Commander Eklind. The government representative falsely got the impression that Eklind may have played a leading role in the 'naval officers revolt' against the government and Prime Minister Olof Palme at this very time, and that he possibly could have been involved in the murder of Prime Minister Palme the following week. Whatever Vice-Admiral Stefenson may have said, he was clearly carrying out the same double policy evidenced during the submarine hunt in 1982. On both occasions, he seems to have cooperated closely with the USA, even though this may have created tension with the Soviet Union, while he presented himself as an advocate for low tension in relation to the Soviet Union.

Because of Admiral Stefenson's 'cautious policy', which seemingly forced his subordinates to release two submarines, Chief of Stockholm Coastal Defence, Brigadier-General Lars Hansson, believed that Stefenson was a Soviet spy or at least informer. The only explanation he could come up with at the time was that Stefenson was actually working for the Russians, and he even started to organize exercises secretly because he was afraid that the information would be handed over to the Russians.[126] After this incident, Swedish security services checked Stefenson out, but he clearly had no contact with the Soviets. Others, such as Commander Hans von Hofsten,[127] believed that the government was cooperating with Moscow and that Stefenson was just following government orders. Chief of OPG (Operations) at the Defence Staff, Lieutenant-Colonel Håkan Söderlindh, said that he received no critical remarks about the Swedish show of force – either from the government or from the Foreign Ministry. He mentioned three representatives from the Foreign Ministry who were briefed at the Defence Staff during the Hårsfjärden incident. None of them argued in favour of a more cautious attitude. Restrictions were given by the Chief of Staff, Vice-Admiral Stefenson.

However, to think that Vice-Admiral Stefenson was cooperating with the Soviet Union is absurd. Stefenson wanted on several occasions to point to the Soviet Union as responsible for the submarine intrusions, while the Commander-in-Chief was sceptical, if not negative. During the Utö incident in 1980, a submarine was believed to have been a Whiskey-class submarine. Stefenson wanted to make this public, while General Ljung demanded 100 per cent certainty.[128] During the Hårsfjärden incident, Stefenson covered up information pointing to the West while preparing or even inventing material (in a memorandum of 18 April 1983[129]) that definitely pointed to the Soviet Union. General Ljung, however, was not convinced in the early phase (see below). In autumn 1983, the Defence Staff, under the leadership of Vice-Admiral Stefenson, stated that the submarine intrusions were continuing and that the Soviet Union was most likely responsible. General Ljung wrote in his diary that he agreed with the first statement, but not with the second. The Defence Staff (and Vice-Admiral Stefenson) wanted, according to Ljung, to point to the Soviet Union without having 'evidence and hardly even indications'.[130] If Stefenson had been cooperating with the Soviet Union, it would have been illogical of him to behave in this way. Furthermore, if Stefenson had worked for the Soviets, it is not possible to explain the close cooperation between Vice-Admiral Stefenson and Vice-Admiral Rudberg, nor how they together, on several occasions, seemingly gave General Ljung selective data or chose to inform him when it was far too late.

I do not believe that Stefenson and, indirectly, Vice-Admiral Rudberg were cooperating with the Soviets. Rudberg was Sweden's top liaison officer with NATO and Swedish Commander-in-Chief in exile in the event of Sweden being occupied.[131] Rudberg had close private ties to Admiral Bobby Inman, former Chief of US Naval Intelligence, former Chief of the National Security Agency and, in 1981, Deputy Director of the CIA.[132] Rudberg and Inman even went on holiday together.[133] When Commander Bobby Inman was US Assistant Naval Attaché to Stockholm in the mid-1960s, he had an excellent Swedish source who facilitated the deployment of listening devices in Swedish waters, a close colleague of Inman told me. He said that the CIA tried to steal this source from the Navy, which is also described by Bob Woodward in his book on the CIA director William Casey.[134] Inman had excellent contacts with several Swedes, and not least with Rudberg. When the US Secretary of Defense, Caspar Weinberger, was in Stockholm in October 1981, Rudberg was the Swedish officer with whom Weinberger had confidential talks. The same happened when British Defence Minister Michael Heseltine was in Stockholm in 1983. Both asked to have Rudberg as their escort officer, he told me. And, according to Rudberg, the defence ministers probably knew about his secret position as Sweden's top liaison to NATO. When Caspar Weinberger was in Stockholm in 1981, he also visited Muskö, where he met with Per Rudberg, with Swedish Chief of the Coastal Fleet Rear-Admiral Bror Stefenson and with Chief of the Naval Base East Rear-Admiral Christer Kierkegaard (see photo). To believe that these three were working for the Soviets is absurd. All of the above incidents are much easier to explain if we think in terms of Western submarines.

When discussing the ceasefires, Rear-Admiral Gunnar Grandin's internal Navy Report states that superior commands (Defence Staff and Naval Base East, or to be more specific Bror Stefenson and Christer Kierkegaard) had decided about the use of depth charges with a total lack of 'necessary technical competence for such a detailed planning of the operations . . . Ceasefires for the mine barrages were also given by higher commands without competence and knowledge.'[135] Stockholm Coastal Defence Staff reported to MBÖ about Defence Staff 'muddle-headedness in orders about the use of force'.[136] The Ekéus Report makes a similar comment.[137] On Swedish Radio in 2001, Vice-Admiral Stefenson spoke about himself as 'clumsy' and the situation as 'confusing'.[138] A Dagens Nyheter comment on my work argued that lack of competence is a more likely explanation than that some Swedish officers would have cooperated with a foreign power.[139]

However, officers will not advance to become Chief of the Navy, like Per Rudberg, or Chief of the Coastal Fleet, like Christer Kierkegaard and Bror Stefenson, if they have a total lack of competence and understanding of naval technology. Emil Svensson has been described as the most competent anti-submarine officer in Sweden. To believe that all these officers were totally incompetent is not very credible. And, as Paul Beaver says, it is naive to believe that Western submarines would have operated in Swedish waters unless somebody in the 'Swedish High Command was aware that there were going to be some intrusions during a given period'.[140] There must be somebody in position to act if necessary. The statements about incompetent commanders are just illogical. Here, it may look as though I am presenting a circular argument: as if the strange orders were explained by the existence of Western submarines. This is not the case. There are large numbers of indications or even evidence pointing to Western submarine operations in Hårsfjärden. When those responsible for 'incompetent' orders releasing some submarines are also responsible for filtering away all information pointing to these Western submarines that is something that must be worth looking into.

Commander Hans von Hofsten and others (see below) have argued that the government was unwilling to use force. The political leadership, according to this hypothesis, had forced the military leaders to let the submarines out. This, however, is by no means confirmed by the statement by former State Secretary for Defence Sven Hirdman, by the diary of the Commander-in-Chief or by the diary of Conservative Party leader Ulf Adelsohn. Both Prime Minister Fälldin and Prime Minister-elect Palme agreed on 5 October to force the submarine to the surface, accepting that this might lead to the submarine's being damaged and crew members lost.[141] Within this framework, the Commander-in-Chief took the decisions about which measures should be used. On one occasion, on 6 October, he turned to Fälldin and Palme after it had been reported that the submarine might detonate its nuclear weapons if hit by Swedish anti-submarine forces. However, both Fälldin and Palme argued that the hunt should continue despite these threats.[142] On 8 October, Palme said that Swedish territory would be defended with all available means. According to Adelsohn, Palme said that there were no restrictions on the use of force and that one submarine had been 'seriously damaged' (see above). General Lennart Ljung himself took the decision to use mines, which were perceived as wartime weapons. Both Fälldin and Palme supported this decision. General Ljung clearly states that the government gave him the right to use force. He criticized some political leaders, not for being too soft but for being too trigger-happy. Or, more to the point, he was unhappy with Conservative Party leader Ulf Adelsohn, who had complained about General Ljung's too-lenient attitude and had had a quarrel with Vice-Admiral Stefenson. Adelsohn's statement about Chief of Staff Stefenson releasing a submarine on 7 October after a ceasefire made Ljung 'check with his own diary and with the Chief of Staff'.[143] After this incident, Stefenson said that he would speak to Carl Bildt, and Bildt had then immediately been in contact with Adelsohn to 'correct' his view.[144] Nothing in Ljung's diary indicates that the political leaders had been less willing to use force. On 22 October, Prime Minister Palme stated that the government already had the option of ordering Swedish defence forces to sink a submarine.[145] The ceasefires were not recommended by the political leaders, but by Ljung's subordinate, Chief of Staff Vice-Admiral Stefenson. All these incidents are much easier to explain if we think in terms of at least two Western submarines – something several sources actually confirm.

If the above analysis is correct, primarily two – actually three, and possibly five – officers systematically conveyed and denied data to the Commander-in-Chief in order to make him derive selected judgements, which made it possible to release two or three submarines. In practical terms, these officers did not primarily belong to the formal Swedish military hierarchy, with the Commander-in-Chief at the top, but to an informal Western security community.[146] Their ties and responsibilities were primarily to the 'Swedish guarantee power', the USA, and they come across as high-ranking E&E officers covertly working for this power. They were certainly thinking about Swedish defence, but to them this defence was identical to the defence of the Western world. Or should we rather think in terms of a deal between the Americans and some senior Swedish industrial and military 'representatives', for example Peter Wallenberg and Per Rudberg, as the Ansa source might suggest. This would mean that the Wallenberg empire and the Swedish military establishment would receive something in return – or had already received something. When Caspar Weinberger was in Stockholm a year earlier, the deal with the Swedes was 'sweetened' by offering the Wallenberg company SAAB the General Electric jet engine and other aerospace technology for *JAS Gripen*.[147] Weinberger also offered the Navy and Rudberg a much more advanced signal intelligence ship, *Orion*, which was far better then the most advanced version the Swedish military planners had presented for the government. However, a deal that includes the testing of Swedish coastal defences presupposes, as in the former case, that these Swedish 'representatives' would perceive themselves primarily as part of the Western security community, and that they would be willing to make a distinction between an informal Swedish power structure and the formal hierarchy with the government at the top. In other words, the government that had direct responsibility to the public was to be kept out of this operation.

THE CRITICS

Almost all journalists and researchers accepted as fact the statement by the Parliamentary Submarine Defence Commission about six Soviet submarines. A few journalists and researchers, however, particularly on the left-wing side, believed that the submarines were underwater ghosts and that the Navy wanted to use them as an argument for a larger budget. I myself did not, at the time, exclude Western involvement, but I believed that the major operations were carried out by the Soviet Union, and I believed that the Submarine Defence Commission Report had substantial information to support its claims.[148] At the time of the Hårsfjärden incident, no academic scholar, no author and only one or two journalists, primarily Anders Hasselbohm, wrote about Western submarines. Hasselbohm seemingly also had good sources.[149] However, nobody was willing to go public, except for former army chief Lieutenant-General Nils Sköld.[150] Hasselbohm was never taken seriously, and Sköld was believed to be senile, even though this happened only a year after he had left office. Later, *Dagens Nyheter* journalist Olle Alsén[151] and freelance writer Tommy Lindfors[152] also wrote about possible Western – or rather US – involvement, but their sources were believed to be even less reliable, and nobody seemed to take their arguments seriously. Some of Hasselbohm's sources, however, have turned out to be remarkably correct. I will primarily discuss two cases.

Soon after the submarine hunt, a source in a NATO country told Hasselbohm that:

> one officer in the Swedish military leadership, somebody who knows, has said that they were definitely sure. Definitely sure! The submarine

at Mälsten originated from the West. And they had more than sound to prove their case. They had several definite pieces of information in combination. I can tell you, they have possibly even seen the submarine.[153]

In his book, Hasselbohm also refers to a 'NATO source', who said:

The whole submarine hunt in Hårsfjärden started with a submarine that entered Hårsfjärden and was observed by two conscripts. This submarine originated from a NATO country. This submarine, which was a conventional submarine, soon afterwards went out of Hårsfjärden, out to Danziger Gatt, close to Mälsten . . . On 11 October, this submarine was damaged by a mine, though not very seriously. About a week later, it was assisted out of the Baltic Sea through Öresund by another submarine. Both submarines went close to each other in a sub-surface position in order to hide that one was damaged and where they came from . . . The midget submarines also came from the West.[154]

The same source told Hasselbohm that they had recorded the sound signature of the damaged submarine at Mälsten and that it proved to be a Western submarine. He said there was no doubt that it was a 'NATO submarine'. He knew this because the tapes were analysed by Norwegian specialists. It was a 'conventional submarine', a mother-sub, able to carry midget submarine(s), he said. It was damaged at Mälsten and, after that, the other submarine was let out.[155] All this – two Western submarines, one damaged on 11 October at Mälsten and one released soon afterwards at the same place – fits perfectly well with the Mälsten war diary, with the naval base war diary and with the statements by Brigadier-General Hansson and Lieutenant-Colonel Svenhager of Stockholm Coastal Defence and Lieutenant-Colonel Kviman at Mälsten. All of this information confirms what Hasselbohm's source says about works on a damaged submarine (which preceded the recording of the sound signature of the submarine).

A Norwegian source told Hasselbohm that the Norwegian Commander-in-Chief, General Sven Hauge – who was in Stockholm at the time of the submarine hunt – 'ordered our intelligence personnel to go to Sweden to help the Swedes. Of course, they were very discreet.'[156] One of Hasselbohm's Swedish sources, 'partly responsible for the submarine hunt', said that Norwegians set up advanced sonars in September to support the Swedes a few weeks before the submarine hunt started. Director Rolf Andersson says that this Norwegian system was deployed on 31 August and 1 September, and the Norwegians were helping him with the calibration a month later. This Norwegian assistance has been confirmed to me by Norwegian senior officers, even though they did not mention the exact time period. Former Norwegian

Minister of Defence Anders Sjaastad has confirmed to me that, after inquiries from General Sven Hauge, he gave his approval for the sending of a couple of sonar experts to Sweden during this time. The final Norwegian analysis, which pointed to a Western submarine, was forwarded to Stockholm immediately after the submarine hunt. Shortly afterwards, General Sven Hauge was informed by a well-connected senior official, the former Director of the Political Division at the Norwegian Foreign Ministry, Einar Ansteensen, that a US submarine had been damaged during the Hårsfjärden hunt. Hauge obviously believed that Soviet submarines had been involved in the submarine hunt, but he then received information both from his intelligence service and from 'diplomatic channels' about a damaged US submarine (see below). In an interview with *Dagens Industri*, General Sven Hauge declared that the submarine was not Norwegian, but added 'I cannot speak for other NATO countries.'[157]

I told former Norwegian Defence Minister Anders Sjaastad (1981–86) that there were clear indications that the Swedish military (naval) leadership – during the 1982 submarine hunt – realized that at least one of the Hårsfjärden submarines originated from the West. I also said that my sources had told me that Norwegian Military Intelligence knew about this. I asked him if Norwegian Military Intelligence had informed him about a Western submarine in Hårsfjärden. He did not answer this question, but he said that Military Intelligence always came to him if there was anything of importance. He said that during the submarine hunt, according to his information, the Swedes believed it was a Soviet submarine, but he remembered very well that Swedish Defence Minister Anders Thunborg later told him that they had nothing on the Soviets.

Hasselbohm's 'NATO source' – who described how a damaged submarine 'was assisted out of the Baltic Sea through Öresund by another submarine' – positively confirms a damaged Western submarine and indicates that it originated from the USA. This latter incident demands a special investigation. One week after the Hårsfjärden submarine hunt was ended, two Western submarines allegedly sailed close to each other through Öresund (the narrow sound between Sweden and Denmark), and, when possible, below the surface, which is illegal. A Swedish intelligence officer told Hasselbohm about the incident just after it happened:

> Suddenly there was a lot of fuss at the staff, because a submarine had passed submerged out through Öresund among the ferries and all the other ships. This is illegal, and it has never happened before . . . [After having revealed this transit, he had to leave his military position. A source with contacts in the Swedish military leadership told Hasselbohm:] two

submarines from the West travelled close to each other. They left the Baltic Sea in daytime submerged through Öresund. I think this is the first time this has happened.[158]

An internal Swedish intelligence report referred to a damaged 'NATO submarine', in other words with a damaged submarine sail, that went out together with another submarine through Öresund, but the submarine had allegedly not been damaged in Swedish waters. There were even photos, Hasselbohm told me.

In May 1984, Anders Hasselbohm published his book *Ubåtshotet: En kritisk granskning av Hårsfjärds-incidenten och ubåtsskyddskommissionens rapport* [The Submarine Threat: A Critical Review of the Hårsfjärden Incident and the Submarine Defence Commission Report]. During the days that followed, he discussed the transit through Öresund with former Chief of the Army, Lieutenant-General Nils Sköld, who had received a copy of the book and responded positively to it. Sköld confirmed Hasselbohm's statement, but he was not willing to go public because of his position at the Defence Ministry and at the Stockholm Conference on European Disarmament, Hasselbohm told me. This contact, however, led to immediate reactions within the Defence Staff. On 18 May a few days after Hasselbohm's book had been published, General Ljung wrote in his diary, apparently referring to Hasselbohm, about individuals questioning that 'the submarines actually were from the Soviet Union' and suggesting that 'maybe, possibly NATO was responsible'. Ljung continued: 'The Chief of Staff [Vice-Admiral Bror Stefenson] and his Deputy [Major-General Bengt Wallroth] are worried about signs from the Ministry [of Defence] indicating that Nils Sköld, who now has a position as consultant for missile affairs, has also moved into other business.'[159]

In late 1987, Hasselbohm turned to Nils Sköld again and asked if he was willing to go public about the passage through Öresund after the Hårsfjärden hunt. In December Lieutenant-General Sköld confirmed publicly for *Dagens Industri* that he, together with the Chief of the Air Force, shortly after the Hårsfjärden incident had complained to the Commander-in-Chief about not receiving information about the submarine hunt. General Lennart Ljung organized a special briefing for the military leadership that was confusing to Sköld. Sköld told *Dagens Industri* that 'shortly after the Hårsfjärden submarine hunt, a damaged submarine, escorted by another submarine, went out through Öresund in a sub-surface position'. Sköld argued that this did not seem to indicate a Soviet submarine and continued:

> With my knowledge that NATO was present in the northern archipelago, and that a submarine, in order not to reveal itself, passed out

through Öresund in a sub-surface position just after Hårsfjärden, then it is not clear that NATO was not involved in Hårsfjärden.[160]

Before the interview was published Hasselbohm asked Sköld if there was anybody else at this briefing who could confirm the passage through Öresund. Sköld said that he would come back to him. Shortly afterwards, Sköld called Hasselbohm and said that he should contact former Chief of the Naval Staff, Major-General Bo Varenius. Hasselbohm called Varenius, and they both had a longer conversation at Hasselbohm's home. Varenius confirmed Sköld's version, but he was not willing to go public about it. Varenius was a senior Coastal Defence officer, and he had been Chief of the Naval Staff for 11 years (1972–83), which included the Hårsfjärden incident. He was interested in Hasselbohm's sources in the West, and he wanted to know exactly which words they had used. Hasselbohm got the impression that Varenius had received the green light to talk to him, and that he would report their conversation, perhaps to the Minister of Defence Roine Carlsson. After the interview with Lieutenant-General Sköld in *Dagens Industri*, Sköld was questioned by the new Commander-in-Chief General Bengt Gustafsson (1986–94). When I spoke with Gustafsson in 2000, he remembered Sköld as saying that the submarine was not just a 'NATO submarine' but a 'US submarine'.

The day after Hasselbohm's interview with Sköld in *Dagens Industri*, Sköld confirmed to *Dagens Nyheter* that the military leadership briefing had brought up the transit through Öresund:

> the transit of the submarine was presented as a fact, but no link was made to the submarine hunt in Hårsfjärden . . . I don't remember exactly how the submarine passed out [the limited depth close to Malmö and in large parts of Öresund would have made it impossible to go all the way in a sub-surface position], only that it was made as 'stealthy as possible'.[161]

On the same day, recently retired (1986) Commander-in-Chief General Lennart Ljung said, also in *Dagens Nyheter*:

> NATO submarines pass rather often through Öresund. I do not *remember* information about a damaged submarine from that time. Neither do I *remember* that we linked the transit of a submarine with the incidents in Hårsfjärden . . . [Directly referring to Sköld's statement, General Ljung continues] I cannot *rule out* that such information was given, but my *memory of it is not clear*.[162] (author's italics)

Why did General Ljung use these words? He could just have denied the incident. To say that one does not *remember* if one let out a damaged Western submarine after Sweden's most dramatic submarine hunt is absurd. This would have been one of the most serious incidents in his life as a military commander. To say that 'I do not remember' or 'I cannot exclude it', as General Ljung said, is almost a confirmation of this incident.

I tried to find out the truth about this incident. One officer with a vital position at OPG at the Defence Staff said that he remembered having read that two submarines had been followed and tracked by the Swedes when they passed Kullen at the northern exit from Öresund – something that had never been stated publicly. He also said that I should contact BOMÖ (Bevakningsområde Malmö), the military authority responsible for monitoring all traffic passing through Öresund. I spoke with the former Chief of BOMÖ, Commander Rolf Nerpin. He said that he did not remember this incident, but that if it had taken place a report would have been sent to the Commander of the Southern Military District and to the Chief of OPG at the Defence Staff. I spoke with both these officers. Vice-Admiral Bengt Schuback, then Commander of the Southern Military District, confirmed that he saw the report at the Southern Military District. He also said that BOMÖ was able to identify any submarine passing Öresund. He then said that he did not remember if he saw this report as Commander of the Southern Military District or as a Chief of the Navy, at the military leadership meeting after former army chief Lieutenant-General Nils Sköld had brought it up. However, the latter possibility seems less likely.[163] He also confirmed that he and the Chief of OPG would have been the ones who received the report from BOMÖ. Lieutenant-Colonel Håkan Söderlindh, Chief of OPG, did not remember this report.

Eric Rylander, a senior officer at FRA, wrote that he received a report soon after Hårsfjärden – probably from the Southern Military District – about a visual observation of two submarines, one with a damaged submarine sail. They were spotted south of Öland (close to Karlskrona) and were heading southwards (towards Poland, Germany or Denmark), which would certainly exclude Soviet submarines. They were believed to be Polish submarines. Rylander never saw this report again, and when he brought it up with Swedish Military Intelligence they denied any knowledge of it.[164] This report is not included in the Naval Analysis Group Report, and it has supposedly disappeared from the Intelligence Archive. However, Polish Whiskey submarines would have gone towards the southeast, towards the submarine base and shipyards of Gdansk. We would accordingly be left with Western subs, probably the same two submarines, including one with a damaged sail, which allegedly passed out through Öresund a few days later. This may be the reason why the report has disappeared. To explain that a Western submarine was damaged in Hårsfjärden would be too difficult.

Ambassador Rolf Ekéus's military expert, Rear-Admiral Göran Wallén, says that 'there is no indication of such an unusual passage'.[165] In BOMÖ's intelligence archive, there is, according the Ekéus Report, no information on the passage of a damaged Western submarine. Neither the former Chief of BOMÖ nor the officers at the Intelligence Unit recall such an incident, the report argues.[166] However, before Wallén had spoken with them, I asked the Chief of the Intelligence Unit about the passage. He said: 'I do not know what I am allowed to tell you', and when I came back to him he told that he had nothing to say. This does not confirm Wallén's conclusion, and the fact that former Chief of the Army Lieutenant-General Nils Sköld, former Chief of the Southern Military District (and former Chief of Staff) Vice-Admiral Bengt Schuback and former Chief of the Naval Staff Major-General Bo Varenius have confirmed a briefing or a written report about this incident should at least make us a little bit more cautious.

One officer told me that this incident with the two submarines passing Öresund took place during the exercise 'Sydfront' (Southern Front) in late September, not after but just before the Hårsfjärden hunt. I don't know if he or the others remember the time of the incident correctly. This officer believed that the passage just before Hårsfjärden may have been confused with another incident: a small submarine or submersible had been towed by a surface vessel through Öresund shortly after the Hårsfjärden submarine hunt. It was observed not far from Kullen at the northern end of the passage. He did not know whether this incident had anything to do with the Hårsfjärden hunt, but he argued that there must have been another reason for the earlier passage with the two submarines going out partly below the surface.

In late autumn 1982, a representative for a company dealing with submarine technology visited a Danish shipyard in Jutland. He said that a small Western submarine or submersible (but not a Danish one) had been repaired at the shipyard. I tried to get this information confirmed, but the source – now in Swedish Military Intelligence (MUST) – was denied permission to speak about it. I went to Danish Military Intelligence (FET). They argued that they do not keep files on allied activities. Information on naval exercises and other activities was destroyed after one to three months. However, FET registered all Warsaw Pact naval transits through the Danish Straits (Store Belt and Öresund), and it keeps this information in classified monthly reports. If one or two Soviet or Warsaw Pact submarines had passed through Öresund in late October 1982 (or in late September), this would have been registered by FET. However, no such information exists.

According to the classified FET Monthly Report on Naval Activities, only one Soviet naval vessel (and no Polish or East German ones) passed out through the Danish Straits in October 1982.[167] The next Warsaw Pact vessel passing out was a Soviet Juliet-class submarine on 20 November.[168]

Nothing of this is found in General Ljung's diary. Ljung wrote some lines or pages every evening – except for the three weeks that followed the Hårsfjärden submarine hunt (16 October to 10 November). These 26 days are written down afterwards 'as he *remembered* them'.[169] Something seems to have happened during these weeks. It seems that a selective memory had become necessary. Nothing is said about the transit through Öresund. The briefing on Hårsfjärden that the Chief of the Army and the Chief of the Air Force had demanded and that he himself had organized is not mentioned in his diary. Nor does he mention anything about the Norwegian analysis of the propeller recordings that was forwarded to Stockholm at that time. Several incidents that point to a Western submarine took place during the weeks when General Ljung 'abstained from' writing his diary, though it must be wondered whether he did in fact write some lines every day but preferred to rewrite them afterwards because the most sensitive information should 'not exist on paper'.[170]

In an interview with General Bengt Gustafsson, General Ljung's successor as Commander-in-Chief, he told me that Ljung had neither in written form nor orally given him any information about the above-mentioned mysterious aspects of the submarine hunts. In recent years, Gustafsson had come to realize that there were many things that Lennart Ljung, for some reason, did not want to tell him. Ljung informed him about most sensitive intelligence matters, but not about either the top-secret operative ties between Sweden and the USA or about the mystery of the submarine hunts, even though the latter had been the single most important issue during Ljung's years. We have to ask why this information was so sensitive that it could not be given to Ljung's successor as Commander-in-Chief. Information on Soviet submarines would obviously not have been that sensitive. However, information on a damaged US submarine could easily have been viewed as 'cosmic', to use NATO terminology.

On 10 January 1983, a couple of months after the submarine hunt, General Ljung wrote in his diary that Henry Kissinger had talked with the Swedish State Secretary for Foreign Affairs, Pierre Schori. As already mentioned, Kissinger said to Schori that 'it was smartly done by the Swedish government to release the submarine the way they did it'.[171] Of course, by first damaging the submarine and then covertly releasing it, the Swedes had been smart enough to demonstrate resolve to defend their territory without causing the foreign power to lose face. But, as stated above, this does not make sense if the foreign power was the Soviet Union. It does seem as though Kissinger was speaking about a Western (or even US) submarine that Sweden had released after having first damaged it.

NOTES

1 SOU (1983), p. 85.
2 CMS2 WD; CMS WD.
3 CÖrlBO WD.
4 CMS Report (11 October 1982).
5 ÖB HWD; LGP HWD.
6 CMS WD; CÖrlBO WD.
7 Bevb 77 LB; Bevb 77 WD.
8 CMS2 WD.
9 Y46 Report.
10 CMS2 WD; CMS WD.
11 CMS WD.
12 Y46 Report.
13 CMS WD.
14 SOU (2001), p. 124.
15 Y46 Report.
16 SOU (2001), p. 124.
17 CÖrlBO WD.
18 Y46 Report; see also Wallén (2002), p. 40.
19 CMS WD.
20 CMS2 WD.
21 SOU (1983), p. 85.
22 SOU (2001), p. 124.
23 Y46 Report.
24 SOU (2001), p. 124.
25 ÖB HWD.
26 SOU (2001), p. 124.
27 Bo Rask Letter (2001).
28 SOU (2001), p. 124.
29 CMS WD; CÖrlBO WD; ÖB HWD; LGP HWD.
30 MAna Hårsfj.
31 CMS WD (12 October).
32 FOA Tape 1.
33 CÖrlBO WD (12 October).
34 CMS WD.
35 MAna Hårsfj, Attach. 61.
36 MAna Hårsfj, Attach. 38, Subattach. 2.
37 Ibid.; FOA Tape 1.
38 SOU (1995), pp. 201–6.
39 Ibid., p. 208.
40 MAna Hårsfj; CM/Grandin (1982); SOU (1983); SOU (1995); SOU (2001).
41 Wallén (2002), p. 45.
42 One full tape covered one hour's recording at normal speed, which corresponds to 2,400 units on the counting system on the tape recorder. One minute corre-

sponds to 40 units on the counting system. According to the FOA report, the sequence of submarine sounds covered 749–893 (144 units or 3.47 minutes), which would correspond to the 18th to the 22nd minute or actually the 20th to the 24th minute of the tape, because there is a difference of two minutes between the counting system and the actual time. Karlsson's commentary took place at 1,250 (about 400 units later), which theoretically would correspond to the 31st minute, but actually took place in the 33rd minute, about ten minutes after the 3.47-minute sequence (MAna Hårsfj, Attach. 38, Subattach. 2; FOA Tape 1). According to the speaker channel, there is a whizzing sound in the 24th minute of the tape. There is also a whizzing sound during the 3.47-minute sequence, but the speaker channel does not report any propeller sound, despite this supposedly being the only clear propeller sound registered. The tape was supposedly stopped after the 3.47-minute sequence, which means that this sequence appeared more than 10 minutes and possibly several hours before Karlsson's commentary.

43 FOA Tape 2.
44 FOA Tape 2.
45 CÖrlBO WD.
46 CMS WD.
47 FOA Tape 2.
48 MAna Hårsfj, Attach. 38, Subattach. 2.
49 Ibid.; SOU (1995), p. 201.
50 FOA Tape 1.
51 CMS WD, CMS HWD.
52 MAna Hårsfj, Attach. 38, Subattach. 2; SOU (1995), p. 201.
53 SOU (1995), pp. 202–3.
54 Ibid., p. 202.
55 MAna Hårsfj, Attach. 38.
56 MAna Hårsfj, Attach. 61.
57 CÖrlBO WD (12 October); MAna Hårsfj, Attach. 38.
58 MAna Hårsfj, Attach. 61.
59 Riste and Moland (1997), p. 226.
60 Somebody may have been less satisfied with the results of the Norwegian analysis, because the tape was handed over to the French. General Ljung writes that Rear-Admiral Gunnar Grandin had given the tape to Paris, and Ljung continues: 'The French analysis seemed to point not just to the existence of a submarine but also to the Soviets' (ÖB TD, 18 November 1982). However, this analysis was apparently not clear enough to be used as evidence or even as an indication of a Soviet submarine in the Defence Staff Report of 18 April 1983 about the national origin of the submarine.
61 Hasselbohm (1984), p. 22.
62 Svensson (1995).
63 Ibid.
64 MAna Hårsfj, Attach. 38.
65 Wallén (2002), p. 44.
66 Ibid.
67 MAna Hårsfj, Attach. 61.
68 Wallén (2002), pp. 43–4.
69 MAna Hårsfj, Attach. 38.
70 FOA Tape 3.
71 MAna Hårsfj, Attach. 38, Subattach. 2.
72 MAna Hårsfj.

73 Ibid.
74 ÖB TD.
75 Wallén (2002), p. 50.
76 SOU (2001), p. 286.
77 CÖrlBO WD.
78 MAna Hårsf RABu; Cato and Larsson (1995); SOU (1995), pp. 245–9.
79 MAna Hårsfj RABu.
80 Cato and Larsson (1995).
81 MAna Hårsfj RABu.
82 Cato and Larsson (1995); SOU (1995), pp. 247–8.
83 MAna Hårsfj RABu.
84 Naval Underwater Museum, e-mail (May 2002).
85 Committee on Undersea Vehicles and National Needs (1996), p. 93.
86 Forman (1999), pp. 165–8.
87 *Jane's Fighting Ships* (1987–88), p. 566; Mooney (1994).
88 Dockery, Kevin (1991) *SEALs in Action*, New York, Avon Books.
89 CÖrlBO WD.
90 MAna Hårsfj RABu.
91 Ibid.
92 Ibid.
93 Cato and Larsson (1995); SOU (1995), pp. 244–9.
94 MAna Hårsfj RABu; CM/Grandin (1982).
95 MAna Hårsfj RABu.
96 ÖB TD (6 December 1982).
97 ÖB TD (14 December 1982).
98 SOU (2001), p. 127.
99 Ibid., pp. 127–8; Wallén (2002), p. 47.
100 Adelsohn (1987), p. 97.
101 SOU (1995), p. 146.
102 Forman (1999).
103 UL (1982).
104 *Dagens Nyheter* (1 February 1994).
105 Wallén (2002), p. 50.
106 MAna Hårsfj.
107 Bynander (1998b), p. 372.
108 Wallén (2002).
109 ÖB TD (7–12 October 1982).
110 Wallén (2002), p. 37.
111 Von Hofsten (1993), p. 83.
112 Wallén (2002); von Hofsten (1993), p. 64.
113 Hellberg (1994).
114 CMS WD (12 October 1982).
115 CM/Grandin (1982), Attach. 2.
116 CÖrlBO WD.
117 MAna Hårsfj.
118 CM/Grandin (1982), p. 130.
119 MAna Hårsfj.
120 MAna Hårsfj, Attach. 25.
121 MAna Hårsfj, Attach. 20.
122 ÖB TD (7–21 February 1986).
123 Interviews with Eklind; see also *Dagens Nyheter* (29 October 1990).
124 ÖB TD (21 February 1986).

125 ÖB TD (19 February 1986).
126 Kadhammar (1987), p. 106.
127 Von Hofsten (1993), pp. 83–4, 110–12.
128 ÖB TD (24 September 1980).
129 SOU (1995), pp. 144–6.
130 ÖB TD (1 September 1983).
131 Holmström (1998a, 1998b).
132 Tunander (1999), p. 186.
133 Hasselbohm (1992).
134 Woodward (1987), p. 206.
135 CM/Grandin (1982), p. 25.
136 SCSK Report (14 October 1982).
137 SOU (2001).
138 Swedish Radio (22 November 2001).
139 Lundmark (2001).
140 Paul Beaver, *Striptease*, Swedish TV2 (7 March 2000).
141 KU 1982/83:30, Attach. 7, p. 166.
142 ÖB HWD; ÖB TD (6 October 1982).
143 ÖB TD (4 January 1983).
144 ÖB TD (4–5 January 1983).
145 KU 1982/83:30, p. 19.
146 Tunander (2000a).
147 Schweizer (1994), p. 163.
148 Tunander (1989), pp. 114–16
149 Hasselbohm (1983a, 1983b, 1984, 1987).
150 Hasselbohm (1987).
151 Alsén (1987, 1990, 1992).
152 Lindfors (1991, 1996).
153 Hasselbohm (1984), p. 20.
154 Ibid.
155 Interview with Hasselbohm.
156 Hasselbohm (1984), p. 22.
157 Hasselbohm (1983b).
158 Hasselbohm (1984), pp. 23–4.
159 ÖB TD (18 May 1984).
160 Hasselbohm (1987).
161 *Dagens Nyheter* (17 December 1987).
162 Ibid.
163 Former Commander-in-Chief General Bengt Gustafsson says that no report was shown to him at the military leadership meeting in 1987. This supports Vice-Admiral Schuback's first statement that he saw the BOMÖ report as Commander of the Southern Military District.
164 Rylander (draft 2002), p. 138.
165 Wallén (2002), p. 47.
166 SOU (2001), p. 125.
167 It is not reported if this was a submarine or a surface vessel, nor if it passed through Store Belt or Öresund. However, anything unusual would have been registered. It was therefore probably not a submarine and certainly not a damaged submarine. It probably passed through Store Belt, because Soviet transits through Öresund were less common (see FET Monthly Report on Naval Activities, 1981–85).
168 FET (Monthly Report on Naval Activities, 1982).

169 ÖB TD (18 October 1982).
170 Tunander (1999).
171 ÖB TD (10 January 1983). The full quote is the following: '"It was smartly done
     by the Swedish government to release the submarine the way they did it." Schori,
     of course, changed his [Kissinger's] mind on this particular point.' After this inci-
     dent, General Ljung decided to brief a number of military attachés on this issue
     as well as his and the Chief of Staff's counterparts in the Nordic countries.

1. US Defense Secretary Caspar Weinberger visiting the underground naval base at Muskö in late September 1981. He is guided (from left to right) by Chief of the Naval Base Christer Kierkegaard, Chief of the Coastal Fleet Bror Stefenson, and by Weinberger's Swedish escort officer, Chief of Navy Vice-Admiral Per Rudberg. A year later, these Swedish officers were the main actors during the Hårsfjärden submarine hunt at Muskö Naval Base. In 2000, Weinberger stated on Swedish TV that the US had used their submarines to test Sweden's coastal defences after Swedish–US navy-to-navy consultations. On the right, the Swedish destroyer *Halland*. (Photo: Albert Håkansson/Pressens Bild)

2. US naval visit to Stockholm on 25–27 September 1982: the cruiser 26 *Belknap*, the frigate *1082 Elmer Montgomery*, and the navy tanker *Monongahela*. At noon on 26 September, a submersible showed its periscope metres from the US ships. It was probably from the *Monongahela*, there to protect the US ships, but, more important, it masqueraded as a 'Soviet submarine' on its way out. (Photo: Hans T. Dahlskog/Pressens Bild)

3. After the first observation of a periscope in Hårsfjärden on 1 October 1982, the Swedish Chief of Staff, Vice-Admiral Bror Stefenson, ordered the navy information division to prepare a press centre for 500 journalists. Soon all major US and European TV-channels and newspapers, altogether 750 journalists, turned up at Berga press centre from where they could watch the Swedes hunting 'Soviet' submarines in the narrow and shallow waters of Hårsfjärden. (Photo: Jan Collsiöö/Pressens Bild)

4. Helicopters and boats hunting 'Soviet' submarines in Hårsfjärden. (Photo: Örjan Björkdahl/Pressens Bild)

5. Fast attack craft dropping depth charge in Hårsfjärden. Some 47 depth charges were dropped, and it was the first time since World War II that the Swedes had used mines against enemy forces. (Photo: Ingemar Berling/Pressens Bild)

6. Fast attack craft *160 Väktaren* – the Swedish vessel that dropped most depth charges during the submarine hunt. On 5 October, it may have damaged a small bottom-crawling submersible. In the afternoon and night of 7 October, the *Väktaren* made clear contact with a submarine, but on both occasions, she was ordered to hold fire. (Photo: by Folke Hellberg/Pressens Bild)

7. At noon on 11 October, a 600-kilo mine was detonated 100 metres west of Måsknuv island after clear indications of a passing 'subsurface object'. A pillar of water rose up some 60 metres above the surface. The underground base at Muskö 15km further north shook. An hour later, a clear yellow dye was sent up about 100 metres south-southwest of the small island, indicating a damaged Western, most likely US, submarine. The sonar operator registered underwater repair works, and several Western officials have later spoken about a damaged US submarine. (Photo: Folke Hellberg/Pressens Bild)

8. Two days after the detonation of the mine west of Måsknuv, another submarine approached the mine barrage. The local mine chief received a cease-fire order directly from the Chief of Staff. But before the submarine had passed through the narrow channel, the local commander ordered helicopter 69 to lead an attack with 16 depth charges without informing the higher command. Seconds before the drop, the naval base entered the frequency and stopped the massive attack. (Photo: Bernt Claesson/Pressens Bild)

9. Press conference with Chief of Navy Vice-Admiral Per Rudberg and Commander-in-Chief General Lennart Ljung. Rudberg and Chief of Staff Bror Stefenson were competent naval officers who briefed Ljung during the incident. But Ljung did not always trust this information and sent his own intelligence people to the naval base. (Photo: Bertil Ericsson/Pressens Bild)

10. The Swedish parliamentary commission (appointed after the Hårsfjärden incident) presented its findings half a year later on 26 April 1983. From left to right: the chairman, former Defence and Foreign Minister, Sven Andersson; Social Democratic MP Maj-Lis Lööv; the military expert, Chief of Staff Vice-Admiral Bror Stefenson; and the Conservative MP Carl Bildt. The commission stated that six Soviet submarines had operated in the Stockholm archipelago, one in central Stockholm and several close to Muskö naval base. However, in the 1990s, it turned out that all the 'evidence' pointing to the Soviets had in fact been invented. (Photo: Leif Engberg/Pressens Bild)

11. Press conference on 26 April 1983, with (from left to right) Prime Minister Olof Palme, Defence Minister Anders Thunborg, and Foreign Minister Lennart Bodström, after the Swedish parliamentary commission had presented its statement about the six Soviet submarines. Palme stated that 'the serious Soviet violations of Sweden's territorial integrity' was 'a serious crime against international law'. (Photo: Bertil Ericsson/Pressens Bild)

12. Soviet Ambassador Boris Pankin after having received a note of protest from Prime Minister Palme. Moscow responded that the note was a 'unfriendly act'. Newspapers wrote about the 'most serious crisis between Sweden and the Soviet Union in modern times'. (Photo: Lennart Nygren/Scanpix)

5

Manipulation of Government Policy

On 13 October, while the dramatic submarine hunt was still going on, Chief of the Navy Vice-Admiral Per Rudberg appointed a committee to investigate the incident under the chairmanship of Rear-Admiral Gunnar Grandin, seconded by former Chief of Stockholm Coastal Defence, Brigadier-General Sven-Åke Adler (Deputy Chairman). The group also included Commander Anders Hammar, Commander Herman Fältström and Lieutenant-Colonel Curt E. Lundh (Secretary), all from the Naval Staff, and Commander L.G. Thomasson from the Eastern Military District. Their task was to investigate the Hårsfjarden incident, analyse the experiences and propose measures for the change of weapons systems, tactics, training and leadership.[1]

Two days later, on 15 October, when the hunt suddenly seemed to be over and the press centre was closed down, the government decided to appoint an official Parliamentary Commission to investigate the incident. Sven Andersson, former Minister of Defence (1957–73) and Minister of Foreign Affairs (1973–76), was appointed as its chairman. The members of the Commission were five MPs: Sven Andersson (Social Democrat), Carl Bildt (Conservative), Lars Eliasson (Centre Party), Maj-Lis Lööv (Social Democrat) and Olle Svensson (Social Democrat). Chief of Staff Vice-Admiral Bror Stefenson, and Sven Hellman from the Ministry of Defence were appointed as experts. The secretary was Michael Sahlin from the Ministry of Foreign Affairs.[2]

On 21 October, the government prepared for a press conference the following day to announce the appointment of the Parliamentary Submarine Commission.[3] At this meeting, Prime Minister Olof Palme, Foreign Minister Lennart Bodström and Defence Minister Börje Andersson were briefed by the Commander-in-Chief Lennart Ljung and by Chief of Staff Bror Stefenson. The notes from this meeting, made by Olof Palme's State Secretary Ulf Larsson, state:

> Meeting on submarines 21 October 1982. OP [Olof Palme], LB [Lennart Bodström], BA [Börje Andersson], UL [Ulf Larsson], PB [Per

Borg], Hans Dahlgren, T[ovio] Heinsoo, ÖB [Lennart Ljung], [Bror] Stefenson.

ÖB (Lennart Ljung): The investigation of the sea floor continues. The barriers are still deployed. There has definitely been one submarine, possibly several. Identification: no indication of nationality. Large amount of force used, even mines, which has never happened before. 'Tough methods. I don't know any other country that has done this in peacetime.'[4]

[Vice-Admiral] Stefenson: autumn 1980 'zero' [beginning of a new activity. The submarines] more provocative, [operate] two and two. Technical news (for example new sensors). Why are they here? 1) Swedish archipelago; it is very difficult to find submarines in the archipelago. 2) Test of our capability/will. 3) Intelligence. All cases (sounds, magnetic et al) indicate one (2?) submarine(s).[5]

At that time, there was, according to Ljung, no information on nationality pointing to the Soviet Union or any other nation. According to Stefenson, the operations were carried out because the Stockholm archipelago is ideal for submarine operations, because of intelligence and because a foreign power wanted to test Sweden's 'capability' and 'will' to defend its territory. These are exactly the words used by American and British officials to explain Western submarine operations in Swedish waters (see below). On other occasions, Stefenson has used the words of his US colleagues, which might indicate that this is the information they gave him. One month before the Hårsfjärden incident, Stefenson told *Dagens Nyheter*: 'Today, our capacity to hunt submarines is so low that the great powers may say: "You cannot defend your territory" . . . The great powers may put pressure on us and say how they want to do instead.'[6] It was hardly the Soviet Union that was worried about Sweden's lack of ASW capacity. In other words, the USA and Great Britain might say, particularly after the stranded Whiskey submarine in Karlskrona, that Sweden could not defend itself against Soviet submarines, but that the USA and Britain could help Sweden to develop such a readiness. These are almost the same words that the Conservative MP Carl Bildt had used in *Svenska Dagbladet* three days earlier. He spoke about continued Soviet intrusions and the stranded Soviet submarine at Karlskrona. Under these circumstances, it is, according to Bildt, 'not at all unlikely that NATO will start to exercise counter-operations in these very Swedish archipelagos where we have demonstrated our inability to keep Soviet submarines out'.[7] It seems that Carl Bildt and Vice-Admiral Stefenson were talking about Western submarines testing Swedish 'capability and will' to defend its internal waters in order to increase this 'capability and will'. Furthermore, it is difficult to understand a Soviet interest in testing Swedish 'will' to defend itself, if these operations had as their immediate consequence that they strengthened this Swedish 'will' to defend itself against the Soviets. Less than one month before the Hårsfjärden operation both Stefenson and Bildt indicated that NATO, or rather the USA and Great Britain, were likely to operate submarines in the Swedish archipelagos in order to increase Sweden's readiness and strengthen its capability to defend itself against the Soviet threat.

At the press conference of 22 October, Prime Minister Olof Palme announced that the 'government already had the option to order the military forces to sink a foreign submarine in Swedish waters. Anyone considering intruding in Swedish territory should, according to the Prime Minister, also consider that the government in the future might use this option.'[8] No further government statement was made until the Commission had published its report half a year later.

On 3 December 1982, Rear-Admiral Gunnar Grandin *et al.* presented their investigation report to the Chief of the Navy:

> There were visual detections, magnetic indications in mine barrages and magnetic sensor systems, radar indications of periscopes, IR indications, received signals [from submarines], and acoustic contacts with active and passive sonar. Among these reports there are several detections of certain submarines: [the observation of a periscope in Hårsfjärden at 12.50 on 1 October, the observation of a submarine sail close to Sandhamn at 18.05–19.00 on 4 October, the sonar contact (Doppler contact) with a submarine at a speed of 8 knots at the northern barrier of Hårsfjärden at 21.35 on 7 October, the visual observations of periscopes in Jungfrufjärden at 15.13–15.16 and close to Nämdö at 16.16 on 9 October, and the sonar contact and recording of propeller sound at 18.00 on 12 October] . . .
>
> In conclusion, this indicates operations with one or several submarines in our archipelago. The submarines, at least one of them, have carried at least one smaller vessel for deep penetration of the archipelago. The kind of activity indicates that one operation has penetrated the Sandhamn area and possibly the waters close to Stockholm, and at least one, possibly two, operations have penetrated the area south of the former one: primarily the Hårsfjärden area but also the area close to Mälsten.
>
> There is no possibility, with any degree of certainty, of analysing how the submarines have moved around in the Stockholm archipelago.
>
> There are probably several explanations for the activity: [1] a systematic mapping of our defence installations; [2] reconnaissance on sea routes and areas of our archipelago that might be used for submarines . . . [3] testing of our readiness against intruding submarines; [4]

following our tests with new defence material; [5] following our training programmes and military exercises; [6] a more general explanation may be preparation for an attack against our forces and our mobilization in an early phase of a war, for example through sabotage.

When it comes to the nationality of the submarines operating in our territorial waters, we know that the submarine in Karlskrona was a Soviet submarine. A number of visual, sonar and passive radar indications point, even during this period, to submarines from the WTO [Warsaw Treaty Organization]. Some indications of received radar signals cannot exclude that submarines of other nationality (NATO) have been in the area outside where the incidents have occurred. The reason for this has probably been to follow the activity.[9]

The Grandin Report confirms many of the statements from the war diaries. There are clear indications of submarines, but arguments supporting a Western operation are much weaker. The explanation of the submarine activity is speculative, and some arguments point also to Western submarines. However, the report believes in a Soviet operation, but it is still ambiguous. According to the report, ceasefires ordered by the military leadership did not follow the usual routines. 'Both ÖrlBO [the naval base] and Kaf [the Coastal Defence forces] argue that some of the best possibilities for a hit got lost because of this.'[10] The Naval Analysis Group Report with all its biased material is included as an attachment. Other parts of the text confirm incidents not recognized in this attachment. The Grandin Report seems to include a lot of ambiguities that are characteristic of an internal report.

The Submarine Defence Commission was dominated by its chairman Sven Andersson, secretary Michael Sahlin, Conservative MP Carl Bildt and military expert Vice-Admiral Bror Stefenson, who all had a deeper knowledge about security policy and military affairs. From interviews with officers briefing the Commission and from General Ljung's diary it seems clear that the others had little or no influence on the development of the investigation. Lennart Ljung wrote in his diary for 8 April: 'During the weekend [9–10 April], the Chief of Staff [Stefenson] is working together with Sven Andersson, Carl Bildt and the secretary Sahlin [Bildt's later State Secretary for Defence] on the final version of the Commission report.'[11] The Submarine Defence Commission used the Naval Analysis Group Report and the briefings by Commander Emil Svensson. Michael Sahlin was a friend of Captain Göran Wallén, Chief of Operations Division, Eastern Military District. This made it possible to use Wallén's expertise more informally for the Commission. Wallén told me that the Commission got the Eastern Military District war diary, which the Commission used for writing the report.[12] Commander Bengt Gabrielsson, Chief of Naval Operations,

Eastern Military District, said that he wrote a thick document as a draft for the Commission. Several paragraphs were used for writing the report. Military professionals were able to write a blueprint for the Commission; however, on essential events, they were less informed. The Defence Staff had turned directly to the local commanders and short-cut the line of information. Gabrielsson said that there were many things they had not been informed about. The same words were used by Major-General Gustaf Welin, Chief of Staff, Eastern Military District. The Commander of the Eastern Military District had been 'shunted aside'. As with the Naval Analysis Group Report, the drafts made by the Eastern Military District seriously biased the final Submarine Defence Commission Report. Furthermore, all ambiguities from the Grandin Report were taken out. The possibility that the ceasefires saved submarines was denied. All submarine activity was described as originating from Warsaw Pact members and almost certainly from the Soviet Union. The activity was described as war preparations, not as 'testing of Swedish capability and will'.

The Submarine Defence Commission Report was presented on 26 April 1983. It created a storm of reactions against the Soviet intrusions. The dramatic submarine hunt was described as only one indication of the Soviets playing with the Swedes. A concluding summary in English follows below:

> The Commission makes clear that it has been fully confirmed that foreign submarines were in the Hårsfjärden area in early October, 1982. It is stated that during this period six foreign submarines, three of which midget submarines of a hitherto unknown character, may have operated in the Stockholm archipelago. The sea floor prints, which have been measured and depicted, indicate that there were two types of partially bottom-crawling midget submarines, one leaving tracked prints, the other leaving prints of *inter alia* a keel. The discovery of these prints and the knowledge accordingly gained concerning the likely properties of these midget submarines have made it possible to reconstruct a likely sequence of events around the Hårsfjärden incident. The discovery has also initiated a renewed scrutiny of earlier incidents which could appear mysterious in certain respects. The discovery and the knowledge gained have underlined the seriousness of the submarine threat facing Sweden.
>
> In the account made of the likely sequence of events it is pointed out that of the six submarines, which may have participated in the total operation, four submarines – of which two were midget submarines – were involved in the penetration of Hårsfjärden, whereas the third large submarine and midget submarine operated in the central Stockholm archipelago. Probably, there were at most one large submarine and two midget

submarines simultaneously in Hårsfjärden proper. The large submarine is thought to have left the area rather soon after its discovery on 1 October. One of the two midget submarines presumably left Hårsfjärden after a few days. However the other, tracked midget submarine probably remained for a longer period of time in Hårsfjärden, causing most of the indications obtained in Hårsfjärden in the beginning of October.

In addition, the Commission reports that evidence has been secured that yet another penetration of the area near Hårsfjärden by a midget submarine took place in the beginning of November. A further number of certain observations show that operations by foreign submarines on Swedish territory have continued even after the Hårsfjärden incident.

The Commission states that during 1982 a considerable increase in the number of submarine violations has taken place. It appears likely that midget submarines have been used in connection with earlier submarine violations during the year, and that foreign submarine activity has been partially organized in a number of larger, coordinated operations. Seen over a long period of time it can be determined that there is a tendency for submarine activities to increase in scope, with an increasing tendency to penetrate Swedish internal waters and to operate in a provocative manner. Also, there is a tendency to spread the operations to a larger part of the year and a larger part of the Swedish Baltic coast, including Norrland.

The Commission underscores the seriousness and unacceptability of these violations in terms of Swedish security and defence policy and Sweden's policy of neutrality. Dealing with aspects of security policy, the Commission analyses conceivable motives underlying the violations. In so doing, the Commission sees fit to strongly question certain motives frequently appearing in the public debate and to point out the probability of motives of a military operational character.

Evidently, a security policy assessment of the submarine violations cannot be made in isolation from the fundamental question concerning the national identity of the submarines. On this point the Commission confirms that neither the sea floor investigations nor any other investigation has yielded proof in the form of objects found or otherwise which could bind a certain state to the violations. However, reports have been presented to the Commission on a large amount of observations of various kinds which, taken together, clearly indicate that the submarines in question originate from the Warsaw Pact, i.e., essentially the Soviet Union. The Commission accepts the conclusion drawn by experts that the violations made at Hårsfjärden as well as other violations during 1982 and, at any rate to an overwhelming degree, during the 1980s as a whole, were made by Soviet submarines.

No observation has been obtained indicating intrusions into Swedish territory by a submarine belonging to a NATO country.

... Finally, the Commission has assessed certain specific experiences gained from the anti-submarine operation carried out during the Hårsfjärden incident. In this context the Commission rejects rumours that the submarines escaped with deliberate Swedish assistance as entirely unfounded. It is determined that the submarines escaped because the nature of the midget submarines was unknown, because available Swedish resources were inadequate and too limited and because the use of anti-submarine weapons was too restricted. Difficulties in applying available weapons systems for the purpose of forcing submarines to the surface were seen to be considerable. Prohibitions concerning the use of mines were ordered for acceptable reasons.[13]

In the Swedish text it is stated that 'the probable sequence of events' was the following:

It can be assumed on safe grounds that the penetration by submarines of the naval base area at Hårsfjärden was only one part of a coordinated operation covering a relatively wide geographical area. This is a pattern that has also been established in the case of other incidents that it has been possible to follow in relative detail.

This coordinated operation would appear to have embraced six submarines in the Stockholm archipelago, of which three were midget submarines of a type not hitherto established.

These submarines probably operated in such a way that a conventional submarine served as some type of mother craft for a mini-submarine. Each submarine probably had well-defined and separate tasks forming part of this operation.

One submarine and mini-submarine taking part in the operation probably operated mainly in the central Stockholm archipelago. After separation from the submarine, this mini-submarine penetrated the area of the inner archipelago. Certain observations may even indicate that this mini-submarine penetrated into the Port of Stockholm during the last week of September. The mother craft returned to the Sandhamn area, where it was to be reunited with the mini-submarine. On the evening of 4 October it was observed and attacked by a Swedish patrol vessel with depth charges just inside Sandön. Contact was then lost on this occasion. This submarine and mini-submarine appear to have left the area after they were reunited at the end of the first week in October.

The main responsibilities of the two other submarines and their respective mini-submarines were in the area of the southern archipelago. Both mini-submarines entered the Hårsfjärden area at the turn of the month. They probably made use of both the approach from the south through Skramsösund, and the northern approach at Huvudholmen. At

12.50 hours on Friday 1 October, two conscripts at Berganäs observed two periscopes of a submarine heading into Hårsfjärden. On the basis of this periscope observation, the conclusion can be drawn that the craft in question was a conventional-size submarine. At this point of time it is certain that one, and very probably two, mini-submarines were already inside the Hårsfjärden area.

The submarine that was detected at 12.50 hours on 1 October, triggering the Swedish anti-submarine operation, may have left the area comparatively soon after it was detected . . . The other observations and indications recorded in Hårsfjärden proper are all considered to have stemmed from the two mini-submarines operating there. The mini-submarine that entered Hårsfjärden past Huvudholmen [in the north] left drag marks from its keel both when entering and when leaving by the same route. This mini-submarine probably left the area only a day or so after 1 October, to be reunited in due course with its mother craft. Both this mini-submarine and its mother craft probably remained in the archipelago area throughout the following week. It is established that a conventional submarine was just south of Oxnö udde, immediately off the northern approaches to Hårsfjärden, on the evening of 7 October. It is also probable that these submarines left the Swedish archipelago by some route other than through the Mälsten approaches during the next few days. It would appear that there was knowledge of Swedish mine detonations in the latter area on board the submarines.

The mini-submarine that left behind the characteristic imprints of caterpillar tracks was in Djupviken, inside Hårsfjärden, on the morning of 1 October. It would appear primarily to have been this mini-submarine that caused the large number of indications inside Hårsfjärden during ensuing days (and nights). It cannot be excluded that this mini-submarine suffered minor damage from a depth charge on one occasion. This mini-submarine probably remained in Hårsfjärden for a relatively long time, after which it left the Hårsfjärden area and, subsequently, the inner archipelago area.

It is established that a conventional submarine was in the waters off Mälsten on 12 October. This may have been the larger submarine, which was waiting for the mini-submarine that left Hårsfjärden last. After this it looks as if all the submarines and mini-submarines had already left the inner archipelago area on their voyage home.[14]

This presentation of the sequence of events is different from the one I have described above. According to the Submarine Defence Commission no submarine (except for possibly the last midget) is believed to have passed out at Mälsten. No submarine is believed to have been damaged by a mine. However, on the question of national origin, the Commission is very clear. The report claimed that all submarines were from the Warsaw Pact, most likely from the Soviet Union.[15] This conclusion was followed by a strong Swedish protest delivered to the Soviet Union.[16] At the press conference, Prime Minister Olof Palme said:

> The government has handed over a note of protest to the Soviet government. In this note, the Swedish government delivers its strong condemnation of the serious Soviet violations of Sweden's territorial integrity. This is a serious crime against international law. These deliberate and illegal attempts to investigate Sweden's territorial waters must be condemned. We have demanded from the Soviet government that it gives such instructions to its own Navy that the intrusions terminate.[17]

The *New York Times* wrote on its first page that:

> Sweden protested today against 'the gross violations of Swedish territorial integrity of which the Soviet Navy has been guilty' and threatened to sink any submarine that enters its waters without permission . . . Swedish Government sent a stiff diplomatic note to Moscow [and] temporarily recalled its Ambassador.[18]

In the records of the conversation between Prime Minister Palme and the Soviet Ambassador Boris Pankin, Palme used an even harsher language.[19] On 5 May, the Soviet response was handed over to Olof Palme. The Swedish protest was described as an 'unfriendly act that would undermine the good neighbour relations . . . Check of records for Soviet submarines from this time showed that they had not been in Swedish waters and had not been closer than 30 km.'[20] *Svenska Dagbladet* said that the language in the note was stronger than in any former crisis, and talked about the most serious crisis for Sweden in modern times.[21] Relations between Sweden and the Soviet Union were icy for several years. A radical change in Swedish public opinion towards the Soviet Union took place (see below).

The Submarine Defence Commission Report was prepared and presented under dramatic circumstances. One month before the report was made public, a submarine hunt took place close to Karlskrona Naval Base in the Blekinge archipelago in southern Sweden and another hunt went on again in the Hårsfjärden area close to Muskö Naval Base. A day after the report was presented, a submarine hunt started in the Hardangerfjord in Norway with the use of a number of depth charges and 24 anti-submarine rockets (see below). The next day another submarine hunt started in the Sundsvall area along the coast of mid-north Sweden, which, together with the Commission Report and the Norwegian hunt, dominated the newspapers. A couple of days afterwards, a submarine was seen in a fjord on the Swedish west coast north of Göteborg, and the day after another submarine appeared in Swedish territorial waters south of Göteborg (the latter surfaced and turned out to be West German).[22] A month later, on the evening of 27 May, three journalists saw 'the top of a small submarine sail' – 1–2 metres wide – for a minute or more in central Stockholm a few hundred metres from the royal castle. They reported their observation to the Defence Staff and they were interviewed the same night. Their description of the submarine sail is similar to the observation made in Stockholm harbour on 30 September. In this case too, there were important naval ships visiting Stockholm – the British frigate *Minerva* and the Royal Yacht *Britannia* with Queen Elizabeth II – as if the small submersible was patrolling these ships.[23]

The strange thing is that all these submarines, except for the West German one, were – like the first Hårsfjärden submarines – first seen on the surface deep inside archipelagos or fjords in relatively densely populated areas. The Swedish submarine captain Nils Bruzelius had already said six months earlier:

> The question that has to be answered is the following: why are the foreign submarines so easily discovered when Swedish submarines, under the same circumstances (in Swedish waters) are almost never discovered. The reasons cannot be that these foreign submarine crews are badly trained. On the contrary, when they have been subject to advanced anti-submarine operations, they have proved to be very capable. The only explanation I can find is quite simply that 'they are discovered because they want to be'.[24]

Some researchers explained this as a Soviet show of force and as political signals to force Sweden to adapt to Soviet interests.[25] The consequences of these activities, however, were rather the opposite, and now, 20 years later, we may have to accept that these incidents had another origin.

On 26 April 1983, after the Submarine Defence Commission had presented its report, the co-author of the Swedish note, Sverker Åström, a senior diplomat and Sven Andersson's former State Secretary for Foreign Affairs, was interviewed on the evening news. He stated:

> There must be very strong motives on the Soviet side . . . [In Russia], all branches of government, and also the Soviet Navy, have had a plan for several years, and I guess they have just continued to fulfil it as if nothing had happened. There is a certain bluntness and stiffness in the system that makes them continue with this . . . If one is an optimist one might say that there is a chance that Andropov will give instructions to

terminate the activity . . . [The intention of the note] is to bring the issue up in the inner circles of the Kremlin.[26]

The major proof for pointing to the Soviet Union seems to have been that only Whiskey submarines were believed to have keels (referring to the marks of a keel on the sea floor southeast of Mälsten). The Hårsfjärden submarine was described as a diesel-powered submarine like the Whiskey, while the American and the British submarines were said to be nuclear. Another proof seems to have been that allegedly only the Soviets, and no other navy operating in the Baltic Sea, had midget submarines. A bottom-crawling midget was also supposed to indicate a Soviet submarine. Member of the Commission Olle Svensson said that he was convinced by Sven Andersson of Soviet responsibility 'after the two of us had gone through the secret file [the Naval Analysis Group Report] with all the documents about the nationality of the intruder'.[27] In a summary of 3 March on confirmed submarine observations the Naval Analysis Group Report presents several unfounded statements: 'There are no midget submarines operative within NATO . . . The analysis concludes: older submarine with two propellers – These are only to be found in the Warsaw Pact.'[28]

At the 26 April press conference several hundreds of journalists appeared. The Chairman of the Commission, Sven Andersson, told them that, according to the conclusions made by the experts, the submarines originated from the Warsaw Pact:

> The many visual observations made by military officers and civilians . . . point without doubt to submarines from the Warsaw Pact. Furthermore, there are two acoustic observations, which both reveal submarines from the Warsaw Pact. Results from our signal intelligence on radars and radio traffic also definitely point to Warsaw Pact submarines. The sea-floor investigation gives the same result . . . No observation has been made indicating intrusions on Swedish territory by submarines originating from NATO. The fact that the Soviet Union has about 45 conventional submarines in the Baltic Sea, while Poland only has four and the GDR none, is one of several elements indicating that the Warsaw Pact in this case is identical with the Soviet Union. The Commission has, after a thorough examination, agreed with the conclusions of the experts.[29]

There was, according to Andersson, a large amount of evidence pointing to the Soviet Union. There was no doubt about the national origin, and Carl Bildt said: 'I cannot think of anything in modern times that has been more serious.' 'We are definitely sure,' he said. 'There is no doubt, [but we cannot reveal everything]. That would damage Sweden.'[30]

At the press conference with a couple of hundred journalists from all over the world, Sven Andersson presented one proof after another clearly demonstrating that the operations were carried out by the Soviet Union. Andersson was, however, more or less, word for word, quoting the report from his military expert, the Defence Staff Report of 18 April 1983. It stated, firstly, that all visual observations had been interpreted as submarines from the Warsaw Pact. Secondly, two acoustic observations had been made. In both cases, the conclusion was submarines from the Warsaw Pact. Thirdly, the results of signal intelligence could not be made public for security reasons. Signal intelligence proved definitely that there were Warsaw Pact submarines. Fourthly, the existence of tracks from midget submarines supported the conclusion that the Warsaw Pact was responsible for the intrusions. It would, according to the Defence Staff Report, be 'almost impossible to keep such systems secret in the West'. In the Soviet Union, however, such a submarine could easily have been hidden.[31]

On 10 October 1983, after some Swedish–Soviet controversies, Prime Minister Palme handed over a memorandum to the Soviet Ambassador Boris Pankin to explain the strong protest against the Soviet Union. A videotape showing prints on the sea floor was enclosed. The material presented in the memorandum was almost identical to the report presented by Vice-Admiral Stefenson and the Defence Staff on 18 April 1983. A few lines were taken out (shown below in brackets). The part concerning the sea-floor investigation was extended compared to that in the Defence Staff Report. The memorandum states the following:

> The Submarine Defence Commission states in its report that it had been informed about a large number of observations and circumstances that altogether give the basis for the conclusion that the submarines intruding in Swedish territorial waters during the Hårsfjärden incident belonged to Soviet naval forces. A conclusion on this material follows below.
>
> 1. Visual observations
> Visual observations were made by both military personnel and civilians. They were questioned as early as possible after the observations, and they made drawings describing what they saw. After that they gave detailed descriptions to make it possible to define submarine class, nationality and behaviour.
>
> [The total number of visual observations (during this period) accepted for nationality and class identification is 16, of which 11 originate from the time of the Hårsfjärden incident.]
>
> All observations from the time of the Hårsfjärden incident lead us

to the conclusion that the submarines belonged to the Warsaw Pact. On two occasions, the submarines were of Whiskey class. On one occasion, the submarine was either a Whiskey, Foxtrot or Juliet. Other occasions (i.e. observations of masts) point to Warsaw Pact submarines even though it has not been possible to define the class.

2. Acoustic observations
After analysis of the acoustic observations, it was possible to draw conclusions about nationality in two cases. One of them took place in August, the other in October in Danziger Gatt during the Hårsfjärden incident.

[It is normal that there were very few acoustic observations. It is only during submarine hunts that this kind of information is received. The usual search method from helicopter is active sonar, which does not give information for identification. Only with the use of passive sonar will it be possible to identify the submarine. Hence the low figure.]

The conclusion is that in both these cases we are dealing with Warsaw Pact submarines. It is possible to identify various sounds; i.e. to identify the number of propellers.

3. Signal intelligence
It is well known that signal intelligence makes it possible to define the kind of radar station that transmits a signal. Knowledge about ship radar makes it possible to define class of ship and usually even nationality. Under certain circumstances it is even possible to define the individual ship.

By taking the bearing of the signal, the position of a transmitter can be defined. It is also possible to get important information by listening to radio traffic between different ships or between ship and base.

[Knowledge about our capability in and results from signal intelligence is of extraordinary value for foreign powers. Because of this, it is not possible to present the extensive material on various radar and radio transmissions that have been recorded. If results from our signal intelligence were published, it would be possible to make comparisons between incidents and results from signal intelligence, which could reveal our signal intelligence organization.]

The result of signal intelligence shows [definitely] that Warsaw Pact submarines were active in Swedish territorial waters during the time of the Hårsfjärden incident.

4. Investigation of the sea floor
After the Hårsfjärden incident, tracks from midget submarines were found on the sea floor. They were video-recorded.

There is an extensive development of sub-surface vessels in various countries. It is well known that the Warsaw Pact countries, particularly the Soviet Union, has great knowledge about sub-surface technology and has a number of small military and civilian submersibles able to move on the sea floor by the use of different methods of propulsion. There is also information about Soviet mini- [or midget] submarines published in books. There is, however, no sign that any Western power in the vicinity of Sweden has mini- [or midget] submarines.

Prints from a larger submarine were also found on the sea floor. These prints show that the submarine had an external keel. In the Baltic Sea, only submarines from the Warsaw Pact have such a keel. The size of this print happened to be the same as the one found after the submarine 137 in Gåsefjärden [Karlskrona 1981].

The existence of prints on the sea floor shows that the intruding submarines belonged to the Warsaw Pact.

The Submarine Commission concludes that all these circumstances, combined with the known pattern of naval operations in the Baltic Sea, show that it is perfectly clear that the intrusions in Hårsfjärden were carried out by submarines belonging to the Warsaw Pact. The fact that the Soviet Union has 45 conventional submarines (mostly Whiskey class) for operations in the Baltic Sea, while Poland only has four old submarines and the GDR to our knowledge none indicates that the Warsaw Pact, in this case, is essentially identical to the Soviet Union.[32]

In this document there is, as already stated by Carl Bildt, 'no doubt'. However, the 1995 Submarine Commission shows that all these arguments were made up to prove Soviet responsibility for the Hårsfjärden operation. There was no evidence supporting these statements. We have to admit that all this information was a construct invented by the Defence Staff under the leadership of the Commission's military expert Vice-Admiral Bror Stefenson.

Firstly, the 1995 Submarine Commission, with access to the same material as the 1983 Commission, did not find any visual information pointing to the Warsaw Pact. According to Sven Andersson and the Defence Staff analysis, several witnesses had seen periscopes and submarine sails. They had made drawings and been shown pictures of Soviet submarines. However, it is not easy to distinguish these Soviet submarines from some Western submarines, and it would demand a specialist. The 1995 Commission states: 'From the reports on visual observations that we have had access to, we cannot make any definite conclusion about nationality.'[33] To say, as the Defence Staff Report did, that an observation has been identified as a Whiskey-, Foxtrot- or Juliet-class submarine is in itself absurd, because of the differences between these submarine classes.

Secondly, of the two pieces of acoustic information described by the Defence Staff Report, one was from August 1982; the other was the 3.47-minute sequence from 12 October discussed above. The Navy Analysis Group argued that the tape recordings proved that the submarines had two propellers and that this indicated Soviet or at least Warsaw Pact submarines. The first recording was analysed by experts from FOA in the winter 1982–83. They found no indication of propellers on the tape. FOA handed in their analysis on 13 April 1983, but still what appeared in the Defence Staff Report of 18 April 1983 and in the Swedish note to the Soviet Union of 10 October 1983 was a Warsaw Pact submarine with two propellers. The tape recording of 12 October 1982 was analysed at FOA the following week. The report of 20 October 1982 stated that a 3.47-minute sequence of the tape included propeller sounds that 'most likely originated from a submarine if the surface was free [from other vessels].'[34] Commander Anders Hammar says that they used Arne Åsklint's analysis: a sound similar to a submarine with two propellers. But Åsklint says that this conclusion referred to a different tape recording. Hammar says now that he was the one that misinformed the Commission, because he himself had been misled about the possible nationality. The only thing we know today is that this 3.47-minute sequence was not tape-recorded around 18.00, nobody knows who tape-recorded it and there is, in general, no correspondence between the tape-recorded sounds and the commentaries on the speaker channel. The Defence Staff presented the 'two propellers' as proof of a Warsaw Pact submarine, while many submarines from NATO countries actually had two propellers. The far more experienced Norwegian Military Intelligence that analysed the FOA tape found it to be neither a conventional nor nuclear Soviet submarine, but probably a submarine originating from a NATO country or, according to one source, possibly the USA. In the early 1990s, the Swedish Ambassador to the USA handed over a copy of the 3.47-minute tape to a friend, General William Odom, a former Chief of the NSA, to let US intelligence make an analysis of it. After this analysis, the latter returned to the Swedish Ambassador and said that it was 'not possible to conclude anything from this tape'. From 1983 to 1995 the tape was presented as the major Swedish proof of Soviet involvement.

Thirdly, there was no signal intelligence pointing to the Soviet Union. This statement was invented by the Defence Staff. Commander Björn Eklind, Deputy Chief of Defence Staff Intelligence and responsible for the signal intelligence briefings of the Commission, said to me that he was surprised at Andersson's statement, because he was not informed that they had anything on the Soviets. At least, there was no Swedish signal intelligence pointing to the Soviet Union, he said, neither from FRA nor from the Swedish Navy. In 1988, after information had turned up in the mass media, Pär Kettis, Director-General of the Swedish Signal Intelligence Agency (FRA), wrote to State Secretary for Defence Nils Gunnar Billinger. Kettis stated that FRA had no information on signals linked to the Hårsfjärden incident. In 1995, FRA wrote to the Second Submarine Commission and said that they had not registered any signals linked to the Hårsfjärden incident. Swedish signal intelligence against the Soviet Baltic Fleet had given no results.[35] When Commander-in-Chief General Bengt Gustafsson became aware of this information he turned to former member of the Submarine Defence Commission, the leader of the Conservative Party Carl Bildt, who said that the signal intelligence information they had did not originate from FRA, but from the Navy. The Navy had five indications of submarine radar appearing in the Grandin Report (and in the naval base war diary): two of them were supposedly Warsaw Pact radar, while three originated from possibly West German submarines. In the Naval Analysis Group Report, one 'West German' radar is excluded (*Visborg*'s report from 08.20 on 5 October). Three of these indications (two Warsaw Pact and one West German) 'may have originated from outside Swedish territorial waters', while the fourth one was the possible West German indication (from Kanholmsfjärden of 30 September). The Defence Staff Report states that signal intelligence definitely indicated Warsaw Pact submarines. However, the two indications that were believed to be within Swedish territorial waters were both classified as possibly 'West German'.[36] Either Carl Bildt has been manipulated or he has himself tried to manipulate General Gustafsson.

Fourthly, the Defence Staff Report states that the sea-floor investigation clearly indicated Warsaw Pact submarines. It would not have been possible, according to the Defence Staff, to keep a bottom-crawling submarine leaving caterpillar tracks on the sea floor secret in the West. This is not true. NATO countries were able to keep both mini- and midget submarines with such a capability secret (see below), while it is still not confirmed if Soviet submarines had this capability at the time. Western navies (West German, French, British and US) had conventional diesel-electric submarines as well as midget submarines. Within NATO, the Baltic Sea was primarily a West German and Danish responsibility. British and sometimes French submarines entered the Baltic Sea overtly. However, according to Danish and British sources, both British and US submarines entered the Baltic Sea covertly. British or US submarines carrying out intelligence tasks or special force operations would enter the Baltic Sea submerged, and the officers at the Danish Naval Command in Århus were supposed to close their eyes (see below). Several of these submarines had a keel similar to the Whiskey. Furthermore, Whiskey submarines and other Soviet submarines may have been able to carry SDVs (Swimmer

Delivery Vehicles) in a 0.5-metre torpedo tube, but there were no indications that Soviet submarines in the Baltic Sea ever carried real midgets, while several Western submarines were able to do that. Soviet surface ships were known to carry midget submarines (see below).

Every single statement made by Sven Andersson, the Defence Staff Report and the Swedish PM to the Soviet Union seems to have been a bluff. Andersson and Stefenson may, for several reasons, have believed that this was necessary under the special conditions in which these incidents took place. Still, all arguments Andersson brought up seem to have been invented by the Defence Staff to prove its case. The alleged signal intelligence information was, according to Ingvar Carlsson (later Prime Minister), 'important background material' for the strong Swedish protest against the Soviet Union.[37] Now, it is clearly established that this information was invented to prove Soviet presence. The same seems to have been the case with one of the Commission's advisers, Professor John Erickson, a British scholar and specialist on Soviet military forces. He stated clearly on Swedish TV that he knew that the Hårsfjärden submarines originated from the Soviet Union (see above). Erickson was invited to brief the Commission together with a Norwegian anti-submarine warfare specialist, Captain Tor Nicolaisen. Erickson was a Professor and Director of Defence Studies at the University of Edinburgh, while Nicolaisen was the Military Assistant to the Norwegian Minister of Defence, Anders Sjaastad. Nicolaisen had received anti-submarine warfare training from the USA and Great Britain and had been project officer for the SOSUS station at Andøya in Northern Norway. He told me that neither he nor Erickson had any specific indications pointing to the Soviet Union, but Erickson believed that the Soviet Union would have been 'willing' to carry out these operations. He had, however, nothing that linked this 'Soviet psychology' with the operations in Hårsfjärden.

Some five years later, it turned out that Olof Palme had never been convinced by the Commission Report, but it was politically impossible for him to deny its results. In 1988, *Dagens Nyheter* wrote that 'Olof Palme was forced to point to the Soviet Union'.[38] The Submarine Defence Commission did not keep the government informed, and Palme was briefed only 10 or 11 days (actually 14 days; see below) before the Commission Report was made public. When the unified Parliamentary Commission pointed to the Soviet Union, the government had no choice.[39] In 1999, former Deputy Prime Minister (and later Prime Minister) Ingvar Carlsson said:

> Because the Soviet Union had violated our waters in Karlskrona [the Whiskey submarine that was stranded outside Karlskrona in 1981], many people believed that it must be Soviet submarines also this time

... Sven Andersson did not inform Olof Palme about the Commission's conclusions until they had tied themselves totally [to a final decision].[40]

In his book, Ingvar Carlsson stated that Sven Andersson informed Olof Palme on 12 April.[41] (Ljung wrote that it was 11 April, the day after the report was finalized[42]). At that time the decision to point to the Soviet Union had already been taken. 'It must have been Sven Andersson's strategy to postpone information for such a long time that the Prime Minister would not be able to influence the Commission,' Carlsson argued.[43] Not even Defence Minister Anders Thunborg was informed. 'The conclusions were presented as a *fait accompli* even to him. This made Olof Palme irritated.'[44] The Minister of Industry and later Defence Minister Thage G. Peterson said: 'Olof Palme thought that the Social Democrats in the Submarine Defence Commission had not enough evidence to come up with these conclusions. I remember that Olof Palme and Sven Andersson had a real quarrel.'[45] In the briefing of 11 April, both Prime Minister Palme and Defence Minister Thunborg were sceptical. Ljung wrote that it had become necessary to bring up extensive and detailed material to convince the two ministers. This material (the Defence Staff Report of 18 April) 'is now put together at the Defence Staff', Ljung wrote.[46] Still, neither Palme nor Thunborg were convinced by this material, but they accepted that the Commission had created a *fait accompli*. The Minister of Justice, Ove Rainer, was against pointing to the Soviet Union despite the conclusions of the Submarine Defence Commission. He said that the evidence or indications pointing to the Soviet Union would not hold water in a trial. Foreign Minister Lennart Bodström had the same view.[47] In 1994, Bodström spoke about the government's decision to point to the Soviet Union as responsible for the intrusions in accordance with the conclusions in the Submarine Defence Commission Report:

> The Social Democratic government was in doubt about the conclusions made by the Submarine Defence Commission Report in spring 1983, but the government yielded to public opinion . . . The party representatives within the Commission were unified. And with the kind of public opinion that dominated, the government had no other alternative than to adhere to the conclusions of the Commission. Wrong? But in politics, you sometimes have to follow public opinion.[48]

Later, he said: 'In conclusion, I would like to say that the government had no choice. It was forced to adhere to the Submarine Defence Commission and accordingly defend it. This was our position.'[49] In an interview I had with Lennart Bodström, he told me that the task of the

Commission was not to point out any specific state, but to study the possibilities for 'improving anti-submarine warfare forces before new submarine intrusions take place'.[50] In an interview with me, former Defence Minister Anders Thunborg said that he did not agree with Sven Andersson. Thunborg said to me that we had nothing on the Soviets, and that he was against pointing to the Soviet Union.[51] In the 1980s, Thunborg kept to the official version and stated clearly that Soviet submarines had penetrated the Swedish archipelago at Hårsfjärden in 1982.[52] However, Thunborg never believed this version. There was no evidence. This was also Anders Thunborg's view at the time of the incidents, former Norwegian Minister of Defence Anders Sjaastad told me. In 1996, Anders Thunborg said:

> As Defence Minister I did not have the same view as the Submarine Defence Commission. I thought they were too self-confident . . . But what could we do? We could not dive ourselves. If we have military authorities that know these things, we have to trust them. We were sorry that the Commission had decided not to contact the government before the report was published. And the driving force behind this position was Carl Bildt, and that I cannot accept.[53]

The Prime Minister, the Deputy Prime Minister (and later Prime Minister), the Foreign Minister, the Defence Minister, the Minister of Industry (later Defence Minister) as well as the Minister of Justice were all against pointing to the Soviet Union, because nobody on the military side had presented any clear evidence supporting this view. Still, the government made the strongest ever protest against the Soviet Union. Sweden recalled its Ambassador to Moscow for consultations. According to Deputy Prime Minister Ingvar Carlsson:

> Olof Palme had two choices: He could have a fight with the Submarine Defence Commission and its chairman Sven Andersson supported by the Navy and most other representatives of the Swedish defence forces, or he could have a fight with the Soviet Union.[54]

In practical terms, Prime Minister Palme had no choice. The Submarine Defence Commission had created a *fait accompli*, because its chairman, Sven Andersson (as well as Carl Bildt), believed that it had become a political necessity.

In 1990, Carl Bildt spoke to the Swedish Royal War Academy. He no longer mentioned any of the 'evidence' that earlier was supposed to point to the Soviet Union as responsible for the 1982 incident. Bildt said that the Commission had no distinct evidence linked to specific observations that made it possible to point to the Soviet Union.

> With the requirements that later became necessary to make a statement
> on nationality – clear and definite evidence linked to a specific obser-
> vation – the Commission did not have enough information to make
> such a statement . . . [However, to the Chairman of the Commission,
> Sven Andersson] it was natural not just to accept this fact. A discussion
> about nationality was viewed as unavoidable, and to publicly point out
> the responsible nation was also perceived as an essential part of a policy
> to terminate these operations.[55]

In other words, Andersson allegedly wanted to tie the Soviet Union to
the incident for political reasons. *Dagens Nyheter* refers to a source
close to Andersson saying that the mass media expectations in Sweden
and internationally made it necessary to come up with a statement
about national origin. Andersson's former State Secretary for Foreign
Affairs, Sverker Åström, had allegedly recommended that Andersson
point to the Soviet Union.[56] Vice-Admiral Per Rudberg told me that,
unlike the government, Andersson was convinced that the Soviet
Union was responsible, and Andersson decided to keep the government uninformed in order to create a *fait accompli* that would force
the government to accept the position of the Commission. Sverker
Åström himself said that Bildt and the military were driving forces
behind the accusations against the Soviet Union. However, the enormous press coverage made it impossible to come out without a scape-
goat. Åström also argues that there were strictly political reasons for
Sven Andersson's decision.[57] Åström was, together with Anders
Thunborg, the co-author of the government protest note strongly criticizing the Soviet Union.[58] Åström wrote later:

> If Moscow had been allowed to go free despite strong indications, the
> Commission would have been split in two, and Bildt, at least, would
> have expressed a different view. It would have been a furious domestic
> political fight – a crisis that foreign interests would have been able to
> profit from. Such a development had to be avoided, and, because of
> this, he [Andersson] was willing to overcome his doubts, and, of course,
> defend his position with force. He was prepared for a conflict with
> Moscow, and they would be able to handle it in the years to come.[59]

Social Democrat and member of the Submarine Defence Commission
Olle Svensson has a similar view on Bildt, as the most active member,
who wanted to profit from the incident politically, but Svensson is also
clear on Sven Andersson's role and the role of the experts (Bror
Stefenson and Emil Svensson's report). Olle Svensson says:

> Most important, we decided not to hide the conclusions drawn by our
> experts. We pointed to the Soviet Union as the intruder! At the office

of the Commander-in-Chief, we were shown a film with the caterpillar tracks of a midget submarine on the bottom of the Baltic Sea, and we were informed about some other observations. Among the experts we have to rely on, this removed any doubt about which military force entered our waters. If we don't speak out, we will be perceived as cowards both at home and abroad. I was in doubt for quite a while, but I was convinced by Sven Andersson after the two of us had gone through the secret file [the Naval Analysis Group Report] with all the documents about the nationality of the intruder.[60]

Sven Andersson's problem was political. If Sweden was unable to identify an intruder, despite all indications and with everyone in the mass media pointing to the Soviet Union, it would be perceived as a weak state possibly adapting to Soviet interests. In his diary on 8 March 1983, General Ljung confirmed that Andersson wanted to point to the Soviet Union for political reasons. Ljung referred to Andersson as saying: 'If we don't come up with a decision on the nationality, we may get a debate with many statements about the Swedes purposely avoiding a conclusion on this issue. This may be perceived as an easy way out politically.'[61] In other words, despite lack of evidence pointing to the Soviet Union, Sweden had to point to the Soviets, otherwise people or even the international community would believe that the Swedes were adapting to Soviet interests. At that time, Ljung himself was not convinced that it was possible to point to the Soviets. A week later, however, on 16 March 1983, he had changed his mind. Hasselbohm's article from the day before in *Dagens Industri* claiming 'NATO involvement' in Hårsfjärden made it necessary to point out the Soviet Union.[62] On 21 April, just a few days before the Commission presented its report, Ljung wrote:

> The nationality question [the Commission accusing the Soviet Union] will not be very controversial . . . [However,] the Commission's statement about a submarine [or midget submarine] being deep inside Stockholm harbour and the possible link that will be made to the ongoing visit of US naval ships may become a difficult issue.[63]

General Ljung was worried that if this latter incident with a periscope a few metres from the US cruiser *Belknap* was brought up, the submarines would be linked to the US naval ships in central Stockholm. It is much more likely that this vessel was released by the US ships than that it was a Soviet midget that had gone some 50 kilometres submerged through the archipelago on a busy waterway with thousands of narrow passages all the way to the Stockholm castle and back. Despite General Ljung's worries, however, this issue was never brought up.[64] After reading General Ljung's diary, the only reason for pointing out the Soviet Union as responsible for the intrusions in Hårsfjärden in 1982 seems to have been political.

Still however, several leading government representatives probably believed in Soviet submarine activities, but they were not willing to protest against the Soviets because this would strengthen the Conservatives' and Carl Bildt's Cold War rhetoric. In a formerly classified document from the Social Democratic leadership meeting on 17 May 1983, Olof Palme argues: 'The debate on foreign policy is about to fall to pieces . . . if they [the Soviets] continue, this will seriously damage our relations. We have to explain this to them. Sooner or later we will sink a submarine.' In the same document, Sten Andersson, later Foreign Minister, says:

> Continued Soviet activity using our coast as their backyard will put us in a difficult political position. The Conservatives will get air under their wings for their propaganda . . . In conclusion, we have to let the Russians understand – through diplomatic and political channels – the consequences of continued intrusions.[65]

The Social Democratic Party had become extremely worried that the Conservative Party would profit from what even they believed were serious Soviet intrusions.

In early autumn 1983, after a summer of continued submarine intrusions (some 200–300 reported observations), Carl Bildt argued at a Parliamentary Foreign Affairs Committee meeting in favour of a statement on the national origin of the intruders. He himself was going to point to the Russians, he told General Ljung.[66] This was also the view of the Naval Analysis Group and the Defence Staff, General Ljung wrote:

> They argue that the submarine intrusions continue beyond any doubt. They also say that everything supports the fact that the submarine activity originates from the Soviet Union . . . I support the first statement [with some reservations] . . . When it comes to the national origin, I cannot agree with the view of the Defence Staff . . . [There is] no hard evidence, hardly even indications.[67]

Despite continued submarine intrusions and despite new dramatic submarine hunts, neither the government nor the Commander-in-Chief was willing to point to the Soviet Union. They may have believed in Soviet activity, but uncertainty at the highest levels is also illustrated by the information the Swedes received from Moscow in connection with the submarine hunt in Karlskrona in February–March 1984. This time neither the government nor the Commander-in-Chief pointed to any state responsible for the intrusions. The Ekéus Investigation writes that during this incident, the Swedish Assistant Under-Secretary for Foreign Affairs (for the Political Division), Ambassador Jan Eliasson, happened to be in Moscow. His Soviet counterpart had asked him, 'Why do the Swedes not use more military force against what they believe are submarines?' The Soviet General Secretary Andropov had let the Finnish President Koivisto bring Prime Minister Palme a similar message: 'Just bomb them.'[68] According to Koivisto, the Soviet leader had said: 'It will suit us very well if the Swedes use live ammunition against the intruding submarines.'[69] This attitude seems illogical if the submarines originated from the Soviet Union, and neither the government nor the Commander-in-Chief wanted to touch the nationality issue in the following years.

Not until General Ljung left office in 1986 did the Defence Staff under Vice-Admiral Stefenson prepare a report claiming Soviet responsibility for the intrusions. This report was presented to the new Minister of Defence Roine Carlsson on 25 November 1987 by the new Commander-in-Chief, General Bengt Gustafsson, and the new Chief of Staff, Lieutenant-General Thorsten Engberg. This report summarized submarine activities since 1982 and spoke of an intruding sub-surface system with an estimated number of ten 30-metre submarines and even more 10-metre submarines or rather SDVs. Operations often involved one or two of the 30-metre submarines and up to four smaller vessels.[70] Only the Soviet Union was believed to have the capacity to produce such a system and to carry out this activity. The report was partly declassified in September 2001.[71] Parts that it was not yet possible to declassify at that date are shown in italic below. The Defence Staff Report stated:

> Western countries *are open. Only very limited resources may exist without our knowledge.* This means that no single [Western] country could carry out this activity. Also within NATO's unified resources such possible hidden resources would be too small. It is out of the question that Western nations would be able to carry out this activity both coordinated and hidden for such a long period of time. This does not exclude individual indications originating from a Western country. The Warsaw Pact countries *are less open.* The production of a sub-surface system with *observed capabilities* presupposes a high level of knowledge about submarine technology. Among the Warsaw Pact countries in our vicinity, it is only the Soviet Union that has such a capacity . . . Other indications on nationality may be *signal intelligence, acoustic information, prints on the sea floor, and the link to other systems.* Of these indications only the prints on the sea floor have given us interesting information in recent years. Since the prints found in Hårsfjärden in

1982, parallel tracks on the bottom have been found in . . . and in Kappelhamnsviken [Gotland] in 1987. According to an investigation, the latest prints are in their character and dimensions the same as the ones found in Hårsfjärden in 1982 . . . In conclusion, all information points to the Soviet Union as the country carrying out foreign sub-surface activity on Swedish territory.[72]

The Commander-in-Chief told the Minister of Defence that, in the general briefing for the government the next day, he intended to point to the Soviet Union as responsible for the intrusions during the last year. According to Prime Minister Ingvar Carlsson, no evidence was presented, and the Commander-in-Chief was probably under hard pressure from the group analysing the incidents. '[A] surprise attack from the Swedish military forces was unacceptable . . . [and Carlsson would] not accept pointing out any nation without definite proofs.' After this, he appointed an advisory group to look into the Defence Staff analysis.[73] This group consisted of Ambassador Hans Dahlgren from the Prime Minister's office, Ambassador Jan Eliasson, Assistant Under-Secretary for Foreign Affairs, and Major-General Bengt Wallroth, Assistant Under-Secretary for Defence and former Chief of Swedish Military Intelligence (SSI). The latter had overall responsibility. According to Wallroth's notes made for the briefing of the government, no bases, no confirmed information on these vessels and no information about their transit from Soviet coasts had been found. According to Wallroth's notes and Dahlgren's draft notes, several countries had a high level of competence and the capability to hide sub-surface systems.[74] Although tracks from a bottom-crawling submarine had also been found in 1987, these were, according to the 'Wallroth Group', not interpreted as proof of Soviet activity. According to a *Dagens Nyheter* interview with a member of the group, there was:

> no proof that these kinds of tracks on the bottom could only originate from Eastern vessels . . . One has to ask oneself how NATO would react if the C-in-C Analysis Group stated that Sweden was subject to extensive submarine intrusions. It would most likely be interpreted that the Soviet Union was moving its strategic positions forward in a way which would demand NATO countermeasures; for example, the West would feel forced to operate in these waters.[75]

Later, Major-General Wallroth confirmed *Dagens Nyheter*'s version, and he did not exclude that several submarine intrusions originated from a NATO country. According to Prime Minister Carlsson, the advisory group confirmed submarine activity in Swedish waters in

1987, but there was no information pointing to a particular state responsible for these operations.[76]

In the early and mid-1980s, very few people knew that the government, the Submarine Defence Commission and the military leadership did not have any evidence pointing to the Soviet Union, and even fewer people knew about indications pointing in the opposite direction. In December 1987, the statement by the former Chief of the Army, Lieutenant-General Sköld, about NATO presence in the Stockholm archipelago and with two 'NATO submarines' passing out through Öresund, as well as the indirect confirmation by General Lennart Ljung, made the Commission Report look awkward. A few days later, Olle Alsén wrote in *Dagens Nyheter* that the Chairman of the Submarine Defence Commission, Sven Andersson, had told him in a tape-recorded telephone conversation:

> It was not possible to identify the periscope sighted in Hårsfjärden on 1 October 1982, and a submarine sail could not be identified as a Soviet submarine – rather the opposite. [The latter statement probably refers to the observation at Sandhamn on 4 October. Both statements are correct if we accept the wording used by the witnesses interviewed for the Naval Analysis Group.][77]

Carl Bildt also confirmed that there had been 'no distinct evidence linked to a specific observation'.[78] By the early 1990s, the Submarine Defence Commission's statements on Soviet responsibility for the intrusions had become devaluated. There was nothing left of Sven Andersson's and Carl Bildt's definite views of ten years earlier. Chief of the Naval Staff Major-General Lars-G. Persson told me about increased doubts also within the Navy:

> In the 1980s, we took Soviet responsibility for granted. Now, people started to have doubts, but we never thought about possible US or UK submarines. The submarine incidents in the 1980s may have been similar to witch-hunts in the 17th century. Even during these witch-hunts the prosecutor had to come up with definite evidence to prove the case.

More and more people became sceptics. In January 1992, the Bildt government started talks with Russia to get the final proof of Soviet intrusions into Swedish waters. The Swedes were able to convince the Russians about the existence of submarines. In January 1993, Captain Emil Svensson, now working as military adviser to Prime Minister Carl Bildt, brought with him two tape-recorded cavitation sounds: one was the 3.47-minute tape from Mälsten of 12 October 1982; the other was a recording from May 1992. The Russian specialists confirmed that the

1982 recording originated from a submarine with about 200 rpm (rotations per minute) if the surface was free from other vessels, but the Russians argued that only one propeller could be identified and the parallel sound that appeared for 17 seconds could not be classified as a separate propeller. The talks with the Russians went on until 1994 without results.[79] Svensson argued that the Mälsten submarine was most likely a Whiskey.[80] However, as already mentioned, the origin of this sequence is unclear. The Norwegian analysis of the 12 October tape excluded a Soviet nuclear as well as conventional submarine, and pointed instead to a Western submarine. If this was the tape that Bildt and Svensson took to Moscow, this would definitely have convinced the Russians that the Swedes were sincere in their beliefs. Afterwards, this seems to have been one of the more peculiar aspects of this game. In July 1994, it was revealed that the May 1992 cavitation sound most likely originated from swimming minks.[81]

In the mid-1990s, new information indicated that two different 'submarine sounds', which had been recorded since the 1980s, turned out to originate from swimming minks and possibly a fish.[82] In August 1994, the Swedish Commander-in-Chief, General Owe Wiktorin, admitted that a cavitation sound that earlier had been described as a 'certain submarine' originated from swimming minks.[83] Three months earlier, FOA had stated that this sound most likely originated from a small source close to the surface, but the Navy had at that time not taken this information into consideration.[84] Another sound classified as 'certain submarine' most likely came, according to FOA, from large numbers of herring, or possibly from another fish.[85] This was later confirmed by a special investigation, the 'Type Sound Report', partly declassified in 2000. According to a former Chief of MUSAC (the Navy Sound Division), it had been a British expert who had told the Swedes in 1984 that this sound originated from a submarine, and the Swedish Navy had accordingly classified it as a 'certain submarine'.[86] The British had, according to a Swedish high-ranking officer, pointed to a similar sound from two smaller Soviet vessels belonging to the Northern Fleet. Now, the FOA analysis concluded that this sound originated, at least on several occasions, from large numbers of herring. Two sounds that the naval authorities had classified as 'certain submarine' turned out to have biological origin. Admirals from NATO countries turned up questioning the credibility of the Swedish analyses.[87] In January 1994, a group of independent critics including former Foreign Minister Lennart Bodström, former Chief of the Army Lieutenant-General Nils Sköld and former Chief of Naval Base South (Karlskrona) Captain Karl Andersson demanded an independent commission.[88] The resulting criticism forced Defence Minister Thage G. Peterson (1994–97) to appoint a new official Submarine Commission in February 1995 with a majority of scientists, under the chairmanship of Professor Hans G. Forsberg and with Major-General Bengt Wallroth, former Assistant Under-Secretary for Defence, former Deputy Chief of Staff and Chief of Swedish Military Intelligence (SSI) and Chief of Swedish Signal Intelligence (FRA), as its secretary. Later, Ingvar Åkesson from the Parliamentary Standing Committee on the Constitution was appointed co-secretary for the Commission. The new Submarine Commission presented its conclusions in December 1995.[89]

The new Commission confirmed a number of submarine incidents. It concluded that most likely there had been a combined operation with different classes of submarines, which included midget submarines. It stated that there had been, beyond doubt, tracks on the sea floor from bottom-crawling vessels and that divers had been sabotaging sub-surface military installations. The 1995 Submarine Commission Report started with a summary of the Commander-in-Chief's statements from 1981 to the early 1990s. A few paragraphs follow below:

> In 1981, the incident that was paid most attention to was the Soviet submarine, known as U137, that stranded on a rock in Gåsefjärden in Karlskrona archipelago on the evening of 27 October. After an investigation of the submarine and an interrogation of the commander, U137 was escorted out into international water on 6 November. In his report, the C-in-C stated that it was very likely that the submarine had carried out a planned intrusion into Gåsefjärden . . . Already before this incident, intrusions had been confirmed in Göteborg's archipelago in March, in Hanöbukten [in the south] in May, and at Utö [in the Stockholm archipelago] in early June . . .
>
> In 1982, the C-in-C stated that foreign submarines had intruded or probably intruded [Swedish] territory on 25 occasions. On 11 occasions, the intrusion was classified as certain. The other 14 occasions were classified as probable intrusions [primarily in June–October]: in the Bay of Bothnia and Södra Kvarken [along the north Swedish coast] and in the Stockholm archipelago . . . [in October] with certain intrusions in the area of Hårsfjärden. A certain intrusion was also supposed to have taken place at Karlskrona in November. Most attention was given to the Hårsfjärden incident . . .
>
> In 1983, the C-in-C reported a large amount of incidents, primarily in July–September . . . At the end of March, one intrusion was supposed to have taken place at Mälsten and another in Hanöbukten. In April–June, intrusions allegedly took place at Rödkallen [in the north] and twice in the Sundsvall area . . . [possibly also] in Södra Kvarken and the Stockholm archipelago. In July–September, after analysis of 40 indications, the C-in-C concluded that intrusions had been made on 18

occasions . . . In September intrusions were supposed to have taken place in the Karlskrona area, in the Stockholm archipelago, in the archipelago of Östergötland, at Gotland and along the north Swedish coast . . .

In 1984, the C-in-C concluded that it was confirmed that sub-surface activity had taken place in the Karlskrona area in February–March. There were a large number of indications of larger and smaller submarines as well as of SDVs and divers. The C-in-C also concluded that sub-surface activity had most likely taken place in July–September [and in October–December] in the archipelagos of Stockholm and Östergötland and possibly in the Karlskrona area . . .

In 1985, the first months were characterized by severe cold, which the C-in-C presumed to be the reason for the small number of reported submarine observations. However, there were some reports from the west coast. Reported indications of sub-surface activity on the west coast continued in the spring and in the summer. A photo of a suspected object [periscope] from Gullmarsfjorden [north of Göteborg] was presented. Sub-surface activity had most likely also been carried out along the coast of the most northern part of Sweden. The C-in-C's reports concluded that such activity had most likely also taken place in the Stockholm archipelago in July–December . . .

Also in 1986, there was severe cold with a lot of ice in the first months of the year . . . In early and mid-February, a number of observations and radar contacts were made at the west coast . . . [In April–June there were indications from the Stockholm archipelago], the west coast and the Bay of Bothnia and from a couple of other areas. In July–September, there were a large number of reports to the military authorities . . . Some observations were made at close distance (50 metres or less) but primarily at a longer range (300 metres or more). The C-in-C concluded that foreign sub-surface activity had taken place . . . [along the north Swedish coast], the West coast, Öresund, Kalmarsund, Bråviken [the archipelago of Östergötland] and in the Swedish part of the Åland Sea . . .

In 1987, the C-in-C concluded that several incidents of sub-surface activity had taken place . . . On several occasions, midget submarines had been used: in the north in the Bay of Bothnia (Törefjärden) and the Sundsvall area, in the south in the Stockholm archipelago, Bråviken area and along the west coast. The C-in-C concluded that six certain and three probable coordinated operations had violated Swedish waters . . .

In 1988, the picture was similar to the one the C-in-C had presented for 1987, but there were fewer indications with real substance. The C-in-C concluded that sub-surface activity had been carried out [most likely along all coasts]. On at least three occasions, there were clear indications of sub-surface activity inside Vaxholm [in the Stockholm inner archipelago] close to Lidingö [in the Stockholm harbour]. Both on the west coast and the east coast force was used several times including depth charges and mines [the submarine hunt at Hävringe in June is particularly mentioned].

In 1989, the C-in-C concluded that the number of reports (about 490) on sub-surface activity had been considerably less than in earlier years, but that the pattern was similar to 1988 . . . with a geographical centre in the Stockholm archipelago . . . also inside Vaxholm [close to the Stockholm harbour]. The C-in-C concluded that no single intrusion had been classified as 'certain'. Foreign sub-surface activity had, however, most probably taken place on about 10 occasions in the areas mentioned above.

In 1990, in early February, Swedish territorial waters were violated by a West German submarine northeast of Simrishamn [in Hanöbukten in south Sweden. The incident] was reported by the German authorities, which apologized for what had happened. The total reports for the year were less than 600: 20 per cent more than in 1989 but less than in 1988 and 1987 . . . The C-in-C concluded that sub-surface activity had most likely taken place on several occasions . . . in south Sweden (primarily in the Blekinge [Karlskrona] archipelago and the archipelago of Östergötland), the east coast and along the north Swedish coast . . .

In 1991, there were 400 reports about possible sub-surface activity. The C-in-C concluded that sub-surface activity had most likely taken place on five occasions, on the east coast of Sweden . . . One operation was supposed to have penetrated the Stockholm area . . .

In 1992 . . . the Commander-in-Chief stated that the pattern of sub-surface activity had been essentially similar to the preceding years . . . [and] that Swedish territorial waters had been violated on at least three occasions . . . The incident that had been given most attention in the mass media was a submarine hunt against what was described as 'certain' sub-surface activity in the area of Oxelösund [close to the Stockholm archipelago (depth charges, anti-submarine shells and a torpedo were used) [90]].[91]

During the severe cold winters of 1984–85 and 1985–86, there were still a number of reports but only from the west coast as if the submarines under these circumstances did not want to enter the Baltic Sea. In other words, they may have originated from states outside the Baltic Sea. Altogether 4,700 reports of submarines were made in 1981 to 1994, including reports on passive and active sonar contacts, radar and IR contacts, magnetic indications, sea-floor investigations and visual observations of periscopes, submarine sails and divers.[92] The reports were collected by the Naval Analysis Group and classified as 'certain submarine', 'probable submarine' or 'possible submarine' (but not unlikely). Under this, there were several groups of possible but less likely submarines. The 1995 Commission presented an evaluation of some of these reports.

During this period, there were 2,587 reports of visual observations. The first visual observation of a 'certain submarine' was made in 1981 with the 'Whiskey on the Rocks' in the Karlskrona archipelago. According to the military reports on visual observations there had, in 1981, been one 'certain' observation, one characterized as 'probable' (and most likely) and seven characterized as 'possible' (but not unlikely) observations (possible but less likely observations are not presented here); in 1982, there were seven 'certain' observations, 15 'probable' and 56 'possible'; in 1983, there were six 'certain' observations, 41 'probable' and 131 'possible' observations; in 1984, there were 11 'certain' observations, 20 'probable' and 61 'possible' observations; in 1985, there were seven 'certain' observations, 33 'probable' and 83 'possible' observations; in 1986, there were six 'certain' observations, 59 'probable' and 99 'possible' observations; in 1987, there were three 'certain' observations, 78 'probable' and 147 'possible' observations. After 1987, there were no 'certain' observations recorded, but, in 1988, still 31 'probable submarines' and 164 'possible submarines'; in 1989, 23 'probable submarines' and 89 'possible submarines'; in 1990, ten 'probable submarines' and 57 'possible submarines'; in 1991, seven 'probable submarines' and 37 'possible submarines'; in 1992, six 'probable submarines' and 28 'possible submarines'. After 1992, there were no observations of 'probable submarine'.[93]

Examples of 'certain submarine'/'certain' sub-surface activity are the following:

1. A minesweeper with several civilian guests was operating in Kalmarsund [between the Swedish mainland and Öland island in southern Sweden] in July [1986]. The weather was beautiful with sunshine and a sea smooth as glass . . . When checking with his binoculars, [the watch-officer] found that the rock was part of a submarine sail with several masts. It was moving. He went to the captain, but the captain only saw a mast slowly disappear in the water. The minesweeper went in the direction of the object. After a few minutes, other people [on the ship] saw an object rather far away. It was photographed . . . The ship went towards the object once again. At a distance of 300 metres, several people saw a periscope that turned to face the ship, increased its speed through the water and disappeared below the surface.[94]

[2.] In September 1983, an inspection officer was checking a mine station in the Stockholm archipelago. He was on an island and saw an object in the water that he first believed was a seal. He checked it more carefully and saw that the object was a diver. Then he saw another two divers. One was sitting on the beach. The divers had a cord with marks on and were busy measuring something. The observer went down to the diver sitting on the beach. The diver saw him, made a sign and then all the divers went into the water.[95]

Examples of 'probable submarine' or 'probable' sub-surface activity are:

[1.] In May 1987, an inspection officer observed an object looking like a submarine sail in a fjord in the Stockholm archipelago. The distance was 200–300 metres and the observation was made for 15–30 seconds. With his binoculars he saw the 'sail' disappear into the water. A black mast was still visible above the surface. The mast moved towards land.

[2.] Early in the morning of a day in June 1990, a local resident saw a submarine in the Stockholm archipelago. He first saw an echo on his radar. When he looked in his binoculars towards the position of the echo, he clearly saw a submarine. Less then 10 minutes later, he was less then 200 metres from the submarine. It then moved rapidly and dived. During most of the time of the observation, the submarine was lying surfaced with a large part of the hull exposed.[96]

[3.] In the morning of a day in August 1986, a Coastal Defence vessel with a crew of three men saw an object in the Stockholm outer archipelago. The object looked like a dark pipe [periscope] and it had a speed of 6–9 knots. It was clear visibility, and the distance was 35–40 metres. Two of the observers saw the object disappear into the water . . .

[4.] In the morning of an October day in 1987, two officers on a merchant ship (on its way to a harbour in mid-Sweden) saw two (connected) objects moving parallel to the ship. The distance to the objects was 200–400 metres. They moved at the same speed as the ship – 10 knots – and created waves. When the ship turned after five minutes to follow the sailing route [towards the harbour], the objects continued into a bay and the contact was lost. The object was also followed on radar . . .

[5.] In the early morning of a day in January 1990, two men in a boat followed an object looking like a pipe [periscope] for 15 minutes on a sailing route towards Stockholm. They focused a spotlight on it at a distance of 30–50 metres. They could see how the pipe created a wave, and then disappeared into the water and, after that, the wave disappeared . . .

[6.] In August 1987, a few people were sailing in one of the large fjords in the Stockholm archipelago. At a distance of 3–4 metres, they observed a periscope exposed for 15–20 seconds. The observation was preceded by a wave moving the sailing boat. The very short distance made it possible to observe the glass on the periscope and how it was mounted.

[7.] In the morning of a day in June 1987, a man was on his way home after having been fishing for herring in the Töre area [Törefjärden in the far north of Sweden]. At a distance of 30 metres, he observed a grey-black 'submarine' surfacing. After that it dived slowly and disappeared. The man observed the object for three minutes. He could have gone into and hit it but decided to wait and observe it.[97]

[8.] In September [1987 in the Bråviken area close to Norrköping], a man was out in his boat ... When he went closer, he saw it was a diver. At a distance of 25 metres, he saw that the diver was sitting on a vessel, because he was sitting straight up while he was moving forward. The diver turned his head and obviously saw the approaching boat, because he went down into the water while moving forward. At the short distance (25 metres), the observer could see his Cyclops and how his diving suit folded in his neck when he turned his head.[98]

Examples of 'possible submarines' or 'possible' sub-surface activity are:

1. On the morning of a day in December 1987, four people at a ferry in the Stockholm archipelago saw a 'submarine sail'. The object was observed for 3–4 minutes at a distance of 4,000–5,000 metres ...

2. In early June 1994, two civilians on Gotland observed, for 15 minutes, a submarine sail and parts of the hull of a submarine at a distance of 3,000–4,000 metres ...

[3.] One morning in July 1986, a family of four people were out in their motor boat in northern Östergötland. Suddenly, at a distance of 20 metres, father and son saw an object for 20–25 seconds that moved in front of the boat until it disappeared into the water. They clearly saw foam and waves, and they estimated the speed at 3–4 knots. The object was cylindrical and behind it was an object that looked like an antenna.

[4.] On one morning in November 1986, an officer and a conscript observed an object moving south between two islands in the Östergötland archipelago. Both men had binoculars. The distance of the object was 250–450 metres. The observation lasted 4 minutes ...

[5.] In June 1988, a couple were in a motor boat at Brämön not far from Sundsvall. They saw an object moving towards the boat at a speed that almost created foam [around it] ... The distance was 100 metres, and the observation lasted one minute. The man in the boat contacted two other boats by radio. They also saw something that looked like a stick. The object was vertical to the sea surface all the time ...

[6.] In June 1987, one person was in a boat on the coast of Norrbotten [in northern Sweden]. In front of him, he saw a 2-metre-long 'rock' at a distance of 100–150 metres. Small waves lapped against the object. It disappeared at a distance of 30 metres. A bubble appeared on the surface. The vision was clear and there was no wind or waves.

When the object had disappeared, there was a plough-like wave moving in the same direction as the object.

[7.] In May 1988, a couple were out in their sailing boat in the Stockholm southern archipelago. At a distance of 500 metres, they saw something that looked like the back of a whale moving towards the boat. The object changed direction and increased its speed with waves in the front and at the back. The couple saw the object for 8 minutes with and without binoculars . . .

[8.] In early September 1991, a man and a woman were out in a boat in the Stockholm archipelago. At a distance of 15–20 metres in front of the boat, they saw something flashing in the water. The man immediately believed it was a diver and decreased the speed of the boat. Both observers saw the diver turn his head and the Cyclops become visible. The man, himself a diver, saw that the Cyclops was of a type not known to him. No bubbles were visible after the dive, but there were two rings in the water where the 'head' had disappeared.[99]

In this text, not only reports about 'certain submarines' but also reports about 'probable' and even 'possible submarines' appear to a large extent credible. Commander Göran Frisk, former Chief of a Fast Attack Craft Division and Chief of the Anti-Submarine Force, said that the Navy, once or twice a year, used to let one Swedish submarine show its periscope in the Stockholm archipelago or somewhere else to test the readiness and the routines of the Swedish military organization. The observations went through the usual procedures but were immediately afterwards taken out of the Naval Analysis Group Report. One Swedish submarine that had been showing its periscope in the Stockholm archipelago was, for example, classified as a 'possible submarine', Frisk said – indicating that a 'possible submarine' does not have to be less real. The classification made by the Naval Analysis Group only tells us something about the perceived credibility of the observations, not if this or that observation refers to a real submarine.

The 1995 Commission went through all this material from the secret files made by the Naval Analysis Group from 1982 onwards. Their critical investigation still confirmed the existence of 'certain submarines'. However, the Commission found no proof for pointing to any particular state of origin. After having looked at all the classified material used by the 1983 Commission and every single argument presented by this commission, the 1995 Commission found none of its arguments convincing. That there were regular, large-scale operations threatening Sweden was confirmed, but the Commission did not find any particular state responsible for these threats.[100]

Mikael Damberg, from the Swedish Defence Ministry, explained the difference between the two commissions in the following way:

the first [1983] Commission was able to identify the nationality of the intrusions into Hårsfjärden, because it based its judgement on a combination of indications and security policy motives. The second [1995] Commission was not able to identify nationality. It did not take any security policy motive into consideration. It only looked at indications.[101]

In other words, in contrast to the views among a number of generals, admirals and political leaders quoted above, he implied that the reason for the 1983 Commission to point to the Soviet Union was that only the Soviet Union would have had an interest in carrying out such operations. Professor Bo Huldt at the Swedish Defence College had been asked to analyse possible motives for the 1995 Submarine Commission, but the Commission had rejected Huldt's study (a later version was published in *Internationella Studier*[102]). Huldt argued that the Soviet Union had had the strongest motives and was most likely responsible for the intrusions. The Commission, however, argued that a motive is not enough if you don't have evidence. This may explain Damberg's statement.

Both the 1983 Commission and the 1995 Commission seem to have presupposed that the material presented to them was the most sensitive material with most clear evidence of submarine activity. This, however, was not the case, and, for the 1983 Commission, this fact was known to its military expert. Most clear arguments for this are: firstly, that the Naval Analysis Group Report under Commander Emil Svensson excluded the most sensitive material and several of the clearest observations; secondly, that somebody had edited the tape recordings and removed the most sensitive information from the tapes; and thirdly, that Commander Bengt Gabrielsson, Chief of Naval Operations Eastern Military District, was asked to write drafts for the 1983 Commission (which he did) without having access to the most sensitive material – something its military expert Vice-Admiral Stefenson was aware of.

Vice-Admiral Stefenson stated to the Ekéus Investigation that there was no evidence pointing to any specific state and that he was surprised that the Commission had pointed to the Soviet Union.[103] I doubt that Stefenson remembered this correctly. As the military expert, Stefenson participated in the work of finalizing the Commission Report.[104] The members of the Commission refer to Stefenson as the one who was able definitely to point to the Soviet Union. The material presented by Emil Svensson and the Naval Analysis Group also definitely pointed to the Soviet Union. Stefenson's own Defence Staff Report of 18 April 1983, which was used for the press conference and for drafting a diplomatic note to the Soviet Union, points to the Soviet Union in every respect.[105] Stefenson stated also to the Ekéus Investigation that 'the signal intelligence information they had did not necessarily point to the Soviet Union',[106] but his report of 18 April 1983 says that 'the result of signal intelligence shows definitely that Warsaw Pact submarines have been active in Swedish territorial waters'.[107] In both the Defence Staff Report (Bror Stefenson) and in the Naval Analysis Group Report (Emil Svensson) information pointing to Western submarines was taken out, while information that could be interpreted as supporting Soviet involvement was used to discuss alternative classes of Soviet submarines – something that made the member of the Submarine Commission Olle Svensson accept the military expert's view about Soviet responsibility for the intrusions.

In 1999, former defence minister Thage G. Peterson, came up with some questions about the submarine intrusions:

> [I]t concerns the American total lack of interest in the Swedish submarine problems, and what the explanation is for this lack of interest. The Baltic Sea area has for decades been and still is of great strategic significance for the USA and NATO. If such serious matters occur as submarine intrusions into the waters of neutral Sweden in this very sensitive area, and the Soviet Union/Russia is believed to be responsible for these intrusions, shouldn't the Americans in that case be interested in what has happened or still is happening? In practical terms, this would be a forwarding of the position of the other military bloc. But the USA has never been concerned about the submarine issue. Isn't that strange? Particularly since the USA and NATO have been covering and still cover the Baltic Sea area with satellites, aircraft and other advanced reconnaissance systems? And have an extensive intelligence activity? But they leave us with our submarine problems. Isn't that strange? . . . In late 1996, I was visited by the US Secretary of Defense, William Perry. We developed good relations, and I liked his friendly and listening attitude. We visited Hårsfjärden together. In the car from Berga, I brought up the submarine intrusions. My American colleague smiled and looked at me with sympathy: 'It may be other things than submarines in the water, and if there is a submarine, it doesn't have to be Russian![108]

NOTES

1 CM/Grandin (1982).
2 SOU (1983).
3 General Ljung wrote in his diary: 'The Prime Minister had gathered the Ministers of Foreign Affairs and Defence and their State Secretaries at Rosenbad [the Prime Minister's office]. A press conference was to be held the following day concerning the submarine defence issue, where the task for the commission

headed by Sven Andersson would be announced. The meeting, chaired by Palme, lasted for an hour and a half. It started with relatively short briefings made by the Chief of Staff and myself on our conclusions, and occasionally our lack of conclusions, regarding the submarine hunt. Palme posed a number of really good questions, which showed that he had rapidly grasped these problems, and that he understood which parts of the activities could mainly be in question at the press conference, etc. It was surprising to note that neither the Minister of Foreign Affairs nor the Minister of Defence in any way interacted in this meeting' (ÖB TD, 21 October 1982).

4 UL, 1982.
5 Ibid.
6 Swedish News Agency *TT* (Tidningarnas Telegrambyrå) (5 September 1982); *Dagens Nyheter* (6 September 1982).
7 Bildt (1982).
8 KU 1982/83:30, pp. 19–20.
9 CM/Grandin (1982), pp. 9–12.
10 CM/Grandin (1982), p. 17.
11 ÖB TD (8 April 1983).
12 See also Wallén (2002), p. 50.
13 SOU (1983), pp. 79–81.
14 Ibid., pp. 34–5; SOU (1983) (unofficial English transl.), pp. 34–7.
15 SOU (1983), p. 80.
16 *Svenska Dagbladet* (27 April 1983); SOU (2001), p. 144.
17 *Rapport*, Swedish TV2; *Aktuellt*, Swedish TV1 (26 April 1983).
18 *New York Times* (27 April 1983).
19 SOU (2001), p. 146.
20 Ibid., pp. 146–7.
21 *Svenska Dagbladet* (27 April 1983).
22 *Svenska Dagbladet* (27 April – 4 May 1983).
23 Hasselbohm (1984), pp. 44–5.
24 Bruzelius (1982), p. 4.
25 Hansen (1984); Leitenberg (1987); McCormick (1990).
26 *Aktuellt*, Swedish TV1 (26 April 1983).
27 Svensson (1993), p. 85.
28 MAna Hårsfj.
29 *Extra Rapport*, Swedish TV2 (26 April 1983).
30 *Rapport*, Swedish TV2 (26 April 1983).
31 SOU (1995), pp. 144–6.
32 Ibid., pp. 155–7.
33 Ibid., p. 276.
34 Ibid., p. 144.
35 Ibid., pp. 160–2.
36 Ibid., pp 139–40, 160–2, 238–40.
37 Carlsson (1999), p. 115; see also SOU (2001), p. 145.
38 Mellbourn (1988c).
39 Ibid.; Mellbourn (1988d).
40 *Aktuellt*, Swedish TV1 (25 October 1999).
41 Carlsson (1999), p. 72.
42 ÖB TD (8, 11 April 1983).
43 Carlsson (1999), p. 72.
44 *Aktuellt*, Swedish TV1 (25 October 1999); see also Carlsson (1999) and Thunborg (2001).

45 Peterson (1999), p. 555.
46 ÖB TD (11 April 1983).
47 Mellbourn (1988c); see also Carlsson (1999), p. 75.
48 *Dagens Nyheter* (6 June 1994).
49 Bodström (1999), p. 162; see also Lampers (1996).
50 See also Bodström (2000), pp. 245–7.
51 See also Thunborg (2001).
52 Thunborg (1986), p. 72.
53 Aland and Zachrisson (1996), pp. 150–1; see also Thunborg (2001).
54 Carlsson (1999), pp. 72–3.
55 Bildt (1990), p. 38.
56 Mellbourn (1988c).
57 Åström (1996).
58 Mellbourn (1988c); Carlsson (1999), p. 74.
59 Åström (1996).
60 Svensson (1993), p. 85.
61 ÖB TD (8 March 1983).
62 ÖB TD (16 March 1983).
63 ÖB TD (21 April 1983).
64 See also Hasselbohm (1984), pp. 42–3.
65 SAP VU meeting (17 May 1983).
66 ÖB TD (16 September 1983).
67 ÖB TD (1 September 1983).
68 SOU (2001), pp. 186–7.
69 Sven Svensson (*Dagens Nyheter*, 21 October 1986).
70 CFö/INT (1987); Försvarsstaben (1987).
71 Försvarsstaben (1987).
72 Ibid., pp. 29–30.
73 Carlsson (1999), pp. 91–2.
74 CFö/INT (1987); Dahlgren (1987).
75 Mellbourn (1988a, 1988b).
76 Carlsson (1999), p. 93.
77 Alsén (1987).
78 Bildt (1990), p. 38.
79 SOU (1995), pp. 200–10.
80 Svensson (1995), p. 41.
81 SOU (1995), pp. 222–7; see also Svensson (1995), p. 38.
82 SOU (1995), pp. 211–27.
83 Carlsson (1999), p. 104.
84 SOU (1995), p. 224.
85 Ibid., pp. 211–22.
86 See also *Reportrarna*, Swedish TV2 (9 September 1998).
87 *Striptease*, Swedish TV1 (9 June 1993).
88 Bergström and Åmark (1999).
89 SOU (1995).
90 Ibid., pp. 231–2.
91 Ibid., pp. 35–43.
92 Ibid., pp. 173–261.
93 Ibid., p. 175.
94 Ibid., p. 176.
95 Ibid., p. 197.
96 Ibid., pp. 177–8.

97 Ibid., pp. 180–6.
98 Ibid., pp. 197–8.
99 Ibid., pp. 178–98.
100 Ibid., pp. 275–81.
101 Quoted in Lampers (1996), pp. 29–30.
102 Huldt (1996).
103 SOU (2001), p. 136.
104 ÖB TD (8 April 1983).
105 SOU (1995), pp. 144–6, 155–8.
106 SOU (2001), p. 136.
107 SOU (1995), p. 145.
108 Peterson (1999), pp. 556–7.

6

The National Origin of
the Hårsfjärden Submarine

SOVIET SUBMARINE OPERATIONS

The 1995 Submarine Commission Report was not able to identify the national origin of the intruding submarines. This provoked the Swedish Ministry of Foreign Affairs on 20 February 1996 to appoint a group to make a study of possible security policy motives for the foreign submarine activity. The lack of evidence pointing to one nation or another made it necessary to classify this report (it was declassified in March 2000). Ambassador Lars-Erik Lundin was appointed the chairman of this study group. The other members were Ambassador Carl-Johan Groth, Professor Rutger Lindahl and Ambassador Lennart Myrsten. The report concluded that the Soviet Union and the Warsaw Pact had the strongest military motives for operations in Swedish waters, while both the Soviet Union and NATO countries may have had political motives for such operations. The authors underlined, however, that the strongest motives were to be found in the East. Only Baltic Sea states were believed to carry out major operations in the Baltic Sea area, and of these states only the Soviet Union, later the Russian Federal Republic, had the capability of operating with several midget submarines and conventional submarines in Swedish waters. The study does not exclude some Western activity, but the main intruder is believed to have been the Soviet Union. The number of Soviet submarines in the Baltic Sea, the actual intrusion of a Whiskey submarine in October 1981, and Soviet interests in the Swedish coastline because of increased tension between the two blocs all pointed to the Soviet Union.[1]

In 1982, the Soviet Navy had about 40 submarines in the Baltic Sea: 15–20 Whiskey-class submarines (76 metres; two propellers), one or two Romeo-class submarines (77 metres; two propellers), six Foxtrot (91 metres; three propellers), four to six Zulu (90 metres; three propellers), one Tango (92 metres; three propellers), six Golf-class ballistic-missile submarines (98 metres; three propellers), three Juliet

229

cruise-missile submarines (87 metres; two propellers) plus possibly a couple of smaller Quebec (56 metres; three propellers).[2] Several of the older submarines may have been in reserve. The Soviets also had a number of oceanographic research submersibles like Tinro 2 (7 metres; one propeller), Sever 2 (12 metres; one propeller) and Benthos-300 (30 metres; one propeller) – most of them in the Black Sea. These submersibles could have been transferred to the Baltic Sea, but none of them are suited to covert intelligence collection and special force operations. Furthermore, the Soviets had four (according to another source 12[3]) deep submergence rescue vehicles, two Project 1837K (11 metres; two propellers) and two Project 1837 (12 metres; one propeller) with the two India-class submarines as mother-subs.[4]

More important, however, Soviet naval special forces used a number of midgets or SDVs including the torpedo-like Sirena (6 metres; one propeller), the advanced Sirena-UME (8.7 metres; one propeller) and several Triton I (5 metres; one propeller) and Triton II (9.5 metres; one propeller). Both these Tritons have a speed of 6 knots.[5] There is supposedly also a larger version of Triton – a dry/wet mini-submarine of about 20 metres for the landing of special force swimmers – as I was told by an intelligence officer. After the Second World War, the Soviets captured the German midget submarine type Seehund (12 metres; one propeller) and the 'human torpedo' Neger (7.5 metres; one propeller). The post-war Soviet midgets may have been a development of these craft.[6] The Soviet Sirena has similarities to the Neger, and the Soviet Elbrus (14 metres; one propeller[7]) has similarities to the Seehund. The Soviets had, according to Swedish Military Intelligence, a couple of small tracked submersibles with about 0.5-metre-wide caterpillar tracks and less than a metre in between them, similar to the German bottom-crawling Seeteufel. A Norwegian admiral told me that, in the 1990s, prints from a bottom-crawling submersible were found in northern Norway. They were believed to originate from a Soviet submersible. However, the dimensions were very different from the prints in Sweden in 1982. In the Norwegian case, each track was narrower and the distance between them was much greater compared to the prints in Hårsfjärden and at Mälsten. In 1987–88 (or from 31 December 1988[8]), there were two Pyranja or Losos (29 metres; one propeller) also fitted for special force operations.[9] They were able to deliver two Sirenas to the target area.

In 1982, Soviet conventional submarines based in the Baltic Sea were able to launch SDVs, the torpedo-like Sirena (a diameter of 0.5 metres) through a standard torpedo tube, but this is no real midget submarine. The research vessel *Akademik Aleksey Krylov* was able to carry a 'midget', a 14-metre 'research submersible' (the Elbrus), in a hidden hangar on the side of the ship. She made her maiden voyage in December 1982.[10] In the Baltic Sea, up to four other surface vessels were at the time able to carry midgets that could exit a flooded section of the ship through a door below the surface, a Swedish intelligence officer told me. These vessels were known by Western intelligence and they never entered Western ports, he said. However, at the time of the Hårsfjärden operation, none of these vessels, actually no Soviet vessel, was even in the vicinity of the Stockholm archipelago.

In the Northern Fleet, the Soviet Navy also had a mother-sub, an India-class submarine (105 metres; one propeller), carrying two rescue vehicles, which could possibly be replaced by offensive midget submarines. In the 1980s, a rebuilt Yankee submarine (125 metres; two propellers) was believed to carry a midget in a hangar behind the sail.[11] In *Modern Submarine Warfare*, David Miller and John Jordan propose that an India-class submarine might have carried Soviet midgets to the Swedish archipelagos,[12] and, theoretically speaking, both the Yankee and the India class could have been transferred to the Baltic Sea, but they never were. In 1982 (or between 1981 and 1985), according to the monthly Danish Military Intelligence Report, neither the Yankee class nor the India class was ever in the Baltic Sea.[13]

During the Second World War, the Soviet Union operated submarines in Swedish waters and sank Swedish and other ships in these waters. In the Bay of Finland, Soviet submarines used a special technique to crawl on the sea floor to avoid submarine nets. Commander Hans von Hofsten quotes the Swedish wartime Naval Attaché to Helsinki, Commander Ragnar Thorén, as saying: 'If you are expecting to find the [Soviet] submarines outside a certain archipelago, you may well find them on guard inside the archipelago in well-defended fjords, which they reached by crawling on the bottom.'[14] A Swedish senior Defence Ministry official said that this information was perceived as the final proof for Soviet intrusions into Swedish waters in the 1980s. It was believed that these Soviet experiences from the Second World War were used to formulate Soviet operative planning in the post-war years.

In 1990, in his address to the Swedish Royal War Academy, Carl Bildt argued that such operations could only, for geographical reasons, be done along the Swedish coast. He believed that the Soviet Navy had carried out anti-ship operations in the Swedish territorial sea and outer archipelago since the Second World War.[15] Finding hiding places for the six Golf missile submarines might also have been an important argument for Soviet operations in Swedish archipelagos. Soviet wartime experience, the large number of Soviet submarines (including midget submarines), the threatening Soviet rhetoric and Soviet security interest in activities along the Swedish coast (for example, because of possible US use of Swedish airbases in time of war) convinced most Swedish academic scholars that the Soviet Union was responsible for almost all intrusions into the Swedish archipelagos in 1980s.[16] Others, primarily US scholars like Robert Weinland, Gordon McCormick and Paul Cole, underlined the Soviet need to reach the Norwegian Atlantic coast by attacking and then passing through central Sweden. The Soviets would land special forces from submarines and attack the political and military elite and thereby paralyse Sweden.[17] In a 1984 study for the Office of the Secretary of Defense, Lynn M. Hansen writes:

> [To be able to make a swift move forward with conventional forces,] the Soviets have been undertaking the special Spetsnaz operations in both Sweden and Norway so that they can move quickly and decisively in achieving naval supremacy in the Baltic Sea by neutralizing Swedish defenses, including the Swedish Navy. The reason for actively violating Swedish territory could be to create the possibility of moving overland across Sweden with several divisions to attack much of Northern Norway ... [These] operations conducted against Sweden and Norway, and probably also all the other Scandinavian countries, were performed by special forces [mini-submarine groups and combat swimmers] characteristically referred to by the Soviets as Spetsnaz.[18]

In 1983, former Director of the CIA Admiral Stansfield Turner said that the Soviet Baltic Fleet had midget submarines as well as naval special forces, and these forces 'have to be given something to do'.[19] Michael MccGwire writes that the Soviets have two interests in the Swedish archipelago, both linked to intelligence and navigational training: 'to prevent it being used to their disadvantage and to use selected parts of it for their own purposes. Thorough peacetime reconnaissance is important to both missions.'[20] In the same year, Carl Bildt argued:

> Operations on this scale, and of this nature, cannot be explained by the intelligence and navigational training tasks often pointed at in the public debate. Intelligence gathering is a task that can be assigned to an isolated submarine trying to get close to Swedish naval manoeuvres or fixed military installations, but it is not possible to ascribe the type of large, coordinated operations observed repeatedly during 1982 purely to intelligence gathering ... The operations are to be seen as preparations for actual missions to be undertaken in case of war ... [C]overt mining is one of the important tasks ... Another possible (indeed probable) mission for these submarines in wartime might be the landing of special purpose forces to undertake sabotage raids against ... vital political and military installations.[21]

Bildt is probably right that the primary purpose is not intelligence gathering, but it is difficult to understand how the show of submarine sails and periscopes in densely populated areas can be interpreted as preparations for covert mining and covert landing of special forces. These preparations might very well have taken place, but the activity in the Hårsfjärden operation and in many other incidents is difficult to explain as such tasks.

Colonel Jonathan Alford (ret.), then Deputy Director of the International Institute of Strategic Studies in London, argued, like Leitenberg and McCormick, that the Soviets by conducting these provocative operations were trying to bully Sweden into a submissive state of mind to make the Swedes understand that they would be unable to resist in time of war. However, he also believed that Soviet submarine intrusions into Swedish waters may have been an attempt to provoke the Swedes to develop an anti-submarine warfare capability to draw resources from the Air Force, which would be of greater significance for the control of the Scandinavian peninsula.[22] The Swedish submarine captain Nils Bruzelius also argued that the Soviets may have operated submarines in Swedish waters in order to provoke Sweden to develop its anti-submarine warfare capability, but to Bruzelius the argument would be to strengthen the Swedes' ability to defend against Western submarines threatening Soviet activity in the Baltic Sea. In a war, West German submarines would most likely operate from Swedish territorial waters to attack the Soviet Sea Lines of Communication along the eastern Baltic coast. If neutral Sweden did not have an anti-submarine warfare capacity, West German submarines could use Swedish waters as a sanctuary, Bruzelius argued.[23] This hypothesis, however, presupposes that the Soviets took for granted that Sweden would stay neutral in a war, something that is not very likely.[24] According to another argument, the Soviet Navy needed to deploy transponders for navigation support in important sub-surface waterways. This seems plausible, and, according to a Swedish former intelligence officer, a Russian source has also indicated that this might have been the case. Signals believed to come from transponders have been picked up by the Swedes at Mälsten and at Långbälingen. However, there is also information pointing to Western deployment of such transponders.

During the submarine hunt in October 1982, Radio Moscow stated that 'the real danger should not be sought under water'[25] indicating that the presence of a US cruiser and frigate – not the covert sub-surface activities – would be the real threat to Sweden, as if possible submarines were of less importance than these surface ships. Radio Moscow could be interpreted as if these submarines originated from the Soviet Union.[26] In March 1984 Alexander Bovin wrote in *Izvestija* and *Dagens Nyheter*:

233

In whose interest is this continued chill between Moscow and Stockholm? Not even the most trained political scholar will be able to explain it to be in the Soviet interest . . . [But he also wrote that] the intensification of NATO's activity in northern Europe and the Baltic region naturally requires the Warsaw Pact to see to its own security. This increases the probability of undesirable incidents. Particularly undesirable incidents. And our military leadership does everything it can to prevent them from occurring. Especially if it concerns the territorial waters or airspace of alliance-free or neutral countries.[27]

These statements combined with the very existence of the provocative but elusive submarine activities were interpreted as a conscious use of submarines to signal Soviet ambitions as well as a criticism of NATO and particularly of the forward US operations and of close Swedish–US cooperation. Scandinavian and particularly Swedish waters were perceived as a grey zone.[28] Some of us saw the 'Soviet activities' in the framework of the general Cold War logic,[29] while others looked upon these activities from a perspective of Soviet offensive operations.[30] There was no independent researcher who believed in the possibility of non-Soviet submarines, or rather only one researcher pointed to the possibility of West German activity.[31]

Some years later, a Soviet general, Vladimir Cheremnikh, First Deputy Commander of Leningrad Military District, told me that Soviet submarines may have operated in Swedish waters in the 1950s and 1960s. He also indicated that this may have happened later, but he would have been informed if there had been any serious incident. A Norwegian admiral told me that on one occasion divers landed in northern Norway and soon afterwards left for the sea again. The divers did not present themselves, but the Norwegian Navy knew that, at that time, at that very place, there was a Soviet submarine just outside, which indicated that the divers originated from Soviet special forces. On other occasions, however, divers landing from submarines turned out to originate from US or UK special forces (see below).

In a Swedish TV programme in autumn 1996, an anonymous former Soviet naval officer said that he had participated in submarine operations in Scandinavian (allegedly in Swedish) territorial waters. All symbols on the submarine were covered with paint. The mother-sub – the conventional submarine – stayed outside while they used the Sirena or the Triton for deep penetration. He said that the Soviets deployed mines and torpedoes in foreign coastal waters, and these weapons could be activated in a war but needed maintenance in peacetime. In the same TV programme, retired Captain Valerjan Asejev, a medical doctor on Baltic Sea submarines, said that special submarine operations were run by the GRU. It was possible to feel immediately when the submarine entered foreign waters, because the senior officers became much more alert. In some incidents, crew members had been hurt and divers had possibly been lost. They also said that Western submarines (US, French and West German) operated in these waters.[32]

In the late 1980s, the Swedish Navy was able to tape-record a Golf II submarine in international water in the Sea of Bothnia, which indicates that it had passed through the Åland Sea either on the Swedish or on the Finnish side. However, there is no confirmed tape recording of a Soviet submarine in Swedish waters. Swedish Commander-in-Chief Bengt Gustafsson said that in May 1987 the Swedish Navy had taken a 'photo' (with a 'Kleinhydrophone') of a small submarine, about 30 metres (or to be more exact 28.5 metres), in Swedish waters.[33] In June 1988, the Swedish Navy had contact with an echo/submarine with a length of 30 metres[34] (or 20–30 metres[35]). Also in 1988, according to Wilhelm Agrell and Christer Larsson, the West German Navy took a photo (with infra-red film) of a submarine of a similar size, possibly the Pyranja, in Soviet waters close to the Soviet naval base of Baltijsk.[36] However, the Pyranja did not exist in 1982, and it was allegedly not operational in May 1987, when the 'photo' (with a 'Kleinhydrophone') was taken.[37] In May 1984, a Swedish minesweeper had contact with a 30-metre-long echo moving faster than the ship in a narrow passage in the Stockholm archipelago.[38] It seems that 30- (or 20- to 30-) metre submarines operated in Swedish waters before the Pyranja was developed. The Swedes believed that there must have been an earlier version of Pyranja. In comments made by US Naval Intelligence on Agrell's and Larsson's article, this was not perceived as very likely. Naval Intelligence did not believe in the Pyranja as a second generation.[39]

From 1985, Swedish Military Intelligence had information about a 28-metre submarine in Soviet waters. It was 6.5 metres high and had a low sail (1.5 metres). These figures are identical to the Cosmos MG-110, and I am not yet convinced that this was a Soviet submarine. On several occasions, the Swedish Navy had also had contact with a 5- to 10-metre midget including the bottom-crawling vessel seen in Hårsfjärden in 1982. The Pyranja was able to carry two SDVs, the 6-metre Sirena, while the Triton could be delivered from a surface ship. These midgets are said to be under the command of GRU and to have Leningrad as a rear base supplemented by a mobile basing system using trailers (not conventional submarines) for transportation to different Baltic ports.[40] However, this does not give an answer to the operations in Swedish waters.

The top-secret Swedish Defence Staff Report of 25 November 1987 stated that the Swedish Navy had experience of an intruding Soviet sub-surface system with up to ten 30-metre submarines each delivering one or two 10-metre midgets or SDVs to the target area. One or more of the latter were believed to be tracked submersibles with bottom-crawling capability. The report argued that the Swedes had several years' experience of these submarines.[41] In 1990, Carl Bildt said that he and the Submarine Defence Commission were probably wrong to believe that Whiskey submarines operated as mother-subs for the 10-metre midgets. New information showed that it was these 30-metre submarines that had this task. The Whiskeys or other conventional submarines most likely did not operate in Swedish internal waters. Bildt mentioned the possibility of eight 30-metre submarines and 14 10-metre submarines – all operating primarily against Sweden.[42] However, in 2002 I have still seen no proof that the Soviet Union had such a system. The information from 1985 is not confirmed, and before 1988 there may not have been a single Soviet submarine of 20–30 metres except for the large submersible and sub-surface laboratory *Benthos-300* with a speed of 1.5 knots, which is not very suitable for offensive operations.[43] Furthermore, according to the 'Government Group' and former Chief of Military Intelligence Major-General Bengt Wallroth, there is no information about these 20- to 30-metre vessels crossing the Baltic Sea,[44] despite the fact that they would be much easier to pick up on transit there than in the Swedish archipelagos. These 30-metre submarines seem to have been deployed from surface ships and dumped into the archipelagos. However, in Hårsfjärden in October 1982 and also on other occasions there was no Soviet ship in the vicinity.

In the 1990s, in connection with the Swedish–Russian talks about the submarine incidents in Swedish waters, Swedish intelligence personnel investigated the issue in Russia and in the newly independent Baltic States. They found nothing, a Swedish intelligence officer told me. There was no infrastructure necessary to support the sub-surface system of a number of 30- and 10-metre submarines. The Soviet Baltic Fleet does not seem to have had such forces. Soviet submarines most likely exercised in Swedish waters, but not in the very complicated inner archipelago, he said. Soviet Military Intelligence, GRU, had a very secret department for carrying out sub-surface espionage or special force operations, but this does not give a satisfactory answer to the operations in Swedish waters, this intelligence officer said. He was not able to explain the combined operations of SDVs and mini-submarines as mother-subs deep into the Swedish archipelagos.

After the stranding of the Soviet Whiskey submarine on 27 October 1981, Danish Military Intelligence reported on Soviet activities and on concentration of a large Soviet force off the Swedish coast. The same reports for October 1982, dealing with all Soviet naval activities in the Baltic Sea area, do not reflect anything in connection with the submarine hunt in Hårsfjärden. In general, Soviet activities in the Baltic Sea were characterized as 'low', and activities along the Swedish coast were not mentioned.[45] The same pattern is found in the Swedish intelligence reports of October 1982 (see above). The only 'hard evidence', the tape-recording from 12 October 1982, turned out to point to the West. Commander Anders Hammar, who made the relevant briefing of the Submarine Defence Commission, says today that he deceived them, because he was misled by his own colleagues.

The above information indicates Soviet submarine activities in Swedish waters, and it would be surprising if Soviet operations had not also been conducted in the 1980s. But the above information does not give a satisfactory explanation – either to the Hårsfjärden incident or to several other high-profile operations in the Swedish archipelagos. Except for the stranded Whiskey submarine in 1981, there are no hard facts and only a few indications pointing to the Soviet Union. We also have to look at other possibilities.

WEST GERMAN SUBMARINE OPERATIONS

In the early 1980s, West Germany had quite a few submarines in the Baltic Sea: six Type 205-class submarines (44 metres; one propeller) and 18 Type 206-class submarines (48.6 metres; one propeller). Both are said to have a 'non-magnetic hull',[46] or actually a hull made of a steel alloy with very low magnetism, a German admiral told me. When passing the sensors of the mines, the magnetic field of the submarine would not be clearly registered. The West German Navy may have had a couple of mini- and midget submarines like the small coastal submarines MSV 75 (21 metres) with a transit range of 2,900 nautical miles and Type 100 (20 metres; one propeller) developed together with the British company Vickers (see below).[47]

During the Second World War, Germany produced several hundreds of midgets of type Seehund, Biber and Molch (all 9–12 metres; one propeller), hundreds of the human torpedo Neger (7.5 metres; one propeller) and a prototype of a bottom-crawling Seeteufel/Elefant (13.5 metres; one propeller), the latter leaving tank-like prints on the sea floor.[48] These small coastal submarines were supposedly able to operate both in harbours and in shallow waters. In the 1980s, the Germans also had a midget submarine Sea Horse II (14.5 metres; one propeller) with a transit range of 400 nautical miles. It was capable of diving 200 metres and carrying four to six men.[49] '[O]ne was procured in 1984 by North Korea through a commercial organization, while the delivery of the second boat, although officially designed for underwater work and inspection, was stopped in 1987 by international pressure.'[50] Emil

Svensson's report mentions a couple of civilian and possible military midget submarines. However, none of them are believed to have been operational.[51]

In a war, West German submarines were supposed to use the Swedish coast as a basing area, because the major German Baltic naval base (at Kiel) would certainly have been destroyed. It was believed that the Soviet lines of communication through Poland would be destroyed in the early phase of a war, and the primary offensive task of the West German submarines was to attack the Soviet Sea Lines of Communication along the Soviet Baltic coast and Poland. In a document of 1963, former Swedish Chief of Staff General Carl Eric Almgren speaks about Swedish coordination with NATO and a plan that 'includes such information that we will not sink each other's submarines or enter each other's minefields'.[52] In other words, Almgren speaks about Swedish plans for coordinating wartime mining and submarine activity with NATO. This means that Swedish submarine operations would either be coordinated by BALTAP in Karup (NATO's Command for the Baltic Approaches in Denmark), or they would be geographically limited to the northern Baltic Sea, with operations in the Bay of Finland and Estonian waters, while West German submarines would operate in Latvian and Lithuanian waters from the area of the Swedish port of Norrköping southwards. According to a Danish admiral, the latter alternative would be more likely in the initial phase of a war.

The West German Rear-Admiral Ansgar Bethge has stated that the primary offensive task for German submarines would be to cut the Soviet Sea Lines of Communication in the Baltic Sea along the Latvian and Lithuanian coasts.[53] To survive, these submarines would have to use the Swedish archipelago as a base area, where they would be supported with ammunition by German depot ships. The latter would not be able to operate in open sea in wartime. They would want to use Swedish naval bases, or, as one German naval officer said to a Swedish admiral as an argument for a naval visit to Karlskrona, 'Karlskrona is such an ideal base in wartime.' The German Navy usually visited small Swedish harbours along the coast, while other navies primarily visited Stockholm and Göteborg. German submarines obviously used port visits (in Norrköping, Västervik, Kalmar and Karlskrona) to make themselves acquainted with the underwater terrain. Furthermore, in a prolonged war, these 'Swedish-based' German submarines would have access to pre-stocked German ammunition in southern Norway. According to a Swedish intelligence officer, the German diesel-electric submarines would also have to use their noisier diesel engines in Swedish waters to avoid Soviet anti-submarine warfare while charging their electric batteries and to use their silent electric engines for attacks against the Soviet Sea Lines of Communication along the Latvian and Lithuanian coast.

In private talks, Swedish naval officers have told me that West German submarines have also been found in Swedish waters and covertly have used Swedish waters as a base area for exercising offensive operations against Soviet vessels along the Latvian and Lithuanian coast.[54] A Swedish intelligence officer told me that, in the early or mid-1980s, West German submarines had exercised offensive operations against Soviet vessels along the Latvian coast and then left for an official port visit to the Swedish harbour of Norrköping, while other West German submarines replaced the first ones. After that, the first submarines went back to the Latvian coast replacing the second group as if the port visit in Norrköping had been part of the exercise. The Germans were training to use Swedish ports as bases where the submarines received fuel and ammunition. As already mentioned, to cut the Soviet Sea Lines of Communication in the Baltic Sea was a primary task for the West German Navy, and this seemingly presupposed German use of Swedish coastal waters. This may be an additional reason for Soviet activities in the Swedish archipelago. The Soviets also had to make themselves acquainted with the underwater terrain. According to an admiral from a NATO country, reductions in Swedish defence spending from the early 1970s and the scaling-down of Swedish anti-submarine warfare capacity gave any intruder free access to Swedish territorial waters. Submarines in the Swedish archipelago may have originated from both the Soviet Union and various NATO countries. Of the incident at Utö (outside Mysingen) in late September 1980, some Swedish officers suspected a Soviet Whiskey submarine as well as a West German Type 206, but the Commander-in-Chief never said anything about the national origin of the submarines.[55]

During the Hårsfjärden incident some West German activities demand a closer look. The believed West German submarine radars, the Bonn telegram on 6 October, the strange behaviour of the West German merchant ship on 10 October and the nervousness of some West German diplomats during this period may all indicate some kind of West German involvement. However, a large amount of indications or even evidence mentioned above fit neither with Soviet nor with German submarines: the prints on the sea floor, the tape recordings, the yellow/green patch, the possible passage of a submarine through Öresund after the Hårsfjärden incident, and the statements about 'the Mälsten submarine'. In *Expressen*, a Swedish high-ranking officer was quoted as saying that the 'Mälsten submarine' was a 'NATO submarine' but not a West German one.[56] In his diary General Ljung characterized *Expressen*'s comment as 'doubtful' (in Swedish, 'tveksam'). He wanted to neither confirm nor deny this statement, although he denied a statement about a West German submarine.[57]

After a Swedish general had had long talks with his West German counterpart, he accompanied him to his aircraft. Before entering the aircraft, the German general said: 'We have also had these tracks from a bottom-crawling submarine.' To the Swedish general, this was of course very interesting, so why did the German general choose to tell him this at the stairs to the aircraft, when there was no possibility of further questions? If he believed that the tracks originated from a Soviet vessel, he would have invited some exchange of information. But he did not. Maybe he wanted to signal that the origin was different from what the Swedish general believed. The Swedish general did not know how to interpret this incident.

There are several observations of West German submarines in Swedish territorial waters – some also in the archipelago – but to my knowledge, except for the above-mentioned possible observation of a Type 206 in 1980, they have all been outside the restricted security zones. During the war, the Germans already had detailed maps of sub-surface waterways and hiding places in the Swedish archipelagos. After the war, the West Germans were able to use their port visits for necessary training in the Swedish archipelago. They may also have trained in navigation in Swedish archipelagos under other circumstances. All this seems to have been satisfactory to the Germans. There is, however, to my knowledge nothing that indicates that the West Germans have tried to provoke the Swedes on purpose. The West German post-war focus on legal activity also makes it less likely that German submarines would have been responsible for the extremely provocative operations in Swedish waters in the 1980s.

Furthermore, it is very difficult to believe that the German Navy would operate deep into the Swedish archipelago risking the lives of their officers and divers. Unlike the British Royal Navy, the French Navy and the US Navy, the German Navy has no, and did not at the time have any, global responsibility, which could have justified a damaged submarine and a loss of personnel. While British, French and US navies are used to losses and able to hide a loss of military person-nel in a remote conflict, nothing of this is applicable to Germany. (The West German need to use Swedish territorial waters in wartime also made such operations extremely risky.) The Royal Navy, the French Navy and particularly the US Navy have been much more willing to accept loss of lives. In 1982, the US Navy lost 562 men, and, in the 1980s altogether 5,865 men were lost, primarily in the USA. Of these losses, 12 men (and 11 marines) were lost in 'unknown/not reported' areas, which indicates that these men were lost in areas where the Navy will not acknowledge having operated.[58]

BRITISH SUBMARINE OPERATIONS

In the early 1980s, the Royal Navy had 13 diesel-electric and demagnetized Oberon-class patrol submarines: *Oberon, Odin, Orpheus, Olympus, Osiris, Onslaught, Otter, Oracle, Ocelot, Otus, Opossum, Opportune* and *Onyx* (90 metres; two propellers) providing the principal submarine delivery units for naval special forces (SBS and SAS swimmer teams).[59] The Royal Navy still had a couple of Porpoise-class diesel-electric submarines like *Walrus* (73 metres; two propellers) as well as some smaller nuclear Valiant-class submarines (87 metres; one propeller) and the earlier *Dreadnought* (81 metres; one propeller).[60] Similar to the Soviet Whiskey submarine, the Oberon profited from the design of the German XXI-class submarines with their cachalot-like form, external keel and two propellers. The Oberon-class submarines were able to carry a midget. The *Odin* (S10) and the *Opossum* (S19) were training with the US submersible *Avalon* in the early 1980s.[61] A photo shows a Royal Navy SDV (13 metres; one propeller) being manoeuvred to fit on its mother-sub, an Oberon-class submarine. Welham also has a drawing showing another British SDV (10 metres; one propeller).[62] The Royal Navy used the Canadian-built *Taurus* (11 metres; two propellers) both as a submarine rescue vehicle and for delivering divers into a target area.[63] Furthermore, British mother-subs have carried US SDVs. Special Boat Squadron (SBS) were using three US SDVs, type MkVIII.[64] From the 1980s, SBS also had at least two different kinds of British-built midgets or SDVs, I was told by an officer who had been training with these vessels. He also said that there was a third more advanced system that might have been the US version. In the late 1970s, SBS founded a very secret Maritime Counter-Terrorist Force, which included a Swimmer Delivery Team.[65] According to Foster:

> Seabased covert operations are nearly always run from a submarine, although this may act as a mothersub for the high-tech mini-subs the SBS has helped to develop over the years. In addition to landing and collecting agents, this area can include pro-active anti-terrorist/piracy operations . . . reconnaissance on specific sabotage targets, if a foreign country shows sign of becoming a little frisky.[66]

From the Second World War, the Royal Navy had a number of small X-Craft (12–15 metres; one propeller) and the even smaller Wellman (6 metres; one propeller). In 1955, 'an X-Craft was involved in an attempt to measure the diameter of the propellers of the new Soviet cruiser' in Kronstadt harbour close to Leningrad. The X-Craft unit was disbanded in 1958.[67] However, the British continued to use small craft of a similar size. From the late 1970s, the Royal Navy most likely had a Piranha mini-submarine (26.6 metres; one propeller) developed by Vickers. It was able to carry a team of ten special force troops. It was specialized for the role of covert missions and was able to penetrate into shallow waters with low risk of detection. It had a submerged speed of up to 9 knots. The Piranha also carried a pair of two-men SDVs (about 7 metres; one propeller). It had a transit range of 1,800 nautical miles, an operational radius of 800 nautical miles and was able to remain on patrol for 12 days.[68] In cooperation with the West Germans, the British Vickers company also developed an even smaller, 20-metre-long coastal submarine (Type 100), able to carry nine men and remain on patrol for 14 days. It has a top speed up to 11 knots.[69]

In 1988, the Swedish Navy made a perfect tape recording of a submarine in central Mysingen more than 10 kilometres north of Mälsten in Swedish internal waters. This is to my knowledge the only tape recording in Swedish internal waters where class of submarine has been identified. I was told that, when this tape was demonstrated to British sound experts, they confirmed that it was an Oberon-class submarine. 'It is one of ours,' a surprised British expert exclaimed. This story (but in less detail) was confirmed by Commander Leif Holmström, former Chief of MUSAC. He said on Swedish TV that they had tape-recorded the sound of a submarine in Swedish internal waters. During his talks with his counterparts in a NATO country, one of them had then confirmed its identity and exclaimed: 'It is one of ours.'[70]

In 1976, the *Opossum* went through the Kiel Canal to the Baltic Sea to trim the submarine for the different salinity and sonar conditions in the Baltic 'in preparation for longer submerged operations by another Royal Navy SSK [*Orpheus* (S11); see below] the following year'.[71] From 1977 up to the early 1990s, a couple of Oberon-class submarines regularly patrolled the Baltic Sea. According to a Swedish naval officer, it went on a yearly basis (two or three times a year) into the Baltic Sea up along the Baltic coast towards Finland and down along the Swedish coast, sometimes into Swedish territorial waters to test Swedish readiness with approval of somebody in the Swedish military leadership. In July 1982, *Onslaught* (S14) passed Öresund on the surface.[72] Later in the 1980s, an Oberon-class submarine was seen surfaced in international waters north of the Åland Islands along the north Swedish coast, a senior Swedish intelligence officer told me. Despite Danish and international law, such intelligence and special force submarines often went submerged through the Danish Straits (Store Belt). According to a Danish general, the Danish Naval Operative Command at Århus (Jutland) was pre-notified to avoid misunderstandings. They were ordered to 'close their eyes', he said. He also said that Oberon-class submarines landed special force troops in foreign countries without their approval. He did not believe that they had done that on Danish territory (at least not in recent years) but most likely had on the Soviet Baltic coast and possibly also in Sweden. A Danish admiral told me that he had given approval for British Oberon submarines to go submerged through the Danish Straits. The passages were made into exercises for testing instruments and personnel. This also made the submerged passages legal, he said. One such submarine was the *Orpheus*, I was told. *Orpheus* was the first submarine 'fitted with a purpose-built five-man chamber that allowed special forces to enter and exit from the submarine when it was dived in a group rather than, as hitherto, one or two at a time'.[73]

I have had most of this information confirmed by two Royal Navy officers, both commanding officers of Oberon-class submarines. A former Chief of Staff to Flag Officer Submarines (chief of submarine operations) said that he used to go up along the Norwegian coast, but he had also made a couple of trips into the Baltic Sea. The submarine went submerged through the Danish Straits and then along the Soviet Baltic coast and back along the Swedish coast. He also confirmed that they had landed SBS troops on the Soviet side, but he could not speak about the Swedish side, because these operations were considered extremely secret. 'We landed SBS troops,' he said. 'I just went where I was ordered to go.' According to his information, these covert trips – in addition to the officially recognized trips – were made twice a year from the late 1970s and during the 1980s. To the Swedes, these submarines would seem to come from the Soviet Union, because their origin would be unknown and they would always come from the waters of Estonia and the Bay of Finland. This Royal Navy officer also said that, when entering Norwegian fjords and when landing SBS troops in Norway, only a few people were informed on the Norwegian side. He also admitted that they went into some fjords without Norwegian approval.

The other Oberon captain, one of Britain's most experienced submarine officers, also confirmed the trips into the Baltic Sea along the Soviet and Swedish coasts from the late 1970s and during the 1980s. In the early and mid-1980s, the Oberon-class submarines were modernized, and they were operational until the early 1990s – exactly the same period when Sweden experienced provocative submarine operations in its own archipelagos. He also said that they did go north of the Åland Islands (to the Sea of Bothnia or possibly even to the Gulf of Bothnia), but he did not want to come up with any details. He said that he could not speak about operations into Swedish waters, as they, as well as some other operations, were still classified. However, it is more than likely that they landed special forces in Sweden, because there would otherwise have been no reason to operate a submarine rebuilt for this specific purpose along the Swedish coast and even in Swedish archipelagos. Of course, this is a very sensitive issue. According to this Oberon captain, there could be a new Cold War and, by speaking about these operations today, there is the risk of compromising future operations. In the 1980s, ministerial approval was given for every single operation, he said. He got his orders directly from the Flag Officer Submarines. They also briefed the Prime Minister's Office regularly about the risks with these operations. It is difficult to believe that the Prime Minister would have been uninformed about the political consequences of these operations. He also confirmed that such submarine operations could be useful in a crisis situation and in a low-intensity conflict.

Norwegian Prime Minister Kåre Willoch (1981–86) told me that they believed that some submarines in Swedish waters may have originated from the West, from the UK and possibly also from the USA, but he said he 'preferred not to be informed about it . . . Of course, Prime Minister Thatcher would never have informed us about these operations; that would have been impolite.' In other words, that would have put him in a dilemma as to whether to be loyal to the Swedes or to the British. However, Willoch believed that the USA and the UK might have carried out such operations, and he may also have been informed in general terms that operations were going to take place. At that time, to operate Western submarines in Swedish waters was a necessity. According to Willoch: 'It would have been negligence in the discharge of one's duties not to do so.'[74]

Both Oberon captains mentioned above spoke about operations on the Soviet and Swedish coasts and about landing SBS troops. The major book about this service, John Parker's (1997) SBS: The Inside Story of the Special Boat Service, does not mention anything of these operations. It is an almost 400-page book on SBS operations during the Second World War, in Northern Ireland, in the Falklands and in the Gulf War. He mentions some training along the Norwegian coast but nothing about operations in Soviet or Swedish waters. The only thing he mentions is a Maritime Counter-Terrorist Force founded in the late 1970s, which 'for reasons of security remains classified and beyond the scope of this book . . . [A] dedicated Swimmer Delivery Team was founded. They trained specifically in the use of motorised underwater tugs and towing craft for the speedy delivery of personnel to an operation.'[75]

Sir Keith Speed (British Minister for the Navy 1979–81 and member of the Parliamentary Defence Committee 1983–87) also confirmed that British submarines were testing Swedish coastal defences. On Swedish TV, he was asked if he could confirm that the testing was conducted in Swedish waters. His answer was 'yes'. He said they used Oberon- and Porpoise-class submarines, because they were 'much cheaper', 'smaller' and 'very quiet'. These operations were, according to Speed, made

> under the umbrella of a bilateral agreement . . . If the Swedish Naval Staff was not happy, and thought that they did not get much out of it, they could raise it with their Foreign Ministry or their government . . . If something happens like the 'Whiskey on the Rocks', it wouldn't be a very good idea to have a British submarine make an exercise ten days after the 'Whiskey on the Rocks' in 1981. It would have been politically sensitive. Let's relax. Perhaps think about it in a few months' time. It is common sense . . . As far as Britain is concerned, there would have been a general agreement that, during a certain period of time, British submarines . . . are going to be in your area of the Baltic . . . We would not necessarily say that we would be precisely here. Because if we told them that, and if we were trying to probe or test your defences, it wouldn't have been very sensible either from your point of view or from ours . . . There might well be penetration dive exercises. Can submarines actually get in and almost surface in the Stockholm harbour? Not quite, but that sort of thing. How far could we get without you being aware of it?[76]

Keith Speed confirmed that British submarines have operated in Swedish waters, and that this was done regularly to test Swedish coastal defences, which means that they had to operate in Swedish inner archipelagos where these defences were located. According to Keith Speed, the British submarines tested Swedish defences by going as far as possible into Swedish waters. He confirmed the use of Oberon-class submarines, but not midget submarines. This view is also supported by Paul Beaver (spokesman for *Jane's* in London):

> During the Cold War, I think you would be naive to think that NATO submarines would not operate throughout the Baltic. Two reasons. One would be intelligence gathering against the Soviet Union, perhaps following the Whiskey-class submarines out of Leningrad or Polish submarines operating out of Gdansk, but also I think there would be an interest NATO would have in testing the Swedish capability to find out how good the Swedish anti-submarine warfare operations were and how quickly they would respond to incursions of their territorial waters . . . I think it would be naive to believe that if you were going to operate within Swedish territorial waters, if you were going to operate deep inside Swedish homeland, particularly in the Stockholm archipelago and around naval bases, then I think you would want to make sure that the

Swedes would not immediately attack you with torpedoes or other sub-marines. So I wouldn't be surprised if there was some secret agreement between the government of Sweden and NATO nations, perhaps on the individual bilateral basis with the British or perhaps with the Germans that would allow a certain amount of intrusions into their [the Swedish] territorial waters as long as that intrusion was notified. In other words, as long as somebody in the High Command in Stockholm was aware that there were going to be some intrusions during a given period.[77]

I indicated earlier that Chief of Staff Vice-Admiral Stefenson, or Chief of the Navy Vice-Admiral Per Rudberg, may have been the officer in the Swedish High Command who was pre-notified of Western intrusions or testing operations in order to avoid a catastrophe. Rudberg has con-firmed that he was the Swedish secret liaison to NATO. And a month before the Hårsfjärden incident, Stefenson said that the great powers (in other words Great Britain and the USA) might put pressure on the Swedes (according to Carl Bildt, by exercising counter-operations in Swedish archipelagos), because the Swedes had proved unable to defend their own waters. In his briefing to the Prime Minister Olof Palme immediately after the Hårsfjärden submarine hunt (see above), Stefenson used almost the same words as Speed and Beaver, but without mentioning anybody as responsible for these operations. His argument about testing Swedish 'capability' and 'will' may very well have been what his British or US counterparts had told him. There is no reason to believe that the Soviet Union would test the 'will' of Sweden. In the same TV programme as Speed and Beaver were interviewed, the Danish Lieutenant-General Kjeld Hillingsø (Commander of BALTAP (NATO wartime supreme commander for Denmark, northern West Germany and the Baltic Sea) 1993–95) used exactly the same words as Stefenson:

> One was interested in testing if Sweden firstly was capable and secondly willing to defend its territory. This was a legitimate NATO interest. The Norwegians and the Danes could say to the other NATO countries: 'We trust the Swedes. They would certainly defend that flank.' However, the great powers and the superpowers preferred to get their own informa-tion, to have it confirmed themselves.[78]

In other words, the USA and the UK were not satisfied with Scandinavian assurances. They wanted to have physical proofs demon-strating Swedish capability and will. This is not much different from the testing, about twice a year, that Swedish submarines did in the 1980s and also in the 1990s as described by Commander Göran Frisk (see Chapter 5), reported by Captain Nils-Ove Jansson in the naval journal *Marinnytt*[79] and confirmed to me by Captain Rodrik Klintebo, former Chief of First Submarine Flotilla. From the late 1980s, a Swedish Navy group also operated a midget submarine in Swedish waters in order to test its own anti-submarine warfare capability.[80] It is always necessary to test the readiness of your own forces. A major difference, however, is that the USA and the UK perceive themselves as having a larger responsibility covering the whole NATO area. And when you are testing the 'will' of the Swedish forces, in other words if the Swedes really are willing to use force, you obviously must be willing to possibly sacrifice some of your own forces. These US or UK tests are, accordingly, more dramatic and more realistic than the Swedish tests described above. In an interview I held with Hillingsø, he said:

> US and UK submarine operations into Swedish waters would, firstly, be realistic training operations; secondly, give important information about Soviet capabilities of operating in Swedish waters; thirdly, convince the Swedish forces to increase their readiness; and, fourthly, strengthen the Swedish morale both within the military forces and in the population as a whole.[81]

The existence of the Royal Navy 'intrusions' has been confirmed by former Swedish Ambassador in London Leif Leifland. He said on Swedish TV that he knew about them.[82] In an interview I had with Leifland after this TV programme, he tried to modify his confirmation. He said that the existence of such Royal Navy operations in Swedish waters was a 'conclusion he made' or a 'feeling he got' after having talked with British naval officers. But he had no proofs, and as Ambassador he had not reported anything to Stockholm.[83] According to Commander Hans von Hofsten, Chief of Staff Lieutenant-General Thorsten Engberg had filtered the information to the Commander-in-Chief and seemingly obstructed a submarine hunt in the same way that Chief of Staff Vice-Admiral Stefenson had done in Hårsfjärden in 1982 and during other incidents.[84] If there was a top-level agreement with the Royal Navy to test Swedish anti-submarine warfare capability, these 'obstructions' are easier to explain.

The Hårsfjärden hunt, however, does not fit perfectly with such a scenario. The request from the Eastern Military District and General Ljung's decision to use mines to damage the submarine and the actual damaging of a submarine on 11 October indicate something else. The most sensitive part of General Ljung's diary seems to have been the part following the submarine hunt. At least, it seems that General Ljung was not informed of any Western intrusion in the first phase of the submarine hunt. That would explain the radical change in Swedish behaviour during these days. The press centre with several hundred journalists was suddenly closed down as if something had happened during the hunt. In other words, if an Obcron-class submarine was involved in Hårsfjärden in 1982, this would have happened without the Royal Navy or any other navy pre-notifying the Swedish Commander-in-Chief.

In 1982, *Oberon* appeared with SBS swimmers deep inside a Norwegian fjord (Lyngen not far from Tromsø and close to the Finnish border) without Norwegian approval. This incident led to the British and Norwegian authorities setting up clear rules for British activities in Norway. In 1985, however, the same submarine turned up in another Norwegian fjord. Just before a submarine hunt was initi-ated, the Norwegian Navy identified the submarine as being the British *Oberon*. Preparations for the hunt were stopped and the Norwegians immediately contacted British naval headquarters. The British naval authorities sent a bottle of whisky to the Norwegian commander and apologized for the incident.

This apology, however, may have been a routine statement. A Norwegian submarine captain told me that US and UK submarines went into Norwegian waters without pre-notifying the Norwegian authorities. He said that, according to UK and US colleagues, there was a programme for entering Norwegian and others waters. When revealed, the blame for the incident may very well have been given to the 'ambitious' submarine captain. A former chief of Norwegian Military Intelligence told me that Royal Navy submarines landed SBS swimmers as a training programme for the Stay-Behinds, and the regular military hierarchy was never informed. This fits well with what the above mentioned Oberon captain said about going into Norwegian fjords without Norwegian approval and that he was just ordered to go to all these locations. His submarine was rebuilt for landing SBS swimmers. He also went along the Swedish coast, where his task would have been the same. The Swedish Stay-Behinds were part of the European-wide Stay-Behind network, and the programme for testing Sweden's capability and may have been a spin-off from the Stay-Behind training programme. The Swedish wartime commander of these forces, Vice-Admiral Per Rudberg, would have been pre-notified.

Perhaps it was an Oberon-class submarine that was involved in Hårsfjärden, but it is rather large to enter such narrow waters. The submarine observed in the outer archipelago at Sandhamn on 4 October may very well have been a relatively large submarine able to carry a midget submarine or small submersible. It was believed that this submarine received the small submersible that had exercised its way out from Stockholm harbour. The sail of the Sandhamn subma-rine was described as a 'large wall' perhaps up to '10 metres high', which fits well with an Oberon-class submarine. It may have been the same submarine that was parked southeast of Mälsten south of the island of Grän on 10–11 October. Oberon has an external keel close to 60 metres, similar to the print found more than 1 kilometre southeast of Mälsten. However, US and Italian Tang-class submarines also have similar characteristics. If the mother-sub was British, the small submersible may still have been American. SBS submarines used three US SDVs. There was a close cooperation concerning these kinds of operations. Several of the above sources indicated that it was American. The large yellow/green dye in the water on 11 October possibly also indicated a US submarine.

FRENCH SUBMARINE OPERATIONS

In the early 1980s, the French Navy had a couple of diesel-electric Agosta-class submarines (68 metres; one propeller), *Agosta* and *Bévéziers,* for landing swimmer teams.[85] The French had some small midgets for the oil industry and for defence purposes.[86] The French allegedly also used a couple of their nine Daphné-class submarines (58 metres; two propellers) for special operations. The Daphné class has a keel similar to the Whiskey or the Oberon, but it is shorter.[87] One of these Daphné-class submarines (or possibly a Daphné-class submarine from another country: Spain or South Africa) is believed to have operated in a Norwegian fjord in 1983, which was followed by a dramatic submarine hunt. A French admiral and former fleet commander told me that, in wartime, their strategic submarines would use Norwegian fjords or Norwegian waters for launching their missiles against the Soviet Union. They might enter Norwegian waters in peacetime to check out conditions for hiding submarines and how sounds were transmitted in the fjords, but the French Navy would not do that without approval from the Norwegian authorities, he said.

The incident in 1983 seems to point in another direction. On 27 April 1983, the day after the Swedish Submarine Commission published its report on the Hårsfjärden incident, a submarine was seen on the surface in Hardangerfjord. Two Norwegian retired naval special force officers saw the submarine for up to 30 minutes with special force swimmers on board (submarine personnel would never leave the submarine sail under these circumstances). They identified the submarine as not being a Norwegian submarine. The Norwegian Navy used several anti-submarine rockets against an echo in the fjord. At 07.30 the following morning the seriousness was underlined by the Norwegian Prime Minister Kåre Willoch speaking on the radio. Hundreds of journalists (including a large number of foreign correspondents) turned up on the shores of the fjord. The Norwegian

249

Aftenposten wrote that nobody could trust Soviet peaceful intentions. The Norwegian *Dagbladet* said that it was serious when the Soviet Union violated the territory of a neutral country, but it was no less serious when the Soviet Union sent submarines into Norwegian fjords. The Swedish *Dagens Nyheter* wrote that the Soviet Union was showing its strength by 'sniffing about in Scandinavian fjords', while *Svenska Dagbladet* argued that Sweden should sever its contacts with the Soviet aggressor.[88] The *New York Times* spoke about a probable Whiskey-class submarine.[89]

A Norwegian senior officer told me that during the hunt in Hardangerfjord, a Norwegian submarine came into contact with a foreign submarine at the entrance of the fjord, most likely the same submarine that had been seen by the two Norwegian special force officers, or another submarine operating together with this submarine (to attract anti-submarine forces away from the most sensitive areas where the first submarine might have been operating).[90] The Norwegians believed that it was a Daphné-class submarine. There was no indication it was a Soviet submarine, but they did not go public about it, this officer told me. Another Norwegian, who at the time had a vital position, has confirmed this information. The submarine was believed to have been one of two Daphné-class submarines believed to have been assigned to a special force organization outside the French Navy. This organization was not under parliamentary control, but under the direct control of the President. One submarine may have been damaged or possibly even lost. Similar to the Hårsfjärden incident in Sweden, this incident created a storm in the international mass media.

The two unclassified versions of the military report on the Hardangerfjord incident do not mention any state responsible for this operation, but they confirm that a submarine may have been damaged and, indirectly, that the submarine at the entrance of the fjord was identified.[91] Another senior Norwegian officer (with access to the classified parts of the military report) has confirmed that the above information is correct. In other words, the submarine had first been seen on the surface of the fjord by two Norwegian retired special force swimmers, but the Norwegian authorities had not been able to identify it. They thought, however, that it was linked to the submarine at the entrance to the fjord, which they believed was a French Daphné-class submarine. A former minister also told me that the French at the time operated in Norwegian waters without government approval. Another former minister told that he remembered that they believed that the Hardangerfjord submarine might have been French. A formerly classified report from August 1983,[92] written by Director-General Finn Molvig (Assistant Under-Secretary for Security Policy), states that it 'goes without saying' that the submarine was from the Soviet Union, as if he had not been informed about any possible French involvement. The information about a possible French submarine seems to have been classified as 'cosmic' and only available to a very few people.

The parallel to the Hårsfjärden incident is remarkable. The submarine appeared on the surface of a fjord in a relatively densely populated area. Maybe it was 'discovered because it wanted to be'. But why would the French President carry out such a risky operation? France has no special responsibility in Scandinavia. To risk a submarine and its crew in this way makes no sense if it wasn't assigned to another organization or state worried about Norwegian or Scandinavian public opinion and readiness. As with the Hårsfjärden incident, it made Scandinavian public opinion aware of the Soviet threat. The Soviets were believed to be the only possible intruder. This information was spread not only in Norway and Sweden but in the Western world in general. And the timing was perfect: one day after the launch of the Swedish Submarine Defence Commission Report. Maybe this operation was carried out as a French deal with another state? The most likely candidate for such a deal is the USA. The USA has such a wider responsibility, while close US ties to Norway make the use of other countries' navy platforms more convenient. The US counterpart in such an operation would most likely be the CIA. Under General Alexandre de Marenches (and his successor) in the late 1970s and early 1980s, French intelligence cooperated closely with US intelligence. A possible French involvement in Hardangerfjord – directly after the release of the 1983 Submarine Defence Commission Report – raises the question of a possible French involvement also during the Hårsfjärden incident. A Daphné-class submarine supposedly passed through the Öresund into the Baltic Sea in the last week of September a few days before the Hårsfjärden submarine hunt started.[93]

However, we may also have to look into the possibility of a South African Daphné-class submarine, for example operating from the US submarine base at Holy Loch in Scotland. A deal with South Africa would be more convenient for the Americans. A loss of life would be less sensitive, and almost nobody would imagine a South African involvement. Hasselbohm has documented that South African naval special force officers were active in Sweden in the early and mid-1980s. One South African agent in Stockholm said in London in September 1982 that submarines were going to turn up in the Swedish archipelagos as if he knew what was going to happen. He clearly had good contacts within the Royal Navy and with senior US officials. According to an alleged document from the Swedish Military Intelligence Service SSI from 1987, a couple of South African agents

251

had been ordered to deploy transponders or navigation aids for submarines in the Baltic Sea in cooperation with the CIA. None of these statements are proof of South African involvement, but there are too many indications of South African naval special force activities in Sweden at the time to exclude such an option.

US NAVY SEAL SUBMARINE OPERATIONS

In the years 1970–84, the principal US Navy delivery unit for special forces or SEALs was the rebuilt USS *Grayback* (SS 574) (102 metres; two propellers). It carried two SDVs (Swimmer Delivery Vehicles or SEAL Delivery Vehicles) and had a capability to deliver more than 60 combat swimmers.[94] *Grayback* had an external keel similar to the French Daphné, the Soviet Whiskey and the British Oberon, but, compared to the others, *Grayback* was larger (58, 76 and 90 metres vs. 102 metres).[95]

From the 1970s, Sturgeon-class submarines like USS *Hawkbill* (SSN 666) (89 metres; one propeller), USS *Gurnard* (SSN 662), USS *Bergall* (SSN 667) and USS *Pintado* (SSN 672), as well as 'special project submarines' like USS *Halibut* (SSN 587) (106 metres; two propellers) and USS *Seawolf* (SSN 575) (103 metres; two propellers) had all operated as mother-subs for Deep Submergence Rescue Vehicles (DSRVs) and/or for other submersibles. The markings on the sail on several of these submarines show that they were 'specifically designed to support the DSRV [or SDV or DSV] on other than rescue missions, [for example] intelligence operations'.[96] From 1982, one Sturgeon-class submarine, USS *Cavalla* (SSN 684), was rebuilt to carry SDVs, while additional Sturgeon-class submarines like USS *William Bates* (SSN 680) were used as mother-subs for DSRVs.[97] In 1988–91, an additional five Sturgeon-class submarines – USS *Archerfish* (SSN 678), USS *Silversides* (SSN 679), USS *William Bates*, USS *Tunny* (SSN 682) and USS *L. Mendel Rivers* (SSN 686) (all 92 metres; one propeller) – were modified into mother-subs for SDVs.[98] According to an admiral from a NATO country, other US submarines had already been rebuilt for carrying SDVs from the early 1980s. In the 1980s, there were several US submarines with the capability to carry SDVs or other submersibles that would operate covertly in foreign waters. In the early 1980s, the four-man SDV, Mk VII (6 metres; one propeller), was replaced by the more capable six-man Mk VIII (6.5 metres; one propeller) and by the two-metres wide two-man Mk IX (6 metres; two propellers). In 1987, there were some 19 units within the two SDV Teams.[99]

In the late 1950s, the US Navy had experimented with a small experimental attack craft, *X1* (15 metres; one propeller).[100] In the

1960s, they developed several small Deep Submergence Vehicles (DSVs) like *Alvin* (7 metres; one plus two propellers), *Turtle* (8 metres; one plus two propellers) and *Sea Cliff* (8 metres; one plus two propellers) that were all available in the early 1980s. From 1970, these vessels were supplemented by two DSRVs, *Avalon* and *Mystic* (both 15 metres; one propeller).[101] Most of these vessels, as well as mother-subs like *Halibut* and *Seawolf*, belonged to Submarine Development Group 1 (in San Diego) that carried out deep-sea research but also espionage operations in foreign countries.[102] Lockheed had a similar DSV, *Deep Quest* (12 metres; two propellers) also based in San Diego. It was developed as a first prototype for the DSRVs.[103] In addition, there were a number of small privately owned DSVs like Rockwell's *Beaver MK4* (8 metres; two plus one propellers).[104] Furthermore, the US Navy has a bottom-crawling nuclear-powered mini-submarine *NR-1* (41.6 metres; two propellers), which belonged to Submarine Squadron 2 (linked to and co-located with Submarine Development Squadron 12 in Groton, Connecticut). *NR-1* is able to stay in a sub-surface position for 30 days. Similar to the deep submergence vehicles, it has external spotlights and a remote-controlled manipulator. It has wheels for going on the sea floor.[105] It has been used for laying SOSUS lines on the bottom of the ocean but also for covert operations in Soviet and friendly waters. It was based in Holy Loch in Scotland while carrying out operations in European waters.[106]

Some US 'special project submarines' carried out secret missions into other countries' territorial waters including planting listening buoys and tapping communication cables. In the 1970s and 1980s, these operations were carried out in the Sea of Okhotsk, in the Barents Sea – by USS *Halibut*, USS *Seawolf* and former Sturgeon-class nuclear attack submarines (like USS *Parche*)[107] – and allegedly also in the Baltic Sea. They operated as mother-subs for the *Avalon* and the *Mystic*. *Seawolf* also operated in tandem with *NR-1* and used submersibles like the *Turtle* and the *Sea Cliff*.[108] The *Seawolf* had the capability to carry these submersibles 'on her after deck'.[109] Norman Polmar wrote in 1987 that the Navy had been reluctant to release photographs of the *Seawolf* from the 1980s, 'because of modifications for her employment in research and special missions'.[110] John Craven, former Chief of Submarine Development Group 1, says that the *Seawolf* was assigned to his organization. It carried out deep-sea research, but this activity was also a cover for espionage operations, which were carried out by a small organization within the official organization. However, this smaller secret organization was also a cover for top-secret special projects that cooperated closely with Naval Intelligence and the DIA, sometimes in competition with the CIA. The whole organization was built up according to a hierarchical structure of 'Russian dolls', and you never knew if you had reached the most secret unit of the organization. Most people working for Submarine Development Group 1 had no idea about the covert projects, Craven said.[111]

Submarine Development Group 1 was also responsible for the diesel-electric submarine *Dolphin* (AGSS 555) (46 metres; one propeller). Other US diesels were *Barbel* (SS 580), *Blueback* (SS 581) and *Bonefish* (SS 582) (all 67 metres; one propeller), *Albacore* (64 metres; one propeller), which belonged to the Atlantic Reserve, the Tang-class submarines *Wahoo* (SS 565), *Gudgeon* (SSAG 567) (both 87 metres; two propellers) and *Darter* (SS 576) (82 metres; two propellers).[112] The latter was a sister ship of *Grayback*. *Blueback* had operated as a mother-sub for *Mystic*.[113] All these diesel-electric submarines were used for espionage, for special forces or for training operations testing the anti-submarine warfare capability of US (and other) forces. In addition, the USA has had one or more Soviet diesel-electric Whiskey submarine(s), probably bought from Indonesia after General Suharto's military coup in 1965. Indonesia received up to 14 Whiskey submarines during 1962–65. In 1977–78, there were three left, and in 1981–82 Indonesia still had two Whiskey submarines.[114] At least one or perhaps several of these submarines were taken over by the USA. The US Navy used one or more Whiskeys to play Soviet submarine(s) in connection with special naval exercises. A high-ranking officer told me that he participated in an exercise with a US Whiskey submarine. In the early 1980s, this submarine may have been used to masquerade as a Soviet submarine. It was kept very secret in the USA, and for obvious reasons not described in *Jane's Fighting Ships* or other naval handbooks. In 1982, the US Navy (and the CIA) seems to have had at least ten diesel-electric submarines.

Operations with 'special project submarines' were financed through and to some extent decided by the National Underwater Reconnaissance Office (NURO), a committee of CIA and Naval Intelligence officers (or rather DIA officers at the Office of Naval Intelligence). NURO was initiated in 1969 and headed by the Secretary of the Navy.[115] Sontag and Drew describe NURO as a liaison agency between the Navy and the CIA, which in the early phase was dominated by the CIA. In the mid-1970s, the CIA lost its day-to-day control of Navy Intelligence activities, and the Navy representative at NURO, Captain James Bradley, Director of Undersea Warfare at the Office of Naval Intelligence, was able to conduct his own special project operations.[116] However, according to Craven, Bradley conducted these special project operations as a DIA officer at the Office of Naval Intelligence.[117] In the 1980s, the general policy and the major decisions about 'special project submarines' were still controlled by NURO, most likely to receive a mutual CIA, DIA and Navy support for these operations (see below). If the Secretary of the Navy was still heading NURO, then it was headed by John Lehman.

When naval special forces were exercising landing operations in 'occupied territories', the CIA was given command of US Navy submarines. Submarines were used to land SEALs in foreign countries to exercise cooperation with local Stay-Behinds. They exercised infiltration and exfiltration directly from larger submarines as well as via SDVs and other smaller vessels. A Norwegian former intelligence officer told me that, already in 1958, they had intruding submarines that operated in south Norwegian fjords in a way totally illogical from a Soviet point of view. The Chief of Norwegian Military Intelligence, Vilhelm Evang, and his staff believed they were American. CIA officers from the US Embassy asked Norwegian Intelligence why they did not protest against the Soviet intrusions. The Norwegians answered that they did not have enough information. In 1967, after a similar incident, the US Deputy Defense Attaché approached a Norwegian Military Intelligence officer. The US attaché said that he had been instructed to ask why the Norwegians had not protested against the Soviet submarine. The Norwegian officer said that he believed it was a US submarine. The attaché said that he actually also believed that this was the case. A couple of days afterwards, the latter called back and said that he had been removed from his position in Norway. He was going to be replaced immediately and transferred to Vietnam. The Norwegian intelligence officer said that he had discussed this incident with Evang, and they were convinced that the CIA had conducted its own operations without informing the attaché at the Embassy.

From about 1960, parallel US operations seem to have taken place in Swedish waters. Two Scandinavians told me that they received information from a US source, which in both cases turned out to be Captain Bernhard Lauff, US Naval Attaché to Stockholm (1960–63). One of these Scandinavians believed that support for these operations was given by the US Office of Naval Research in London, and by its chief, Captain J.K. Sloatman, with whom he used to meet occasionally. On 24 October 1966, a submarine on the Swedish west coast, in the archipelago north of Göteborg, showed its periscope and sail. By using a cable with two 50-kilo weights, a Swedish mine sweeper made physical contact with the submarine ten metres below surface, where the sea depth was 29 metres. This contact was maintained for two hours. Commander Nils Bruzelius has argued that this was most likely a US George Washington-class Polaris submarine lying on the bottom.[118] Commander Wilhelm Carlstedt, who was responsible for the Swedish operation, said that he received clear orders from his 'top leadership' not to attack the submarine with live ammunition until it had gone further out.[119] From around 1960, US submarines, possibly under CIA command, seem to have conducted some very secret operations in both Norway and Sweden. Two other Norwegian intelligence officers have told me that, in the 1980s, both US and UK submarines conducted operations in Norwegian fjords as part of a top-secret programme. However, several, and perhaps all, of the most senior naval officers were never informed. To the Navy, similar to what happened in the 1960s, these submarines were believed to be Russian. These operations appear as a test of the Norwegian Navy and the Norwegian coastal defences, while they convinced public opinion of the Soviet danger. Also in similar fashion to the 1960s, CIA officers approached high-ranking Norwegian officers (while demanding a safe room) to tell them about intruding Soviet (midget) submarines. However, the concrete information presented by the Americans was not reliable.

In 1984, US Chief of Naval Operations, Admiral James Watkins, set up a 'terrorist' force, the 'Red Cell' or the Navy Security Coordination Team (NSCT) – recruited from former members of the anti-terrorist SEAL Team Six – to test security and readiness at US Navy bases worldwide to convince the officer corps of the reality of the insurgent danger. The idea was launched by Secretary Lehman's confidant Vice-Admiral James Lyons, Deputy Chief of Naval Operations for Plans, Policy, and Operations.[120] The members of the 'Red Cell' acted as terrorists and dressed like terrorists until it was closed down in 1992 after some scandals. They used violent actions: planted bombs in secure areas, hijacked aircraft, attacked surface ships and submarines in harbours, wounded US personnel and took hundreds of hostages including base commanders. They entered US installations at home or abroad in order to test their security, and, more important, to create an awareness of the terrorist threat, which has been described in detail by Admiral Lyons, by former commander of SEAL Team Six, Commander Richard Marcinko,[121] and by the former commander of SEAL Team Three, Commander Gary Stubblefield.[122] To most Americans the terrorist threat had no reality. It was necessary to be 'physical', to quote Admiral Lyons. 'We had to change their mindset, to raise people's awareness,' Lyons said.[123]

According to Commander Marcinko, the Navy had for years used Soviet equipment including Soviet aircraft, while playing enemy forces against its own forces. Now, according to Marcinko, they also had to prepare for a terrorist threat.[124] An admiral from a NATO country told me that, already in the 1970s, SEALs used a Soviet cover to play enemy forces to make the threat appear more real. In the 1970s and 1980s, SEAL team officers operated in Soviet uniforms, with

Soviet weapons and communication systems and they even had a Soviet Whiskey submarine. SEAL Team Six, established in November 1980 (and possibly its parent unit SEAL Team Two), had been used for the purpose of testing US or friendly coastal defences. In Europe, these coastal operations were under the command of Supreme Allied Commander Europe (SACEUR). In the late 1970s, his name was General Alexander Haig.

General Haig later became Secretary of State under President Ronald Reagan, while Caspar Weinberger was Secretary of Defense. As a former State Secretary, Haig visited Sweden in March 1983, a couple of months after the Hårsfjärden incident. Haig supposedly told a surprised Swedish top official, 'it is good that you let the submarine out' (see below). Weinberger had visited Sweden exactly a year before the Hårsfjärden incident. He had had meetings with senior Swedish naval officers. In an interview for Swedish TV, Weinberger confirmed that these testing operations were carried out in the NATO area, and he confirmed that they were carried out in Swedish waters after consultations with the Swedes. However, these consultations were not at the level of ministers. He never discussed this issue with the Swedish Prime Minister or Defence Minister. It was Navy-to-Navy consultations, Weinberger said. The Commander-in-Chief, General Bengt Gustafsson (1986–92), stated afterwards that he was never informed. He was quite upset.[125] Later, he spoke about himself as a 'useful idiot'. The following is a longer quote from the interview (see Appendix II for more of the interview):

> *Weinberger:* My understanding is that there were consultations and understandings that there were going to be various tests or there were going to be attempts to ensure that the defences in the Swedish areas were effective . . . [T]o my knowledge, there was no direct intrusion or testing of Swedish waters or defences without consultations with the Swedes . . .

> *Swedish TV*: At what level were these consultations?

> *Weinberger*: Generally, they were Navy to Navy, the US Navy to the Swedish Navy, I believe. The Swedish Navy is part of the Swedish government and the US Navy is part of the US government. Responsible officials on both sides would have discussions, consultations, and agreements would flow from that, to make sure that they get all the help needed to protect the sovereignty of their waters. If for example Sweden had said that you must not have any intrusions of that area in this month that would certainly have been honoured and respected by NATO.

Swedish TV: But other areas would then be OK?

Weinberger: Well, it depends entirely on the response of the officials in charge of the negotiations. What I am saying is that at no time, to my knowledge, did NATO simply send a submarine directly into Swedish waters without consultations and prior discussions and agreements that that could be done. Under those circumstances, it was not a pressing problem. It was part of a routine, regular, scheduled series of defence testing that NATO did and indeed had to do to be responsible and liable. [The Soviet Whiskey submarine in 1981] was a clear violation, and submarines can get in where they are not wanted, and that is exactly why we made this defensive testing and these defensive manoeuvres to ensure that they would not be able to do that without being detected . . . The mission of NATO was to not permit Soviet invasion or attacks. The consultations and discussions we had were designed – with all countries, not just Sweden – to ensure that NATO was able to perform this mission and had ample opportunities to test through manoeuvres and other activities as to whether the defences were adequate and whether or not the Soviets were requiring any new capabilities that would require any changes in their defences or anything of that kind.

Swedish TV: How frequently was it done in Sweden?

Weinberger: I don't know. Enough to comply with the military requirements for making sure that they were up to date. We would know when the Soviets required a new kind of submarine. We would then have to see if our defences were adequate against that. And all this was done on a regular basis, and on an agreed-upon basis.[126]

There is no doubt that Weinberger, in this interview, spoke about regular submarine operations in Swedish waters carried out by US or perhaps Royal Navy or other Western submarines. On the day the interview was broadcast on Swedish TV, Swedish Defence Minister Björn von Sydow said he was surprised, but added: 'I have no reason to question what a former US Defense Secretary is saying.'[127] The following day, Swedish Prime Minister Göran Persson stated in the Swedish Parliament: 'If there are any documents I don't know, but I know that a former Secretary of Defense, a US Secretary of Defense, in a long interview, in a clear wording has presented a rationale for what, according to his view, NATO apparently did in our waters.'[128] One hour after the interview with Weinberger, Associated Press held an interview with Sir John Walker, former head of Britain's Defence Intelligence. He said that NATO wanted to test Swedish anti-submarine forces: 'If you were going to operate inside the Stockholm archipelago, you wanted to make sure that the Swedes would not attack you with torpedoes.' And

Walker added that NATO was 'allowed a certain amount of intrusions during a given period'.[129] Both Weinberger and Walker spoke clearly about 'NATO'. However, this does not necessarily mean NATO as a formal organization, but rather US or UK operations in cooperation with one or more allies, I was told shortly afterwards by General Vigleik Eide, former Norwegian Commander-in-Chief and former Chairman of the NATO Military Committee. He said that these operations would have been too sensitive to carry out through the NATO system. After having received a US briefing, NATO Secretary-General George Robertson came up with a similar hint. He said in a Swedish TV interview:

> It is not a matter for NATO. It is a matter between [stop]. If people wish to go back to the history between Sweden and the individual countries that own individual submarines [stop]. If retired secretaries of defense want to sound off that is their prerogative and their memory will be tested. It is not a matter for me.[130]

Weinberger speaks about the necessity of testing Swedish coastal defences to assure that these defences were up to date, and to assure that the Soviets would not easily enter Swedish waters. 'The consultations and discussions we had were designed . . . to assure that NATO . . . had opportunities to test through manoeuvres and other activities as to whether the defences were adequate and whether the Soviets were requiring any new capabilities that would require any changes in their defences . . . Besides that one intrusion of the Whiskey-class submarine, there were no violations, no capabilities of the Soviets [here he changes the direction of the sentence] to make an attack that could not be defended against, and that was the mission of NATO.' Weinberger seems to state that essential activities in Swedish waters after the 'Whiskey on the Rocks' in 1981 were carried out by Western submarines with the understanding of somebody on the Swedish side. These testing operations were seemingly also necessary to understand what technology the Soviets would develop.

After this interview, a senior US Navy Intelligence officer said: 'I wonder why he let himself get into such a discussion. He should have avoided it (my opinion).' This retired US Navy officer also said that he himself was never informed about these operations even though he had an important position at the time. After the interview with Weinberger, a US senior official told me almost the same, but he argued that he had been briefed about these operations:

> I don't know why Weinberger said what he did. Covert submarine operations are the most secret thing we have . . . The decisions were taken

by a committee of DIA and CIA people [most likely NURO], but I will neither confirm nor deny any operations in Swedish waters.

A high-ranking CIA officer confirmed to me that US operations in Scandinavian waters were sometimes run by NURO, and he spoke about the 1982 incident in Swedish waters as 'something of an underwater U-2'. He had, however, never himself been involved in these operations, he said, but he knew the people involved in it. Caspar Weinberger's Assistant Under-Secretary, Dov Zackheim, said after the interview with Weinberger that neither he nor anyone else in the administration would confirm or deny anything of what Weinberger had said. And publicly Zackheim said: 'If the former Secretary of Defense wants to say this, it is up to him.'[131] In a letter to Ambassador Ekéus's Investigation in 2001, an anonymous source confirmed Weinberger's statement:

> In the early 1980s, we routinely received a number of Swedish military/political delegations (NB not diplomatic) for 'near-top consultations' . . . [one] talked about your problem with Soviet subs and literally invited us to test the Swedish defence with a 'free-in-out guarantee'. Your naval people wanted this to have your government shift budgets from air to naval defences. So CW [Caspar Weinberger] promised that you'd have some subs to play with. That Whiskey sub must have been a real heaven sent gift for them though everyone here had a good laugh over the gullible Swedes!

As a final comment he states: 'In short, this verifies the interview.'[132] On the Swedish side, it is not yet clear who was informed, but it may only have been a couple of people within the Navy – perhaps the same people who were responsible for the ceasefires and the de-escalation of the submarine hunt in Hårsfjärden in 1982. These were also the same officers who met Weinberger exactly one year earlier in October 1981.

The above-mentioned high-ranking CIA officer described a damaged submarine in 1982 in Hårsfjärden as 'something of an underwater U-2', which points to the significance of this incident. Similarly, a senior US Navy officer actually told the *éminence grise* of the Norwegian Foreign Ministry, Einar Ansteensen, that the damaged submarine in Hårsfjärden was American. 'It was a sad story,' he said. Ansteensen was well connected. He was the maker of ministers of defence and foreign affairs in Norway and had been at NATO Defence College in Rome. He had been the director of the ministry's Political Division and the Policy Planning Division in the 1960s and 1970s. During the Hårsfjärden incident, he was at the Embassy in Stockholm. He reported the damaged US submarine to his Commander-in-Chief General Sven Hauge, but he did not inform General Ljung and the Swedes, he told me. The US Navy officer had told Ansteensen that US submarines went on a regular basis into the Baltic Sea but not north of a certain latitude in order not to create trouble for the Finns. Ansteensen said that US submarines operated covertly in the Baltic Sea, not in Finnish waters, but he confirmed that they operated in Swedish waters.[133] When I, during a car trip in 1993, mentioned that a US submarine had been damaged in the Stockholm archipelago in 1982 to former Director of the CIA and former US Secretary of Defense James Schlesinger, he said: 'I recall the incident but I don't remember the details.'

What characterizes these operations is their ultra-secrecy, the direct links between lower commanding officers and top military commanders and the direct political involvement. On the US and British side, it probably was just some special force officers, a few submarine captains and some people at the very top level who knew about these operations. The above-mentioned captain of a Royal Navy Oberon submarine told me that ministerial approval had been given for every single operation. He himself had briefed the Prime Minister's Office on the risks. The link was direct from the captain to Flag Officer Submarines and the First Sea Lord to the Prime Minister. Commander Richard Marcinko reported directly to Chief of Naval Operations Admiral James Watkins.[134] SEAL operations testing the readiness of NATO forces were under the direct command of SACEUR, while only four or five senior officers were informed in the host country (see below). The Navy's NURO representative, the DIA officer Captain James Bradley – responsible for the top-secret spy operations in Soviet territorial waters – had a direct link to Henry Kissinger through General Alexander Haig.[135] The historian of the Reagan administration Peter Schweizer describes how the Director of the CIA, William Casey, left Rome and turned up in Stockholm in his own aircraft. He had a meeting and lunch with a couple of Swedish military officials. Thus, there seems to have been a direct link between the CIA leadership and the local commanders.[136] When Glenn Campbell, Chairman of the President's Intelligence Oversight Board, described Casey, he said: 'He loved putting things together making them happen in the field.'[137] A former Deputy Commander (for Intelligence) US Naval Forces Europe said that he did not know about these operations: 'However, the Agency crowd and the SOF people [Special Operation Forces] didn't inform me anyway. After all I was only the Navy's chief Intel officer for the region.' In the early 1980s, the SEALs got an ultra-secret portable satellite communications system – for their commando operations – linked into the White House FLASHBOARD crisis alert network under the supervision of Lieutenant-Colonel Oliver North in close cooperation with Vice-President George Bush and CIA Director William Casey. 'SEAL

Team Six [was] tasked by the Secretary of Defense and the White House' with a direct link to the Vice-President and the CIA Director, which implies the importance and the delicate nature of these operations.[138]

In August 1982, Vice-Admiral Lee Baggett, Jr. presented the first Naval Special Warfare Master Plan.[139] In a few years, there were several new 'mother-subs' (carrying SDVs). According to General James Lindsay, Commander of Special Operations Command, the number of SDVs had increased [radically] to 15, or in 1987, according to Kevin Dockery, 19 (Mk VIII and Mk IX).[140] A new form of dry and warm SDV, Advanced SEAL Delivery System (ASDS), was developed. This cigar-like ASDS (20 metres; one propeller) with 2.5 metres in diameter let the eight 'SEALs remain relaxed and dry, and avoid loss of body heat'.[141] Rear-Admiral George Worthington, former commander Naval Special Warfare Command, states that the radical build-up started in the early 1980s, the budget for the SEAL teams increased drastically[142] and almost all these resources were put into the SDV-mothersub concept.[143] In 1987, an Assistant Secretary of Defense for Special Operations was established.[144] In the mid-1990s, according to official figures, US special forces conducted between 2,000 and 3,000 deployments, including secret operations, in more than 130 countries each year.[145]

We have to ask: which experiences motivated this radical build-up and reorganization of the special forces? It cannot have been the mistakes from Iran in 1980 or the more or less unsuccessful operation in Grenada in 1983. The radical change and build-up must have been justified by some highly classified and extremely successful operations – operations the commander of SEAL Team Three, Commander Gary Stubblefield, confirms have taken place:

> [He describes some covert operations in the early 1980s, some] really smart interesting training in the NATO and Atlantic theatres . . . We set up and worked with support networks, E&E networks and we started getting smart about going into foreign areas. All that involved looking like people who weren't in the US Navy and doing things that people in the US Navy weren't supposed to do.[146]

The first part of the paragraph indicates training for the Stay-Behinds, but the second part indicates something more, and seems to refer to the same operations that Caspar Weinberger discussed with direct reference to Sweden. The only operations Commander Stubblefield talks about that could have justified a radical change in naval special warfare and a dramatic increase in the number of midget submarines and 'mother-subs' seem to have been 'covert training' operations in the NATO theatre – either as formal members of the Navy or as a force with an assignment for other branches of government outside the Department of Defense (in other words, the CIA):

> [In these operations, the US Navy SEALs looked like nothing in the US Navy forces even if they were caught or found dead in foreign areas:] 'there are no uniforms, no ID-cards, and no connection to the armed forces or government of the United States.[147]

Lieutenant Joseph Maguire has described how swimmers from SEAL Team Two trained at harbour penetration from submarines in the Baltic Sea in the early 1980s. He tells about a penetration exercise on the German Baltic coast to establish contact with an E&E net, but this is 'probably the only one we can tell you about', Lieutenant Maguire said.[148] Commander Stubblefield mention that he, in the early 1980s, participated in an extremely secret group called the 'Special Development Unit' that he couldn't talk about.[149] At this very time, the SEALs started to operate SDVs and 'mother submarines' in cold water. This was the reason for the development of a new SDV system. The bad experience of the cold-water environment forced the Navy to develop the ASDS.[150] However, if we are talking about covert training operations in the cold waters of the NATO theatre, where the US Navy SEALs were operating under cover of being 'the opposite' and doing things they were not supposed to do, we are obviously talking about Scandinavia. Stubblefield seems to describe how the US Navy SEALs, in the early 1980s, carried out unconventional warfare operations, 'some really smart training' in Scandinavian waters, where they masqueraded as Soviet forces.

An officer from a NATO country and former Chief of Military Intelligence confirmed to me that what I have written about US Navy SEALs' covert military training operations in the 1980s is a good description. He had no criticism on that part. According to a Joint Chiefs of Staff report on special operations: 'SEAL delivery vehicle personnel . . . specialize in operating SDVs and would most likely provide infiltration and exfiltration support'.[151] Successful infiltration and exfiltration are a must for naval special warfare.[152] In Norway, I have met former SEALs speaking Norwegian fluently, and Norwegian-speaking E&E networks have also operated in Norway. Sometimes they have been revealed quite easily, a Norwegian senior officer told me. In several cases, SEALs and E&E networks operated covertly in Norway with Norwegian military leadership approval. In Norway, SEALs were usually delivered from submarines, but they were sometimes dropped from small aircraft, a senior intelligence officer told me. In training operations (no physical confrontation), SEALs have simulated attacks on ordinary Norwegian naval forces in order to test their readiness. Only four or five military officers on the Norwegian side were informed beforehand (the Commander-in-Chief, the Chief of the Navy, the Chief of Military Intelligence, the Commander of the Military District and his assistant). Former Norwegian Defence Minister Anders Sjaastad confirmed to me that he was informed in general terms and, in case of allied special force operations against Norwegian forces, he was probably informed in every single case, he said. There was government approval for these operations.

Two Norwegian intelligence officers said that the USA and the UK not only had such a secret formalized training programme for special force submarines and E&E networks, but also had a separate top-secret programme for submarine operations in Norwegian waters. Norwegian individuals with very close ties to the USA or the UK, for example the Norwegian Chiefs of Military Intelligence, were informed beforehand. This was done outside the formal military hierarchy. A couple of times, a specific US Los Angeles-class submarine was identified in Norwegian fjords (Sognefjord and Bjørnafjord [Hardangerfjord]). To my knowledge, this information did not reach the most senior officers, but the Chief of Intelligence was informed in case he was loyal to the Americans, one of them said. This programme seems to have been handled by informal US contacts with a low profile. The former programme was primarily a training and testing programme, while the latter was also an intelligence-collecting programme, he said. I was told by a high-ranking CIA officer that such a programme was run by NURO.

Former Chiefs of Norwegian Military Intelligence have told me that top-secret submarine and landing operations run by the CIA were formalized and conducted within the framework of the Stay-Behinds. True, the regular military hierarchy was not informed, but the Chief of Intelligence would have intervened in case of emergency. However, this programme was, according to their knowledge, a training programme for the special forces and the Stay-Behinds, not an intelligence-collecting programme. 'But I may not have been fully informed', one of them said. There were at least one, probably two, top-secret US submarine programmes for entering Norwegian fjords, and corresponding programmes would have been run in Swedish waters. They were run outside the regular military hierarchy, but like other submarine operations in the Eastern Atlantic, they were coordinated at Northwood outside London by COM-SUBEASTLANT and his US Deputy. When these operations were conducted in territorial waters of other states, local contacts were necessary. In these cases, informal networks of local officers loyal to the USA and the UK seem to have operated in parallel to the formal national hierarchies.

The SEAL commander Captain Richard Marcinko has written that they operated 'clandestinely in friendly countries without their permission'.[153] In 1984, John McWethy, the Pentagon correspondent of the ABC TV channel, said:

> American submarines are repeatedly violating territorial waters of other nations while gathering intelligence. Most of the top-secret missions are into the waters of the Soviet Union, but according to both active duty and retired military sources, some missions have been run into the territorial waters of those nations considered friendly to the US. Even friendly countries, sources say, sometimes do things they don't want the US to know about, things that could inadvertently threaten American security. The missions are conducted by specially equipped nuclear powered attack submarines and in some cases by a nuclear powered mini-sub called NR-1 (MINI-SUB). It has a seven-man crew, wheels on its underside for crawling along the bottom and is described by the Navy as a research vessel.[154]

A few weeks before ABC made its comment on US secret missions in friendly waters, Admiral John L. Butts, Chief of Naval Intelligence, had been questioned by the House of Representatives' Subcommittee on the Department of Defense. Butts referred to US spy operations on the Soviet Navy and described information from these operations. The committee asked Butts if he could confirm that the submarine intrusions into Swedish waters were carried out by the Soviets. Butts responded that the Soviet submarine in Karlskrona in 1981 was 'genuine'. In 1982 'the Swedes had several submarine contacts' close to the Muskö Naval Base (referring to the Hårsfjärden submarine hunt). However, his following paragraph on the national origin is classified.[155] Although the Swedes had pointed to the Soviet Union, the paragraph is classified, indicating that Western or perhaps US submarines operated in friendly Swedish waters. Admiral Butts also spoke about a Soviet programme for a new 'small submarine called Uniform. This is sort of like our NR-1. There is no chance that the Soviets could have operated this sub or anything like it near the Swedish home waters.'[156] In other words, one submarine operating in Hårsfjärden might have been the US NR-1 or something similar, but it cannot have been a Soviet submarine, because the Soviets did not have anything like it at the time.

Soon after Admiral Butts had made his statement for the Subcommittee on Defense, information on US submarine operations into friendly waters, including the use of the NR-1, was leaked to ABC. According to ABC, 'military sources' said that the USA violated other countries' territorial waters for

> three primary reasons. One, to gather information on underwater coastal and harbour defences, thus gauging a country's ability to detect

intruders. Two, to plant listening buoys in key waterways. And three, to gather first-hand intelligence on new ships, particularly submarines and missile launchers from the sea.[157]

The first and possibly the second argument are clearly of interest for covert submarine operations into friendly waters. '[G]auging a country's ability to detect intruders' also implies a testing of the equipment and readiness of the friendly country. After this TV programme, the Swedish Naval Attaché to Washington, Captain Hans Tynnerström, said to *Svenska Dagbladet* that the USA was testing its systems and the readiness of its friends.[158]

During the submarine hunt in Karlskrona in February–March 1984, more detailed information was received on only one submarine: it had supposedly one driving propeller with five blades.[159] This may possibly indicate a US Sturgeon class or Los Angeles class. Prints found at Klintehamn on the island of Gotland in June 1986 fit with wheels from *NR-1*. A small bottom-crawling submarine with wheels left a 1,100-metre-long parallel print close to the shore. The prints looked like prints from a car that had been driving on the sea floor. The submarine had at least two pairs of wheels. It did not dive until it reached a depth of 16 metres,[160] which would indicate a larger mini-submarine and most likely *NR-1*. No other submarine of this size is known to have wheels for crawling on the bottom. This seems to indicate that a US 'specially equipped nuclear powered attack submarine' as well as *NR-1* actually operated in Swedish waters in the 1980s.

Statements and other information indicate that *NR-1* may have operated in Swedish waters in October 1982. Operations in friendly waters were, according to ABC, conducted by *NR-1* and by 'specially equipped nuclear powered attack submarines'. One such submarine may have been USS *Seawolf*, which operated together with *NR-1* in Libyan waters in 1986.[161] In 1974, it was equipped for special project operations,[162] and it was also rebuilt with a compartment for SEAL divers.[163] It operated together with DSV *Turtle*,[164] and, as already mentioned, the *Seawolf* was able to operate as a mother-sub for the *Turtle* and other submersibles. It was the only submarine that has explicitly been given that role. In 1983, the *Seawolf* received a medal for excellence in 'Battle Efficiency' and another medal for excellence in 'Damage Control', indicating some serious damage. In 1983, she was in a shipyard recovering from some kind of damage (allegedly from a storm).[165]

In the early to mid-1980s, the CIA used US Navy platforms like the DSV *Turtle*, but also Lockheed's *Deep Quest*, I was told by a Navy Intelligence officer. The *Turtle* was modified in 1980 so as to be able to operate for longer periods of time.[166] In 1978–80, the *Deep Quest* was refitted with a fuel cell power system for the US Navy, which made it able to operate for a greater length of time (96 hours).[167] One source, who has experience from both the *Turtle* and the *Deep Quest* in Scandinavian waters in the early and mid-1980s, confirmed that *Turtle* received its award for excellent bravery in espionage 30 August to 5 November 1982 for an operation in Scandinavian waters. In practice, this would mean Swedish waters. We have reasons to believe that the *Turtle* acted as a 'decoy',[168] masquerading as a Soviet vessel in the Hårsfjärden operation. This might explain why some observations fit so well with the *Turtle*. And, if the *Turtle* was in Scandinavian or Swedish waters in September–October 1982 it is not unlikely that the *Seawolf* was used as its mother-sub. Prints on the sea floor at Huvudholmen do not indicate the *Turtle* or the *Deep Quest,* but they fit relatively well with some other US submersibles.

A source with knowledge of passages through the Danish Straits told me that a specific US submarine entered the Baltic Sea in early September and left in late October – almost exactly the time needed for operations in Hårsfjärden. It was also said that this submarine had special forces on board, which means it entered the Baltic Sea submerged at Store Belt. According to the same source, it was the same British and US special force submarines that regularly entered the Baltic Sea in the early 1980s. I don't know which submarines participated in these operations. However, in 1982 the US Navy did not have many submarines to choose from. Except for the *Seawolf*, there were a couple of Sturgeon-class submarines, for example USS *Bergall*, that had operated as mother-subs of DSRVs, and the USS *Cavalla*, which had been rebuilt in 1982 for carrying special forces and SDVs.

USS *Bergall* received an award for an operation conducted between 24 July and 1 December 1982, while USS *Cavalla* was awarded for an operation between 1 August 1982 and 31 December 1983.[169] *Cavalla* conducted overseas operations and received an award for excellent bravery for operations in direct support of Chief of Naval Operations Project 098-7. According to a document signed by Secretary of the Navy John Lehman: 'the ship conducted the first ever full mission profile Naval Special Warfare operations from a nuclear submarine. These hazardous operations were completed using techniques developed by USS CAVALLA.'[170]

I don't know where these 'hazardous operations' were conducted, but if we accept the statement that 'the same US special force submarines regularly entered the Baltic Sea in the early 1980s', one of them might have been USS *Cavalla*. Another may have been USS *Seawolf* or USS *Bergall*, which both operated as mother-subs and received awards for operations during these months. Either they were run by the CIA within the framework of the Stay-Behinds or they were run by NURO for other purposes. However, these operations may have had another background. From around 1960, the US Office of Naval Research was deeply involved in sound analysis in the Baltic Sea. The head of the London office at that time, Captain J.K. Sloatman, travelled frequently to Stockholm and also to Helsinki.[171] In 1960, a Neptune pilot visiting Stockholm told my source that he dropped sonar buoys in the Baltic Sea. These sonar buoys (dropped by helicopter) were later replaced by a system of bottom-fixed sonars, which most likely demanded submarine support. In the mid-1960s, thanks to the excellent relations between the US Assistant Naval Attaché to Stockholm, Commander Bobby Inman, and a Swedish source, such a system could be deployed in Swedish waters by agreement with the naval leadership in Sweden.[172] According to a senior US Navy Intelligence officer, a system of US sonars existed in the Baltic Sea, in Swedish waters, in the early 1970s, and US Naval Intelligence had daily access to data from these installations. Commander Inman's excellent asset in Sweden had facilitated these arrangements. As mentioned in Chapter 4, the CIA had tried to 'steal' this Swedish officer. However, Navy Intelligence had been able to keep him, and Bobby Inman's success in Sweden was important for his carrier, this senior US intelligence officer told me.[173]

The US Navy operated in the Baltic Sea more or less on a yearly basis in connection with NATO exercises. In *The US Maritime Strategy*, in the section from the US Marine Corps, General P.X. Kelley and Major Hugh K. O'Donnell, Jr. confirm intentions to operate in the Baltic Sea in time of war. Amphibious forces could land in 'the eastern Baltic'.[174] In 1989, in a discussion I had with Robert Komer, former US Under-Secretary of Defense and a critique of *The US Maritime Strategy*, he said: 'One option for the US Marine Corps was to land three divisions on the Soviet Baltic coast. These forces would have to be transported over the Baltic Sea, for example, from Karlskrona in Sweden.' These forces would need submarine escort, and, most likely, the US Navy forces prepared for such an option. It is also likely that the Americans were interested in the six Soviet Golf missile submarines able to cover the whole Central Front from the southern Baltic Sea. Officially, however, the US Navy did not operate submarines in the Baltic Sea and stated that, within NATO, the Baltic Sea was a West German and Danish responsibility.

US submarines operated covertly in the Baltic Sea in connection with espionage and special force operations. In such operations, landing special forces in various foreign countries, was, according to an article in *US Naval Institute Proceedings*, a role 'even more covert than electronic intelligence collection'.[175] These covert operations do not seem to have been made with the approval of the Swedish government or even of the Commander-in-Chief. Another US Navy officer, a former US attaché, confirmed to me that such operations would not have been carried out by the Navy but rather by the CIA using Navy platforms. He was, however, afraid that my writing about these operations might lead to a 'backlash', creating problems for US–Swedish relations. But why were these testing operations much more dramatic in Sweden? Why did the Americans and the British carry out such operations, in Sweden, as if there was a real war? There are a number of coastal countries in NATO or in the Atlantic theatre. Nowhere did these testing operations and training for the Stay-Behinds develop into warlike situations as in Sweden. However, unlike Einar Ansteensen's statement of the position in the early 1980s, there seem, on later occasions, to have been operations in Finnish waters, but the Finns are said to have avoided the game by keeping quiet, following the policy of most other countries.[176] An admiral from a NATO country told me that the Finns never went public with information on intruding submarines in order to avoid an awkward debate.

NATO countries were not always informed about allied submarine activities in their own waters. In these NATO countries as well as in Finland, it was a general policy not to reveal anything about intruding submarines. A submarine hunt might easily appear as a demonstration of impotence: it is not easy, and, even worse, it may prove to be an allied submarine. A Norwegian senior intelligence officer, Trond Johansen, said that he tried to convince the Swedes to keep a low profile, but the Swedes were not willing to listen to him, he said. A group of officers in the Swedish military leadership made a conscious decision to go public about the submarine intrusions partly as an instrument in their struggle with the political leadership. On 1 October, on the very first day of the Hårsfjärden submarine hunt, Chief of Staff Vice-Admiral Bror Stefenson ordered the information division to prepare for a press centre for 500 journalists. This is very large for a small country. After the first observation of a periscope, he prepared for a huge international mass media event. The tension between the more social-democratic political elite and some ambitious military officers (and perhaps industrial leaders) made these officers try to prove their case by demonstrating the seriousness of the threat. In a lunch discussion with the former US Secretary of Defense James Schlesinger, I asked him about his view of Sweden during his years in the administration. His response was short and concise: 'Which Sweden? The "political Sweden" or the "military Sweden"? The military were planning to get the USA involved as soon as possible' (see below).

ITALIAN SPECIAL FORCE SUBMARINES

In the early 1980s, the Italian Navy had several submarines for special force operations. Except for the US Navy, only the Italians had naval forces capable of carrying out complex operations with SDVs, mini-submarines, other small submarines and special force swimmers. In 1982, the Italian Navy had 11 conventional submarines: four Sauro-class submarines (64 metres; one propeller), four Toti-class (47 metres; one propeller) plus two ex-US Tang-class (87 metres; two propellers) and one ex-US Guppy-class submarine (99 metres; two propellers).[177] In addition, the Italian naval special forces COMSUBIN[178] (Commando Raggruppamento Subacqui ed Incursori) had a number of mini- and midget submarines. They were small manoeuvrable crafts that could carry eight to 25 commandos and were especially effective for special force operations. The Cosmos SX 756-W class submarines (25 metres; one propeller) were used in the 1970s and 1980s. They had a transit range of 1,600 nautical miles and were able to carry two SDVs: CE2F-X60 (7 metres: one propeller). The mother-sub had a maximum speed of 8.5 knots.[179] The Cosmos MG-110 (28 metres; one propeller) and Cosmos 120-ER (30 metres; one propeller) from the 1980s are even more capable. The latter has a range of up to 2,500 nautical miles at 3.5 knots and 1,800 nautical miles at 7 knots, with an endurance of up to 20 days.[180] In the mid-1980s, the Italian company Maritalia had three mini-submarines in different sizes between 25 and 30 metres. One or more were most likely also used by COMSUBIN. All these submarines were capable of carrying two SDVs. The 27-metre submarine had a maximum speed of 18 knots and was capable of operating submerged for 14 days.[181] Maritalia also produced a 9- to 10-metre 3GST9 with a range of about 200 nautical miles at 6 knots and 100 nautical miles at 8 knots, which actually was the forerunner of the current ASDS project for an advanced SDV for the US Navy SEALs. It can dive below 400 metres.[182]

The Italians are the only ones who have produced and for years have used a sub-surface system with a number of 25- to 30-metre submarines, each able to carry two almost-10-metre SDVs. The system intruding in Swedish waters in the early and mid-1980s, as it is described by the Defence Staff Report of 25 November 1987, is identical to the system used by COMSUBIN. In the Hårsfjärden operation, the description of the submarine seen on the surface at Dalarö on 4 October is like that of a Cosmos SX 756-W (or possibly a Cosmos MG-110). The drawing shows three square objects on top of the hull, very similar to the Italian Strazza Navigation sonars for navigation in narrow waters. It had a high mast – much higher than the sail – just behind the sail. The length of the vessel is described as two-thirds of the local (Ornö) ferry (at the time two of these ferries were 28 metres while one was 37 metres). This would make a total submarine length of 20–25 metres, or rather about 25 metres, because the propeller area would certainly be submerged. All this information fits well with the Cosmos SX 756-W. No other submarine fits this description. The observer of a periscope and mast on 1 October described the distance between them as 1–1.5 metres, which also fits a Cosmos submarine. It also has a small propeller that creates high turns per minute at low speed. The high mast on the Cosmos (as well as on the later Pyranja) is erected from a horizontal position along the top of the hull to a vertical position just behind the sail. Later in the 1980s, this erection manoeuvre had been observed several times in Swedish waters, I was told by an intelligence officer. The first occasion was in the far north at Töre close to Piteå. The insiders called it 'Piteåpitten' (the 'Piteå cock').

The large submarine sail seen at Sandhamn on the evening of 4 October was described as a 'large wall' with diesel engines. It might possibly have been a British Oberon-class submarine, but it could as well have been an Italian or US Tang-class submarine. In the Hårsfjärden submarine hunt, a third possible Italian vessel is the small bottom-crawling submersible that might have been used by COMSU-BIN. The observers' descriptions of several of the Hårsfjärden submarines are consistent with the descriptions of Italian submarines. However, it is impossible that this operation was an exclusively Italian affair, but an Italian contribution to a US-commanded operation is more than plausible. The Americans often use platforms and individuals of other nationalities to avoid exposure, and the Italians had special forces that cooperated intimately with their US and UK counterparts. The Italians also had a number of small vessels useful for operating in Swedish waters.

The Italians have produced a large number of the small Cosmos submarines. From 1955 Cosmos constructed and sold at least 63 submarines of the earlier version SX 506 (23 metres; one propeller). Twelve were exported to Pakistan and two to Colombia, but most receivers are not known.[183] Later versions like the Cosmso SX 756-W and the MG-110 have also been sold to several countries.[184] According to Annati:

COSMOS is probably the largest specialized producer world-wide of underwater craft for special operations, and in more than forty years of activity it has supplied its chariots [SDVs] and midgets to very many navies all over the world. Over the years technological advances have seen the midgets increase in displacement from 40t in the 1970s to over 110t for the most recent version ... The COSMOS 110t midgets are 'true' submarines capable of launching torpedoes . . . as well as conducting

271

covert surveillance tasks. Their main purpose, however, is the deployment of combat swimmers (up to eight) with inflatable assault boats or two two-man chariots . . . [The latest SDV] is the CE2F/X100 model. It can stand the depth of 100 m when transported on the back of a parent submarine and ensures submerged range of 50nm at a maximum speed of 4.5 kts. The two-man free-flooded cabin can be closed by two sliding canopies.[185]

In 1978, the Italian Navy launched a surface ship, *Anteo*, which carries a midget submarine, *Usel* (8 metres).[186] As with the techniques the Italians used during the Second World War,[187] several small submarines or midgets may have been transported on civilian ships. In Gibraltar in 1940, the Italians used a civilian tanker, *Olterra*, anchored in the port 'as departure base for operations with the maiale',[188] the 'human torpedo', the small sub-surface vessel or SDV. Vice-Admiral Gino Birindelli, former Commander-in-Chief Allied Naval Forces South Europe, describes these operations as 'both a technical and a tactical surprise', because this small submersible was a technical invention, but more importantly it was used in an original manner with a civilian tanker as a departure base.[189] Before the submersible leaves the tanker, the special section is flooded; thereafter the submersible leaves through an underwater door. After completion of the operation it returns the same way.[190] Smaller conventional submarines can also be transported in this way, as demonstrated by photos from the US Office of Naval Intelligence.[191] In the 1970s, in order to enter the Mediterranean covertly, the 42-metre *NR-1* was transported, hidden under a large tent, across the Atlantic on the rebuilt Landing Ship Dock (LSD) USS *Portland* (169 metres; 13,600 tons). During the hidden transport the sail of *NR-1* was painted black for a covert operation at the Libyan coast.[192] Midgets and small submarines with a limited speed or range were transported to the area of operations, preferably on a rebuilt surface ship to avoid detection. This technique made it possible to go through a narrow passage without the opponent knowing about it. It is not unlikely that the larger versions of the Cosmos or perhaps Maritalia mini-submarines have been transferred into the area of operations by a merchant ship, for example by a rebuilt civilian tanker in order to achieve a 'tactical surprise'. Also in the 1980s, small Italian vessels could 'be carried into the vicinity of the enemy harbour by . . . merchant ships', it is stated in an editorial comment to Birindelli's article.[193] Such a modification of a large tanker is not uncommon and by no means difficult, I was told by a senior naval officer. He also said that one such a tanker that, at the time, operated for the Office of Naval Intelligence (and probably for NURO) was the 40,000-ton *Mormacsky* (length 210 metres).[194]

This is of some importance, because, on the afternoon of 9 October 1982 in connection with the Hårsfjärden submarine hunt, the US tanker *Mormacsky* was spotted by the reconnaissance aircraft *GYP* in the area outside the Swedish archipelago, just outside the area of the submarine hunt.[195] Unlike Soviet ships covertly transporting midget submarines, the US *Mormacsky* was in the area. It would have been able to rescue US submersibles or other small vessels. This same tanker has also appeared in connection with other submarine operations, this senior naval officer told me. There is no doubt that *Mormacsky* has been used for such covert operations.

The Cosmos submarines have a limited range and, in a US–Italian operation, to use a US 'civilian' tanker is in many ways ideal. This would certainly create a 'tactical surprise', to quote Vice-Admiral Birindelli. Nobody in Sweden would think about these submarines as possibly being Italian. Several observations of the typical Cosmos mast erected from a horizontal position also support this hypothesis. This would mean that the 25- to 30-metre Cosmos submarines with their 7-metre SDVs (later supplemented by the 10-metre 3GST9s) were deployed in the Baltic Sea off the Swedish coast, entered the archipelago and sent the SDVs into the naval bases and harbours, while the tanker delivered its oil or other petroleum products in a harbour somewhere in Scandinavia or Finland. After that, the tanker could return to a given position outside the archipelago to pick up its submarines. In order not to create suspicion, the tanker, in this case *Mormacsky*, has to carry out its regular business. In other words: 'Every project must have a cover project that must be true', to quote John Craven.[196]

The Swedish Defence Staff report of 25 November 1987 spoke about a system of 30-metre submarines/mother-subs carrying 10-metre small sub-surface vessels[197] (or sonar echoes of 25–30 metres[198] and 5–10 metres[199]). This system can, to my knowledge, only have come from the COMSUBIN in Italy and been transferred to Swedish waters by a civilian ship, most likely a rebuilt tanker, for example the US *Mormacsky*. This would explain why there is no indication of these small submarines in the Baltic Sea on their transit route from the Soviet Baltic coast to Sweden and back[200] even although contact with these submarines would have been much easier to receive on the open sea. Sweden was able to follow the small West German submarines in the Baltic Sea on the Soviet Baltic coast and their transit to the Swedish coast, but the Swedes never received contact with these 30-metre submarines despite their regular appearance in the Swedish archipelagos. These vessels seem to have been dumped into Swedish waters, and, in the case I have studied, it was not done by a Soviet ship.

Before I was given access to Rear-Admiral Christer Kierkegaard's war diary (the naval base war diary) for the Hårsfjärden incident, a couple of young officers from Swedish Military Intelligence had blacked out all entries on Western civilian ships even although this information is in no way classified material. When you are able to read both the declassified material and the still classified sections, which are blacked out, you read these sections as though they are underlined. Interestingly enough, much of the blacked-out information was actually about civilian ships. This procedure does not make sense unless at least one civilian vessel was directly involved in the operation. It also indicates that one senior officer instructing the young intelligence officers knew that this was the case (see for example retired Admiral Bror Stefenson's instructions to Commander Lars-Erik Hoff about the possibility of declassifying information on the NOTVARP operation). *Mormacsky* might have been 'a departure base for operations' with, for example, Italian Cosmos submarines and the bottom-crawling tracked submersible, and/or a base ship for receiving US small submersibles like the *Turtle* that might have been released by USS *Monongahela* in the centre of Stockholm two weeks earlier.

The presence of *Mormacsky* outside the Swedish archipelago would explain the observations of vessels described as Cosmos submarines in the Hårsfjärden area, and it might also explain a regular presence of a system of 30-metre and 10-metre submarines in Swedish waters in the 1980s. This also makes the presence of an Italian bottom-crawling submersible very likely. The Italian naval special forces have – or had at least at the time – one 'midget submarine', an oval submersible (about 10 metres) with a bottom-crawling capability. In the naval community, it is called a 'toad', because it is able to jump in the water. It leaves double tracks on the sea floor like the ones registered in Hårsfjärden. It has instruments for cutting and a twin-arm manipulator for moving objects, similar to the American *Turtle* and *Sea Cliff*. It may function as an underwater base for special force swimmers, one senior officer said. He saw it in the barracks of the COMSUBIN base Varignano at La Spezia. This bottom-crawling submersible was transported on a civilian vessel, he said. It may possibly have been 'borrowed' by others or used in joint exercises, this senior officer told me. Or, as Annati states, several of the small Italian vessels have been sold to other Western navies and they are kept very secret.[201] This Italian bottom-crawling submersible has never been described in *Jane's Fighting Ships* or in any other open source.

When tracked prints from a bottom-crawling submersible were found in Scandinavian waters and seemingly indications from a similar vessel were found both in Norway and in Sweden, this senior officer first worried about some Soviet–Italian collaboration. However, when he investigated the problem this hypothesis was soon dismissed.

COMSUBIN's close ties were clearly to the Americans. There were always two US Navy SEALs at the Varignano base, and they had access to everything, one special force officer at Varignano told me. While many Italians at Varignano did not have access to the barracks, the SEAL officers did. The contrast between the advanced COMSUBIN equipment and material from the conventional forces was striking. In Varignano, much of the most advanced Italian SDV equipment may have been financed by the Americans, he said.

The COMSUBIN loyalties were clearly not with the Soviets. Officers at Varignano speak with respect about the Fascist leader Benito Mussolini, this special force officer told me. Prince Junio Valerio Borghese – the wartime leader of the Italian naval special forces, Decima Flotiglia MAS, and one of the most prominent Fascist leaders during the Cold War – was still their hero. War heroes from Decima MAS, like former commander of the Italian naval special forces Vice-Admiral Gino Birindelli, were honoured with gold medals at the COMSUBIN base at Varignano.[202] During the war, Decima MAS had had its own police force and kept its own intelligence units in other countries as if it was an independent state. From 1943, it operated under SS overall command as an SS Sonderverband. At the very end of the war, Borghese turned himself over to James Jesus Angleton and the OSS. Borghese was later recruited by or at least working closely with Angleton and the CIA, and he participated in several military 'coup attempts' in the 1960s and 1970s in order to manipulate Italian politics, supposedly in cooperation with the CIA.[203] In these 'political operations', he was collaborating with his colleague and former NATO Commander-in-Chief Naval Forces South Europe, from 1973 President for the Fascist party MSI, Vice-Admiral Birindelli. Some of these networks also kept close contacts not just with the British and the Americans but also with the South Africans, which might explain possible South African involvement in the Hårsfjärden operation. In the early 1980s, after an Italian legal investigation of covert CIA–SISMI operations, SISMI generals and agents were rescued by their South African and CIA contacts.[204]

If the Italian 'toad' (or, for example, an Italian Cosmos submarine) was involved in the Hårsfjärden operation, and if it (or one of them) was damaged on 5 or 7 October, this would possibly explain SISMI participation at the meeting in Geneva on 8 October 1982 and the leak to Ansa about Swedish negotiations with a foreign power in Geneva on 9 October – in the middle of the submarine hunt. SISMI had earlier carried out similar kinds of operations in other fields. To use submarines and special force operations for testing other forces is in many ways ideal, and, in the 1980s, to use an unknown submarine would immediately put the blame on the Soviets. We do not know if the bottom-crawling submersible in Hårsfjärden was this Italian vessel, but a similar submersible has been seen on the Swedish west coast and also on the Norwegian side. Furthermore, the tracked prints in Hårsfjärden do not fit with the prints of a supposed Soviet version seen in northern Norway (see above).

COMSUBIN is one of the most well-trained of naval special forces.[205] They are willing to accept great risks. The American SEALs used to have joint exercises with their Italian counterparts. SEAL officers expressed interest in the Italian submarines, but the US Navy was unwilling to buy them.[206] Because of this, joint operations seem to have become a practical solution. The Italians operated very close to the Americans and the British, an Italian intelligence officer told me. The tracked prints on the sea floor in Hårsfjärden may originate from a joint US–Italian (or less likely British–Italian) operation. An observation of a possible Cosmos SX 756-W would also support this hypothesis. This would explain the Italian knowledge of and participation in the alleged US–Swedish negotiations during the Hårsfjärden submarine hunt as well as the Italian interest in my own research.[207] At least, the above-mentioned Italian submersible is the only one I know that seems to fit the tracks in Hårsfjärden. One source said that the US operations in Swedish waters were even run from Italy, which would explain why this meeting took place in Geneva. Furthermore, leading representatives of the Italian special forces, Prince Valerio Junio Borghese, Vice-Admiral Gino Birindelli, Director of SISMI General Giuseppe Santovito and his predecessor Admiral Eugenio Henke were close to four Americans mentioned in this book, former SACEUR and Secretary of State General Alexander Haig, Director of the CIA William Casey, Secretary of the Navy John Lehman and his Chief of Naval Operations Admiral James Watkins.[208] The most important Italian and American high officials deciding about naval covert action belonged to one single network.

NOTES

1 Lundin *et al.* (1996).
2 IISS (1982–83), pp. 115–16.
3 Kemp (1996), p. 224.
4 *Jane's Fighting Ships* (1987–88); Mooney 1994.
5 Annati (1996), p. 88; Lähteinen (1997), pp. 92–3; see also Malachite and Dvigatel brochures.
6 Fock (1996), p. 176; Kemp (1996), p. 218.
7 *Jane's Fighting Ships* (1987–88).
8 Kemp (1996), pp 224–5.
9 Annati (1996), p. 88; SOU (2001), pp. 296–9.

10 FET Monthly Report (1983); *Jane's Fighting Ships* (1992–93), p. 548.
11 Welham (1989), p. 162.
12 Miller and Jordan (1987), p. 178.
13 FET Monthly Report on Naval Activities (1981–85).
14 Thorén (1992), pp. 38–51.
15 Bildt (1990), p. 32.
16 Agrell (1986); Tunander (1987), pp. 97–101; Tunander (1989), pp. 114–17.
17 Hansen (1984); Weinland (1986); McCormick (1990); Cole (1990).
18 Hansen (1984), pp. vii–viii, 5.
19 Quoted in Leitenberg (1987), p. 142.
20 MccGwire (1987), p. 302.
21 Bildt (1983), p. 167.
22 Alford (1984), pp. 304–6.
23 Bruzelius (1982, 1995).
24 Tunander (1999, 2000a, 2000b).
25 Lindahl and Lundgren (1982), p. 4.
26 Tunander (1989), p. 115.
27 Bovin (1984).
28 Tunander (1989), pp. 120–4.
29 Agrell (1986); Tunander (1987, 1989).
30 Hansen (1984); Leitenberg (1987); McCormick (1990); Cole (1990).
31 Tunander (1989), pp. 115–16.
32 *Reportrarna*, Swedish TV2 (22 October 1996); *Reportrarna*, Swedish TV2 (5 November 1996).
33 Agrell and Larsson (1990), p. 22.
34 SOU (1995), p. 231.
35 SOU (2001), p. 222.
36 Agrell and Larsson (1990), p. 22.
37 Kemp (1996), p. 224.
38 SOU (1995), p. 234.
39 US Naval Intelligence comments on Agrell and Larsson (1990).
40 Agrell and Larsson (1990), pp. 22–3.
41 Försvarsstaben (1987).
42 Bildt (1990), pp. 40–1.
43 Mooney (1994).
44 CFö/INT (1987).
45 FET Monthly Report on Naval Activities (1981–82).
46 *Jane's Fighting Ships* (1981–82), p. 191.
47 Hasselbohm (1984), pp. 114–19, 144–7.
48 Fock (1996); Kemp (1996), pp. 183–214.
49 Annati (1996), p. 89; Hasselbohm (1984), pp. 123–7.
50 Annati (1996), p. 89.
51 Svensson (1995), pp. 45–6.
52 Quoted in Petersson (1999), p. 179.
53 Bethge (1986).
54 See also Tunander (1989), p. 116.
55 SOU (2001), p. 56.
56 Brännström and Persson (1983).
57 ÖB TD (15 March 1983).
58 Department of Defense (1991), pp. 3, 30.
59 Welham (1989), p. 157.
60 *Jane's Fighting Ships* (1981–82), p. 559–60.

61 Forman (1999), pp. 244–5.
62 Welham (1989), pp. 174–7.
63 Taurus (2002): http://www.submersiblesubmarines.com/uvi%20test%20Folder/
    uvi%20test/pages/submersible%20taurus.html;
    http://www.sub-find.com/taurus.htm.
64 Annati writes: '[Three US SDVs, MkVIII, are] in service with the British Special
    Boat Squadron under the designation of Mk8Mod1 . . . [It] is probably the best
    SDV ever built in terms of range, payload and electronic equipment. It is cred-
    ited with a maximum range of 36 nm at 6 kt, reduced to 15–18 nm under combat
    conditions. The standard crew of two can be supplemented by a further four
    combat swimmers accommodated in two compartments protected by sliding
    canopies' (1996, pp. 88–9).
65 Parker (1997), p. 273.
66 Foster (1998 [1987]), pp. 155–6.
67 Kemp (1996), p. 217.
68 Fock (1996 [1982]); Hasselbohm (1984), pp. 112–14; Welham (1989).
69 Hasselbohm (1984), pp. 114–16.
70 *Rapport*, Swedish TV1 (21 November 2001).
71 Ring (2001), p. 141.
72 Försvarsmakten (10 March 2000).
73 Ring (2001), p. 133.
74 Interview with Willoch, 5 March and 1 June 1999.
75 Parker (1997), p. 273.
76 *Striptease*, Swedish TV2 (11 April 2000). After this TV programme, Swedish
    Military Intelligence asked the British Ministry of Defence about 'British subma-
    rine operations in Swedish waters'. In response to the Swedish request, the Naval
    Staff Directorate (British Ministry of Defence, 2000) stated that 'I can assert
    happily and unequivocally that no UK submarine operated submerged within
    Swedish territorial waters in the 1980s.'
77 *Striptease*, Swedish TV2 (7 March 2000).
78 Ibid.
79 Jansson (1996).
80 Öhman (1990).
81 Interview with Hillingsø, 12 March 1999.
82 *Reportrarna*, Swedish TV2 (9 September 1998).
83 Interview with Leifland, 5 May 1999.
84 Von Hofsten (1993), pp. 88–96; Kadhammar (1987). In 1986, Captain Hans
    Tynnerström, Chief of Naval Base East, was carrying out a submarine hunt not
    far from the base. Suddenly, he received a telephone call from Vice-Admiral Bror
    Stefenson, now Commander of the Eastern Military District, who said that
    '[General] Lennart [Ljung] had ordered him to terminate the hunt'. Tynnerström
    said that he wanted to have a written order. He never got it.
85 Welham (1989), pp. 95, 158.
86 Annati writes: '[The Havas company has several different models,] all of which
    are peculiar for their small dimensions and light weight . . . The smallest vehicle
    in the HAVAS range is the two-man TTV-2, which can be transported and deliv-
    ered by a submarine through the standard 533 mm torpedo tubes. Mk-5 is an
    older and smaller two-man vehicle with sliding canopies, while the Mk-8 and
    Mk-9 are larger, traditional SDVs, shaped more or less like giant torpedoes
    (about 900 mm dia) and with a crew of two combat swimmers. They are said to
    have a range of 40 nm and be capable of a top speed of 6 kt' (1996, p. 87).
87 Miller and Jordan (1987), pp. 110–11.

88 Höjelid (1991), pp. 57–9.
89 *New York Times* (28 April 1983).
90 See Sontag and Drew (1999), pp. 356, 363.
91 Norwegian Ministry of Defence (1983a, 1983b).
92 Norwegian Ministry of Defence (1983c).
93 Hasselbohm (1984), p. 41. In relation to France, Ljung's diary contains two references of possible interest. In 1982, on 18 October, three days after the submarine hunt had ended, Prime Minister Palme and General Ljung had a talk with Prime Minister Pierre Mauroy, who was on a one-day official visit to Stockholm. One month later, on 18 November, the Swedish Navy investigation under Admiral Grandin gave the tape recordings from Danziger Gatt (Mälsten) to the French without informing the Commander-in-Chief or the Prime Minister. General Lennart Ljung wrote in his diary that this was a very sensitive issue, but he also asked himself what the consequences of French knowledge of the Swedish analysis would be (ÖB TD). If Ljung believed it was a French submarine, this comment would be rather strange.
94 Welham (1989), pp. 160–1.
95 *Grayback* played an important role for the landing of SEALs during the Vietnam War. It was the only US submarine home-based outside the USA in Subic Bay in the Philippines (Bosiljevac, 1990). Even after the Vietnam War, the Director of the CIA, Stansfield Turner, had to sign approval for every single operation, he told me. *Grayback* was retired in 1984 and the following year replaced by two Ethan Allen-class submarines, *Sam Houston* (SSN 609) and *John Marshall* (SSN 611) (125 metres; one propeller), each able to carry 67 combat swimmers and two SDVs (Welham, 1989; *Jane's*, 1990–91). In 1994 *Sam Houston* and *John Marshall* were replaced by two Benjamin Franklin-class submarines: the *James K. Polk* and the *Kamehameha* (both 130 metres; one propeller) (*Jane's*, 1992; Kemp, 1996, p. 215). According to Peter Darman (1994, p. 114), the US Navy also used two other Ethan Allen-class submarines, *Thomas A. Edison* and *Thomas Jefferson* for this purpose. They were all reclassified from SSBNs to SSNs in 1980–81 (www.navsource.org/archivesubidx.htm).
96 Craven (2001), p. 276.
97 Forman (1999), pp. 215–47; *Jane's Fighting Ships* (1975–76).
98 *Jane's Fighting Ships* (1990–91), p. 734.
99 Dockery (1991), pp. 234–9. See also Annati (1996), p. 88. The Mk VIII (speed 4–7 knots) 'is a "wet" submersible designed to carry four swimmers and a crew of two in a fully flooded compartment . . . The pilot and navigator sit [in front] side by side . . . ; the rear compartment is accessed through a separate sliding hatch. Constructed of composite material' (Genat, 1994, p. 42), this SDV is about 6.5 metres long and 1.3 metres high and wide, while the Mk IX (former EX-IX) is 6 metres long and about 2 metres wide with twin propellers. Both SDVs have Doppler navigation system and obstacle-avoidance sonar (Dockery, 1991; US Navy SEALs, 1974).
100 Kemp (1996), pp. 218–22.
101 *Jane's Fighting Ships* (1990–91), p. 795.
102 Sontag and Drew (1999), pp. 65–91; Craven (2001).
103 Forman (1999), pp. 115–21; Naval Undersea Museum (e-mail, 2002).
104 Forman (1999), pp. 88–92, 98–100, 165–8.
105 Polmar (1987), p. 362.
106 Vyborny and Davis (2002), pp. 176–204.
107 Sontag and Drew (1999).
108 Ibid., p. 338.

109 Polmar (1987), p. 73.
110 Ibid.
111 Craven (2001), pp. 128–42.
112 *Jane's Fighting Ships* (1981–82); Polmar (1981).
113 Forman (1999), p. 219.
114 *Jane's Fighting Ships* (1977–78, 1981–82). One possible alternative is that the Americans have taken over Whiskey- and possibly also Romeo-class submarines from Egypt. The Egyptian Navy received up to 1966 eight Whiskey- and six Romeo-class submarines (*Jane's Fighting Ships*, 1981–82; 1987–88).
115 Sontag and Drew (1999), p. 117; Richelson (2001), p. 135.
116 Sontag and Drew (1999), pp. 117, 289.
117 Craven (2001), p. 131.
118 Bruzelius (2002), pp. 230–1.
119 *Reportrarna*, Swedish TV2 (22 October 1996).
120 Lehman (1988); Vistica (1995), pp. 89–90, 189–90; Video: *Red Cell* (1993).
121 Video: *Red Cell* (1993).
122 Stubblefield (1995), pp. 147–54.
123 Video: *Red Cell* (1993).
124 Ibid.
125 *Striptease*, Swedish TV2 (7 March 2000).
126 Ibid. Immediately afterwards, the US Department of Defense denied any involvement in operations along the Swedish coast. The Swedish Prime Minister's Office made an immediate investigation. The same was the case with the Swedish Commander-in-Chief. After a couple of weeks, they presented their conclusions. Swedish Defence Minister Björn von Sydow stated: 'The American response leaves no doubt. There has been no such activity' (29 March 2000). The C-in-C investigation was signed by General Owe Wictorin (31 March 2000) and made by Stefan Ryding-Berg and Lieutenant-General Hans Berndtson. They had not been able to confirm any of the statements made by Weinberger. This investigation found it unlikely that the statements made by Weinberger as well as the ones made by myself were true. My statements were made on prime-time news in a conversation with Swedish former Prime Minister Ingvar Carlsson (the TV news following the interview with Caspar Weinberger).
127 Associated Press, 8.38 p.m., 7 March 2000.
128 *Rapport*, Swedish TV2 (8 March 2000).
129 Associated Press, 8.38 p.m., 7 March 2000.
130 *Aktuellt*, Swedish TV1 (29 March 2000).
131 *Dagens Nyheter* (9 March 2000).
132 Anonymous letter, Ekéus Investigation files, 2001 (no. 28, 20 March).
133 Interview with Ansteensen, 19 December 1998; 18, 25 January 1999.
134 Video: *Red Cell* (1993).
135 Sontag and Drew (1999), pp. 230–4.
136 Schweizer (1994), pp. 160–5.
137 Ibid., p. 160.
138 Dockery (1991), p. 207; Lofthus and Aarons (1994), pp. 463–4. In 1984, Lieutenant-Colonel Oliver North, the CIA Director William Casey and Vice-President Bush's crisis unit allegedly used this portable and undetectable communications system for carrying out the Iran–Contras operation (Lofthus and Aarons, 1994).
139 Worthington (1996), p. 62.
140 Lindsay, quoted in Wilson (1988); Dockery (1991), p. 242.
141 Buff (2000), p. 1; see also West (1998).

142 Worthington (1996), p. 62
143 Dockery (1991), p. 233; Stubblefield (1995), pp. 124–5.
144 Worthington (1996), p. 62.
145 Department of Defense (1995, 1996).
146 Stubblefield (1995), p. 134.
147 Ibid., p. 145.
148 Kelly (1995), p. 247.
149 Stubblefield (1995), p. 11.
150 Kelly (1992), p. 289; Buff (2000).
151 Joint Pub 3-05.3 (1993), p. II-2.
152 Ocean Studies Board (1997), p. 11.
153 Marcinko and Weisman (1994), p. 330.
154 *World News Tonight*, ABC (21 March 1984).
155 Department of Defense (1984b), p. 676.
156 Ibid., p. 680.
157 *World News Tonight*, ABC (21 March 1984).
158 *Svenska Dagbladet* (24 March 1984).
159 Kierkegaard Report 1984.
160 SOU (1995), pp. 250–2; Cato and Larsson (1995).
161 Sontag and Drew (1999), p. 356.
162 Ibid., p. 277.
163 Craven (2001), p. 137.
164 Sontag and Drew (1999), p. 338.
165 Ibid., p. 356; www.seawolf-ssn575.com/ssn575/uss_seawolf_history contin-
    ued.htm.
166 Forman (1999), p. 192.
167 US Congress (1986), p. 27; Forman (1999), p. 121.
168 Committee on Undersea Vehicles (1996), p. 12.
169 Sontag and Drew (1999), p. 425. Several submarines received awards for excel-
    lent bravery in espionage for the autumn of 1982. USS *Parche* received the
    highest award, Presidential Unit Citation (PUC), for operations in 1982. USS
    Puffer received the second-highest award, Naval Unit Commendation (NUC),
    for operations in periods of 1982–83. USS *Cavalla* received the same award for
    an operation from 1 August 1982 to 12 December 1983, and USS *Permit* and
    USS *Batfish* for operations ending in September 1982. USS *Bergall* received the
    Meritorious Unit Commendation (MUC) for an operation starting on 24 July
    and ending on 1 December 1982. USS *Guitarro* received the same award for an
    operation from 1981 ending in December 1982, while USS *New York City*
    received it for an operation in 1982. The DSV 3 *Turtle* received an MUC for an
    operation from 30 August to 5 November 1982 (Sontag and Drew, 1999,
    pp. 425, 433).
170 The Secretary of the Navy (1984).
171 Private letters from J.K. Sloatman, from 1961.
172 Hasselbohm (1992).
173 See also Woodward (1987), p. 206.
174 Kelley and O'Donnell (1986), p. 26.
175 Friedman (1992), p. 108.
176 See for example Lähteinen (1997).
177 *Jane's Fighting Ships* (1981–82), pp. 255–6.
178 COMSUBIN is subordinate not to the Italian Navy but to the Italian
    Commander-in-Chief. A task force may be commanded by a political represen-
    tative or a civil servant or a military officer depending on the task.

179 *Defence Today* (June 1980), p. 293.
180 Annati (1996), p. 87.
181 Compton-Hall (1988), pp. 98–9.
182 Compton-Hall (1989), pp. 35–7; Annati (1996), p. 87.
183 Corlett (1974), p. 16.
184 *Jane's Fighting Ships* (2000–01).
185 Annati (1996), pp. 86–7.
186 *Jane's Fighting Ships* (1992–93), p. 325.
187 Compton-Hall (1987), p. 39; Compton-Hall (1988), p. 88; Kelly (1992), p. 192.
188 Birindelli (1980), p. 292.
189 Ibid.
190 Compton-Hall (1988), p. 87.
191 Harms (2000), pp. 3–5.
192 Vyborny and Davis (2002), pp. 151–5.
193 *Defence Today* (June 1980), p. 293.
194 Lloyd's Register of Shipping 2001.
195 CÖrlBO WD.
196 Craven (2001), p. 129.
197 Försvarsstaben (25 November 1987).
198 SOU (1995), p. 234; SOU (2001), p. 222.
199 CÖrlBO WD (6 October 1982).
200 CFö/INT (1987).
201 Annati (1996), p. 86.
202 Nesi (1996).
203 Bale (1995), pp. 250–511; Ferraresi (1996), pp. 19–20.
204 Ferraresi (1996), pp. 11, 140; *Africa Confidential* (15 April 1987).
205 Darman (1994), p. 115.
206 Marcinko and Weisman (1994), pp. 44–5.
207 After I started to look into the submarine hunt in the Stockholm archipelago, Italian intelligence officers showed interest in my work. I was contacted by one Italian intelligence officer dealing with submarine activities. Another Italian officer made a less civilized approach. After one incident, a high-ranking Norwegian officer turned to the Italian Defence Attaché and asked about that Italian officer. Immediately afterwards, the US Defense Attaché approached the Norwegian officer and asked if he was 'cooperating' with me. Another US attaché, a former assistant to the US Secretary of the Navy, approached me. The only thing he asked me about was my contacts in Italy, indicating that this was of some special interest. It seems that some Italians are very interested in my research and that the Americans are kept fully informed. Possibly, there is a US–Italian link, explaining some of the activities in the Swedish archipelagos in the 1980s.
208 Bale (1995), pp. 505–6; Lernoux (1989), pp. 297–301.

7

Submarine Ghosts and Psychological Warfare Against Sweden

In the early 1950s, US and British aircraft carried out reconnaissance operations over the western Soviet Union via Danish, Norwegian and Swedish airspace. The Swedish Defence Staff noted that US aircraft went in and out of Soviet airspace over the Baltic republics. British aircraft dropped agents in the Baltic republics. On the evening of 28 April 1954, several US aircraft entered Swedish and Danish airspace. The aircraft were observed at several places along the Swedish west coast and in southern Sweden as a whole. During the night, some aircraft patrolled outside Göteborg, Malmö and Copenhagen, while others, after having been refuelled by the former, went in over Sweden, the Baltic Sea and deep into the western Soviet Union including Novgorod, Kalinin, Smolensk and Kiev. The Soviet air defences were, at the time, not able to intercept the US aircraft. When the latter aircraft returned to the Malmö–Copenhagen area, they were once again refuelled, and after that they all left, probably for the US Strategic Air Command's bases in the UK. A week after this incident, the Swedish Defence Staff wrote in a classified report that the aircraft were either American or British. The Danish Minister of Defence, Rasmus Hansen, stated at a confidential party leader meeting that he could not exclude that the aircraft were American, but this should not be reported to the Parliament or to the public.[1]

A couple of weeks earlier, US Secretary of State John Foster Dulles had announced the new US doctrine of massive retaliation. This operation of 28 April 1954 demonstrated the credibility of the US doctrine. It was an exercise to prepare US forces for a third world war as well as a demonstration of force to deter the Soviet Union from any aggression. In Scandinavia and particularly in Sweden this operation had a different meaning, which has been studied by Swedish historian Wilhelm Agrell. The foreign aircraft were observed in southern Sweden during the whole night. The airports at Malmö and Copenhagen tried to get in contact with the mysterious aircraft without success. On 29 April, the evening newspapers wrote about the incident: 'The military observers are convinced: the aircraft are Russian', 'Why didn't Swedish fighter aircraft do anything?' and 'There were continuous intrusions for eleven and a half hours.'[2] To the public, it was obvious that the 'mysterious aircraft' were Russian, and that they had intruded deep into Swedish territory on purpose. In the Swedish Parliament, despite the analysis made by the Swedish Defence Staff, Swedish Minister of Defence Torsten Nilsson said that it had not been possible to identify the purpose or nationality of the aircraft. In the Danish case, there was no interest in having a debate about US intrusions. The consequence, however, was that this US or US–British operation was interpreted as a Soviet demonstration of force. The debate was turned into a question about why Swedish aircraft were not willing or able to intercept the Russians.[3]

In other words, this US or US–British demonstration of force not only had a psychological impact in this country, but to the Danes and Swedes the consequence was primarily psychological. The fact that the Swedish and Danish authorities classified information on this operation made the public believe that the 'mysterious aircraft' were Soviet ones. The incident was automatically turned into a campaign against the Soviet Union. Two years earlier, in June 1952, Soviet air defence had shot down a Swedish signal intelligence aircraft as well as a Swedish reconnaissance aircraft close to the Soviet territorial border in the Baltic Sea.[4] Now, the Soviets seemingly were operating deep into Swedish territory without the Swedes being able to do anything. As with what happened during the Hårsfjärden operation and during the subsequent Hardangerfjord operation, the lack of evidence and the lack of clear information were in themselves interpreted as confirmation of Soviet aggression. The intrusions involving several Scandinavian countries confirmed the general character of the threat. Everything that pointed to US or UK involvement was highly classified, making the public point at the perceived enemy. By intruding into Swedish airspace or Swedish waters with unidentified and 'mysterious forces', the USA and the UK were able to create a realistic Soviet threat against Scandinavia. Similar to the 'ghostlike aircraft' that appeared in Swedish airspace in the 1950s, 'ghostlike submarines' appeared in Swedish waters in the 1980s. These 'psychological operations' may, initially, have been an extra benefit or a spin-off from already-planned intelligence activity primarily against the Soviet Union. However, after an initial analysis of the Swedish response, these operations may have been turned into true psychological operations (PSYOP).

One reason for US covert activities in Swedish waters in the early 1980s could possibly have been to remove or redeploy some secret listening systems deployed along the Swedish coast from the late 1960s or early 1970s (see Chapter 6). Former Swedish Naval Attaché to the USA Captain Hans Tynnerström told me that in the early or mid-1980s, Sweden bought US listening buoys and deployed them in Swedish waters. These systems may possibly have been a replacement for some of the secret US systems, which then had to be removed. The psychological operation would then have been a spin-off from this very secret activity. This is a hypothesis presented by the author Tommy Lindfors.[5] If the above information is true, Swedish reactions to initial support operations – including the use of US special forces and midget submarines – may have been analysed in the USA and found useful as a form of psychological warfare to change Swedish perceptions.

However, the operation in 1982 inside Muskö Naval Base or in Hårsfjärden was most likely not linked to American sonars or similar equipment. It may have been a form of reconnaissance, as stated by a high-ranking CIA officer. It may have been intelligence collection and reconnaissance on specific sabotage targets, because Sweden showed the 'sign of becoming a little frisky'.[6] But more important, it was a test of Swedish capability and readiness as discussed by former Defense Secretary Caspar Weinberger, former Chief of Defence Intelligence Sir John Walker and former Navy Minister Sir Keith Speed. Or to quote former commander of BALTAP, Lieutenant-General Kjeld Hillingsø: the Americans and the British wanted to test 'if Sweden firstly was capable and secondly willing to defend its territory'. But these tests would also, according to Hillingsø, strengthen morale within the military forces and in the population as a whole. In other words, it is not possible to clearly distinguish these tests of the Swedish defence systems and military readiness from PSYOPs that have the object of influencing public opinion and Swedish government policy. Despite official Swedish rhetoric about intruding Soviet submarines, this was actually an issue discussed by a Swedish Defence Ministry official and his NATO counterpart at that time, I was told by the latter. The submarine operation in the Stockholm archipelago in 1982 was thought of as a possible Western psychological operation. If it was a PSYOP with the intention not only of testing Swedish systems and readiness but primarily of convincing Swedish public opinion of the reality of the Soviet danger in order to change Swedish policy, this was one of the most successful operations of the Cold War.

To test the readiness of your own forces is often a necessity, and the means for doing that are often the same as the ones used in intelligence collection. In late October 1985, the Swedish signal intelligence ship *Orion* was on patrol outside the Soviet naval base of Baltijsk, the captain of the ship, Commander Björn Eklind, told me. While listening to the Soviets, the ship received indications of naval activity some hundred kilometres north of Baltijsk. Covered by the fog and by a false 'Soviet' radar (which showed the characteristics of a Soviet radar), *Orion* went up to the area of the Soviet naval exercise. Then *Orion* changed to its original radar and took the first pictures ever of a Kilo-class submarine in the Baltic Sea. The Russians were taken by surprise. A Soviet minesweeper went towards the Swedish ship and even hit it while trying to force *Orion* to leave the area. After this incident, *Orion* returned to the Stockholm archipelago and the naval base at Muskö, but once again it was using its 'Soviet radar'. This created an alarm in the Swedish signal intelligence system, and there was a lot of fuss at the lower levels of the FRA. At higher levels, the position of *Orion* was known, and the information about an approaching Soviet ship was dis-confirmed. However, the use of *Orion*'s 'Soviet radar' gave an opportunity for an excellent test of the Swedish defence system.

The deceptive cover used for an intelligence operation against the Soviets was also used for testing Swedish defences and readiness. Once or twice a year, the Swedish Navy used submarines that covertly oper-ated in Swedish archipelagos to test the readiness of Swedish coastal defences and the procedures of the local and regional military staffs.[7] Submarines were, of course, also used for intelligence purposes against the Soviet Union. Similarly to *Orion*, US naval platforms most likely used Soviet-type radar as well as Soviet uniforms, weapons and communication systems both for intelligence purposes and for testing US and others' readiness and defence capability. There are, however, three differences: firstly, while the Swedes like other smaller states only tested their own forces, the USA and the UK accepted a respon-sibility for the whole NATO area including Sweden, which means that the Swedes experienced confrontation with an alien force; secondly, while the Swedes were testing their own routines, procedures and technological capability, the USA and the UK also tested the Swedish will to resist, which means they accepted the risk of losing their own submarines; thirdly, the existence of these tests was highly classified, and, in Sweden, the knowledge of them existed most likely only as oral information between less than a handful of people making all this submarine activity appear in the mass media as well as in secret Swedish documents as 'real Soviet activity'. In other words, the extreme secrecy of these operations made them into primarily psycho-logical operations to raise awareness of the Soviet threat and to change Swedish political views.

In Sweden, the 1982 submarine incident in Hårsfjärden and the following incidents in the 1980s radically changed Swedish public opinion. As with what happened with the US aircraft in 1954, the sub-marines in Swedish waters were transformed into 'material facts' demonstrating Soviet aggression. The physical realities changed the 'emotions and the objective reasoning' in Sweden. In 1976, 6 per cent of the Swedish population perceived the Soviet Union as a direct threat and 27 per cent perceived the Soviet Union as a threat or unfriendly to Sweden. These figures refer to a study by the Swedish Board of Psychological Defence.[8] In spring 1980, after the Soviet invasion of Afghanistan, these figures increased marginally to 8 per cent and 33 per cent. After the Soviet Whiskey submarine had been stranded on an island in the Karlskrona archipelago in October 1981, 34 per cent of the Swedish population perceived the Soviet Union as a direct threat and 71 per cent perceived the Soviets as either a threat or unfriendly to Sweden. After the Hårsfjärden incident and the presentation of the Submarine Defence Commission Report (and the Swedish protest against the Soviet Union), this change became even more dramatic with 42 per cent looking at the Soviet Union as a direct threat and 83 per cent as a threat or unfriendly towards Sweden, and those high figures were maintained for several years. Not until 1987 did the last figure fall below 70 per cent. The submarine incidents in the early and mid-1980s seem to have totally changed Swedish views about the Soviet Union. In the 1970s, the Soviet threat had no reality to the Swedes. The physical experience of intruding submarines created an awareness in line with US perceptions. The number of Swedes perceiving the Soviet Union as 'friendly' was reduced from 10–15 per cent in the 1970s to 1–2 per cent in 1983, while the corresponding figures for a 'friendly' USA were swinging between 20 and 40 per cent, seemingly unrelated to any submarine hunts.[9]

The perception of an immediate Soviet threat also changed the demand for an increased defence budget. In 1975–76, 16–19 per cent of the population argued that Sweden should strengthen its military defence. In spring 1980, this figure had increased marginally to 22 per cent. After the stranded Soviet submarine in October 1981, 42 per cent of the population believed in the necessity of strengthening military defence, while, after the Submarine Defence Commission Report in spring 1983, this figure had increased to 46 per cent. In the following years, up to 1987, despite an increase in the defence budget, this figure decreased just a little and remained around 35 per cent.[10] The submarine incidents made it possible to increase the Swedish military budget and direct public opinion against the Soviet threat.

US DOCTRINES FOR PSYOP AND MILITARY DECEPTION

The test of readiness and the effort to convince public opinion of the reality of the present danger was unofficial but internally stated US policy for '*friendly* countries'. This seems to have been particularly important for friendly countries 'lulled into a false security' like Sweden in the 1970s with only a few per cent of the population perceiving the Soviet Union as a direct threat. In the British case, SBS swimmer teams would conduct 'reconnaissance on specific sabotage targets, if a foreign country shows sign of becoming a little frisky'[11] – something that definitely was perceived as true in the case of Sweden. A supplement to a US Army Field Manual from 1970 may give us an interesting parallel. It states that host countries (HC) may be lulled into a false security:

> In such cases US Army Intelligence must have the means of launching special operations, which will convince HC governments and public opinion of the reality of the insurgent danger and of the necessity of counteraction. To this end US Army Intelligence should seek to penetrate the insurgency . . . [and] to launch violent and non-violent actions according to the nature of the case.[12]

The US Navy 'terrorist' team, the 'Red Cell' (see Chapter 6) was set up in 1984 for a similar purpose. They put out bombs and kidnapped personnel at US bases that had been 'lulled into false security'. It was, according to Vice-Admiral James Lyons, important that US forces got 'physical' experience of the terrorist threat in order to 'raise the awareness' and 'increase the security'. 'We had to change their mindset', Admiral Lyons argued.[13] According to former 'Red Cell' officer Steve Hartman: 'To enhance the security [by demonstrating the base security weaknesses] was not the primary mission. It was just part of the cover.'[14] The mission of the 'Red Cell' was primarily psychological.

At the same time, a similar operation was launched by a US Army special force unit in cooperation with Belgian Stay-Behinds. They attacked a NATO base with bombing and shooting in order to test its military readiness. They wounded one of the guards. The Communist terrorist organization CCC (Cellules Communistes Combattantes) was announced to have been responsible, and photos were presented that showed weapons in an apartment allegedly belonging to the CCC. Later, however, it was revealed by a member of Belgian Stay-Behinds that US Army special forces organized the operation and he himself had been involved in the logistics. CCC had nothing to do with the case.[15] In Italy, similar deception operations have been used several times by groups connected to Italian Stay-Behinds organized by SISMI in cooperation with the CIA. Attacks on friendly forces were used to test their readiness, making them, as well as the public, aware of the enemy.[16] US and Italian structures established to counter a Communist takeover in Italy were instead used several times in the

1960s, 1970s and 1980s to create a *fait accompli* to change Italian politics. One of the most important Italian figures in these operations was Prince Junio Valerio Borghese, former chief of the naval special forces, Decima MAS, in Fascist Italy.[17] Even in the 1990s, officers from the Italian naval special force COMSUBIN looked upon him as their hero.

Here, we may find some of the answers to our questions. One naval special forces officer from Fascist Italy, later Commander-in-Chief of Allied Naval Forces South Europe, Vice-Admiral Gino Birindelli, argued in 1980 that the transport of small sub-surface vessels to forward positions in foreign harbours by the use of merchant ships created a 'tactical surprise'.[18] The US tanker *Mormacsky* may very well have had such a role in the transport of small US submersibles and Italian midgets during the Hårsfjärden incident. To the Swedes, these small vessels with their very limited range were automatically believed to originate from the Baltic Sea area, and accordingly from the Soviet Union,[19] which 'convinced the host country government and public opinion of the reality of the Soviet threat'. However, unlike the Italian wartime 'tactical surprise', the US–Italian 'tactical surprise' in Sweden in the 1980s may have been carried on for ten years. COMSUBIN had a symbiotic relationship with the US Navy SEALs, and, according to SEAL Commander Gary Stubblefield, in covert operations it would not be possible to identify SEALs as US forces.[20] The use of Soviet uniforms for such operations has been confirmed by Western admirals.

At the time, the US Navy had one or more Whiskey submarines that they kept very secret. They were used for playing Soviet submarines during special exercises and most likely for testing the readiness of US or friendly forces. However, to my knowledge, there is no indication of a Whiskey submarine during the Hårsfjärden operation, but such a masquerade seems to have been typical of the above-mentioned SEAL operations. The US Navy used Soviet-type aircraft in special exercises, and the SEALs used Soviet weapons, uniforms, communication systems and submarine(s) for this kind of task. The US Navy Deception Groups for the Atlantic and the Pacific organized electronic as well as psychological deception in cooperation with the CIA and US Navy SEALs.[21] A US Joint Chiefs of Staff report states: 'Navy SEALs are equipped and trained to conduct UW [unconventional warfare, whose] primary focus is on political and psychological objectives.'[22] Captain Thomas N. Lawson, Deputy Commander of the Naval Special Warfare Command, says: 'SEALs are the perfect choice if the United States wants to neutralize something, or send a message, without acknowledging US responsibility.'[23]

To dress in enemy uniforms or act as enemy forces is an old military skill. In 1788, Swedish King Gustav III allegedly started his war against Russia by using Swedish troops in Russian uniforms to attack the regular Swedish troops.[24] On 31 August 1939, Nazi Germany used SS men in Polish uniforms to attack a German radio transmitter at the Polish–German border to justify the German war against Poland. To convince neutral journalists, the Nazis showed dead concentration-camp prisoners dressed in Polish uniforms – who supposedly had been shot by German troops – scattered around the radio station.[25] In 1944, the Nazi special force commander, Otto Skorzeny, supposedly used 2,000 American-speaking Germans 'dressed in American uniforms and equipped with captured American tanks, trucks and jeeps', which 'caused a lot of worry and a great deal of trouble' in the Allied Headquarters.[26] In March 1962, US Chairman of Joint Chiefs of Staff General Lyman Lemnitzer, proposed a number of 'pretexts which would provide justification for US military intervention in Cuba. . . . Land friendly Cubans in uniform "over-the-fence" to stage attack on [the US Guantanamo] base. . . . Capture Cuban (friendly) saboteurs inside the base. . . . Blow up ammunition inside the base. . . . Sink ship near harbor entrance. . . . We could develop a Communist Cuban terror campaign in the Miami area . . . and even in Washington. . . . Exploding a few plastic bombs in carefully chosen spots, the arrest of Cuban agents and the release of prepared documents substantiating Cuban involvement . . . Use of [US-captured Soviet] MIG-type aircraft by US pilots [against the Dominican Republic] could provide additional provocation.'[27]

In more democratic countries like the USA, PSYOP and deception – or in other words 'perception management' – is important, because operations have to be publicly justified. By using Cuban military uniforms, Soviet aircraft and manufactured documents proving Cuban involvement in terrorist attacks, all indicators would point to Cuba. This PSYOP would 'influence the emotions, motives, objective reasoning and ultimately the behaviour of foreign governments'. The target here is the US public as well as the international community. And the Joint Chiefs continued: 'World opinion and the United Nations forum should be favourably affected by developing the international image of the Cuban government as rash and irresponsible, and as an alarming and unpredictable threat to the peace of the Western Hemisphere.'[28]

This Operation Northwoods had the written approval of the Chairman of the Joint Chiefs of Staff General Lyman Lemnitzer, but the Joint Chiefs were never able to convince Defense Secretary Robert McNamara and President John F. Kennedy about launching the operation and starting a full-scale war on Cuba. Two years later, however, a more carefully calibrated PSYOP and deception operation was able to mobilize congressional and public support for a US full-scale war in Vietnam.[29] In the Tonkin incident of August 1964, the CIA and US Navy SEALs used small Norwegian-built swift boats, PTFs, to attack targets along the coast of North Vietnam, which provoked a North Vietnamese attack on the US destroyer *Maddox*, which had been ordered to operate close to the shore just outside while listening to the North Vietnamese communication. This attack became the pretext for launching the major escalation of the Vietnam War.[30] The night-officer at the Pentagon, later Captain Robert Bathurst, told me that he decided to call the Chief of Naval Operations and wake him up in the middle of the night. A Vietnamese attack on a US ship was a 'big thing', but, like almost everybody else in the Pentagon as well as outside, Bathurst knew nothing about the background for the attack.

In the 1990s, US doctrine stated that US forces should not be used to deceive its own people: 'Deception operations will not intentionally target or mislead the US public, the US Congress, or the US news media.'[31] However, nothing excludes deception operations against US allies and friends. US Joint Doctrine for Military Deception states:

> *Deception seeks to create* or increase *the likelihood of detection of certain indicators* in order to cause an adversary to derive an incorrect conclusion. Cover stories provide plausible explanations for activities that cannot be hidden . . . While the goal of OPSEC [operative security] is normally to reduce the adversary's ability to see certain indicators, *deception normally seeks to increase the visibility of selected indicators.*[32]

The same doctrine writes that these selected indicators will portray a deception story:

> The story must correspond to the deception *target's perceptions* . . . The adversary must be able to *verify the veracity* of the story. The story must, therefore, take into account *all of the adversary's intelligence sources* . . . Means [for example 'electronic and physical decoys' should be] tailored to the adversary's intelligence collection capability.[33]

The doctrine states about the deception and PSYOP targets:

> The deception must *target the adversary's decision maker* capable of taking desired decisions . . . Similar to military deception, *military PSYOP is a systematic process of conveying tailored messages* to a selected foreign audience . . . *Groups* that might be suitable for targeting by PSYOP in support of deception operations *include* adversary command groups, planning staffs, specific factions within staffs, non-military interest groups who can influence military policies and decisions, and intelligence systems analysts . . . Dedicated PSYOP dissemination assets can discreetly convey intended information to

selected target audiences through appropriate 'key communicator' backchannel networks.[34]

Doctrine for Joint Psychological Operations describes PSYOP as:

> Planned operations to convey selected information and indicators to foreign audiences to influence their emotions, motives, objective reasoning and ultimately the behaviour of foreign governments, organizations, groups and individuals . . . so that their behaviors and actions will promote the attainment of US national goals . . . PSYOP actions convey information not only to intended target audiences but also to foreign intelligence systems . . . [and should] *operate 'inside' an adversary's decision cycle* . . . It is possible to *systematically convey and deny data to opposing intelligence systems with the objective of causing opposing analysts to derive selected judgements.*[35]

US deception operations target the political and military leadership in foreign countries, while PSYOPs also target a wider audience including news media and the intelligence organizations. Indications of sub-surface decoys masquerading as Soviet submarines are picked up by the intelligence service of the host country. Instead of reducing the adversary's ability to detect a periscope, deception seeks to increase the visibility of these indicators and lets them be verified by other indicators, through 'back-channel networks', and by assets operating 'inside' the adversary's decision cycle, all supporting the general story. This information is reported to the political and military leadership, which has to rely on these reports. Member of the Submarine Defence Commission, MP Olle Svensson, describes how the military expert (Bror Stefenson) and the Naval Analysis Group Report (Emil Svensson) had convinced him that the submarines originated from the Soviet Union, although there was no indication pointing to the Soviets (see Chapter 5). And despite the fact that the Social Democratic government had accused the military leadership of not being able to present enough evidence pointing to the Soviets, the political leaders actually believed the information they received. According to a protocol from a Social Democratic leadership meeting on 17 May 1983, at least Olof Palme and later Foreign Minister Sten Andersson believed in Soviet intrusions, but after April 1983 they were reluctant to point to the Soviets because this would have supported the Conservative Party propaganda. Andersson stated: 'In conclusion, we have to let the Russians understand – through diplomatic and political channels – the consequences of continued intrusions.' Olof Palme said: 'The debate on foreign policy is about to fall to pieces.'[36] By sending some 'sub-surface decoys', US deception and PSYOPs had neutralized the Palme government in less than a year.

In the 1990s, the principal adviser and coordinator for US PSYOP was the Assistant Secretary of Defense (for Special Operations/Low Intensity Conflict).[37] Colonel Alfred Paddock, former Director of Psychological Operations in the Office of the Secretary of Defense, argues that, since the birth of PSYOP, it had been married with the special forces.[38] In littoral areas of foreign countries, US Navy SEALs have the responsibility for carrying out such operations. Sub-surface activities in Swedish waters presented a realistic threat, they were adapted to Swedish intelligence capabilities and they seemed to have combined cover stories and tailored messages to the Swedish Military Intelligence and to civilian analysts in order to 'verify the veracity of the story', to confirm ambitious Soviet operations on Swedish territory. If the above-mentioned sub-surface activities in Swedish waters were organized by the CIA and the DIA and carried out by a SEAL task force they were, in fact, extremely successful. These operations strengthened Swedish readiness and bolstered its military defence, they turned the whole nation against the Soviet Union and they turned the Swedish military organization and particularly the Navy against the controversial Prime Minister Olof Palme, who preferred a continued dialogue with Moscow.

Former State Secretary General Alexander Haig said in February 1983 that he 'knew' that the submarines in 1982 in Hårsfjärden 'were nuclear-armed Soviet submarines that the Swedish government let out on international water, a move the Pentagon in the USA and the leadership in Moscow appreciated'.[39] Afterwards, this seemed pretty strange, because it is almost impossible to believe that the Swedish military leadership would have missed a chance to prove a Soviet presence. And several years later, in the late 1980s, the military leadership would have done anything to expose the Soviets. Perhaps Alexander Haig used his invitation to Sweden in February 1983 to leak out a cover story to the Swedes to put the blame on the Soviets and indirectly on the Swedish government that had 'released the Soviet submarines'. This story explained a lot of mysterious incidents during the submarine hunt: the leaks about a damaged submarine, the order to let a submarine out and the sudden close-down of the military press centre. Or, to quote a senior intelligence officer from a NATO country: 'In a case like this, I would have prepared a cover story that would explain the incident if anything should go wrong.' Haig's story appears to be a cover story providing 'plausible explanations for activities that cannot be hidden'.[40]

Furthermore, this story has some similarities with the telegram sent from Bonn to the Swedish Defence Staff early on the morning of

6 October. A man in Hamburg, an alleged Soviet civilian captain, had said that the submarines in Swedish waters were nuclear-armed Soviet submarines and that they would detonate their nuclear weapons if attacked by the Swedes. According to former West German Defence Attaché Colonel Bachelin, this captain had already on earlier occasions come up with false information. It was a mistake to have sent the telegram, Bachelin said. However, this captain may also have been part of a deception operation to put the blame on the Soviets at the same time as the operation may have been trying to save a Western submarine desperately trying to get out. A threat of a nuclear detonation would: firstly, test the Swedish willingness to use force even though confronted with a nuclear threat; and secondly, or rather alternatively, create a ceasefire that would save the submarine.

THE TAILORED MESSAGES OF THE MILITARY ANALYSTS

There are also several examples of civilian or military analysts who have presented totally false stories that would contribute to the manipulation of Swedish public and military forces, either through professional military publications or 'through appropriate "key communicator" back-channel networks'. In November 1983, the Swedish industrialist Peter Wallenberg handed over a British intelligence report to Commander-in-Chief General Ljung. This document stated, though it was totally unfounded according to Ljung, that:

> the political side [the government] had tried on purpose to make the submarine hunt inefficient and that they [the government] had released submarines on purpose . . . Furthermore, it was stated that the Ministry of Defence had on purpose tried to prevent the [Swedish] Navy from receiving an efficient anti-submarine force. It is also indicated that there probably would appear some kind of Swedish–Soviet pact in the near future.[41]

In 1984, CIA operative Lynn M. Hansen wrote – in a public and widely used study for the US Office of the Secretary of Defense – that the submarine operations in Swedish waters were Soviet Spetsnaz operations (see Chapter 6). In the foreword to *Jane's Fighting Ships* (1984–85), Commander John Moore wrote:

> While 25 countries, including the USSR, are discussing the easing of international relations in the various meetings in Stockholm, only a few miles away Soviet penetration of Swedish territorial waters continues unabated. As the talks meander on so Soviet submarines and converted merchant ships are landing reconnaissance parties from the Kronshtadt-

based Spetsnaz units throughout the Swedish coastline. This flagrant contravention of international law has continued since 1962, the present total of such incursions having now passed the 150 mark. All areas of the Swedish coast have been visited, from Haparanda in the north to Malmö in the south. The equipment of this elite group, trained in techniques of raiding, sabotage, reconnaissance, and political murder, includes small submarines and each group has its quota of assault swimmers, some of whom are defecting nationals of the country being visited.[42]

In *Jane's Fighting Ships* (1985–86), Commander Moore refers to the 1983 Submarine Defence Commission Report and the Karlskrona operation in 1984. He argues that Soviet Spetsnaz forces operated in Swedish waters by the use of

> larger submarines outside the skerries as well as smaller vehicles and divers within the skerries area ... [Wartime tasks] would be assisted by the swift elimination of the Swedish Government and High Command by the specialist assassination group of the Baltic Fleet Spetsnaz brigade ... [And] the incursions continue, while the Swedish Navy struggles to overcome years of governmental neglect.[43]

The Soviet naval operations in Scandinavia are among the most important things going on in the world just now, Moore told *Dagens Nyheter*.[44] In early 1986, former British Naval Attaché to Stockholm Commander M.G.M.W. Ellis wrote in *US Naval Institute Proceedings* about the Hårsfjärden operation, and the tracks from a bottom-crawling submarine. Commander Ellis believed that signal intelligence information was the most likely proof of Soviet involvement.[45] In January 1986, John Erickson, the already-mentioned British scholar and adviser to the Submarine Defence Commission, stated on Swedish TV news that the Swedish government had released a Soviet submarine after negotiations with Moscow.[46] The Swedish Navy had caught a Soviet submarine – most likely a midget submarine – in Hårsfjärden in 1982, but the Navy let it leave after diplomatic contacts with Moscow, he stated in *Dagens Nyheter* the following day. Professor Erickson criticized the Swedish military leadership for not being willing to reveal documents on the dramatic submarine hunt and on the diplomatic game behind the release.[47]

Soon after that, two US researchers, Milton Leitenberg[48] from the Washington-based CSIS and Gordon McCormick[49] from Rand Corporation, wrote books that, like Erickson, clearly identified the Soviets as the intruders and put the blame on the Swedish government for releasing the submarines and doing nothing to stop the Soviet submarine activity. Leitenberg was certainly just a scholar following the stream of mass media, but he has undoubtedly played a major role in forming the scholarly view. Senior defence analysts such as Robert Weinland and Michael MccGwire present Leitenberg's book *Soviet Submarine Operations in Swedish Waters 1980–1986* as 'a definitive analysis of Soviet submarine intrusions into Swedish internal waters'.[50]

John Moore and Richard Compton-Hall wrote in 1986 in their large volume, *Submarine Warfare*:

> Divers and midget submarines have been spotted at a number of locations along the Swedish coast, and there can be no real doubt about where they come from . . . The indications are that Soviet midget operations are conducted on quite a large scale . . . Why, one asks, are these incursions aimed, primarily as it appears, at Sweden? The answer is surely that Sweden is the route to south Norway.[51]

Marc Berkowitz's article on Soviet naval Spetsnaz forces in *Naval War College Review* (1988) uses the Hårsfjärden operation of 1982 and the Karlskrona operation of 1984 as the only examples of offensive naval Spetsnaz operations during the Cold War. Soviet activity in Swedish waters is described as general naval training, as intelligence gathering and as psychological warfare 'to gradually wear down the Swedish Government's will to resist'.[52] In their book *Modern Submarine Warfare* of 1987, David Miller and John Jordan present one example of the Soviet Spetsnaz forces' use of mini-submarines: the Hårsfjärden operation in Sweden in 1982. The book even shows a drawing of 'such a mini-submarine', and argues that these small vessels were 'taken to the vicinity of their targets by mother-ships, probably the India-class submarines'.[53] Richard Compton-Hall's major work of 1988, *Submarine vs. Submarine*, refers to the tracks in Hårsfjärden and the Commander-in-Chief's report of 1987. The book also has a fiction section on Soviet midgets in Swedish waters.[54] Michael Welham's *Combat Frogmen* of 1989 uses the Hårsfjärden incident as the only evidence for offensive Soviet Spetsnaz operations with several mini-subs – two of them 'left tracks on the sea bed'.[55] Paul Kemp's *Underwater Warriors: The Fighting History of Midget Submarines* speaks about physical evidence for Soviet offensive midget operations, but he has only one reference, a Swedish officer who mentions these tracks on the sea floor 'in the middle of a sensitive military installation'.[56] Edward Luttwak and Steven Koehl's *The Dictionary of Modern War* has a paragraph about mini-subs, using the tracks in Hårsfjärden as the definitive evidence: 'Soviet naval Spetsnaz are believed to have used at least two different kind of mini-subs to probe the harbors and inshore defenses of Sweden and Japan; one type is known to have tank-like tracks, to crawl along the bottom.'[57]

To the defence analysts and to the scholarly community, the ambitious Soviet submarine operations in the Swedish archipelagos have become a fact like any other fact, and who is the deceiver and who is the deceived in this game is difficult to know. But let us have a closer look at Leitenberg's scholarly technique. In the case of the Hardangerfjord operation, we know that the Norwegian Commission and Norwegian Military Intelligence suspected a French Daphné-class submarine and not a Soviet submarine. Leitenberg's presentation is very different:

> The most well-known submarine incursions in Norwegian waters took place . . . in Hardangerfjord from April 27 to May 6, 1983. The 1983 Hardanger events began exactly 24 hours after the Swedish SDC [Submarine Defence Commission] released its public report in Stockholm, and, as the operation continued, it overlapped with a major submarine operation that was taking place in Sweden. Norway has never officially identified the state to which the submarines belong, claiming that motor sound recordings were absent. Norwegian naval officers have implied unofficially at various times, however, that they could only be Warsaw Pact vessels, which in practice means the USSR or Poland . . . The Hardangerfjord submarine was allegedly a diesel-powered vessel and, from a reported 30-minute visual identification, was suspected of being a Whiskey-class submarine . . . Soon after these ASW operations, a Norwegian military officer was quoted as publicly stating that the Norwegian navy 'could have destroyed Soviet submarines . . . that enter[ed] territorial waters this spring, but chose not to do so for political reasons.' . . . By coincidence, some 10 ships of NATO's Standing Naval Force Atlantic (STANAVFORLANT) were only a few miles away in Bergen harbor all during this submarine hunt and could easily have supplied helicopter as well as other additional ASW support. Nevertheless, Norwegian authorities decided that only national forces should be used.[58]

By using some rumours from the mass media, Leitenberg creates a story that not only identifies the submarine as a Soviet vessel but also puts the blame on the government for not doing anything about the Soviet intrusion. The same technique is used in the Swedish case. Leitenberg wrote:

> Despite his public threats on three occasions between the spring of 1983 and December 1985 regarding the possibility of sinking a submarine, [Prime Minister] Palme was firmly resolved not to do so . . . The best understanding of the purpose of these submarine operations was that they represented some kind of exercise – manoeuvres of specialized units – and contingency planning . . . [and] either primarily or secondarily to

297

exert political pressure on Sweden . . . to force Sweden to acquiesce to Soviet military movements within its territory both in times of peace and of war . . . Other external Soviet military programs, in Afghanistan or in Africa, can be documented by the international community, properly credited to the Soviet Union and assessed in terms of the goals of Soviet foreign policy. The submarine operations in Swedish waters are both covert and denied . . . The operations are the first Soviet military–political initiatives against a Western European state since the Berlin crisis of 1960–1961.[59]

The submarine operations in Swedish waters are presented as major Soviet military operations, and Leitenberg believes they should, at least partly, be understood in the perspective of a political initiative to change Swedish neutrality. In a report of 1990 for the US Air Force, *Stranger than Fiction: Soviet Submarine Operations in Swedish Waters*, Gordon McCormick argues that these ambitious Soviet operations continued up to the end of the decade with up to more than 30 per year.[60] In recent years, Professor Gordon McCormick (for Special Warfare/Low-Intensity Conflict at the Naval Postgraduate School, Monterey) has been close to the SEAL community. He has been adviser to special force students writing on SEAL operations, and he certainly knows about some of these activities. However, in a letter I received from a US Naval Intelligence captain, he stated that McCormick's study 'does NOT carry the imprimatur of the US Navy'.

In the 1980s, in the yearly review of Soviet naval activity for the House Armed Services Committee, the directors of Naval Intelligence (Sumner Shapiro, 1980–82; John Butts, 1983–86; William Studeman, 1987–88; Thomas Brooks, 1989–91) discussed Soviet naval operations all over the world, in the South China Sea and Vietnam, in the West Indies and Cuba, in the Mediterranean including the cooperation with Libya and Syria, and various exercises in the Black Sea and the Baltic Sea, but nothing is mentioned about operations in Swedish waters. Soviet capabilities and offensive activities are described in detail on more than a hundred pages in total, but none of these directors of Naval Intelligence presents the operations in Swedish waters as being of Soviet origin.[61] While described by Leitenberg as the 'first Soviet military-political initiative against a Western European state since the Berlin crisis' and by John Moore as 'one of the most important things going on in the world just now' (translated from Swedish), they were of no interest to US Naval Intelligence. In a review of Soviet naval activities for 1982, Rear-Admiral Butts underlines Soviet expansionism, and mentions a new destroyer in the Baltic Sea, and even a Soviet port visit to Bombay, but there is nothing about Soviet operations in Swedish waters.[62] Very differently, McCormick writes:

Since 1980, Swedish sources indicate that an average rate of between 17 and 36 foreign operations are being conducted per year . . . More often than not, *these operations now involved the use of multiple submarines, mini-submarines, and combat swimmers operating in a coordinated manner.*[63] (italics McCormick)

In an interview, McCormick argued that the Swedish Navy had never got the political green light to use necessary force. The goal of the Swedish government had never been 'to sink a Russian submarine or force it to the surface . . . There is no way that a submarine could operate in these narrow passages without being sunk if somebody really tried to get it.'[64] He argued, similarly to the above-mentioned British intelligence report, and to John Erickson and Milton Leitenberg, that the Swedish government was responsible for the release of Soviet submarines, and if the Swedish Navy had had the right to use force at the right moment, there wouldn't have been any submarines in Swedish waters. It is not clear to me if McCormick knew about the US operations and wanted to deceive the Swedish and the international community, or if he was deceived himself by reports in newspapers and by interviews with Swedish naval officers. His view has been supported by many naval officers lacking access to more sensitive information. Vice-Admiral Stefenson's ceasefires were believed to have been ordered by the government.[65] And everybody believed that Commander Emil Svensson's Naval Analysis Group Report had presented the most qualified information and not hidden this for the government. Naval officers and others (who knew about evidence indicating a release) mobilized against a 'compliant' government and particularly its Prime Minister Olof Palme.

PSYOP TO UNDERCUT SUPPORT FOR AN UNDESIRABLE GOVERNMENT

A local special force commander from Hårsfjärden 1982 told me that he, on 13–14 October, followed the counter-order for a drop of depth charges on radio. He heard with his own ears how a submarine was released. 'To me it was obvious that it was Russian. I was convinced that Prime Minister Palme had released a Soviet submarine', he said. After the Hårsfjärden submarine hunt, a lot of rumours circulated among naval officers. Many officers had experienced contact with foreign submarines at close range but the authorities seemingly showed a cowardly attitude. The decision makers seemingly preferred to let the submarines out and, according to the naval officers, ministers and army officers did not take the threat sufficiently seriously. One major reason for the cautious attitude among the political leaders may have been the Naval Analysis Group Report that had filtered away much of the sensitive information. The clear figures were blotted out in the fog and we were left with shadows of one or another submarine ghost. After a while, this created a conflict of trust between the political leaders and many naval officers, and large parts of the population followed the naval officers' critical view. In autumn 1985, a number of naval officers carried out a 'revolt' and went public with their criticism of the government. In November 1985, Commander Hans von Hofsten wrote a statement signed by 12 naval officers. Chief of the Army Lieutenant-General Nils Sköld writes about this 'naval officers' revolt':

> It was as a matter of fact an organized campaign by large groups within the Navy primarily directed against the former government. In practical terms, Sweden was believed to be at war with the Soviet Union. Hundreds of midget submarines operated in Swedish waters. This was presented as a fact.[66]

Naval officers turned against the Prime Minister, and a number of naval commanders expressed publicly that they no longer had trust in the Prime Minister. According to this group, he no longer took the Soviet threat seriously enough.[67] However, the initiative was not just von Hofsten's. One initiator was also the *Svenska Dagbladet* journalist Lars Christiansson (later Press Secretary for Prime Minister Carl Bildt), who called these officers to confirm their support for these ideas without telling all of them that they were going to appear as signatories of a statement in *Svenska Dagbladet*. The 'naval officers' revolt' was an invention by primarily two individuals, von Hofsten and Christiansson, even though the criticism against the government was widespread within the Navy. The day after this statement was published, Swedish TV asked Olof Palme if it wasn't worrying that so many naval officers did not trust him. Palme answered: 'It is more important that I can trust the officers of this country.'[68] On 5 December 1985, after almost three years of icy relations, Prime Minister Palme stated that he was going to Moscow in April 1986 to initiate a dialogue with the Soviet leadership. In January 1986, the leader of the 'naval officers' revolt', Commander von Hofsten, wrote an article in *Dagens Nyheter* ('corrected' by the Chief of the Navy, Vice-Admiral Bengt Schuback) with the title: 'The Soviet Republic of Sweden?'[69] One of the signatories, von Hofsten's former superior, Captain Cay Holmberg, said in a TV interview that von Hofsten had participated in a meeting with police officers. They had 'discussed the problem if one could trust Palme or not, and how it would be possible to manage this by removing Palme in one way or another'.[70] Former Foreign Minister Sten Andersson said that 'in leading circles within the Swedish military, you found hatred of Olof Palme'.[71] He also said that it was a group within the Swedish security service (SÄK) that operated against Olof Palme and looked upon him as a security risk.[72] In a TV interview, the Minister of Defence, Thage G. Peterson, said that, in the months before Olof Palme's planned visit to Moscow:

> military circles directed a well-organized attack against Olof Palme. They were afraid that Olof Palme was going to sell out Swedish independence and freedom to the Soviet Union. The fact that leading representatives of the Navy did not trust their own Prime Minister must have been a frightful burden for him to carry.[73]

In his memoirs Defence Minister Peterson says that he reported this information about the naval officers to the investigation of the murder of Olof Palme.[74] Olof Palme was shot dead on 28 February 1986 one month before his planned trip to Moscow.

By classifying essential information as top-secret or even higher – or keeping it just as oral information – the general view of the submarine intrusions has been totally manipulated. Naval officers with experience of the submarine hunts were confronted with a government that lacked understanding, because essential information was also withheld from the government. Certain decisions were taken at a lower level and the government did not receive relevant information in the most sensitive matters. This created a sharp conflict between many naval officers on the one hand and the government on the other, which Defence Minister Peterson interpreted as a possible background for the assassination of the Prime Minister. To classify essential information, as in the case of the US aircraft in the 1950s and the submarines in the 1980s, is not just a question of necessary military secrecy in hiding operative planning; it is also an important aspect of psychological warfare. In many cases, the action is hidden, and people are only able to register the reaction, which makes them draw a totally incorrect conclusion.

In the early 1980s, William Taylor, a US military specialist on PSYOP in China and Vietnam, started to focus on Sweden and made several studies on Swedish public opinion and decision-making process. He argued that West Germany was moving towards a 'neutral' position, and he warned Europe of possible 'Swedenization'.[75] In 1982, he stated that in Western Europe, unlike 'other areas in the world, it will not be armed conflict. Rather, conflict will take the form of psychological warfare.'[76] In order to change the Swedish and European mentality, he advocated threats at the lower level of the conflict spectrum that would shift loyalties in support of the USA. As a credible threat and a potential PSYOP in the European area, Taylor mentioned the possibility of 'assassinat[ing] a key leader in a democratic country'.[77] He advocated the use of special forces and particularly the use of psychological warfare to change the perceptions of governments and populations. He also mentioned the British Second World War experience of using the enemy submarine campaign to involve the USA on the allied side.

In Western Europe after the Second World War, war became increasingly unlikely. Power struggles in democratic countries accordingly tried to find new forms at the lower end of the conflict spectrum: for example by the use of psychological warfare. For a great power or a superpower to dominate a democratic state, it had to control or change the mindset of its population and its government, and this was no longer possible by the control of the mass media. In contrast to the authoritarian state, the democratic states of Western Europe have no monopoly of the mass media to form the minds of their citizens. Instead, creating a 'false reality' has become a suitable alternative. It is no longer possible primarily to manipulate the mass media but rather to manipulate the experience of people, which will turn up as news on TV and in newspapers. In other words, a major power has to create decoys or indicators that will be interpreted in a false way to change the mindset of the people. When the existence of foreign submarines had been accepted by the Swedish public – because sufficiently many people had themselves experienced (seen with their own eyes periscopes and submarine sails) – journalists accepted 'Soviet intrusions' as a fact. There were different explanations for these intrusions, but there was a consensus about their existence. The Soviet Union was the dominating power in the Baltic Sea region. People were automatically pointing to the perceived enemy. It was not possible to imagine that a friendly nation could have been responsible for these operations. And after the Soviet Whiskey submarine had stranded in the Swedish archipelago in 1981, no one would doubt the Soviet origin of the continued submarine activities. Even Lars Werner, the party leader of the Swedish Communist Party, VPK (The Left-wing Party, the Communists), said that the Commission had 'substantiated that Soviet submarines had intruded Swedish waters . . . Sweden had the full right to protest against the Soviet Union.' Werner expressed his support for the strong protest against the Soviet Union.[78]

The ambitious submarine campaign totally changed the psychological climate in Sweden. It created 'facts' that prepared the population for a war against the Soviet Union, but it also undercut the support of an undesirable government. No one doubted the Soviet origin of the continued submarine activities, and, combined with leaks to the press about the government purposely releasing submarines, large parts of the population turned against its own 'conciliatory government'. It is impossible that US and British leaders would not have understood that. As already mentioned, the SEALs had a satellite link to the White

House. US and British covert submarine operations in the 1980s appear as a form of PSYOP in line with Taylor's proposal: 'Psychological operations to induce the government and/or population to resist Soviet intervention or psychological operations to undercut support of an undesirable government.'[79]

THE SECRET WAR AGAINST SWEDEN

As in diplomacy, actions are often more potent than words, because, to quote Thomas Schelling: '[actions] carry some evidence of their own credibility'.[80] The use of force in peacetime, particularly something as 'ghostlike' as submarines, will definitely influence the target audience. Similarly to the US aircraft in the 1950s, the submarines of the 1980s were both visible and not. They appeared through indications, as 'shadows' or 'ghosts' that created uncertainty – as a hidden enemy appearing everywhere. To use submarines is ideal for creating threats at the lower end of the conflict spectrum. To believe that the responsible groups would not have been aware of this seems naive. And similarly to the US aircraft in the 1950s, the submarines in the 1980s were also able to shift Swedish loyalties more in support of the USA and US objectives in the area. Edward Luttwak said that these submarine 'incidents were certainly very helpful'.[81] He argues, however, that democratic countries would make a 'clear distinction between psychological operations in war, even if limited war, and the psychological dimension of the conduct of diplomacy'.[82] The Reagan administration in the early 1980s had a different view. As underlined by Fred Iklé, Under-Secretary of Defense for Policy (1981–88), psychological warfare became increasingly important in the early and mid-1980s, because this administration perceived PSYOPs in peacetime as a continuation of war by other means. It did, for several reasons, not make this clear distinction between war and peace.[83] Chief of Naval Operations Admiral James Watkins stated that we are living in an 'era of violent peace'.[84]

According to former DCI (Director of Central Intelligence) Stansfield Turner, '[a]lmost any covert action to help win the war was considered acceptable, and the more the better. Translating that attitude to peacetime conditions of the 1980s was a serious mistake.'[85] After interviews with several representatives for the Reagan administration, Peter Schweizer states that this administration was involved in a number of high-risk operations in the Soviet periphery, not only in the Third World but also in Europe. Sophisticated psychological operations were supposed to create uncertainty in the Soviet leadership.

Bomber forces tested the Soviet periphery, sometimes several times a week, which created chaos on the Soviet side.[86] It is likely that the submarine operations in Swedish waters were part of the same game. A main goal of these operations may have been to create internal confusion in Moscow, for example make the political leadership distrust its own military forces, while tearing Sweden from its excessively neutral position, possibly even by making it into a platform for offensive operations. These PSYOPs would also thwart Sweden's 'global policy' as well as the idea of Sweden as a neutral player on the European scene. According to Peter Schweizer, Casey, as DCI, turned up with his own aircraft in Stockholm, where he had a meeting with some Swedish officers, and with someone in the Defence Ministry. He was an operator, and he was willing to take great risks.[87] Or to quote a former chief of Military Intelligence in a NATO country: 'Casey was completely mad.' To the Reagan administration and particularly to the DCI William Casey, submarines and SEALs were, even in peacetime, the perfect choice when the administration wanted 'to send a message without acknowledging US responsibility'.[88]

In the early 1980s, the submarine incidents showed that Sweden was not able to guarantee its own security. They totally changed Swedish public opinion. They demonstrated the importance of NATO, and the impotence of Olof Palme's disarmament initiatives and foreign policy proposals. The submarine intrusions into Swedish archipelagos close to major Swedish naval bases and densely populated areas made Palme's initiative look pathetic. The Palme Commission Report on Common Security of June 1982, which included a dialogue with the Soviets, appeared to be of no relevance. Palme's global political initiatives and his European and Nordic disarmament initiatives were no longer credible. While telling others how to solve their security problems, he wasn't able to defend the integrity of his own country. In practical terms, the Swedish example became devaluated. To reveal a US involvement would have put Swedish–US ties and Swedish access to US weapons technology into question. If these provocative submarine activities started as a US/UK test of Swedish readiness and later were developed as an instrument to manipulate Swedish public opinion including the opinion within its government and its military forces, it became impossible to reveal this to more than a handful of people (or perhaps just to two individuals, for example Vice-Admiral Per Rudberg and Vice-Admiral Bror Stefenson).

After Olof Palme was elected as Prime Minister in 1982, the submarine operations became more provocative and increased in number and scale. A major argument for US/UK operations in Swedish waters may have been to destabilize the Olof Palme government. In private talks this issue was also discussed among senior military officers, an admiral from a NATO country told me. This idea is supported by the fact that Vice-Admiral Stefenson and Vice-Admiral Rudberg tried to de-escalate the Hårsfjärden submarine hunt on 7 October, the day before the Palme government took office. During the Fälldin government – the first week of the hunt – at least 45 depth charges were dropped (and four mines were detonated). During the Palme government – the second week of the hunt – only two depth charges were dropped (and one mine was detonated) and this limited use of force was carried out by the Coastal Defence base at Mälsten, which was not totally under Stefenson's and the naval base's control. To most military officers and to the public it would appear as if the Palme government was acting in a more conciliatory way and was willing to accept a 'Soviet presence'. There may have been other reasons for de-escalating the submarine hunt, but from the point of view of destabilizing the Palme government such a decision makes perfect sense. It would in practical terms demonstrate that it was impossible to have the Palme government.

Most importantly, however, these peacetime psychological operations may also have been preparations for a wartime contingency. In the initial phase of a major war, it is possible that US Navy special forces might masquerade as Soviet Spetsnaz forces and fabricate a 'Soviet attack' on Sweden in order to receive Swedish support right from day one. Sweden had had close informal ties to the USA since the early 1950s. In a secret National Security Council Document of 1960, in the section on guidelines for Scandinavia, it is stated:

> In event of a general war . . . [the US intention is to] assist Sweden, without prejudice to US commitments to NATO, to resist a Soviet Bloc attack against Sweden. In event of a Soviet Bloc aggression against Sweden alone be prepared to come to the assistance of Sweden as part of a NATO or UN response to the aggression . . . this language is intended to provide the basis only for unilateral US planning and not for planning within NATO.[89]

'State Department Guidelines for Policy and Operations – Sweden' from June 1962 uses the same language, including US unilateral planning for the same contingency. 'This document was in force through the 1970s, and probably in one form or the other up to 1989'.[90] General Carl Eric Almgren, former Chief of Staff (1961–67) and Chief of the Army (1967–76) told a government investigation that, from the early 1960s, Swedish airbases were prepared to receive US aircraft.[91] According to former Assistant Under-Secretary of Defence Ingemar Engman (1972–79), in the event of a third world war the Prime Minister, the Defence Minister and the Commander-in-Chief intended to give the green light for US aircraft to be evacuated from West

Germany to Sweden from the very first day of a war. To the Swedish leadership in the 1960s, this was a primary option.[92] The US aircraft in West Germany were under US and not under NATO command, and in the event of a war these aircraft could be redeployed to Sweden as part of a bilateral Swedish–US arrangement. From the early 1960s, a top-secret secure line was established between the Swedish Defence Staff and the US Air Force Headquarters in Wiesbaden to facilitate this operation. US attack and fighter aircraft would be redeployed from West Germany to the offensive 'unsinkable aircraft carrier' of southern Sweden with direct access to the Polish Lines of Communication, the Central Front and the Soviet heartland rather than to the defensive 'unsinkable aircraft carrier' of Great Britain. With this option, the Soviet Union would suddenly be extremely vulnerable, and it would have to divert its forces and go for a more defensive strategy. This option was of vital importance to the USA. According to Engman, Sweden was not believed to be able to stay out of a war in the long run, and this would have been the only possibility for Sweden to receive US support.[93] Later, Admiral Elmo Zumwalt spoke about an 'unofficial alliance' with Sweden,[94] and John Owen at the North European Office at the US State Department spoke about Sweden as 'plugged into NATO'.[95] In the 1970s and 1980s, US military forces and the Swedish Navy and Air Force intensified their common war preparations, while the political leadership seemed to lean more and more towards a neutral position in a war in order to avoid early destruction, because US use of Swedish airbases would certainly invite a Soviet nuclear attack. In November 1984, General Ljung wrote that SACEUR General William Rogers worried about Sweden's 'political line'. Henry Kissinger had the same view. Sweden was now, according to Kissinger, 'denied essential information', Ljung wrote.[96] However, the problem was the government and the Prime Minister. There had always been tension between some military officers and the political leadership. In the 1970s and even more in the 1980s, this tension became increasingly difficult.[97] When I asked former Secretary of Defense James Schlesinger about his view on Sweden, he responded: 'Which Sweden? The "political Sweden" or the "military Sweden"? The military were planning to get the USA involved as soon as possible.'[98]

In the 1980s, Swedish Prime Minister Olof Palme started to speak about a Nuclear Weapons-Free Zone. He certainly knew that the Soviet first priority was to destroy the NATO forces on the Central Front to reach the English Channel, not to mobilize a large force, particularly an air force and naval force, for a 'Swedish–Baltic Front'. The Soviets wanted to extend a buffer zone in northern Norway to defend the Kola bases, but an immediate attack on Sweden was not necessary as long as Sweden kept to its neutrality,[99] which, in case of a short war, might have saved Sweden. Or to quote Michael MccGwire: 'The Soviets are going to be very short of forces if war comes. And the last thing they'd want to do is to get bogged down in an unnecessary war on the northern flank.'[100] However, a Swedish decision to stay neutral, to avoid early destruction, would have kept the Swedish Air Force and Navy from entering the war, and it would have denied a forward deployment of US aircraft, which from day one would totally have changed the strategic equation. Schlesinger's statement indicates that it was believed that the 'political Sweden' would avoid a war if not attacked by the Soviets, while the 'military Sweden', or at least vital groups within the Swedish military forces, planned for a direct Swedish involvement. That Sweden would stay out of a war if not attacked was also the understanding within NATO.[101] And even though the Soviets certainly also had plans for an attack on Sweden in an early phase, they would try to avoid a new US–Swedish front. From this perspective, Swedish Prime Minister Palme would have denied the US forces a vital advantage. To create a Swedish perception of a 'Soviet attack' by the use of submarines, SDVs and Navy SEALs masquerading as Soviet Spetsnaz forces was the logical US move: both to facilitate a Swedish demand for US intervention and to facilitate the takeover by the Swedish pro-US elite. Similarly to the Joint Chiefs of Staff proposal of March 1962 of a US covert landing of 'Cuban' arms caches on the beaches of the Dominican Republic and a US use of MiG-type aircraft with US pilots to attack the Dominican Republic to create the impression of a Cuban attack on the country, the Americans in the 1980s would have prepared for an attack with submarines and Navy SEALs masquerading as Soviet forces to create the impression of a Soviet attack on Sweden.

A 'swift elimination of the Swedish Government and High Command by the specialist assassination group', as described above by Lynn Hansen and John Moore, would immediately make Swedish military leaders ask for US support. And to facilitate this operation, it would be necessary, even in peacetime, to prepare Swedish Military Intelligence and public opinion for the coming of a Soviet Spetsnaz attack in the very first minutes of a war. US peacetime operations with submarines and special force swimmers in Swedish archipelagos should accordingly also be understood as a psychological preparation for a wartime contingency. There is no proof yet that this was the US intention, but this option was, according to high-ranking officers in NATO countries, far from unlikely, and given the general strategic framework the US sub-surface activities in Swedish waters are very logical. They would 'raise the awareness' of a possible imminent Soviet attack. To enhance security by carrying out 'test operations', as described by Caspar Weinberger, Sir Keith Speed and Sir John Walker, may 'not have been the primary mission'. It may just have 'been part of the cover', to paraphrase former Red Cell officer Steve Hartman. When I interviewed former Minister of Defence Anders Thunborg, he said: 'In the event of war, we had several options and the decision making was in our hands.'[102] However, it is not likely that the Americans would have felt confident with such uncertainty. Or as a Norwegian Defence Ministry official told me: 'Sweden tried to ride two horses, but instead it may have fallen in between them.'

The operation in Hårsfjärden may have been a preparation for a wartime contingency with major implications for a European war. However, even the peacetime consequences of these operations may have been vital for European political change, particularly in northern Europe, where the role of Swedish Social Democracy was still important. The year 1982 was the one when the other Scandinavian states Norway and Denmark, as well as West Germany, Holland and Belgium, had a harsh debate on the deployment of medium-range missiles. The West German Chancellor Helmut Schmidt supported the deployment of the missiles, but he became more and more isolated in his own Social Democratic Party. In Norway, the Labour Party became ever more critical towards deployment, and a Conservative Party proposal in support of the missiles passed in Parliament by only one vote.[103] The anti-missile opinion within the Social Democratic parties was strong, and the 'Soviet submarine intrusions' deep into Swedish archipelagos and Norwegian fjords would most likely have changed this opinion in favour of accepting deployment. The Soviet threat was perceived as extremely worrying. The Hårsfjärden hunt was prime news on US and European TV channels and first-page news in US and European major newspapers. The German Liberal Party was at this very time discussing a change of alliance from the Social Democrats to the Christian Democratic Party, which made the pro-American Helmut Kohl the new Chancellor. The provocative 'Soviet submarine intrusions' against a neutral country with close ties to the German Social Democrats definitely facilitated such a change. In other words, it changed the general German policy more in line with the US administration of the 1980s.

US decision makers may also have believed that activities along the Swedish coast could influence European views on the controversial gas pipeline from the Soviet Union. Up to the early 1990s, the massive submarine intrusions into Swedish waters were seemingly used to justify a hard-line policy against the Soviets. In 1990, *US News and World Report* expressed doubts about the much-publicized defensive strategy of Mikhail Gorbachev, while he was playing a risky game in Swedish waters. Referring to McCormick's Rand report, they argued that the Soviet subs came in all sizes – about 30 a year – but Sweden refused to point a finger at Moscow. They asked: 'Why are the Swedes so timid?'[104] Later the same year, Jack Anderson and Dale van Atta wrote in the *Washington Post*, referring to CIA sources, that the submarine 'incidents in Swedish waters have continued at a rate of 30 or more a year, and they have become even more daring'. This Soviet arrogance was, according to Anderson and van Atta, an argument for not taking Gorbachev's 'courting of Western Europe' seriously.[105] From a US point of view, provocative submarine intrusions deep into Swedish waters may have been instrumental for several reasons. Or to quote Luttwak once again: these 'incidents were certainly very helpful'.[106]

If the submarine operations in Hårsfjärden 1982 were under CIA/DIA command using Navy SEAL task forces, which resulted in a seriously damaged submarine and one, possible two, lightly damaged submarines or submersibles, then this would explain why the SEALs at this very time received an undetectable satellite communications system linked into the White House. All intelligence officers I have spoken with say that this would have been a White House operation, not just a military operation. If the SEALs carried out strictly military operations, it would have been enough to have a portable communication link to the Pentagon. Obviously, the SEALs carried out unconventional operations that also had major political implications – operations supervised by Oliver North at the White House FLASHBOARD crisis alert network.[107] There may be several kinds of operations that have had such implications, but there is little doubt that the SEALs became a political instrument of the White House used to change popular feelings as well as government politics in various countries.

In this delicate game, the lack of a visible Soviet threat was supplemented by a covert US activity representing the 'real Soviets'. Masquerading as Soviet forces, the US teams seem to have been able to create what Baudrillard[108] called a 'hyperreality' with its own invented history adapted to real conflicts. US actions seem to have formed a Swedish 'hyperreality' that corresponded better to US perceptions of the real world than the 'reality' the Swedes had formerly believed in. In a democratic country, propaganda in its traditional form is not very credible, because it is countered by counterarguments and by experience. Instead, experience and real physical incidents have to be created as a 'false reality' or 'new reality' to make public opinion as well as political and military leaders aware of a 'hidden reality': the Soviet threat. According to Schelling, 'words are cheap and not inherently credible . . . [while actions] carry some evidence of their own credibility'.[109] Indicators have to be 'physical' to change the mindset, to quote Admiral Lyons. Or once again to quote the US Defense Department documents on special forces and deception: '[they should seek] *to create* or increase *the likelihood of detection of certain indicators* in order to cause an adversary to derive an incorrect conclusion' and 'to influence their emotions, motives, objective reasoning and ultimately the behavior of foreign governments' to shift their loyalties to support the USA and US objectives in the area.[110] All indicators created should support the 'deception story', and, if anything should go wrong, 'cover stories provide plausible explanations for activities that cannot be hidden'.[111]

In Western democratic countries, public opinion has become extremely important. Foreign policy is formed by public opinion and the mass media's presentation of actual incidents. To create incidents, where your own forces operate under cover of being the opposite, may create the necessary public indignation at the right moment to change public opinion and enable the carrying out of a specific policy in the name of the international community. US forces under cover of being Soviet forces seem to have operated in Sweden to change both Swedish government policy and public opinion. It made Prime Minister Palme's international political initiative impotent. It made the idea of Swedish political neutralism in security issues difficult, and it turned large parts of the population, not least within the military forces, against the conciliatory government. If this is true, this must have been one of the most successful covert operations of the Cold War.

NOTES

1 Agrell (2000), pp. 123–7.
2 Ibid., p. 124.
3 Ibid., pp. 124–6.
4 Ibid., pp. 113–15, 254–6.
5 Lindfors (1996), pp. 229–62.
6 Foster (1998 [1987]), p. 156.
7 Jansson (1996).
8 Stütz (1987), p. 64.
9 Ibid., p. 64.
10 Ibid., p. 83.
11 Foster (1998 [1987]), p. 156.
12 BBC Special, *Gladio Part III, The Foot Soldiers* (10 June 1992).
13 Video: *Red Cell* (1993).
14 Ibid.
15 BBC Special, *Gladio Part III, The Foot Soldiers* (10 June 1992).
16 Ibid.
17 Bale (1995).
18 Birindelli (1980), p. 192.
19 See for example Lundin *et al.* (1996).
20 Stubblefield (1995), p. 145.
21 Dwyer (1992), pp. 107–32.
22 Joint Pub 3-05.3 (1993).
23 Quoted in Kelly (1992), p. 285.

24 Lindqvist (1997), pp. 360–1.
25 Owen (1978), pp. 24–5.
26 Ibid., p. 183.
27 Joint Chiefs of Staff (1962), pp. 5–9.
28 Ibid., p. 2.
29 Bamford (2002), pp. 81–91, 295–301.
30 Edwards (1992), pp. 56–62; Shultz (1999), pp. 189–92. Shultz (1999, pp. 191–2) writes: 'On July 30, four [SEAL] boats headed north to bombard North Vietnamese targets . . . Both missions shelled their targets – a gun emplacement and military structures and a communication station – before returning south with North Vietnamese Swatows in hot pursuit.

'These attacks played a key role in Hanoi's decision to attack *Maddox* . . . The North Vietnamese strikes led to the Gulf of Tonkin Resolution, which set a stage for an escalation of US involvement in the Vietnam War. However, the incident did not result in an actual decision to escalate. The Johnson administration had already determined that it was necessary. The incident was the vehicle through which the president was able to act on what he already had decided.'

Maddox was never hit by the Vietnamese, and the attack on *Maddox* may just have been one of several incidents useful to justify an escalation. However, firstly, the policy of deploying *Maddox* just off the coast of North Vietnam while secretly attacking the coast would sooner or later have led to an incident that would make an escalation acceptable also to the public. Secondly, a report of a second attack on *Maddox* two days after was most likely manufactured by the US authorities. According to Bamford (2002) and according to Vice-Admiral James B. Stockdale (1998, pp. 15–17), who covered the area from the air during this incident, it never took place.
31 Joint Pub 3-58 (1996), p. I-4.
32 Ibid., pp. II-4, IV-6.
33 Ibid., Appendix A, pp. A-2, A-3, A-4.
34 Ibid., pp. I-3, II-3, II-4.
35 Joint Pub 3-53 (1996), pp. I-1, I-5, I-7, IV-2, GL-4.
36 SAP VU meeting (1983).
37 Joint Pub 3-53 (1996), pp. vi, II-1.
38 Paddock (1989), pp. 58–65.
39 *Göteborgs-Posten* (17 February 1983).
40 Joint Pub 3-58 (1996), p. II-4.
41 ÖB TD (23 November 1983).
42 *Jane's Fighting Ships* (1984–85), p. 121.
43 *Jane's Fighting Ships* (1985–86), p. 137; see also 1986–87, p. 123.
44 Moore interviewed in *Dagens Nyheter* (23 August 1984).
45 Ellis (1986), pp. 94–101.
46 Erickson on *Aktuellt*, Swedish TV1 (12 January 1986).
47 Erickson in *Dagens Nyheter* (13 January 1986).
48 Leitenberg (1987).
49 McCormick (1990).
50 Leitenberg (1987), back cover.
51 Moore and Compton-Hall (1986), p. 222.
52 Berkowitz (1988), pp. 14–15.
53 Miller and Jordan (1987), p. 192.
54 Compton-Hall (1988), pp. 86, 156–62.
55 Welham (1989), p. 54.
56 Kemp (1996), p. 223.

57 Luttwak and Koehl (1991), p. 395.
58 Leitenberg (1987), pp. 19–20.
59 Ibid., pp. 109, 155–57.
60 McCormick (1990).
61 Department of Defense (1981–89).
62 Department of Defense (1983).
63 McCormick (1990), pp. v, 24, vi.
64 Holmström (1988).
65 Von Hofsten (1993), pp. 83–4.
66 Sköld (1999), p. 165.
67 *Svenska Dagbladet* (10 November 1985).
68 Swedish TV (11 November 1985).
69 Von Hofsten (1993), pp. 118, 200–4.
70 *Striptease*, Swedish TV2 (31 March 1999).
71 *Striptease*, Swedish TV2 (12 October 1999).
72 *Striptease*, Swedish TV2 (31 March 1999).
73 *Norra Magasinet*, Swedish TV1 (21 February 1996).
74 Peterson (1999), p. 557.
75 Taylor (1982b), p. 415.
76 Taylor (1983), pp. 44–5.
77 Taylor (1982a), p. 120.
78 Lars Werner, on *Rapport*, Swedish TV2; *Aktuellt*, Swedish TV1 (26 April 1983).
79 Taylor and Maaranen (1982), p. 475.
80 Schelling (1966), p. 150.
81 *Striptease*, Swedish TV2 (31 March 1999).
82 Luttwak (1989), pp. 163–4.
83 Iklé (1989), pp. 3–11.
84 Watkins (1986), p. 5.
85 Turner (1985), p. 173; see also Gates (1997), p. 213.
86 Schweizer (1994), pp. viii, 8.
87 Ibid., pp. 160–5.
88 Kelly (1992), p. 285.
89 NSC 6006/1 (6 April 1960), p. 8; SOU (1994): 11 (Bilagor), p. 140.
90 SOU (2002), p. 710; SOU 2002, Appendix 5: 'Guidelines . . .'.
91 Interview with Almgren (1993) for SOU 1994: 11.
92 Engman said that he received this information as a close adviser to Defence Minister Sven Andersson (1957–73), not as a senior official at the Defence Ministry. He believes that no civil servant was informed. Only the military supreme commanders and chiefs of staff and a handful of political leaders knew: Prime Minister Tage Erlander (1946–69), Defence (1951–57) and later Foreign Minister (1962–71) Torsten Nilsson and Defence (1957–73) and later Foreign Minister (1973–76) Sven Andersson as well as the later Prime Minister Olof Palme (1969–76 and 1982–86) and Andersson's State Secretary and later Defence Minister Anders Thunborg (1983–85). Foreign Ministers like Östen Undén (1945–62) and Krister Wickman (1971–73) were, according to Engman, never informed. Engman came in 1967 from the Military Intelligence Service IB (later SSI) to the Defence Ministry to be responsible for defence material, research and the classified accounts. In 1974, he was a candidate to replace Birger Elmér as Chief of IB (1957–74), but he continued as Assistant Under-Secretary of Defence for Defence Material (Tunander, 1999, pp. 178–9; Tunander, 2000b, pp. 434–5).
93 Interview with Ingemar Engman (1993) for SOU 1994: 11; Tunander (1999), pp. 178–9.

94 Quoted in Zackheim (1998).
95 Quoted in Leifland (1997), p. 108.
96 ÖB TD (21 November 1984).
97 Tunander (1999), pp. 169–203; Tunander (2000a), pp. 98–101.
98 Discussion with James Schlesinger, 16–18 June 1993. In my notebook, I wrote that Mr Schlesinger said: 'Which Sweden? The "political Sweden" or the "military Sweden"? The military wanted us to come as soon as possible.' I called Mr Schlesinger on 16 November 1998 and asked if I could quote him on that. He confirmed this statement but wanted to change the last sentence: 'The military were planning to get the USA involved as soon as possible.'
99 MccGwire (1987), pp. 132–53.
100 Quoted in Leitenberg (1987), p. 146.
101 Petersson (2002), pp. 73–88.
102 Tunander (1999), p. 198.
103 Tamnes (1997), p. 124.
104 Stanglin with Bartal (1990), p. 41.
105 Anderson and van Atta (1990).
106 *Striptease*, Swedish TV2 (31 March 1999).
107 Lofthus and Aarons (1994), pp. 463–4.
108 Baudrillard (1975).
109 Schelling (1966), p. 150.
110 Joint Pub 3-05 (1998), p. II-8.
111 Joint Pub 3-58 (1996), p. II-4.

Appendix I

Sources – Archival Material and Interviews

This volume is based upon interviews with a number of the main actors from the Hårsfjärden submarine hunt together with other senior officers and political leaders, as well as upon texts primarily from formerly classified Swedish documents: private diaries, war diaries, intelligence reports, internal investigations and other military documents. This work has been supplemented with information from memoirs and a couple of popular and academic studies, together with Swedish and other newspapers. The combination of archival material and interviews has been most important for my work. I have not used US, UK or Russian archives, because I believe it is unlikely that relevant information will be found in these archives at such an early stage.

ARCHIVAL MATERIAL

I have used the hearings on the Hårsfjärden submarine hunt for the Swedish Parliamentary Standing Committee on the Constitution (KU 1982/83:30) and an attachment that includes an interview with Sven Hirdman, Ambassador and former State Secretary for Defence (KU 1982/83:30, Attach. 7). Hirdman was one of the few Swedish specialists on small US submersibles and one of the few Swedes with contact in this community.[1] I have also used the official report of the Swedish Parliamentary Submarine Defence Commission (SOU 1983), which was under the chairmanship of Sven Andersson, former Minister of Defence and Minister of Foreign Affairs, with the Conservative MP Carl Bildt as a main contributor, Bildt's later State Secretary for Defence Michael Sahlin as its secretary, and Chief of Staff Vice-Admiral Bror Stefenson as its military expert. Andersson's commission was appointed immediately after the Hårsfjärden incident, and it presented its report on 26 April 1983. I have also used the report of the later 1995 Submarine Commission (SOU 1995), which was appointed by Minister of Defence Thage G. Peterson because of renewed debate on the submarine incidents in the 1990s and major criticism of the first official version. The chairman of this commission was Professor Hans G. Forsberg with former Chief of Military Intelligence Major-General Bengt Wallroth and Ingvar Åkesson from the Parliamentary Standing Committee on the Constitution as its secretaries. Furthermore, I have used the report from Ambassador Rolf Ekéus's investigation (SOU 2001), which was appointed by Prime Minister Göran Persson. Ekéus had access to the Military Intelligence Service archives, and he carried out a large number of interviews with civil servants and former ministers but primarily with military officers. As an expert to the Ekéus investigation I had access to much of the archival material. Parts of the material is now declassified (Ekéus Investigation Files) and stored in the Swedish National Archive. As with the 1983 Commission, Ekéus had one of the chiefs of operations, Rear-Admiral Göran Wallén, as his military expert.

The Swedish War Archive gave me access to former Commander-in-Chief General Lennart Ljung's diary (1978–86), which consists of three volumes. For the Hårsfjärden incident, this diary exists in both a hand-written version (ÖB HWD) and a typed version (ÖB TD). The two versions are often very different. The hand-written version is shorter, but seemingly more accurate. The typed version is much longer and has obviously been adjusted. Ljung let his secretary, Margareta Hård, type out his original hand-written manuscript, and it was not always the most interesting things that she typed out, she informed me. Ljung has obviously adjusted the text, particularly the typed version, to suit the public. In 1990, it was more or less ready, and he went to the Swedish War Archive to discuss the practicalities of handing over the manuscript. Soon afterwards, Ljung died from cancer. His son checked with the Defence Staff and handed it over to the Military Security Service to let them make a security examination. It was kept at the Defence Staff for four years before being requested by the War Archive and made available for researchers. The personnel at the War Archive know nothing about any censorship or changes in the text made by the Security Service. We know from the Hårsfjärden case, however, that Ljung's hand-written text has been 'corrected', or rather rewritten, in his typed version.

Other major sources are Rear-Admiral Christer Kierkegaard's war diary for Muskö Naval Base (CÖrlBO WD) and his intelligence reports (CÖrlBO INT). The war diary follows the submarine hunt minute by minute with about ten but sometimes up to 50 entries per hour. The war diary reports observations and indications as well as orders. It was written by hand and printed out later. The same is the case with Lieutenant-Colonel Sven-Olof Kviman's war diary for the mine troops and for the Coastal Defence base at Mälsten (CMS WD).

This document has been very useful. The hand-written version (CMS HWD) has been an important supplement. Some incidents at Mälsten are presented in special reports (CMS Reports). There is also an important report from the helicopter Y46 (Y46 Report) and a war diary from patrol boat 77 (Bev 77 WD). In addition, the protocol of the tape-recorded sounds from the bottom-fixed sonar system at Mälsten (MAFU Report) and the protocol of the speaker channel from these tapes (FOA Tape 0–6) provide important information. Under the Chief of Mälsten were the local chiefs of the single mine barrages, including the Chief of MS2, Johan Eneroth and his war diary (CMS2 WD). The Coastal Defence base at Mälsten received orders from and reported directly to Muskö Naval Base, but Mälsten also received orders and reported in general terms to Stockholm Coastal Defence Staff in Vaxholm. The report from the Coastal Defence Staff (from Brigadier-General Lars Hansson and his Chief of Staff Lieutenant-Colonel Jan Svenhager) documents these orders (SCSK Report). The above-mentioned reports and war diaries often supplement and confirm each other. They have given me important insights. However, they do not give a total picture of the activities of the time. A number of pieces of information may not appear in these documents because, in intensive 'battle situations', priority is given to operative activity, not to notes made for war diaries. Many indications may also turn out to be false indications, and the material has to be analysed afterwards. Like the Mälsten Coastal Defence Base, all local commands and ships made their own war diaries and they reported directly to Muskö Naval Base. However, I have only been able to locate a few of these war diaries. For example, I made an effort to find the war diary for the submarine rescue vessel *Belos*, but this document does not exist in any of the Swedish military archives. It is either in private hands or has been destroyed. According to some sources, much of this material has actually been destroyed.

Both the naval base at Muskö and the Coastal Defence Staff in Vaxholm were supposed to report to the Commander of the Eastern Military District, Lieutenant-General Bengt Lehander, who formally speaking should have been the supreme commander for this kind operation. It is accordingly logical that the war diary of the Eastern Military District (MBÖ WD) should be used, as it was, for drafting the Submarine Defence Commission Report (SOU 1983). Captain Göran Wallén, Chief of Section 1 (Operations) Eastern Military District, and later military expert to Ambassador Rolf Ekéus, was a friend of Michael Sahlin, the secretary of the Submarine Defence Commission, which facilitated this cooperation. However, more sensitive information never reached the Eastern Military District. This information was given directly to the Chief of Staff (see below). Chief of Staff Eastern

Military District Major-General Gustaf Welin argued that they were shunted aside by the Defence Staff, which actually made the war diary of the Eastern Military District less relevant for understanding the day-by-day unfolding of events.

At the Defence Staff, the division receiving information from and preparing orders for operations – including anti-submarine operations in the archipelago – was OPG (Operativt Genomförande [Carrying Out Operations]). Chief of OPG Lieutenant-Colonel Håkan Söderlindh wrote the Defence Staff war diary (COPG WD), also called the Commander-in-Chief war diary, which documents orders to and information received from the commanders in the field. I have not had access to this war diary, but, for the more sensitive hours on 13–14 October, the pages in both the hand-written and typed versions have disappeared (SOU 2001, p. 118). Söderlindh also wrote the highly classified 'green-sealed report' (higher than top-secret) on the Hårsfjärden incident for the Minister of Defence Börje Andersson. However, this report has seemingly been destroyed. Furthermore, most sensitive information seems to have been forwarded directly to the Chief of Staff without passing through OPG, sometimes because the Chief of Staff, Vice-Admiral Bror Stefenson, went by helicopter to the naval base to act as a 'local commander' while short-cutting the line of information, sometimes because he seems to have received information directly from his 'private chief of intelligence' at the naval base, Chief of the Naval Analysis Group Commander Emil Svensson.

On 1 October, when the Hårsfjärden hunt started, Commander Svensson and his group were put at the disposal of the Chief of the Naval Base, Rear-Admiral Kierkegaard. Svensson seems to have received much of the most sensitive information. According to his own testimony, the sceptical approach of Commander Björn Eklind, Deputy Chief of Defence Staff Intelligence, had made it necessary for Stefenson and Vice-Admiral Rudberg to create their own intelligence organization that could follow the events. Emil Svensson was their natural choice to head this group. Other members of the group were Lieutenant-Colonel Rolf Malm, Commander Anders Hammar and Lieutenant-Commander Nils-Ove Jansson. This so-called Naval Analysis Group (Marinens Analysgrupp) made a special report about the day-by-day events in Hårsfjärden. This main report (MAna Hårsfj) exists in several versions (one from 29 October 1982, one from December 1982 and one supplementary version from February 1983). They have a number of attachments including interviews with observers (MAna Hårsfj Attach.). There are also three larger attachments: one on the unfolding of events at Mälsten put together by Lieutenant-Commander Ebbe Sylvén, one on the Defence Research Establishment (FOA) Report of the tape-recorded sounds at Mälsten (MAna Hårsfj FOA) drafted by Bengt

Granath, Director of the Passive Sonar Division at FOA, and one on the report from the sea-floor investigation (MAna Hårsfj RABu) made by Commander Dick Börjesson and Lieutenant Kent Pejdell. This latter attachment is supplemented by a report on the sea-floor print for SOU 1995 made by Cato and Larsson. The main Naval Analysis Group Report classifies the observations as '[certain] submarine', 'possible submarine' or 'not submarine', or as something in between these categories. In many respects, this report supplements the war diaries, but it has also to a large extent been filtered. Some of the most clear indications, or even evidence, of submarines have been excluded from this report, even though, according to the naval base war diary, Svensson received this information. This filtered report was used by the Defence Staff and the Submarine Defence Commission (SOU 1983), which created a distorted version of the whole incident. My comparison between the above-mentioned war diaries and reports has been supplemented by interviews with important actors and by notes and diaries made by some of these actors.

The main report by the Naval Analysis Group is included as an attachment to the Swedish Navy's internal investigation on this submarine hunt. The investigation was chaired by Rear-Admiral Gunnar Grandin, with Brigadier-General Sven-Åke Adler as his deputy (CM/Grandin, 1982). Already during the submarine hunt (13 October), Grandin was asked by the Chief of the Navy, Vice-Admiral Per Rudberg, to make an investigation. The report was presented for the Chief of the Navy on 3 December 1982. The main report and the attachments are often contradictory, because different authors were responsible for different parts. A couple of attachments deal with weapons systems and development. Attachment 2 covers the day-by-day events and is identical to the Naval Analysis Group's special report on day-by-day events, indicating that a member of the first group, Commander Anders Hammar, was also a member of the second. The Grandin Report has been very useful when writing about these events.

I have used a memorandum on the Hårsfjärden submarine hunt written by Rear-Admiral Christer Kierkegaard, Commander Lars-Erik Hoff and Commander Rolf Blomquist (Kierkegaard, Hoff and Blomquist, 1990), an article in the Swedish *Royal Naval Society Journal* by Rear-Admiral Göran Wallén written in a dialogue with myself (Wallén, 2002) and retired Captain Emil Svensson's report from the Swedish–Russian submarine dialogue in the early 1990s, while Captain Svensson was the military adviser to Prime Minister Carl Bildt (Svensson, 1995). Some comparative information has been used from the Commander-in-Chief report on the Karlskrona submarine hunt of 1984 (Kierkegaard *et al.*, 1984). This latter report was written under the chairmanship of Rear-Admiral Christer Kierkegaard, with later

Lieutenant-General Lars-G. Persson and Lieutenant-General Gustaf Welin as members, and with later Deputy Commander-in-Chief Rear-Admiral Frank Rosenius as its secretary. This report exists today in a shorter 'revised version'.

I have also had access to the notes from the meetings between, on the one hand, Commander-in-Chief General Ljung and Chief of Staff Vice-Admiral Bror Stefenson and, on the other hand, Prime Minister Olof Palme (and his closest advisers). These notes were written down by Palme's State Secretary Ulf Larsson (UL 82; UL 83). Furthermore, I have used Lieutenant-General Lars-G. Persson's hand-written diary for the Hårsfjärden submarine hunt (LGB HWD), Brigadier-General Lars Hansson's 'Diary' as it was presented by the magazine Z five years later (Kadhammar, 1987) and the diary of the Conservative Party leader Ulf Adelsohn (1987). Leading Social Democrats' analysis of the submarine activity is expressed in the minutes from the Social Democratic Party Executive Committee meeting from May 1983 (SAP VU 1983). I have also used the memoirs of Ingvar Carlsson (1999), former Prime Minister and leader of the Social Democratic Party, the memoirs of former Foreign Minister Lennart Bodström (2000), an academic report on the 'Bodström case' by Lars Olof Lampers (1996), and an academic report and article about the Hårsfjärden submarine hunt written by Fredrik Bynander (1998a; 1998b). There are also several articles by Olle Alsén, Christer Larsson and Wilhelm Agrell, and books by Agrell (1986), Anders Hasselbohm (1984), Milton Leitenberg (1987) and Tommy Lindfors (1996), who all cover these events. Most important, however, have been Jonas Olsson's interviews with former US Secretary of Defense Caspar Weinberger, former Chief of BALTAP Lieutenant-General Kjeld Hillingsø, and former British Minister of the Navy Sir Keith Speed.

ACTORS AND INTERVIEWS

I have interviewed most of the actors from the submarine hunt in Hårsfjärden. Several of them have given extensive interviews. Others have been more restrained. Many actors have probably not told me everything and, with some, I have only had short telephone conversations. Still, these interviews have given me essential pieces of information, which have supplemented the archival material. However, almost all of the most senior actors are no longer alive, including former Prime Minister Olof Palme; former Defence Minister Börje Andersson; the Chairman of the 1983 Submarine Defence Commission (and former Minister of both Defence and Foreign Affairs) Sven Andersson; former Commander-in-Chief General Lennart Ljung; former Chief of the

Army Lieutenant-General Nils Sköld; former Commander of the Eastern Military District Lieutenant-General Bengt Lehander; former Chief of Naval Staff Major-General Bo Varenius; former Chief of Naval Base East Rear-Admiral Christer Kierkegaard; the co-chairman of the Navy's internal investigation Brigadier-General Sven-Åke Adler; and former Norwegian Commander-in-Chief General Sven Hauge, who was in Sweden during this incident. This has made it difficult to get a true picture of what happened at the top level. However, many other actors are still alive, and I have interviewed most of the officers mentioned below.

On 1 October, when the submarine hunt in Hårsfjärden started, there was a major pre-scheduled reshuffling of positions among the military personnel. Chief of Staff Vice-Admiral Bengt Schuback (CFst) became Commander of the Southern Military District (MBS) and replaced Lieutenant-General Sven-Olov Olsson, who became Chief of the Air Force (CFV); Chief of the Coastal Fleet Rear-Admiral Bror Stefenson (CFK) was promoted to vice-admiral and replaced Admiral Schuback as Chief of Staff (CFst); Chief of Staff, Western Military District, Captain Jan Enquist was promoted to rear-admiral and replaced Admiral Stefenson as Chief of the Coastal Fleet (CFK); Rear-Admiral Ola Backman became Chief of Navy Material (at the Swedish Defence Material), replacing Rear-Admiral Gunnar Grandin, who retired and became chairman of the Navy investigation of the submarine hunt; Chief of Defence Staff Planning Division Major-General Bengt Lehander was promoted to lieutenant-general and became Commander of the Eastern Military District (MBÖ), where he replaced Lieutenant-General Gunnar Eklund, who retired; Captain Göran Wallén was made Chief of Section 1 (Operations), Eastern Military District, where he replaced Lieutenant-Colonel Birger Jägtoft; Chief of Operation Division 4 (OP4) at the Defence Staff Brigadier-General Lars Hansson was made Chief of Stockholm Coastal Defence (CSK), where he replaced Brigadier-General Sven-Åke Adler, who retired and became Rear-Admiral Grandin's co-investigator; Chief of Defence Staff Operations (at Operation Division 2, OP2) Lieutenant-Colonel Urban Sobeus was replaced by Lieutenant-Colonel Håkan Söderlindh (from the Coastal Defence School); and his Chief of the Readiness Unit, Lieutenant-Colonel Hans Wärn, was replaced by Major Ulf Mähler; Chief of Section 1 (Operations), Naval Base East, Commander Per-Gunnar Svensson was replaced by Commander Rolf Blomquist from the Military Staff School; Lieutenant-Colonel Rolf Malm was replaced as Chief of Naval Intelligence by Lieutenant-Commander Nils-Ove Jansson, who also became a member of the Naval Analysis Group. Many other replacements were also made. All of this happened on 1 October.[2]

Other major figures in this submarine hunt were Commander-in-Chief General Lennart Ljung (ÖB); Chief of the Navy Vice-Admiral Per Rudberg (CM); Chief of Naval Staff Major-General Bo Varenius; Chief of Staff, Eastern Military District, Major-General Gustaf Welin (SCÖ); Chief of Defence Staff, Operation Division 5 (OP 5, Intelligence), Captain Ulf Samuelsson (who a few months earlier had replaced Major-General Bengt Wallroth, who was promoted to Chief of SSI and was soon to become Deputy Chief of Staff); Deputy Chief of Defence Staff Intelligence (OP 5) Commander Björn Eklind; Chief of Defence Staff Security Division Commander Erland Sönnerstedt; Chief of the Navy Information Division Commander Sven Carlsson; Chief of the Navy Unit at the Defence Staff Operation Division (OP 2) Lieutenant-Commander Carl-Johan Arfvidson; Chief of Naval Operations, Eastern Military District, Commander Bengt Gabrielsson (CSjöop); Chief of Naval Base East Rear-Admiral Christer Kierkegaard (CÖrlBO); Chief of Staff, Naval Base East, Commander Lars-Erik Hoff (SCÖrlBO); Chief of the Tactical Division, Naval Base East, Commander Nils Modig; Chief of Intelligence, Naval Base East, Commander Mauritz Carlsson; Chief of the First Helicopter Division at Berga Commander Eric Hagström; Chief of the Coastal Fleet First Submarine Flotilla Captain Rodrik Klintebo; Chief of the Attack Craft Division, Commander Gilbert de Wendel; Chief of the Coastal Defence Regiment KA1 Colonel Lars-G. Persson (CKA1); Chief of Staff, Stockholm Coastal Defence, Lieutenant-Colonel Jan Svenhager; Chief of Section 1 (Operations), Stockholm Coastal Defence, Lieutenant-Colonel Jan-Axel Thomelius; Chief of the Mine Troops and Commander of Mälsten Coastal Defence Base, Lieutenant-Colonel Sven-Olof Kviman (CMS); his deputy Captain Per Andersson; Chief of the Naval Analysis Group Commander Emil Svensson (CMAna); Chief of the Mine-Clearing Division and head of the sea-floor investigation that was carried out after the submarine hunt (later Chief of the Navy) Commander Dick Börjesson; his co-investigator and Chief of the First Diver Division Lieutenant Kent Pejdell; the captain of *Belos*, Lieutenant-Commander Björn Mohlin.[3]

PRINCIPLES FOR INTERVIEWS

As a student of naval strategy, I had already met a few of the above officers when I started to write this book. They were able to introduce me to other officers who had vital positions during the Hårsfjärden hunt. This also made it possible for me to meet many low-ranking officers with direct experience of the incident. In several cases, however, I just called the relevant officers because of their position at the time, which may have made them more cautious when talking with me. Some of the above officers have only given short comments. Others have given extensive interviews. Only two officers refrained from talking with me. I have considered these interviews as being on record. It is almost impossible to write about an incident if the actors could not be mentioned by name. However, in a couple of cases, when the information given was of a more delicate nature, I refrained from following this rule to avoid family tragedies. If I am not specific about whom an individual has given information to, he has spoken with me during interviews between 1995 and 2002. In general, I have not mentioned the date of the interview. One simple reason is that this would increase the number of references by up to a thousand. In cases of anonymous interviews, to give the date would sometimes also have made it easy to locate the individual. Almost all interviews have been carried out since 1995, when I started to collect information for this book. The majority of the interviews were carried out between 1998 and 2002, when I received close contact with officers directly involved in the Hårsfjärden operation. A few interviews were conducted on earlier occasions for other purposes, and some of those have been published before. However, these interviews were repeated with the same individuals afterwards.

I had a number of confidential interviews with civilian officials and military officers from various NATO countries. In these cases, I only mention the seniority of the officers or officials, and usually if they are an admiral or a general or belong to the CIA or other intelligence services. In some cases, I have met these officers, diplomats, NATO officials, former ministers or representatives from the intelligence community at seminars or international conferences. In other cases, I have been introduced to them by friends or by officers I already knew. Some individuals I have known for years and had regular talks with, like the above-mentioned Einar Ansteensen, who suddenly, after ten years, told me about US submarines in Swedish waters. One might argue that I have been persistent in my talks with US, British, Norwegian and Danish officers, but, compared to the interviews with Swedish officers, I have been less systematic. I have used the occasion when it has been presented to me. From a methodological point of view, this comes closer to an anthropological approach or a praxis used within the intelligence community: 'to just hang around', or rather to try to understand the way of thinking and to pick up some information here and there. For example, if one senior US officer, who was responsible for briefing his superior about submarine operations in Swedish waters, tells me about the US office conducting these operations, this should be understood as background information. It was certainly never meant for publication or quotation, and he would deny ever having said it. However, if you receive similar background information several times from several sources, you cannot neglect it. You have to present this information in one way or another. As long as the kind of source is presented and as long as these statements, in general terms, are supported by statements on record, and supplemented by archival material, I cannot see why this information should not be mentioned. Also, there does not seem to be an alternative to this method, because the relevant information will usually not appear in declassified documents or in interviews on record. If we just accepted the latter techniques, we would come up with a totally biased picture, which would have little relevance for the understanding of recent history. In this case, I believe, a traditional approach would give us not just a biased but a false picture, because 'perception management' including psychological operations also targets the scholarly community. Most sensitive information will not be declassified or will not appear on paper.[4] To generalize from declassified documents or interviews on record would by definition lead us nowhere as long as the responsible officials have made no mistakes.

Some of the officers and officials I have interviewed I have only met once or twice. Others have given more extensive interviews. Some of them have been commanders-in-chiefs, national chiefs of intelligence or the assistants or deputies to these chiefs, some have been naval intelligence officers, or national and regional chiefs, some have been national operative commanders or national chiefs of the navy, and some have been submarine commanders or senior anti-submarine officers; others have been civilians: prime ministers, defence ministers, senior national or NATO officials and directors of the CIA or their chiefs of division. Several senior officers – chiefs of the navy, chiefs of intelligence and senior submarine officers – have also reviewed my manuscript. Some officers have become close friends during these years. Although my contacts with these officers are known by the intelligence community and the security services, and although some statements may easily be located to them because of the very few people able to present a certain statement, they have asked not to be mentioned by name to avoid inconvenience. I have accepted that. However, I have felt free to give the names of officers and officials who have died during this process. One reason for inconvenience is certainly the worry within responsible authorities that certain statements would be linked publicly to the names of relevant civilian officials or military officers who are still alive.

NOTES

1 Hirdman (1969).
2 Swedish Defence Organisation, 'Rulla' (1982), 'Rulla' (1983).
3 Swedish Defence Organisation, 'Rulla' (1982), 'Rulla' (1983).
4 Tunander (1999).

Appendix II

Interview with Caspar Weinberger

(*Striptease*, Swedish TV2, 7 March 2000)

> *Swedish TV*: Did NATO have a motive for making an intrusion into Swedish waters?

> *Weinberger*: It would certainly be part of NATO's activities as a defensive alliance to ensure that there were defences in all parts of the area against Soviet submarine attacks. And there were undoubtedly instances where NATO was trying to ensure that there were adequate coastal defences maintained as part of the whole alliance defensive line. I noticed the former Prime Minister Carlsson made some statements about NATO preparing for war. This is quite wrong. NATO was preparing to defend against an attack being launched. NATO had no offensive capabilities and no offensive intentions.

> *Swedish TV*: But according to my information NATO tested the Swedish defence?

> *Weinberger*: I think they tested all defences from time to time to see if there were gaps that could encourage the Soviets; particularly after the Soviet submarine intrusion, they would be very likely to test, yes. [. . .]

> *Swedish TV*: But isn't it a political risk to send NATO submarines into Swedish waters?

> *Weinberger*: Well, I think there were consultations with the Swedish government. I don't know of any time when there was an intrusion of which the Swedish government was not aware.

> *Swedish TV*: So there was an agreement?

> *Weinberger*: Well, I don't know if there was an agreement, but there were consultations. It was generally understood by the countries, both

325

NATO and non-NATO members, that part of the NATO mission was to ensure there was capable defence against any kind of attack, primarily from the Soviets, which was the only country at that time that was capable or had any intentions of making an attack. In the course of carrying out that mission, in being sure we did have effective defences in order, it was necessary to test those from time to time. Just like if you want to know if a weapon is effective you have to test that weapon.

Swedish TV: But on what level was this agreement with Sweden?

Weinberger: I don't know if there was any specific agreement with Sweden. As far as I know there were consultations. I am not aware of any objections on the part of Sweden, or any of the other countries, except Libya; there it was an obvious objection to certain claims of freedom of navigation. I don't recall any formal agreement with Sweden. There may have been some before I took office in 1981, and there may have been some agreement before this time. But I know there was a mission of NATO to ensure that its defences were in order. [. . .] And indeed past history demonstrates that enemies of the alliance would be perfectly capable, and did use Swedish waters and anything else they found necessary. That was certainly the case in World War II. In the Cold War period, with the NATO alliance including Germany, the situation was obviously different, because we had a different enemy: the Soviet Union with hostile intentions and a huge navy and a very large submarine fleet, which was not only capable of intruding into Swedish waters but has done so many times. Obviously, it would be part of NATO's defensive mission to ensure that they have defences against that, should the Soviet Union have tried, as part of a general attack against the West, to launch any sort of attack against the Swedish area . . .

Swedish TV: But when NATO submarines made the intrusions into Swedish waters did they expect the Swedish Navy to use depth charges?

Weinberger: My understanding is that there were consultations and understandings that there were going to be various tests or there were going to be attempts to ensure that the defences in the Swedish areas were effective, and there was not to my knowledge any kind of confrontation between Sweden and NATO forces at any point.

Swedish TV: But the Swedes were chasing submarines all the time?

Weinberger: Well, it is normal for a country to ensure that its sovereign waters are not intruded, not invaded. And NATO's job was basically to protect all those waters against an attack, because an attack up there, that had succeeded, would threaten much more directly European sectors of NATO. But to my knowledge, there was no direct intrusion or testing of Swedish waters or defences without consultations with the Swedes. You are speaking of an agreement: I don't think there was any agreement, but I think there were consultations, which led to an understanding that – for an individual case, for a specific situation, a particular manoeuvre – it would be an agreement that that could be done. It was very much in Sweden's interest to have their waters protected, and it was certainly widely known that NATO was not going to invade Sweden or anything of that kind so there would be a very obvious interest on the Swedish government's part to make sure that they had all the help they needed, if they needed any, to protect their waters.

Swedish TV: On what level were these consultations?

Weinberger: Generally, they were Navy to Navy, the US Navy to the Swedish Navy, I believe. The Swedish Navy is part of the Swedish government and the US Navy is part of the US government. Responsible officials on both sides would have discussions, consultations, and agreements would flow from that, to make sure that they get all the help needed to protect the sovereignty of their waters. If for example Sweden had said that you must not have any intrusions of that area in this month that would certainly have been honoured and respected by NATO.

Swedish TV: But other areas would then be OK?

Weinberger: Well, it depends entirely on the response of the officials in charge of the negotiations. What I am saying is that at no time, to my knowledge, did NATO simply send a submarine directly into Swedish waters without consultations and prior discussions and agreements that that could be done. Under those circumstances, it was not a pressing problem. It was part of a routine, regular, scheduled series of defence testing that NATO did and indeed had to do to be responsible and liable. [It would have been irresponsible] if they hadn't done it.

Swedish TV: Were midget submarines included in these tests?

Weinberger: I don't know the level. I don't know the particular instruments used – whatever was discussed and consulted about. We had all different kinds of submarines. We also had to know where all the Soviet submarines were at any time, and we also had the capability of doing that. But that required that our large submarines were mobile and moving around and they did. But we did not intrude upon the sovereignty of any

NATO member or any other country. What was done was done based on the idea that this was part of the defence preparations that had to be made and had to be checked and brought up to date, to be kept up to date, and it was very much to Sweden's advantage and very much to NATO's advantage that this was done. My understanding is that this is what these consultations were all about, and I am not aware that Sweden at any time protested or that there was any intrusion that had not been earlier discussed and agreed upon, and what is agreed upon is not an intrusion.

Swedish TV: Have you discussed this with the Swedish Defence Minister or Prime Minister?

Weinberger: Did I? No, I did not. But I am sure there were standing instructions, and the Navy would not go into areas where they were . . . The general instructions to the Navy were; first, they were under NATO command – the units that were assigned to NATO (we had other units, of course). The procedure was that NATO would make the arrangements and permissions and other things that were necessary in order to perform the kind of testing that NATO had to do to ensure that NATO could carry out their mission, which was to defend against Soviet attack.

Swedish TV: When this 'Whiskey on the Rock' submarine was in the middle of a restricted area it took 12 hours for the Swedish Navy to notice it.

Weinberger: Well, it was a clear violation, and submarines can get in where they are not wanted, and that is exactly why we made this defensive testing and these defensive manoeuvres to ensure that they would not be able to do that without being detected. That particular submarine was in Swedish waters. It went aground in an area where it could not be denied that it was in Swedish waters. It was quite visible to everybody, and it was exactly the kind of thing that NATO was trying to test the defences so as not to permit it to happen. It was very much in Sweden's interest that that would not happen.

Swedish TV: All the people in Sweden believe that there were only Soviet submarines that made the intrusions into Swedish waters?

Weinberger: I think it was quite obvious that the submarines that came in that were not Soviet submarines, as I understand, came in after consultations and understandings that they would do particular tests that the Swedish government agreed they should do. I would not call that intrusions.

Swedish TV: What kind of cooperation was there between Sweden and NATO during these years?

Weinberger: Satisfactory. The mission of NATO was to not permit Soviet invasion or attacks. The consultations and discussions we had were designed – with all countries, not just Sweden – to ensure that NATO was able to perform this mission and had ample opportunities to test through manoeuvres and other activities as to whether the defences were adequate and whether or not the Soviets were requiring any new capabilities that would require any changes in their defences or anything of that kind. So, the result of all that I think was very satisfactory. Besides that one intrusion of the Whiskey-class submarine, there were no violations, no capabilities of the Soviets to make an attack that could not be defended against, and that was the mission of NATO, and it required the cooperation of many countries, which we had, and I would say it was completely satisfactory.

Swedish TV: What you are saying is that you are not denying that US midget submarines went deep into Swedish archipelago areas?

Weinberger: It is not a matter of admitting or denying. It is a matter of discussing the preparations that were taken to make sure defences were adequate against Soviet attack. I have no idea whether midget submarines were used or large submarines or attack submarines or nuclear or whatever. The point was that it was necessary to test frequently the capabilities of all countries, not only in the Baltic [Sea] – which is very strategic, of course – but in the Mediterranean and Asiatic waters and all the rest . . . defences against the Soviet capabilities and Soviet intentions. We had to know what their intentions were. We had to gather intelligence. We had to test from time to time to make sure that our defensive planning was adequate and up to date and capable of resisting any changes in Soviet strength and Soviet capabilities, and that was done on a regular basis. And it was not just done in the sea. It was done on air defences and on land defences, and it was done to protect possible landing areas. The whole thing was satisfactory, and when I say satisfactory I mean there was no Soviet invasion. That was the test.

Swedish TV: How frequently was it done in Sweden?

Weinberger: I don't know. Enough to comply with the military requirements for making sure that they were up to date. We would know when the Soviets required a new kind of submarine. We would then have to see if our defences were adequate against that. And all this was done on a regular basis, and on an agreed-upon basis.

Appendix III

Swedish Naval Forces Mentioned in Chapter 3

Submarines
Shu Sjöhunden (sonar) 51 metres
Shä Sjöhästen (not in use) 51 metres
Näc Näcken (not in use) 55.5 (49.5) metres

Destroyers
J18 Halland (only sonar) 121 metres
J19 Småland (retired) 121 metres
J23 Hälsingland (retired) 112 metres

Fast Attack Craft (Missile)
(Depth charges and reconnaissance)
P 154 Mode (36 metres)
P 158 Mysing (36 metres)
P 159 Kaparen (36 metres)
P 160 Väktaren (36 metres)
P 161 Snapphanen (signal intelligence)

Fast Attack Craft (Torpedo)
T 123 Capella (41 metres)

Minelayers
M 03 Visborg (Coastal Fleet Staff Ship) 92 metres

Minesweepers
M 68 Blidö (42 metres)

Salvage ship (Submarine Rescue)
A 211 Belos (58 metres)

Tenders
A 241 Urd (22 metres)
A 248 Pingvinen (33 metres)

Tugs
A 323 Hercules (20 metres)
A 324 Hera (20 metres)
A 326 Hebe

Mapping vessels (Sonar)
Leaderboat Mb 95
Plus four small support vessels

LCMs
A 333 Skagul (35 metres)
A 651 (21 metres)

Coastal Defence Patrol Craft
(Depth charges and reconnaissance)
Bevb 66 (21 metres)
Bevb 73 (21 metres)
Bevb 77 (21 metres)

Coast Guard (Patrol Craft)
TV 103 – 107 (27 metres)

LCAs (Coastal Defence Transport)
321
334

ATB (Ammunition Transport Boats)
ATB2 (30.4 metres)

Motorboats (Reconnaissance)
Mb 404
Mb 406
Mb 409
Mb 410
Mb 457
Mb 464
Mb 477

Helicopters
Y 44
Y 46
Y 64
Y 68
Y 69
Y 70
Y 71
Y 72

Coast Guard Reconnaissance Aircraft
SE-GYP

References

OFFICIAL DOCUMENTS

Committee on Undersea Vehicles and National Needs (1996) *Undersea Vehicles and National Needs*, Marine Board Commission on Engineering and Technical Systems, National Research Council, Washington, DC, National Academy Press.

Department of Defense (1981) 'Soviet Naval Threat', by Rear-Admiral Sumner Shapiro, 26 February, *Hearings on Military Posture and H.R. 2970 and H.R. 2614 Before the Committee on Armed Services House of Representatives Ninety-seventh Congress*, Part 3 of 6 parts, *Seapower and Strategic and Critical Materials Subcommittee Title 1*, Washington, DC, US Government Printing Office.

Department of Defense (1982) Written statement of Director of Naval Intelligence, Rear-Admiral Sumner Shapiro, 2 March, *Hearings on Military Posture and H.R. 5968 [H.R. 6030] Before the Committee on Armed Services House of Representatives Ninety-seventh Congress*, Part 4 of 7 parts, *Seapower and Strategic and Critical Materials Subcommittee Title 1*, Washington, DC, US Government Printing Office.

Department of Defense (1983) Written statement of Director of Naval Intelligence, Rear-Admiral John L. Butts, 24 February, *Hearings on H.R. 2287 [2969] Before the Committee on Armed Services House of Representatives Ninety-eighth Congress*, Part 4 of 8 parts, *Seapower and Strategic and Critical Materials Subcommittee Title 1*, Washington, DC, US Government Printing Office.

Department of Defense (1984a) Prepared statement of Director of Naval Intelligence, Rear-Admiral John L. Butts, 28 February, *Hearings on H.R. 5167 Before the Committee on Armed Services House of Representatives Ninety-eighth Congress*, Part 3 of 7 parts, *Seapower and Strategic and Critical Materials Subcommittee Title 1*, Washington, DC, US Government Printing Office.

Department of Defense (1984b) *Department of Defense Appropriations for 1985: Hearings Before a Subcommittee of the Committee on Appropriations, House of Representatives, Subcommittee on the Department of Defense (Part 2)*, Washington, DC, US Government Printing Office.

Department of Defense (1985) Prepared statement of Director of Naval Intelligence, Rear-Admiral John L. Butts, 21 February, *Hearings on H.R. 1872 Before the Committee on Armed Services House of Representatives Ninety-ninth Congress*, Part 3 of 7 parts, *Seapower and Strategic and Critical Materials Subcommittee Title 1*, Washington, DC, US Government Printing Office.

Department of Defense (1987) Prepared statement of Director of Naval Intelligence, Rear-Admiral William O. Studeman, *Hearings on H.R. 1748 Before the Committee on Armed Services House of Representatives One Hundredth Congress, Seapower and Strategic and Critical Materials Subcommittee Title 1*, Washington, DC, US Government Printing Office.

Department of Defense (1988) Prepared statement of Director of Naval Intelligence, Rear-Admiral William O. Studeman, *Hearings Before the Committee on Armed Services House of Representatives One Hundredth Congress, Seapower and Strategic and Critical Materials Subcommittee Title 1*, Washington, DC, US Government Printing Office.

Department of Defense (1989) Prepared statement of Director of Naval Intelligence, Rear-Admiral Thomas A. Brooks, *Hearings Before the Committee on Armed Services House of Representatives, Seapower and Strategic and Critical Materials Subcommittee Title 1*, Washington, DC, US Government Printing Office.

Department of Defense (1991) *Worldwide U.S. Active Duty Military Personnel Casualties, October 1, 1979–June 30, 1991*, Washington, DC, US Government Printing Office.

Department of Defense (1995) (Secretary of Defense, William J. Perry) 'Special Operations Forces, Current and Recent Operations', in *Annual Report to the President and Congress* (February), http://www.defenselink.mil/execsec/adr_intro.html.

Department of Defense (1996) (Secretary of Defense, William J. Perry) 'Special Operations Forces, Current and Recent Operations', in *Annual Report to the President and Congress* (March), http://www.defenselink.mil/execsec/adr_intro.html.

Hoff, Lars-Erik (2000) 'Kommentarer kring ub-skydd den 30 sept 1982 m.a.a. Krister Larsson (KL), Dagens Eko, förfrågningar om min uppfattning om bedömningar och beslut vid ÖrlBO stab angiven tid', 13 March, Stockholm, Försvarsstaben.

Joint Chiefs of Staff (Chairman Lyman Lemintzer). Memorandum for the Secretary of Defence (Subject: Justification for US Military

Intervention in Cuba), 13 March 1962 on 'Operation Northwoods'. (This declassified document includes a 'Report by the Department of Defence and the Joint Chiefs of Staff Representative on the Caribbean Survey Group to the Joint Chiefs of Staff on Cuba Project' from 9 March [on the 'Justification for US Military Intervention in Cuba']; an Enclosure A ['Memorandum for the Secretary of Defence']; an Appendix to Enclosure A ['Memorandum for Chief of Operations, Cuba Project; Subject: Justification for US Military Intervention in Cuba']; and an Annex to Appendix to Enclosure A [Pretexts to Justify US Military Intervention in Cuba']. See <http://www.gwu.edu/~nsarchiv/news/20010430/doc1.pdf>.

Joint Pub 3-05.3 (1993) *Joint Special Operations: Operational Procedures*, 25 August, Washington, DC, Joint Chiefs of Staff.

Joint Pub 3-58 (1996) *Joint Doctrine for Military Deception*, 31 May, Washington, DC, Joint Chiefs of Staff.

Joint Pub 3-53 (1996) *Doctrine for Joint Psychological Operations*, 10 July, Washington, DC, Joint Chiefs of Staff.

Joint Pub 3-05 (1998) *Doctrine for Joint Special Operations*, 17 April, Washington, DC, Joint Chiefs of Staff.

KU 1982/83:30, Konstitutionsutskottets betänkande [parliamentary hearing] (including an attachment on the Hårsfjärden submarine hunt, KU 1982/83:30, Attach. 7).

NSC 6006/1 (6 April 1960), National Security Council, 'US Policy towards Scandinavia (Denmark, Norway and Sweden)', included in SOU 1994:11, *Om kriget kommit . . . – Förberedelser för mottagande av militärt bistånd 1949–1969*, Betänkande av Neutralitetspolitikkommissionen, Bilagor (Stockholm: Statens Offentliga Utredningar, 1994).

Norwegian Ministry of Defence (1983a) *The Hardangerfjord Submarine Incident April/May 1983*, Oslo, Ministry of Defence.

Norwegian Ministry of Defence (1983b) *Analyse av Operasjonene i Sunnhordland 27 April–6 Mai 1983*, Oslo, Ministry of Defence.

Secretary of the Navy, Washington (1984) 'The Secretary of the Navy takes pleasure in presenting the Navy Unit Commendation to USS Cavella (SSN 684)', The Naval Archive, Washington.

SOU 1983:13 (1983) *Att möta ubåtshotet: Ubåtskränkningar och svensk säkerhetspolitik*, Betänkande av ubåtsskyddskommissionen, Stockholm, Försvarsdepartementet.

SOU 1983:13 (1984) [Unofficial translation] *Countering the Submarine Threat: Submarine Violations and Swedish Security Policy*, Stockholm, Ministry of Defence.

SOU 1995:135 (1995) *Ubåtsfrågan 1981–1994: Rapport från kommissionen* [Report from the Submarine Commission], Stockholm, Försvarsdepartementet.

SOU 2001:85 (2001) *Perspectiv på ubåtsfrågan: Hanteringen av ubåts-frågan politiskt och militärt*, Stockholm, Försvarsdepartementet.

SOU 2002: 108 (2002) *Fred och säkerhet – Svensk säkerhetspolitik 1969–89* (Stockholm: Statens Offentliga Utredningar, Utrikes-departementet, 2002). An appendix shows a document from US Department of State: 'Guidelines for Policy and Operations – Sweden', June 1962.

Svenska försvarsväsendets (Swedish Defence Organisation) (1982) 'Rulla', Stockholm, Försvarsstaben.

Svenska försvarsväsendets (Swedish Defence Organisation) (1983) 'Rulla', Stockholm, Försvarsstaben.

US Congress (1986) Office of Technology Assessment, *Marine Applications for Fuel Cell Technology: A Technical Memorandum*, OTA-TM-O-37, February, Washington, DC, US Government Printing Office.

US Navy SEALs (1974) *US Navy SEAL Combat Manual* (0502-LP-190-0650), project editor R.G. Bereton LCDR (US Navy), 1 January 1974.

DECLASSIFIED OR PARTLY DECLASSIFIED WAR DIARIES, DIARIES AND OTHER DOCUMENTS FROM THE HÅRSFJÄRDEN SUBMARINE HUNT

Bevb 77 LB (1982) Däcksloggbok för HMS Bevb 77 från 1982-09-10 till 1982-21-10 [Patrol boat 77 Log-Book for 8–21 October 1982].

Bevb 77 WD (1982) Bevb 77: Krigsdagbok 30/9–21/10 [Patrol boat 77, War Diary 30 September to 21 October]. Several pages in the diary are missing.

CÖrlBO INT (1982) CÖrlBO Underrättelseorienteringar [Chief of Naval Base East, Intelligence Briefings], October.

CÖrlBO WD (1982) CÖrlBO Krigsdagbok [Chief Naval Base East, Rear-Admiral Christer Kierkegaard, War Diary], 27 September–15 October.

CMS WD (1982) CMS Krigsdagbok [War Diary of Chief of the Mine Troops and Chief of Mälsten Coastal Defence Base (Chief MS under Stockholm Coastal Defence) Lieutenant Colonel Sven-Olof Kviman], 6–15 October.

CMS HWD (1982) CMS Krigsdagbok [Hand-written War Diary of Chief of the Mine Troops and the Chief of Mälsten Coastal Defence Base (CMS under Stockholm Coastal Defence) Lieutenant-Colonel Sven-Olof Kviman], 6–15 October.

CMS2 WD (1982) CMS2 Krigsdagbok [War Diary of Chief of the Mine Barrage MS2 (under the Chief of Mälsten Coastal Defence Base) Lieutenant Johan Eneroth], 14 October.

CMS Reports, Special reports about incidents at Mälsten Coastal Defence Base on 11, 12 and 14 October 1982, signed Sven-Olof Kviman and Per Andersson.

CM/Grandin (1982) 'Granskning av ubåtsjaktverksamheten mot bakgrund av händelserna i Stockholms skärgård', av Gunnar Grandin (ordförande) och Sven-Åke Adler (vise ordförande) för Chefen för Marinen 3 december 1982 [Swedish Navy internal investigation on the Hårsfjärden submarine hunt by Rear-Admiral Gunnar Grandin (Chairman) and Sven-Åke Adler (Vice-Chairman) for the Chief of the Navy, 3 December].

CM/Grandin, Attach. 2 (1982) 'Händelseförloppet', Bilaga 2 i 'Granskning av ubåtsjaktverksamheten mot bakgrund av händelserna i Stockholms skärgård', av Gunnar Grandin (ordförande) och Sven-Åke Adler (vise ordförande) för Chefen för Marinen 3 december 1982 [Attachment 2, Swedish Navy internal investigation on the Hårsfjärden submarine hunt by Rear-Admiral Gunnar Grandin (Chairman) and Sven-Åke Adler (Vice-Chairman) for the Chief of the Navy, 3 December].

FOA Tape 0–11, Protocol for the speaker channel on the tapes recorded at Mälsten 11–28 October 1982. (The tapes had one channel for each of the four microphones plus one speaker channel for comments from the sonar operator.) The tapes were sent to FOA and were called 'FOA 0'–'FOA 11'. Protocol made by Chief of MUSAC Peter Gnipping, June 2001, for Ambassador Rolf Ekéus's Submarine Investigation, Ekéus Investigation Files, Stockholm, Riksarkivet.

LGP HWD (1982) Lars-G. Persson, Dagbok (Handskriven) [The Handwritten Diary of Lieutenant-General Lars-G. Persson], 27 September–15 October.

MAFU Report (1982) Protocol from the tape recording of underwater sounds in the Mälsten area from the so-called 'FOA testing station'. The report was made by Rolf Andersson from FMV (Swedish Defence Material), 11–12 October.

MAna Hårsfj (1982) Marinens Ananlysgrupp Rapport från Hårsfjärdsincidenten [Naval Analysis Group Report for the Hårsfjärden Incident under Captain Emil Svensson]. The report covers the period 27 September–15 October.

MAna Hårsfj FOA (1982) Marinens Ananlysgrupp Rapport (Attachment 38, Subattachment 2). FOA's rapport om bandinspelningar vid Mälsten: Ananlysresultat sammanfattning, 20 October [FOA report on the tape-recorded sounds at Mälsten 11–14 October].

MAna Hårsfj RABu (1982) 'Resultat av Analys av Bottenundersökningar' [The Sea-Floor Investigation], included in the Naval Analysis Group Report (see above).

ÖB HWD (1982) ÖB Lennart Ljung, Dagbok (Handskriven) [Handwritten Diary of the Commander-in-Chief, General Lennart Ljung], 30 September–15 October, Stockholm, Krigsarkivet [Stockholm War Archive].

ÖB TD (1978–86) ÖB Lennart Ljung Dagbok (Utskriven) [Typed Diary of the Commander-in-Chief, General Lennart Ljung], Stockholm, Krigsarkivet [Stockholm War Archive].

SCSK Report, 'Ubåtsincident Hårsfjärden' [Submarine incident Hårsfjärden]. Report of day-to-day decisions at Stockholm Coastal Defence Staff in Vaxholm under Chief of Staff, Lieutenant-Colonel Jan Svenhager. The report covers the period 5–14 October.

UL (1982) Notes made by Prime Minister Olof Palme's State Secretary Ulf Larsson at high-level meetings, October 1982.

Y46 Report (1982) Drawing and notes made by the personnel on the helicopter Y46 after its reconnaissance trip to Mälsten-Måsknuv on 11 October 1982.

DECLASSIFIED OR PARTLY DECLASSIFIED REPORTS OR NOTES MADE AFTER THE SUBMARINE HUNT

Bo Rask Letter (2001) Letter about methods used by submarines to attract attention in case of emergency (in Sweden, NATO and the Soviet Union) for Ambassador Ekéus's Submarine Investigation, written by Commodore Bo Rask, Chief of First Submarine Flotilla, Swedish Royal Navy, 19 July, Ekéus Investigation Files, Stockholm, Riksarkivet.

British Ministry of Defence (2000) Response to questions regarding British submarine operations in Swedish territorial waters in 1980s, Letter signed by Captain John Gowere, 11 May, Naval Staff Directorate, Ministry of Defence.

Cato, Ingemar and Larsson, Bengt-Åke (1995) *Rapport för ubåtskommissionen [SOU 1995]: Bottespåranalys av insamlat material från Hårsfjärden 1982, Klintehamn 1986, Kappelhamnsviken 1987 och Gustaf Dahlén 1988*, 1 December, Stockholm.

CFö/INT (1987) Notes for the government briefing in December 1987 by the 'Government Group' (Jan Eliasson, Hans Dahlgren and Bengt Wallroth) headed by Major-General Bengt Wallroth, Chief of the International Division, Ministry of Defence (CFö/INT), 'Undervattensverksamhet: förekomst, omfattning och inriktning tidsmässigt och geografiskt (det s.k. "mönstret" i verksamheten) samt nationalitetsbestämning', Ekéus Investigation Files 50:3, Stockholm, Riksarkivet. The document was handed over to the Ekéus Investigation by Deputy Foreign Minister Hans Dahlgren on 5 April 2001.

Dahlgren (1987) Draft notes made by Ambassador Hans Dahlgren for the 'Government Group' briefing of the government, 7 December, 'Om nationalitetsbestämning', Ekéus Investigation Files 49:3, Stockholm, Riksarkivet. The document was handed over to the Ekéus Investigation by Deputy Foreign Minister Hans Dahlgren on 5 April 2001.

Ekéus Investigation Files (2001) Riksarkivet, Stockholm (Swedish National Archive). These files include some 269 documents: notes, letters and reports (notes from interviews are still classified).

FET (1981–85) Forsvarets Efterretningstjeneste, Rapporter om Flådeaktivitet [Danish Military Intelligence Service Monthly Reports on Naval Activities], January–December, Copenhagen.

Försvarsmakten [Swedish Defence Forces] (2000) 'Incidentrapporter inte längre hemliga' [Incident Reports No Longer Secret], *Försvarsmakten: Nyhetsmeddelande*, 10 March, Stockholm, Försvarsmakten.

Försvarsstaben (1987) Rapport om undervattensverksamhet som riktats mot vårt land [Report about sub-surface activity against our country], signed Bengt Gustafsson and Thorsten Engberg, 25 November, Stockholm, Försvarsstaben.

Interview with Carl Eric Almgren, 1993, for the Neutrality Policy Commission, SOU 1994:11, Neutralitetspolitikkommissionens utfrågning av Carl Eric Almgren 3 december 1993, Regeringskansliets förvaltningskontor, Stockholm, Centralarkivet.

Interview with Ingemar Engman for the Neutrality Policy Commission, SOU 1994:11, Neutralitetspolitikkommissionens utfrågning av Ingemar Engman 1993, Regeringskansliets förvaltningskontor, Stockholm, Centralarkivet.

Kierkegaard, Christer *et al.* (1984) Utredning angående ubåtsincidenten i Karlskrona februari–mars 1984 [Investigation of the submarine hunt in Karlskrona February–March 1984], Chairman Rear-Admiral Christer Kierkegaard, Gustaf Welin, Lars-G. Persson, H. Hansson and Secretary Frank Rosenius, 3 May.

Kierkegaard, C., Hoff, L.-E. and Blomquist, R. (1990) PM 27 December: 'Hårsfjärdsincidenten 1982: Erfarenheter och reflektioner i ett snart 10-årigt perspektiv' [The Hårsfjärden Incident 1982: Experiencies and Reflections from a Perspective of Almost 10 Years], signed by Rear-Admiral Christer Kierkegaard, Commander Lars-Erik Hoff and Commander Rolf Blomquist.

Lundin *et al.* (1996) 'Den främmande undervattensverksamheten på svenskt territorium under perioden 1980–1995 sedd ur ett säkerhetspolitiskt perspektiv' (Classified report for the Foreign Minister signed by Ambassador Lars-Erik Lundin, Ambassador Carl-Johan Groth, Professor Rutger Lindahl and Ambassador Lennart Myrsten), Stockholm, Utrikesdepartementet [Ministry of Foreign Affairs].

Norwegian Ministry of Defence (1983c) 'Ubåtskrenkelsene: Noen Sikkerhetspolitiske Refleksjoner', Notes from Director-General Finn Molvig to the Minister of Defence, 8 August, Oslo, Ministry of Defence.

Ryding-Berg, Stefan and Hans Berndtson (2000) 'Förberedande undersökning avseende vissa uppgifter i massmedia' [Preliminary Investigation of Some Information in the Mass Media, signed by the Commander-in-Chief, General Owe Wiktorin], 30 March, Stockholm, Försvarsmakten, Högkvarteret.

SAP VU meeting (1983) Minutes from Socialdemokratiska Arbetarpartiets Verkställande Utskott. (Executive Committee of the Social Democratic Party) meeting, 17 May 1983. Arbetarrörelsens arkiv (Labour Movement Archive), Stockholm.

Svensson, Emil (1995) 'Slutrapport Ubåtssamtalen' [Final Report: The Submarine Talks [with the Russian Counterpart]], Emil Svensson, Ordförande [Chairman], 24 January.

UL (1983) Notes made by Prime Minister Olof Palme's State Secretary Ulf Larsson at high-level meetings, May 1983.

STATEMENTS AND INTERVIEWS ON TV

Sven Andersson, *Extra Rapport*, Swedish TV2 (26 April 1983).

Olof Palme, *Aktuellt*, Swedish TV1; *Rapport*, Swedish TV2 (26 April 1983).

Carl Bildt, *Rapport*, Swedish TV2 (26 April 1983).

Sverker Åström, *Aktuellt*, Swedish TV1 (26 April 1983).

Lars Werner, *Aktuellt*, Swedish TV1; *Rapport*, Swedish TV2 (26 April 1983).

Ulf Adelsohn, *Aktuellt*, Swedish TV1 (5 March 1984).

John McWethy, *World News Tonight*, ABC (21 March 1984).

John Ericson, *Aktuellt*, Swedish TV1 (12 January 1986).

James Lyons, *Red Cell: Secret SEAL Terrorist Operations* (Video) (1993), Boulder, CO, Paladin Press.

Richard Marcinko, *Red Cell: Secret SEAL Terrorist Operations* (Video) (1993), Boulder, CO, Paladin Press.

Thage G. Peterson, Norra Magasinet, Swedish TV2 (21 February 1996).

Valerjan Asejev, *Reportrarna*, Swedish TV2 (22 October 1996).

Wilhelm Carlstedt, *Reportrarna*, Swedish TV2 (22 October 1996).

Leif Leifland, *Reportrarna*, Swedish TV2 (9 September 1998).

Ingvar Carlsson, *Aktuellt*, Swedish TV1 (25 October 1999).

Caspar Weinberger, *Striptease*, Swedish TV2 (7 March 2000).

Kjeld Hillingsø, *Striptease*, Swedish TV2 (7 March (and 11 April) 2000).

Paul Beaver, *Striptease*, Swedish TV2 (7 March (and 11 April) 2000).
Sven-Olof Kviman, *Aktuellt*, Swedish TV1 (7 March 2000).
Ingvar Carlsson, *Aktuellt*, Swedish TV1 (7 March 2000).
Bengt Gustafsson, *Striptease*, Swedish TV2 (7 March 2000).
Göran Persson, *Rapport*, Swedish TV2 (8 March 2000).
George Robertson, *Aktuellt*, Swedish TV1 (29 March 2000).
Björn von Sydow, Swedish TV2 (29 March 2000).
Keith Speed, *Striptease*, Swedish TV2 (11 April 2000).

BOOKS AND ARTICLES IN ACADEMIC AND PROFESSIONAL JOURNALS

Adelsohn, Ulf (1987) *Partiledare: Dagbok 1981–1986* [Diary of the Conservative Party Leader Ulf Adelsohn 1981–1986], Malmö, Gedins Förlag.
Agrell, Wilhelm (1986) *Bakom ubåtskrisen: Militär verksamhet, krigsplanläggning och diplomati i Östersjöområdet* [Behind the Submarine Crisis: Military Activity, War Planning and Diplomacy in the Baltic Sea Area, Stockholm, Liber.
Agrell, Wilhelm (2000) *Fred och fruktan: Sveriges säkerhetspolitiska historia 1918–2000* [Peace and Fear: Sweden's Security Policy History 1918–2000], Lund, Historiska Media.
Aland, T. and Zachrisson, B. (1996) *Berättelser om Palme*, Stockholm, Norstedts.
Alford, Jonathan (1984) 'The Northern Flank as Part of Europe: Some Thoughts about Nordic Security', *Krigsvetenskapsakademins Handlingar och Tidskrift*, 6, pp. 299–307, Stockholm, Royal Academy of War Science.
Annati, Massimo (1996) 'Underwater Special Operations Craft', *Military Technology*, 3, pp. 85–9.
Bale, Jeffrey McKenzie (1995) *The 'Black' Terrorist International: Neo-Fascist Paramilitary Networks and the 'Strategy of Tension' in Italy, 1968–1974*, Ann Arbor, MI, UMI Dissertation Service (UMI Number: 9529217).
Bamford, James (2002) *Body of Secrets: How America's NSA and Britain's GCHQ Eavesdrop on the World*, London, Arrow Books, Random House.
Baudrillard, Jean (1975) *The Mirror of Production*, St Louis, MO, Telos.
Bergström, Lars and Åmark, Klas (eds) (1999) *Ubåtsfrågan: En kritisk granskning av den svenska nutidshistoriens viktigaste säkerhetspolitiska dilemma*, Uppsala, Verdandi.
Berkowitz, Marc J. (1988) 'Soviet Naval Spetsnaz Forces', *Naval War College Review*, vol. XLI, no. 2, Spring, pp. 5–21.
Bethge, Ansgar (1986) 'Developments in the Northern Flank from the

Perspective of West German Strategy and Security Policy in the Post-war Period: Developments and the Mission of the German Navy', Oslo International Symposium, 10–14 August, *Perspectives on NATO and the Northern Flank*, Oslo, Norwegian Institute for Defence Studies.

Bildt, Carl (1983) 'Sweden and the Soviet Submarines', *Survival*, XXV (4), July/August, pp. 165–9.

Bildt, Carl (1990) Ubåtskränkningarna mot Sverige: bakgrund, mönster och motiv (Inträdesanförande 12 April 1990 av riksdagsman Carl Bildt), *Kungliga krigsvetenskapsakademiens handlingar och tidskrift*, pp. 29–56.

Birindelli, di, Gino (1980) 'The Occult Component of Naval Warfare: The Role of the Raiders in Modern Naval Operations', *Defence Today*, July, pp 289–93.

Bodström, Lennart (1999) 'Politik och ubåtar' [Politics and Submarines], in Lars Bergström and Klas Åmark (eds), *Ubåtsfrågan: En kritisk granskning av den svenska nutidshistoriens viktigaste säkerhetspolitiska dilemma*, pp. 151–64, Uppsala, Verdandi.

Bodström, Lennart (2000) *Mitt i Stormen*, Stockholm, Hjalmarson & Högberg.

Bosiljevac, T.L. (1990) *SEALs: UDT/SEAL Operations in Vietnam*, New York, Ivy Books.

Bruzelius, Nils (1982) 'Sveriges territorialhav: En motorväg för ubåtar' [Sweden's Territorial Sea: A Highway for Submarines], *Marinnytt*, 5–6.

Bruzelius, Nils (1995) 'Ett motiv till ubåtskränkningarna' [A Motive for the Submarine Intrusions], *Tidskrift i sjöväsende*, 1.

Bruzelius, Nils (2002) 'Flottan som aldrig siktades vid Vinga – De strategiska robotubåtarnas operationsområde vid den svenska västkusten' (The Area of Operations of the Strategic Missile Submarine Along the Swedish West Coast), *Tidskrift i Sjöväsendet*, no. 3, pp. 222–34.

Buff, Joseph J. (2000) 'ASDS: One MINISUB, Many Roles', 4 Quarter, http://www.udt-seal.org/asds.html.

Bynander, Fredrik (1998a) *Crisis Analogies: A Decision Making Analysis of Swedish Hårsfjärden Submarine Incident of 1982*, Research Report 29, Swedish Institute of International Affairs.

Bynander, Fredrik (1998b) 'The 1982 Swedish Hårsfjärden Submarine Incident: A Decision-Making Analysis, *Cooperation and Conflict*, 33 (4), pp. 367–407.

Carlsson, Ingvar (1999) *Ur skuggan av Olof Palme* [Out of the Shadow of Olof Palme], Stockholm, Hjalmarson & Högberg.

Cohen, Eliot A. (1986) 'US Strategy and the Northern Flank: A Coalition Warfare Approach', in Sverre Jervell and Kåre Nyblom (eds), *The Military Buildup in the High North: American and Nordic*

Perspectives, pp. 3–19, Lanham, MD and London, Center for International Affairs Harvard University/University Press of America.

Cole, Paul M. (1990) *Neutralité du Jour: The Conduct of Swedish Security Policy Since 1945*, Ann Arbor, MI, UMI Dissertation Service.

Compton-Hall, Richard (1987) 'Re-emergence of the Midgets', *Military Technology*, 10, pp. 39–46.

Compton-Hall, Richard (1988) *Submarine vs. Submarine: The Tactics and Technology of Underwater Warfare*, New York, Orion Books.

Compton-Hall, Richard (1989) 'The incredible shrinking submarine', *New Scientist*, 1 April.

Corlett, R.C. (1974) 'Mini-Submarines: Project 70 and Cosmos Compared', *Navy International*, July.

Craven, John P. (2001) *The Silent War: The Cold War Battle Beneath the Sea*, New York, Simon & Schuster.

Darman, Peter (1994) *SAS: The World's Best*, London, Sidgwick & Jackson.

Dockery, Kevin (1991) *SEALs in Action*, New York, Avon Books.

Dwyer, John, B. (1992) *Seaborn Deception: The History of US Navy Beach Jumpers*, New York, Praeger.

Edwards, Steve (1992) 'Stalking the Enemy's Coast', *US Naval Institute Proceedings*, February.

Ellis, M.G.M.W. (1986) 'Sweden's Ghosts?', *US Naval Institute Proceedings*, March, pp. 95–101.

Ferraresi, Franco (1996) *Threats to Democracy: The Radical Right in Italy after the War*, Princeton, NJ, Princeton University Press.

Fock, Harald (1996) *Marine Kleinkampfmittel: Bemannte Torpedos, Klein-Uboote, Klein Schnellboote, Sprengboote – Gestern, heute, morgen*, Hamburg, Koehlers Verlagsgesellschaft [1982].

Forman, Will (1999) *The History of American Deep Submersible Operations 1775–1995*, Flagstaff, AZ, Best Publishing Company.

Foster, Nigel (1998) *The Making of a Royal Marines Commando*, London, Pan Books, Macmillan, [1987].

Friedman, Norman (1992) 'Understanding Submarine Design', *US Naval Institute Proceedings*, February, pp. 108–9.

Gates, Robert M. (1997) *From the Shadows: The Ultimate Insider's Story of Five Presidents and How They Won the Cold War*, New York, Touchstone, Simon & Schuster.

Genat, Robert (1994) *US Navy SEALs: In Colour Photographs*, Europa Militaria, 16, Ramsbury, Crowood Press.

Hansen, Lynn M. (1984) *Soviet Navy Spetsnaz Operations on the Northern Flank: Implications for Defence of Western Europe*, STRA-TECH STUDIES SS84-2, Study prepared for the office of the Secretary of Defense/Net Assessment, Center for Strategic

Technology, Texas Engineering Experiment Station of Texas A&M University System.

Harms, Norman E. (2000) 'Merchant & Military Vessels of World War II: Reviewed', Part 1, Scale Specialities CD-Rom History Series, ONI 208-J, Supplement 2: Far Eastern Small Craft [1945].

Hasselbohm, Anders (1984) *Ubåtshotet: En kritisk granskning av Hårsfjärds-incidenten och ubåtsskyddskommissionens rapport*, Stockholm, Prisma.

Hirdman, Sven (1969/70) 'The Militarization of the Deep Ocean', *SIPRI Yearbook of World Armaments and Disarmament*, London, Gerald Duckworth (Stockholm, Almqvist & Wiksell).

Hofsten, Hans von (1993) *I kamp mot överheten: Örlog och debatt*, Stockholm, T. Fischer & Co.

Höjelid, Stefan (1991) *Sovjetbilden i nordisk press: Svenska, norska och finländska reaktioner på sovjetiskt agerande*, Lund, Studentlitteratur.

Huldt, Bo (1996) 'Ubåtskränkningarna: frågor om bakgrund och motiv', *Internationella Studier*, 1.

Iklé, Fred (1989) 'The Modern Context', in Carnes Lord and Frank R. Barnett (eds), *Political Warfare and Psychological Operations: Rethinking the US Approach*, pp. 3–11, Washington, DC, National Defense University Press/National Strategy Information Center.

International Institute of Strategic Studies (IISS) (1982–83) *Militærbalansen 1982–1983* [The Military Balance 1982–1983], Norwegian edn, Oslo, Den norske Atlanterhavskomié.

Jane's Fighting Ships (from 1974–75 every year to 2001–02), Jane's Information Group.

Kelley, P.X. and O'Donnell, Hugh K. (1986) 'The Amphibious Warfare Strategy', *Naval Institute Proceedings*, Supplement: *The US Maritime Strategy*, pp. 18–29.

Kelly, Orr (1992) *The Untold Story of Navy SEALs: Brave Men, Dark Waters*, New York, Simon & Schuster.

Kelly, Orr (1995) *Never Fight Fair – Navy SEALs' Stories of Combat and Adventure*, Novato, CA, Presidio Press.

Kemp, Paul (1996) *Underwater Warriors: The Fighting History of Midget Submarines*, London, Cassell Military Paperbacks.

Lähteinen, Jussi (1997) 'Ubåtarnas territorialkränkningar: Erfarenheter i Sverige och Finland', *Krigsvetenskapsakademins Handlingar och Tidskrift*, 4, pp. 83–125, Stockholm, Royal Academy of War Science.

Lampers, Lars Olof (1996) *Bodströmaffären och det säkerhetspolitiska debattklimatet i Sverige 1982–1985*, Stockholm, Statsvetenskapliga Institutionen, Stockholms Universitet.

Lehman, John F. (1988) *Command of the Seas*, New York, Charles Scribner's Sons, Macmillan.

Leifland, Leif (1997) *Frostens År: Om USAs diplomatiska utfrysning av Sverige*, Stockholm, Nerenius och Santérus Förlag.

Leitenberg, Milton (1987) *Soviet Submarine Operations in Swedish Waters 1980–1986*, The Washington Papers/128, CSIS, New York, Praeger.

Lernoux, Penny (1989) *People of Good: The Struggle for World Catholicism*, New York and London, Viking, Penguin Group.

Lindahl, Rutger and Lundgren, Claes (1982) 'Moskvaradions syn på ubåtsjakten i Stockholms skärgård' [Radio Moscow's View of the Submarine Hunt in the Stockholm Archipelago], *Meddelanden*, 99, Stockholm, Beredskapsnämnden för psykologiskt försvar.

Lindfors, Tommy (1996) *Under ytan: Ubåtar och svensk säkerhetspolitik*, Göteborg: Daidalos.

Lindqvist, Herman (1997) *Historien om Sverige: Gustavs dagar*, Stockholm, Norstedts.

Lofthus, John and Aarons, Mark (1994) *The Secret War Against the Jews: How Western Espionage Betrayed the Jewish People*, New York, St Martin's Griffin.

Lord, Carnes and Frank R. Barnett (eds) (1989) *Political Warfare and Psychological Operations: Rethinking the US Approach*, Washington, DC, National Defense University Press/National Strategy Information Center.

Luttwak, Edward N. (1989) 'Comments', in Carnes Lord and Frank R. Barnett (eds), *Political Warfare and Psychological Operations: Rethinking the US Approach*, Washington, DC, National Defense University Press/National Strategy Information Center.

Luttwak, Edward N. and Stuart L. Koehl (1991) *The Dictionary of Modern War: A Guide to the Ideas, Institutions and Weapons of the Modern Military Power Vocabulary*, New York, Gramercy Books.

Marcinko, Richard and Weisman, John (1994) *Rogue Warrior II: Red Cell*, New York, Pocket Books, Simon & Schuster.

MccGwire, Michael (1987) *Military Objectives in Soviet Foreign Policy*, Washington, DC, Brookings Institution.

McCormick, Gordon H. (1990) *Stranger than Fiction: Soviet Submarine Operations in Swedish Waters*, R-3776-AF, A Project AIR FORCE report prepared for the United States Air Force, Rand Corporation, January.

Miller, David and Jordan, John (1987) *Modern Submarine Warfare*, London, Salamander Books.

Mooney, Brad (1994) 'Manned Submersibles', in Richard Seymour *et. al*, *Research Submersibles and Undersea Technologies*, Baltimore, MD, World Technology Evaluation Center (ARPA), Loyola College of Maryland, http://itri.loyola.edu/subsea/toc.htm, June.

Moore, John E. and Compton-Hall, Richard (1986) *Submarine Warfare: Today and Tomorrow*, London, Michael Joseph.

Nesi, Sergio (1996) 'Un Eccezionale Raduno a la Specia dei Due Battaglone "Lupo" e "Barbarigo" al Varignano', Riconoscimenti e Meriti della Decima Mas, Gennaio, http://www.italia-rsi.org/farsixa/riconoscimenti%20xa.htm.

Ocean Studies Board (1997) *Oceanography and Naval Special Warfare: Opportunities and Challenges*, Washington, DC, National Academy Press.

Owen, David (1978) *Battle of the Wits: History of Psychology and Deception in Modern Warfare*, London, Leo Cooper.

Paddock, Alfred H. (1989) 'Military Psychological Operations', in Carnes Lord and Frank R. Barnett (eds), *Political Warfare and Psychological Operations: Rethinking the US Approach*, pp. 45–65, Washington, DC, National Defense University Press/National Strategy Information Center.

Parker, John (1997) *SBS: The Inside Story of the Special Boat Service*, London, Headline.

Peterson, Thage G. (1999) *Resan mot Mars: Anteckningar och minnen*, Stockholm, Bonniers.

Petersson, Magnus (1999) 'Sverige och Väst: Det säkerhetspolitiska samarbetet mellan Sverige, Norge och Västmakterna 1949–1969', in Lars Wedin and Gunnar Åselius (eds), *Mellan byråkrati och krigskonst: Sverige strategier för det kalla kriget*, pp. 165–234, Stockholm, Försvarshögskolan Acta B19.

Petersson, Magnus (2002) '"She would not fight unless attacked": Några kommentarer rörande NATO:s syn på Sverige 1949–1965', *Kungliga krigsvetenskapsakademins Handlingar och Tidskrift*, 3, pp. 73–88.

Polmar, Norman (1981) *Ships and Aircraft of the US Fleet*, 12th edn, Annapolis, MD, Naval Institute Press.

Polmar, Norman (1987) *Ships and Aircraft of the US Fleet*, 14th edn, Annapolis, MD, Naval Institute Press.

Richelson, Jeffrey T. (2001) *The Wizards of Langley: Inside CIA's Directorate of Science and Technology*, Boulder, CO, Westview Press.

Ring, Jim (2001) *We Come Unseen: The Untold Story of Britain's Cold War Submariners*, London, John Murray.

Riste, Olav and Moland, Arnfinn (1997) *Strengt hemmelig: Norsk etterretningsteneste 1945–1970* [Top Secret: Norwegian Intelligence Service 1945–1970], Oslo, Universitetsforlaget.

Rylander, Eric (draft 2002) Unpublished paper on Swedish Signal Intelligence Agency FRA.

Schelling, Thomas C. (1966) *Arms and Influence*, New Haven, CT, Yale University Press.

Schlesinger, James R. (1982) 'U.S. National-Security Challenges for the 1980s', in William J. Taylor and Steven A. Maaranen, *The Future of Conflict in the 1980s*, pp. 11–18, Lexington, MA, Lexington Books.

Schweizer, Peter (1994) *Victory: The Reagan Administration's Secret Strategy that Hastened the Collapse of the Soviet Union*, New York, Atlantic Monthly Press.

Shultz, Richard H. (1999) *The Secret War Against Hanoi: Kennedy's and Johnson's Use of Spies, Saboteurs and Covert Warriors in North Vietnam*, New York, HarperCollins.

Sköld, Nils (1999) 'Arméns synvinkel' [The View of the Army], in Lars Bergström and Klas Åmark (eds), *Ubåtsfrågan: En kritisk granskning av den svenska nutidshistoriens viktigaste säkerhetspolitiska dilemma*, pp. 165–9, Uppsala, Verdandi.

Sontag, Sherry and Drew, Christopher, with Annette Lawrence Drew (1999) *Blind Man's Bluff: The Untold Story of American Submarine Espionage*, New York, HarperCollins.

Stockdale, James B. (1998) 'The Gulf of Tonkin: A Personal Observation', *Naval Intelligence Professionals Quarterly*, Fall, pp. 15–17.

Stubblefield, Gary (1995) *Inside the US Navy SEALs*, Oskeola, WI, Motorbooks International.

Stütz, Göran (1987) *Opinion 87: En opinionsundersökning om svenska folkets inställning till några samhälls- och försvarsfrågor hösten 1987*, December, Stockholm, Styrelsen för psykologiskt försvar.

Svensson, Olle (1993) *Maktspel synat: På Erlanders, Palmes och Carlssons tid*, Stockholm, Norstedts.

Tamnes, Rolf (1997) *Oljeålder: Norsk Utenrikspolitisk Historia 1965–1995*, Vol. 6, Oslo, Universitetsforlaget.

Taylor, William J. (1982a) 'Psychological Operations in the Spectrum of Conflict in the 1980s', in William J. Taylor and Steven A. Maaranen (eds), *The Future of Conflict in the 1980s*, pp. 113–29, Lexington, MA, Lexington Books.

Taylor, William J. (1982b) 'Scenario: The Nordic Region in the 1980s', in William J. Taylor and Steven A. Maaranen (eds), *The Future of Conflict in the 1980s*, pp. 411–16, Lexington, MA, Lexington Books.

Taylor, William J. (1983) 'The Future of Conflict: US Interests', *The Washington Papers*, 94, Washington, DC, Center for Strategic and International Studies, Georgetown University.

Taylor, William J. and Maaranen, Steven A. (1982) 'Conclusion: Thinking About Strategy', in William J. Taylor and Steven A. Maaranen (eds), *The Future of Conflict in the 1980s*, pp. 459–80, Lexington, MA: Lexington Books.

Thorén, Ragnar (1992) *Ryska ubåtskriget i Östersjön 1941–1945* (Den svenska marinattachén i Helsingfors 1942–1945 Ragnar Thorén rapporterar med förord av Hans von Hofsten), Stockholm, Meddelande från Militärhistoriska avdelningen vid Militärhögskolan, 6.

Thunborg, Anders (1986) 'The Need to Maintain Sweden's Defense Efforts', in Sverre Jervell and Kåre Nyblom (eds), *The Military Buildup in the High North: American and Nordic Perspectives*, pp. 67–73, Lanham, MD and London, Center for International Affairs, Harvard University/University Press of America.

Tunander, Ola (1987) *Norden och USAs maritima strategi: En studie av Nordens förändrade strategiska läge* [The Nordic Countries and US Maritime Strategy: A Study of the Changed Strategic Position of the Nordic Countries], Försvarets Forskningsanstalt [Swedish Defence Research Establishment], FOA Rapport C 10295-1, 4 September.

Tunander, Ola (1989) *Cold Water Politics: The Maritime Strategy and Geopolitics of the Northern Front*, London, Sage.

Tunander, Ola (1999) 'The Uneasy Imbrication of Nation-State and NATO: The Case of Sweden, *Cooperation and Conflict*, **34** (2), pp. 169–203.

Tunander, Ola (2000a) 'The Informal NATO or NATO als Gemeinschaft: The Case of Sweden', in J. Peter Burgess and Ola Tunander (eds), *European Security Identities: Contested Understandings of EU and NATO*, Oslo, PRIO Report, 2, pp. 81–101.

Tunander, Ola (2000b) 'A Criticism of Court Chroniclers', *Cooperation and Conflict*, **35** (4), pp. 431–40.

Turner, Stansfield (1985) *Secrecy and Democracy: The CIA in Transition*, London, Sidgwick & Jackson.

Vistica, Gregory L. (1995) *Fall from Glory: The Man Who Sank the US Navy*, New York, Simon & Schuster.

Vyborny, Lee and Davis, Don (2002) *Dark Waters: The Insider's Account of the NR-1, The Cold War's Undercover Nuclear Sub*, London, Ebury Press, Random House.

Wallén, Göran (2002) 'Hårsfjärden 1982: Fakta i målet', *Tidskrift i Sjöväsendet*, 1, pp. 33–50.

Watkins, James D. (1986) 'The Maritime Strategy', *US Naval Institute Proceedings*, **112** (1), January (Supplement), pp. 2–17.

Weinland, Robert G. (1986) 'Soviet Naval Buildup in the High North', in Sverre Jervell and Kåre Nyblom (eds), *The Military Buildup in the High North: American and Nordic Perspectives*, pp. 22–44, Lanham, MD and London, Center for International Affairs, Harvard University/University Press of America.

Welham, Michael (1989) *Combat Frogmen: Military Diving from the Nineteenth Century to the Present Day*, Wellingborough, Patrick Stephens.

West, Leslie (1998) 'The ASDS Advantage: Navy SEALs Set for Major Leap Forward in Undersea Mobility', *Sea Power*, July.

Woodward, Bob (1987) *Veil: The Secret Wars of the CIA 1981–87*, London, Simon & Schuster.

Worthington, George (1996) 'Whither Naval Special Warfare?', *US Naval Institute Proceedings*, **122** (1), January.

Zackheim, Dov S. (1998) *The United States and the Nordic Countries During the Cold War*, Lecture to the Nordic International Studies Association seminar, 6 March, Copenhagen.

ARTICLES IN NEWSPAPERS AND MAGAZINES

Agrell, Wilhelm and Larsson, Christer (1990) 'Den hemliga ubåts-basen', Z, 25 January, pp. 28–34.

Alsén, Olle (1987) 'Indicierna som försvann', *Dagens Nyheter*, 21 December.

Alsén, Olle (1990) 'Tungomål och tystnad som vapen', *Dagens Nyheter*, 2 March.

Alsén, Olle (1992) 'Ubåtar från Nato fick fri lejd i skärgården', *Arbetet*, 9 June.

Anderson, Jack and van Atta, Dale (1990) 'The Soviets vs. the Swedes', *Washington Post*, 6 May.

Associated Press, Harald Möllerström (2000) 'Weinberger: Sweden Let Subs in', 8.38 p.m., 7 March.

Åström, Sverker (1996) 'Passiv USA-attityd till ubåtar bör utredas: Märkligt att ubåtskommissionen inte efterlyst uppgifter från ryska besättningar', *Svenska Dagbladet*, 10 January.

Bildt, Carl (1982) 'Kränkningarna direct utmaning: Carl Bildt (m) svarar försvarsministern om insatserna mot främmande ubåtar', *Svenska Dagbladet*, 2 September.

Bovin, Alexander (1984) 'Vem tjänar på denna ständiga kyla?', *Dagens Nyheter*, 27 March (published in *Izvestija* the following day).

Brännström, Leif and Persson, Ulf (1983) 'Nato spionerade på ubåts-dramat', *Expressen*, 15 March.

Eriksson, Erik (1982) 'Ni kan få se en ubåt när som helst', *Stockholms-tidningen*, 12 October.

Hasselbohm, Anders (1983a) 'Analys av motorljuden: Minst en Nato-ubåt fanns i Hårsfjärden', *Dagens Industri*, 15 March.

Hasselbohm, Anders (1983b) 'Jakten på Hårsfjärden: Marinen fick hjälp av Norge för att identifiera ubåtsljuden', *Dagens Industri*, 16 March.

Hasselbohm, Anders (1987) 'Fem år och två månader efter Hårsfjärden kommer bekräftelsen: Skadad ubåt smög ut genom Öresund', *Dagens Industri*, 16 December.

Hasselbohm, Anders (1992) 'Undervattensspionage godtogs', *Dagens Nyheter*, 2 February.

Hellberg, Anders (1994) '"Inga ubåtar i Hårsfjärden": Minorna hade kunnat skada civila båtar, säger viceamiral Bror Stefenson', *Dagens Nyheter*, 1 February.

Hofsten, Hans von (1986) 'Sovjetrepubliken Sverige?', *Dagens Nyheter*, 21 January.

Holmström, Mikael (1988) 'USA-kritik av Sveriges försvar: Ni låter ubåtarna smita!', *Ny Teknik*, 18, August.

Holmström, Mikael (1998a) 'Marinchef i exil skulle försvara riket', *Svenska Dagbladet*, 22 March.

Holmström, Mikael (1998b) 'Ministrar kände till plan på exilstab', *Svenska Dagbladet*, 23 March.

Jansson, Nils-Ove (1996) 'Erkänt eko med okänd nationalitet', *Marinnytt*, January, p. 9.

Kadhammar, Peter (1987) 'Vi tvingades släppa ubåtten: Dagbok från ubåtsjakten' [We Were Forced to Release the Submarine: Colonel Lars Hansson's Diary from the Submarine Hunt], Z, 25 November, pp. 99–107.

Larsson, Christer (1987) 'Den stora ubåtsfällan' [The Great Submarine Trap], *Ny Teknik*, 21.

Lindfors, Tommy (1991) 'Vi lät ubåten komma undan', *Dagens Nyheter*, 22 December.

Lundmark, Lennart (2001) 'Konspiration? Snarare slarv', *Dagens Nyheter*, 29 November, p. B3.

Mellbourn, Anders (1988a) 'Regeringens experter ger ÖB bakläxa: "Ubåtskränkningar har inte ökat"', *Dagens Nyheter*, 16 January.

Mellbourn, Anders (1988b) 'Regeringens ubåtsexperter: ÖB's grupp dålig på källkritik', *Dagens Nyheter*, 17 January.

Mellbourn, Anders (1988c) 'Efter ubåtsrapporten 1983: Palme tvingad peka ut Sovjet', *Dagens Nyheter*, 6 March.

Mellbourn, Anders (1988d) 'Säkerhetspolitiska bedömare eniga: Svårt hitta motiv för ubåtskränkningar', *Dagens Nyheter*, 8 March.

Öhman, Anders (1990) 'Hemlig grupp avslöjar ubåt', *Dagens Nyheter*, 9 March.

Stanglin, Douglas with David Bartal (1990) 'A Cold-War Hangover: Soviet Subs are Still Playing a Risky Game with the Swedish Navy', *US News and World Report*, 19 February, p. 41.

Svensson, Sven (1986) 'Mauno Koivisto på trådagarsbesök: Tiger omframtiden', *Dagens Nyheter*, 21 October.

Thunborg, Anders (2001) 'Ohållbart att peka ut Sovjetunionen', *Dagens Nyheter*, 6 May.

Wilson, George (1988) 'US Unveils Mini-Submarine Unit', *Washington Post*, 4 March.

Index

Made in the USA
San Bernardino, CA
04 August 2018